T0354866

The Snake, 20/20

Odie Hawkins

authorHOUSE®

AuthorHouse™
1663 Liberty Drive
Bloomington, IN 47403
www.authorhouse.com
Phone: 1 (800) 839-8640

Published by AuthorHouse 06/01/2020

ISBN: 978-1-7283-6330-1 (sc)
ISBN: 978-1-7283-6329-5 (e)

Library of Congress Control Number: 2020909922

Print information available on the last page.

Any people depicted in stock imagery provided by Getty Images are models, and such images are being used for illustrative purposes only. Certain stock imagery © *Getty Images.*

Cover Graphics Art Credit
Cedric Adams, Artist
https://www.facebook.com/cedricadamsart/ and https:// www.youtube.com/watch?v=6bKq8q7OOvk

Cover design by AuthorHouse Design Team

Photos by: *Zola Salena-Hawkins*
www.flickr.com/photos/32886903@N02

Model: Rashid Bahati
rashid@bahatifoundation.org
www.bahatifoundation.org

This book is printed on acid-free paper.

Dedicated to Chief FAMA Aina Adewale-Somadhi and BaBa Ifabowale Somadhi, courageous people, visionaries.

To G. Adesina Hood, my daughter; to Merilene M. Murphy, my friend, and to Queen Zola Salena for her beauty, strength and Insight....

Without their help I could not have done this.

AŞE

Contents

CHAPTER 1

"We weren't ready for Chicago. Chicago was too cold, too cold in ways that had nothing to do with the weather.

Down home we had farmed, raised a few cows, we had chickens, pigs, a decent home and, despite the crackers, a decent lifestyle.

In Chicago things changed. People moved fast, talked fast, acted fast. I think that's what took your great Aunt Sylvia into those drugs. I don't honestly believe she really knew what they were, what they could do to your soul.

Let's be real, comin' from where we came from, in Deepest Georgia, the strongest non-alcoholic drug we knew anything about was mary-juana. O.K.? Sometimes, some of the old people smoked it in their corn cob pipes.

Now we come up North and here we are, surrounded by people selling and using gorilla tranquilizers, elephant knockout drops, substances that could curl your toe nails back, <u>real</u> <u>drugs</u>.

It was especially devastating for Sylvia, I think, because she was the basic reason for our family fleeing to the North, to Chicago. Stop me, if you've heard this."

Kojo smiled, nodded no, as though he had never heard this story, one that he had listened to since he was a little boy; that was the only encouragement his Grandfather needed, with the aid of three fingers of Chivas Regal.

"In some ways our whole family was messed around by our move. It would be impossible to explain what happened. Look at it this way; we were living in Georgia, had been there since our 'importation', when was that? 18 something or other? Generations...."

And now, after all these years of maintaining our pride and dignity, we're forced out of our homes because some silly, drunk ass White boy pinches my sister's behind and my brother Jerome punches his lights out."

Kojo sipped his pineapple soda, stared at the faraway look that misted his Grandfather's eyes. He had heard the story often, of how the Brown family had been forced to flee this little town in Georgia or be assassinated by the KKK, because the family had too much pride.

But he could never get ready for the haunted look that came into the old man's eyes.

"Can you imagine? A whole, entire family forced to leave their home, their belongings, everything, because we wouldn't allow the White folks to treat us any ol' kinda way."

Kojo nodded, agreeing with his Grandfather's outrage. The truth of what he was talking about wouldn't register. As often as he had heard the story, as much as he empathized, he simply couldn't make himself understand the conditions that existed in his Grandfather's time.

In his day, White people ran from Black people, not the other way around, but as his father frequently pointed out to him, "Remember, Kojo, this is history...."

"Yeahh, the conditions of that time required every Negro...uhhh... Black man, woman and child to be a Superman. There was so much operating against us; the cold weather, the courts, the government, the Depression, racism, you name it.

I believe it was the stress of these conditions that caused your Grandmother to have three miscarriages in a row.

Finally, as the saying goes, Mrs. Queen Esther Brown kicked in with our first man-child, your Daddy, and then the other three, your uncles."

Kojo mentally reviewed his "Uncle Tape"; Amen, Kwabena and Kalo.

"I don't know what kind of vow Queen Esther had taken or made, or any of that, but right after Kofi was born, she went down and changed her name to Tanina Oshaleshay-Brown.

I was so proud of her I could've busted wide open. I had always wanted her to change her name but she was so proud of being Queen Esther. Sooooo proud."

The old man paused to take a sip of his whisky, something Kojo noticed that he did frequently, whenever he mentioned his wife, as though he were pouring a libation down his throat in tribute to her memory.

"Yessuh, right after Kofi, the dam opened up... Your uncles came swinging into the world. We had an outdoorin for 'em, just the way they have in West Africa, to introduce the new born to the community."

"Granddad, you make me think of about a lot of things, you know? I don't know if I've ever asked you this..."

Kojo took note of the alert gleam in the old man's eyes, he loved to be questioned.

"How did you come into the 'Africentricity', 'way back then?"

The gleam brightened....

"That's a daggoned good question, Kojo. And you're right, you've never asked me that before. Now then, I don't want to be guilty of shootin' from the hip, so let me think on this for a minute..."

Kojo smiled at the old man settling back in his favorite reading chair, a low slung barber shop deal he had designed himself.

The man is so, so hip. He's got to be 85 at least, but look at how lean and keen he is.

"Since your grandmother's passing, I've only had one vice, I like to take a little nip every now 'n then."

He was unhurried, unbothered by the frenzy of "modern life".

"Ahhhh, nothing but fools rushing to see how fast they can kill themselves."

Kojo's eyes wandered around the rook filled with books that he had spent so many hours in, reading or listening to his grandfather and his uncles.

"Well, let me start off by saying this. It was always there for us, don't let 'em lock you outside of Africa, they been trying to do that since they brought us over here.

It was like the air we breathed, it was in the atmosphere. While other children in our town were going around hanging their heads because they were dark skinned and had nappy hair, we celebrated it in our house!

I don't think I'd ever be able to put my finger on a moment that would say.... 'yeah! right There.' 'That's when it happened.' It wasn't like that.

My Daddy's parents insisted on him knowing the true role Afirca, Africans had played in the context of world history. World history, not African-American slave history, world history!

It wasn't a hobby, it was serious stuff, believe me.

By the time I was ten I had been exposed to as much of our Creole culture, and our African culture and heritage as most adults, probably more than most..."

"You say Creole?"

"I don't mean it in the New Orleans sense of the word, I'm talking about us as a New World people. It would've been highly unlikely that we would've had Native American ancestors, or Swiss, or Polynesian, or any of those other strains in our bloodliness, if we had been allowed to remain in Africa, minding our own business.

In my mind these 'admixtures' make us a Creole people."

"Oh, I see, said the blind man."

The two men exchanged coded winks at their little "In" joke.

"But, getting back to your question. It was always there.

How it came about is something that bears some serous looking into, but it was always there. Makes me think of that experiment the Russian scientist made, guy named Pavlov. Remember him?"

"Wasn't he the one who did the experiments with the dogs? Conditioning them to salivate when they heard a bell announcing dinner?"

"That's the boy. Now, the thing he did was very, very interesting. He rang this bell, then fed the dogs, rang the bell, fed the dogs, rang the bell, fed the dogs...

Naturally, most of them got hooked on the conditioning process, which is the basis for modern advertising. But they never tell us about the rebellious little black dog that washed out of the conditioning program, the one who said... 'Hey, this is bullshit. I aint gonna start slobbering every time they ring a bell. What if they don't have any food?'

I kinda have the feeling that our family is from that kinda bloodline, the maverick bloodline. We didn't buy into the normal bell-ringing slobber-slobber routine.

Now, once again, the big question is why? There was every reason to go for the okeydoke, the people all around us were sopping it up like molasses.

Like our names, for example. I was named Kwame 'cause I was born on Saturday, like they do in Ghana.... but my mother insisted on naming my sister Sylvia, after her mother, which is kind of traditional too. And Jerome, for greatgranddad.

Yessuh, we started off with a foundation and built on it. There's a rumor, just a rumor, that one of our ancestors was off the boat a week, had picked up a newspaper somewhere and taught himself how to read.

He knew that reading was going to be the key to survival in this place. Like I said... it's just a rumor, but I've been hearing it all my life."

Kojo smiled at the sight of his grandfather leaning back in his chair, delicately sipping his drink. He sips, he doesn't drink, he sips.

A full minute passed before the old man opened up again.

"So, now then, when are you leaving for the conti-nent.?"

He always divided the syllables when he spoke of Africa and made "conti-nent" sound as though it should be capitalized.

"Well, if the 'well' don't go dry and the creeek don't rise, I'll be on the bird come Monday morning."

Grandfather Brown gave up a belly laugh. He loved to hear his old sayings bounced back at him.

"Hahh hahh hah.... I heard that, I heard that. Been awhile since you was on the conti-nent, huh?"

"About eight years ago, when Dad and Momma gave me the all expenses paid trip to Ghana."

The old man took a sip of his drink, in memory of the occasion.

"What was that like, Kojo, frankly speaking, man to man? Your first trip to the conti-nent?"

"That's a little bit like the question I asked you a few minutes ago..."

"How's that?"

"It's a question you've never asked me before."

"Oh, I see..."

"Said the blind man."

They reached out to each other to shake hands, enjoying each other's company.

"What was it like? Well, let me try to give you a picture...."

Subconsciously he slumped back in his chair, a younger version of his grandfather and father. A kaliedescope whizzed across the surface of his mind. The sights, sounds, emotions of being in Ghana, West Africa, after so many years of being given the best information available about Africa and Africans.

"Got to keep one important thing in mind. I was seventeen years old that summer. Remember?"

"Never will forget it."

Never will forget it. The whole family was there to see me off. Some of them cried, thinking about the experience they knew I was going to have.

"Number one, the trip seemed like it was going to last forever. And this was on a superfast bus in the sky. It gave me a deeper insight to what it had been like to come from over there to over here on a slave ship..."

The old man nodded solemnly.

"Hour after hour I couldn't do anything but sit there and try not to crack up, thinking about how we had been transported from Africa to America.

Now here I was, <u>flying</u> back. The irony of it was enough to make you feel crazy."

Once again the old man nodded, remembering the first of his several trips to the "conti-nent."

"I'd like to be able to say I felt a deep, deep sense of being back home when I stumbled down the stairs off the 'plane.

But it wasn't that. In some ways, being back on the conti-nent was almost anti-climatic."

His grandfather nodded, smiled and sipped.

"I don't mean anti-climatic in the sense of..."

"I know what you mean, go on...."

"I felt I belonged there from the first minute and things got better as the days went on. A number of people had told me about the heat. I didn't find it any more unbearable than Chicago in the summer.

And the people seemed so familiar. I was always being surprised when someone turned away from me to speak to someone else in Ga, Twi or whatever."

"Did you meet a girl?" The grandfather asked, crossed his legs and allowed a sly expression to glaze his face.

"I met two. Lemme tell you about 'em. One was a devout-churchgoing sister and the other one was an iconoclastic secondary school girl...."

"She was a what?"

"She was a bohemian type."

"Oh."

"Comfort Lartey was the same age I was..."

"Which one was this?"

"This was the secondary school girl. And Grace Vivian Hlovor was the the devout churchgoing sister. She was about my age too, maybe a year older.

Funny how it happened. I met them a couple days apart. Let me start with Comfort. Comfort lived down the street from this family that rented me a room in the section of Accra called Osu."

"I know it well."

"You couldn't help but notice Comfort. The girl was stacked, granddad, the girl was stacked. I mean stacked!"

"I know what "stacked" means, Kojo, believe me I do... go on!"

Kojo loved his grandfather's warmth and enthusiasm, his interest in life made him seem superanimated.

"Aside from having this gorgeous body, she had a dynamite head on her."

"You mean....?"

"Uhh, nawww, I mean she had a helluva mind..."

"Ohhh..."

"The first time I spoke to her she invited me to a radical lecture, a speech by some guy with a Don King haircut."

Kojo paused, like a professional comedian, to give his grandfather some laughtime. He had never known a man who loved a laugh as well as his grandfather, especially if he painted the right image for his funny bone.

"Two hours later we were in my room, making outrageously loud teenaged love."

"I hope you used a rubber?"

"O yes, yes, indeed, lots of 'em."

"Ain't that incredible about those African girls? They can go to church eight hours a day and still be natural...."

"Well, the way Comfort put it was like this.... "this is what the Lord wants us to do or else we wouldn't be doing it.""

7

It was a crazy, crazy summer, believe me. The contradictions threw me for a few minutes. Here I am with Comfort, the bohemian, who wants to make love all the time and come back to America with me, and Grace, the conservative, equally beautiful, but reluctant to do anything, past kissing, I said she was reluntant, not rigid.

Comfort didn't believe in anything that the European brought to Africa; "Far as I'm concerned it's all a crop of crap!"

Grace, on the other hand, was completely brainwashed. She believed in European superiority, European ideals, the whole kaduza. We argued a lot.

We talked about everything, the three of us; I spent a lot of time running from one to the other. I guess you could say I was definitely in a polygamous mode that summer."

"Kojo, you too much, boy, you know that?"

The comment caused them both to laugh, and after the chuckles died, they were quiet for a moment. The young man gathering random thoughts, the old man waiting.

"It was romantic, no doubt about it, but there was a whole lot more, a whole lot more. I can remember waking up from nightmares, feeling like my chest was being crushed by something, many nights.

It wasn't so much a nightmare as something else. It took me a year to realise that I had been feeling the pressure of a slave ship on my body, the way our people had been packed in those hell holes.

Despite what you, Grandma, Mom and Dad had laid on me about Africa, despite all of that, there were times when I have this strange feeling of being 'way back up inside myself, like someone who was looking at himself from centuries past.

In some weird way I think that feeling, more than any other is what took me into film. I thought about writing for awhile, but I kept seeing visions, films in my mind.

After that summer I knew I was going to get into films; I wanted to give my version of what the 'African-African-American Experience' is about."

Kojo drained the dregs of his pineapple soda and stared into his grandfather's eyes. The old man's eyes fascintated him, the milky fringes around the irises, the flecks of orange and grey that showed in different lights.

"My Grandfather's Eyes." The title of the film sent a shiver down his spine. All the moments I've spent with this wonderful old dude, absorbing his vibes, feeding on his energy and wisdom.

"So, what's the deal now?"

The old dude wasn't dreaming he was right there.

"Well, to really tell you the truth, I don't really know what the deal is, I can't really say. I just feel a need to be back in that space again, to recap some of the emotions and energy I tapped into when I was 17."

The old man pursed his lip for a moment and looked into a distant corner.

"Well, you know what they always say, Kojo; 'The fire you go back to is always ashes.'"

"I'm willing to take that chance. After all the ashes I've been through over the past eight years there has to be a fire somewhere."

Kojo could remember moments in his life when he didn't truly understand what that meant. It didn't register until he got into the U.S.C. Film School, coping with the institionalized racism of that institution.

Somehow, at that point, he understood that his grand father's blessings carried the promise of a spiritual shield.

He could recall times when the thought of carrying his grandfather's blessings pulled him over the hump.

The old man stood and folded his grandson into his chest.

"Go on back to the conti-nent and give 'em my regards, I'll be making my last trip there in a couple more years."

They held each other at arm's length to stare into each other's face. Kojo felt the urge to cry but couldn't bring himself to release the tears.

"Yeahhh, that's the way you have to think, Kojo, when you hit your low eighties."

"O, I see...."

"Said the blind man. Ha, ha, ha."

Kojo drove north on Vermont, feeling the urge to check the city out before he left. Vermont and Imperial. The red light gave him a chance to take it all in.

Vermont and Imperial, two blocks from the first apartment we lived in when we first moved here.

The gorgeous sunshine gave the streets a brassy, orange glare. June 10th, 1996. He pulled away from the light cautiously, people ran the traffic light frequently at Vermont and Imperial.

A few blocks away, Locke High School. It always seemed easier to daydream in Los Angeles, it had something to do with the sunshine. He made an impulsive right turn at Manchester, going East to the freeway.

Be nice to trip to the ocean for a minute. From Chicago's Lake Michigan to California's Pacific Ocean.

Yeahhh, this is better; I can speed a little and not have to do the stop 'n go number.

"EL-A"; he felt he knew it as well as anyone after ten years of whipping around the freeways.

The miles curling in front of him made him think of an endless track. Are we moving or is the freeway moving? Anything was possible in Los Angeles. Locke High School, the "new boy."

"Let's give it to you straight, Kojo, they say that Locke is a bad high school."

"Uhh, Dad, Momma, I just transferred from DuSable, on Chicago's baaaaddd Southside, remember?"

Fifteen years old, the "new boy", the feisty "newboy."

"We gonna kick your ass, sucker!"

"Whose first?"

He smiled at the memory of the half dozen fights he was forced into, and that he won because of his knowledge of the African-Brasilian martial art called Capoeira.

"Kojo, you have to think of yourself as a primary defense system, what that means is that you can be buck nekkid and still be able to defend yourself."

As a fifteen year old "new boy", he had been practising Capoeira for eight years. It had become a part of his lifestyle. He started each day off with forty-five minutes of Capoeira.

"Heyyy, brother, what was that whirly bird shit? You looked like a helicopter when you kicked Bunco in the jaw."

Kojo Bediako Brown, the son of Kwame and Nzinga Oshalishe Brown. He felt blessed to have them as his parents, to have the grandparents he had, they were a powerful support system.

"Don't ever surrender, Kojo, you can never tell when help is going to come."

Winding 'round the bend that would give him his first clear look at the ocean, heading north on Highway One, one of his favorite drives, he felt exhilarated.

It was a feeling he could never prepare himself for, but one that always slid in on him when he drove up Highway One, with the ocean bordering his left, for days.

He clinched into the flow-of-speed-traffic, mindful of the fact that he was passing thru three police jurisdictions (jurisdictions?), his mind wandering across a collage of emotional landscapes.

The move from the Southside of Chicago to Golden California.

"I'm going to be totally honest with y'all, I just never believed that African people were supposed to live in the snow. We're moving to California."

The slow drive across the country spilled itself across his mind, the opening of the Africentric Bookstore on 103rd Street, in the heart of Watts.

"Whoaaa, c'mon now, brotherman, them people don't even read the newspapers, what makes you think they'll buy books?!"

School Daze. Locke <u>was</u> a bad school, low ranked, filled with underachievers, gang bangers, druggies and an elite that took great pride in being able to say that they had come in on top of all that.

Kojo pulled into his favorite seaside reastaurant, the gymnasium sized place with the picture windows facing the ocean.

California Dreaming and the Pacific Ocean

"Would you care for a cocktail, sir?" The clean diction, the bright smile, the deep tan, the gorgeous busom, the cornstalk colored hair. Almost a caricature of the White Californa beach girl.

"Let's make it a Guiness Stout."

"And would you care to order now?"

"In a bit...."

"Be right back."

He took critical note of the waitresse's swivelling hips as she danced away from his booth.

White girl. Never had a white girl.... never thought about them.

He stared at the calm ocean, gently lapping at the pilings of the restaurant. The sun glazed the water, drawing him into the hypnotic ebb and flow of the movement.

Yeahh, Dad made a wise decision. Chicago was the birthplace, but so cold. So cold. He could recall going back to that atmosphere for two weeks, to attend a couple funerals, and felt stifled by how closed in life was/had been.

CHAPTER 2

Everybody was always on guard; their doors double/triple/quadruple locked, their windows barred, their attitudes closed....

"Hey, look at it this way, cuz, it's about survival man, survival. You from California, y'all don't know nothin' 'bout this kinda stuff..."

He was forced to agree, even though he didn't agree. Los Angeles, California could be as dangerous, freaky, ill tempered, schizold, crazed, mad minded as any ghetto block in Chicago had ever thought to be, but the sun shining on the television newscasts and all the Romantic Ads, ("See Calfornia, Experience the pleasure"), denied the reality of a hard life.

"It is lovely, isn't it?"

Kojo turned to face the feverish blue eyes of the waitress.

"Yeahhh, you got that right."

They stared into each other's face for a hard moment trying to figure out what the other was thinking.

"Uhhh, would you like to order now?"

"How 'bout one of your "ONE MAN" pizzas?"

She shared his ironic vibe, quickly jotted it down on her pad.

"That's a great choice, I'll sprinkle a little extra mozarella on it for you."

"Good. And bring some tobasco with it."

Once again the glittering smile, the ruffed hair, the carefully "dimensioned" body swiveled away. He did a slow Pan of the restaurant. Middle of the road, middle classed, White bread eatin' Protestants, (as defined by the Sociocomedianne Carol Burnett), a few Black families trying to make their children aware that the Pacific was for everybody, clots of Asians here and there.

Yeahhh, it would be easy to see how someone "Back East" in the snow would look at this. it was sun, sea, sand, and an earthquake, from time to time.

They didn't seem to take the drive by shootings, the gang/drug related death rates, the racism, the environmental death rate (smog, smog, smog, etc.), the absence of drinkable water, AIDS, psychoses bred by the craziness of the Moment, the desperate urge to keep up, the car/vehicle smash up devastation...

O well, what the hell, yu can't win 'em all.

He strolled along the beach, pausing to pick up interesting stones and shells, from time to time.

"Well, Mr. Brown, the committee has carefully reviewed your project and I'm reluctant to say.... we'll have to reject it."

"Why?"

"Mr. Brown, I'm sure you're familiar with the committee's policies regarding student films."

"Why....am I being....rejected?!"

"Now please, Mr. Brown, control yourself!"

"I want you..... to tell me why....?"

"If you insist...."

"I insist."

"Well, to put it briefly, we have no authority available, to deal with the premise of your proposed documentary."

"So, what you're saying is that you can't find a White man who knows something about the presence of Africans in 18th century Hawaii, I listed four historians..."

"But they were all Black."

"Does that automatically invalidate their credentials?"

"Now, just a minute, Mr. Brown, there's nothing personal about any of this...."

"I'm sure."

Four years of intensive, attempted cultural imperialism - brain washing at U.S.C.

If it hadn't been for my folks I would've dropped out after the first year...

"Now just hold on a minute, son you can't drop out of school because of racism. You have to think of a better reason than that.

Let's face it, if you feel that dropping out of school because of racism will accomplish something, then you ought to rationalize a way for African-Americans to "drop out" of America."

He sat on a clump of boulders near the shore line, lost in thought, his camera eyes recording the soft velvet hues of the afternoon sun.

"Mr. Brown, I think our committee has been extremely lenient with you. We have allowed you to do your film, as you requested, without the advice of a faculty advisor.

But, we are having second thoughts about the...uhhh...direction your project has taken. It seems that you have made a blatantly anti-White film..."

Four years of it. Why does it have to be considered anti-White simply because it's pro-African?

Four years of it. He sprawled back on the rocks. I guess I showed their stinking, prejudiced asses a thing or two.

Twenty-five years old; four critically received short films, a dozen well done documentaries, assistant director on two top grossing feature films, thirty (forty?) industrial training type movies, another half dozen juicy possibilities staring him in the face.

Nawww, I ain't doing too bad, so far. The only problem is the Big Bucks. He sat up slowly and stared at the sun slowly melting into the sea.

The Big Bucks were dodging his grasp. The Big Bucks were needed for his feature film, the one he craved for.

Kojo rolled the words around in his head; independent producer-writer-director. Independent. Yeahhh, that's where my cookie is.

I don't want to do a Spike Lee. I want to do a Kojo Bediako Brown. And that's exactly what I'm going to do as soon as I get back from Africa, from the 'conti-nent'".

Kojo stared out at the milky white clouds surrounding the plane.

Well, I'm on my way....after the parties, the dancing, the good times, the libation.

"We pray to our Ancestors, we pray to the Orisha, we pray to God that our son will reach his destination safely and that he will remain in good health and accomplish all that he has set out to accomplish."

Thanks, Granddad, thanks. And thanks, uncles, thanks, family.

He shuffled around uneasily in his seat, his hip pocket stuffed with $2,500.00, another $2,000 in travelers checks in his valise and $3,000.00 more in his checking account.

Beautiful family, they were real about life....

"Once we get past all the romance, we have to start talking finance."

Thanks, Mom, thanks Dad.

"Now, Kojo, I don't want you to think I'm trying to urge you into doing something you haven't thought about doing, but take a good look at one of those African sisters whilst you're over there..."

"Why only one, Momma?"

"Well, hey, let's get real 'round here, how many daughters-in-law do you think I can handle?"

He settled his head back against the seat and closed his eyes. Kojo Bediako Brown, Grandson of Kwame and Tanina Oshalishe Brown, son of Kofi and Nzingha.

A bright flare of sun washed across his eyelids, reminding him of Chicago and the days when he tramped through freezing rains, snow, ice, the cruelty of life in the ghetto.

"Dad, is it really true that we're middle class? I mean, you know, what people call middle class?"

"No, we're not middle class, Kojo we're African-Americans. You see, designations like upper-upper, lower-upper, middle, middle-middle and all the rest were designed by White folks for White folks.

The reason I'm saying this is because no matter how much money an African in America has, he's still subject to being treated in an undesirable way, to put it mildly."

"Yes, I know, somebody is always running around screaming – 'Things are better than they was!'"

"Well, hell, they couldn't get any worse, they had to get better."

"So, we're not middle-class...?"

"I'd say that we are super-class 'cause we're African-Americans, that puts us in an class by ourselves. What makes you ask a question like that anyway?"

"One of my friends at school started talking about us, you know, like you and Momma have good jobs and stuff."

"Oh, so that's supposed to mean we fit into some kind of category."

"I guess so. My friend said that we could definitely afford to live in a better neighborhood."

"There are no better neighborhoods than this one. We all know each other and we look out for each other.

Remember, Mr. Bell coming over to help me get my car started last week? Remember Mrs. Adams and the block club ladies coming in to bring some goodies to your mother when she fractured her wrist? Sort of a 'We care' visit.

Of course, we have a few rats running around but it's that way in any environment. But, you see, Kojo, the point is this; the minute some of us luck up onto any kind of money we immediately want to move away from our own people, like we've suddenly become afraid of each other or something.

Be careful of false perceptions, they can blind you to the truth!"

The soft drone of the 'plane and the filtered sunlight eased him into a twilight sleep.

"C'mon, Kojo, the performance starts at 8, we don't want to be late."

He smiled at the memory in his twilight dream, of his father in his Ghanaian kente, his mother in her kaba and himself in his blue and gold caftan.

Performance of the Ballets Africain from Guinea, the Nigerian National Drum Ensemble, the National Drama Company of Ghana, the National Dance Ensemble of Senegal, Kutero lessons ("kun ba ding da") with brother Mosheh, Capoeira Regional classes with Mestre Henrique, plays, art exhibitions, festivals, jazz clubs and concerts, whatever was authentically Africentric.

"Kojo, don't ever be ashamed of being an African-American. Always remember we are the ones who made this country a world class power, with the sweat, blood, strength and bones of our ancestors, not the Europeans."

He came out of his twilight sleep with a simple theme in his mind...
I've got to give them some grandchildren, soon...

Many hours later, after the stopover in London and the pregnant pause in Kano, Nigeria, he stared down on the city of Accra.

Wonder what's changed in eight years?

He followed the stream of people into the immigration lines. Once again the dreamy feeling of being in a strange place that was so familiar that he didn't feel lost, disoriented or out of sync, struck him.

He took note of the modernized look of the terminal, but also noticed that the organized chaos seemed to be at the same level it had been eight years ago.

"Welcome to Ghana."

The voice from within the immigration kiosk sounded metallic, bored. Wonder how many times a day she has to say that?

"Thank you."

His attention was drawn to the excited voices of a group of African-Americans on his left.

After retrieving his passport from the immigration kiosk, with the obligatory thirty days visa stamped on the appropriate page, he stood over to one side, casually observing the tour group.

He knew it would have been grossly impolite, may be even patronizing to laugh at the sisters and brothers, but that's what he felt like doing.

Maybe it's just in me to see something funny about any group of people milling around, waiting for the program to be called out.

He intensified his observation; about thirty people, obviously middle-class (sorry, Dad). His Camera-eye isolated clusters of different attitudes.

There, the imperial couple, the man leaning on an oversized walking stick, kente cloth of every type blazing in the dull gleam of the air terminal lights.

Three schoolteacher types, probably on summer sabbaticals, hair braided to the bone, braceleted on all four limbs.

The quartet of hyper-excited, spoiled youngsters. They were probably forced to take the trip. Bet they'd rather be playing Nintendo somewhere.

The tall, elegantly dressed, darkskined sister, looking around for an African man to seduce.

The look of the group screamed - "FIRST VISIT TO THE MOTHERLAND".

He created an instant satire, the Camera isolating African-American attitudes. Why should the African-American visit home always be treated so stifly, so humorlessly?

He questioned his motives for wanting to do a satirical-film-comedy-of-errors on the group.

I shouldn't be so cynical. How many of us have had the kind of upbringing I've had, where the Africa thing was always kept in perspective.

"They ought to abolish the term "tourist" for African-Americans returning to Africa. And while they're about it, it wouldn't be a bad idea to deal with dual citizenship for those of us in the Diaspora."

He made his way through the usual customs rigamarole - "Anything to declare?"

He had requested that his father's friends, the Chinebuahs, shouldn't pick him up at the airport.

"But why not?"

"Well, number one, we know that there is always a possibility that the 'plane won't arrive on time."

"Well wait."

"Uhh, I would actually prefer the experience of making my own way in, just as I did the first time I came..."

"Oh, I see..."

One had to be brutally firm in the face of Ghanaian hospitality, or else it could overwhelm one. He felt lucky to be able to pick up both of his bags from the revolving baggage rack, after only a few turns.

Careful now, Kojo, musn't start making judgements, see it the way it is, the way you did the first time.

Bags in hand he eased himself through the customs inspection, paying as little attention to the inspection of his bags as the inspector paid.

Just think, I could be bringing ten kilos of cocaine in here.

The organized chaos on the inside gave way to less organization on the outside. He had only a few moments to take note of the African twilight before the hustlers moved in.

"Taxi, sah?! Taxi?" I will take you! I will take you! "I am called Kwame, I am your driver."

There was a cool about the man that he liked, and the fact that he heard his grandfather's name.

"Awright, brother, it's you. Let's go. I'm chartering your taxi for two hours."

The driver cast a shrewd look in his direction. The man has obviously been to Ghana before. Kojo smiled at the scene they were leaving behind as he followed the driver to his taxi.

It could be Mexico and "Black", as blasphemous as that might sound.

The driver placed his bags in the boot of his car, jumped in behind the wheel and waited for instructions.

Kojo checked his watch. 6 pm, time for all the things happening in Accra to happen, Tuesday night. He made an impulsive decision to hang out for a couple days, tune himself into the vibe.

Hell with the Chinebuahs, I'll be there when I get there.

He knew everything would be cool, no matter what he did, that's the way it was if you were a man in Ghana.

"Kwame?"

"Yessah?"

"Kwame, I want you to take me to Adabraka, and then to LaBone and then to Osu, and then maybe a couple other places."

"Yessah."

"And let's skip the "sah" bullshit."

"Yessah."

Nothing new on the food stands in Adabraka, off of Kwame Nkrumah Circle, popularly called, simply, "the Circle" or "Circ".

21

Black Star Square, Accra, Ghana

Wowww....looks like some of this stuff has been here since I was here the last time.

He strolled through the cooked food market, pausing to check out the ugly smoked fish, the beautifully glazed turkey butts, the bits and pieces of things he couldn't immediately identify.

"Buy my food, it is good! Here! Stop here!"

The women who sold the food were perched on wooden stands above the pedestrian heads. Why?

"Auntie, why do you have your food way up there?"

The woman stared down from her six foot high perch...

"You want smoked fish? Turkey meat? Very good!"

"Yeah, I want some fish, but I want you to tell me why you sell your food way up there?"

The woman frowned, looked away as though she were embarrassed and finally said, "It is to keep the young ones from stealing the food."

Kojo bought a couple pieces of fish he didn't really feel the appetite for, and strolled around the raucous market sobered by the woman's information.

I don't remember people stealing anything when I was here before. He looked around the food market with a different attitude. There was a carnival atmosphere, with the bright lights, the brawling music, the crowds, but the undercurrent was serious.

There was no uneaten food tossed on the ground, none of the waste that would be found at an American Carnival, no glitzy, tricky, money sponging games. No one wanted to spend money on anything that wasn't "real".

He wandered back to his "chartered taxi" filling up on atmosphere, beginning to feel hungry, not simply "snakish", but hungry.

"LaBone."

"LaBone, sah?"

"Yeahh, LaBone, the Chinese restaurant."

"Hin-lone?"

"That's the one."

Hin-lone-LaBone, driving through the once familiar streets he was beginning to feel in touch with the scene.

Adabraka, the Circle, LaBone and the Chinese restaurant, one of the few Chinese places that didn't corn starch everything to the stretching point.

Hinlone. He asked for a corner table and checked the time. I've been here an hour already, back on the "conti-nent" for a whole hour.

"What region is your food from?"

"Chinese food from China."

The memory of his attempt at cuisine research made him smile. He did a slow Pan of the people drinking and eating.

"Chinese food from China, o.k!"

And yes, it was o.k., it was more than o.k., it was delicious; the spiced bits and pieces of this and that, the duck.

He sipped his ABC, well chilled..... Ahhhhhhh.....finished it and moved on.

Osu. Osu was where he enjoyed himself, where he wanted to live, if and when he moved to Ghana.

Bywels, the weirdly structured Indian owned bar that pretended to understand what Jazz was about, "Jazz, every Tuesday at Bywels."

He perched on the too tall bar stool, (who in the hell thought of having a barstool at the same level as the bar?), and looked around; Bywels in Osu.

What a hip place this could be if the owner had any idea of what jazz was supposed to be about. He smiled into his beer, thinking of the night he hd been there when a male vocalist was singing a really interesting version of "The lady is a Tramp" in Ga, as the owner periodically interrupted his efforts to pump the sale of lottery tickets.

"Come pleeezzz, buy two tickets! Thrrrree hundrrred cedis each one. Who can say? You may be the lucky Winnerrr of anew 'frrridge or something ever morrree useful! Come pleeezzz!"

"And that's why the lady is a Tramp..."

There had to be irony in there somewhere.

The Shalizar. The Shalizar, 'round the corner from Bywels was an authentic drinking bar. No one attempted to sing anything, unless it was one of the cassettes piled up next to the boom box, and there were no lottery announcements.

It was an authentic, down-to-earth-drinking bar. Ga heard more often than English, chilled beer and local gin and brandy.

Men, (mostly), came in, purchaed their tots of gin, poured them down their gullets, splattered a few drops on the gound in memorial service to their ancestors and stutterstepped back out into the streets, their cares temporarily dismissed.

The two sisters who owned the Shalizar welcomed him warmly, but not effusively. They were too cool for that.

"So, you are back, long time."

"You are welcome."

Eight years ago, the first place in my life where I could buy a legal shot-of-gin.

"Yeah, long time."

Four tots of gin later, the senior sister put in an appearance with a bowl of banku and okro stew.

"Please sit down and eat."

Wash your right hand and dig into it. He ate with gusto, there was no other way to do it. Banku and okro stew. Midway through the lucious flavors he stood back from himself and shot the scene.

African-American-Diaspora-son-of-Africa-eating-in-the-local-joint.

He had forgotten how good banku and okro stew could be. He dug his fingers into the banku, used the slightly sour corn dough as a shovel for the flavors of the okro stew.

Okro stew, they call it here. Okro/okra. He dug into the mixture, enjoying and appreciating the flavors that he had almost forgotten. This wasn't glazed turkey butt or salted fish, it was live-real-done-right now food.

Yeahhhh, this is Ghana, I'm back home now f' real. This ain't Chinese food.

The girl who brought him the bowl of water and soap to wash his hands, after his enthusiastic appreciation of the meal, smiled shyly at him.

Whatshername? She was a little girl when I saw her the last time, and now look at her, she's a woman. How old? She must be sixteen, at least.

He sat at his favorite table in the rear of the bar and stared out of the wood slatted window at the evening's activities. Nothing had changed in any substantial way; men, women, children flowed past, laughing, talking, arguing, joking, singing, playing, enjoying the cool night air.

He felt sleepy, lulled into an acute state of low profile elation.

Jet-lag coming on, with all this good chop inside me. How much did I eat? How many tots? Time for me to chill out.

"See you guys later, I gotta go get some sleep, my first night in town. Oyiwaladonn..."

The Ghana Garden Hotel. He woke up listening to roosters crow. The Ghana Garden Hotel was centrally located. He could change money two streets away, call the Chinebuahs to tell them that he had arrived and that he would be with them on Friday.

And then I'll call Comfort. Wonder if she's still driving people crazy at the Ministry?

Room No. 206, the same room, maybe the same foam mattress. He stared up at the fan in the ceiling, feeling his body for mosquito bites. The Ghana Garden Hotel had been the location for his introduction to malaria.

He made an involuntary shudder, recalling the onset of the illness. A brief, flu-type weakness and then a total wipeout; no appetite, no strength to speak of, no will to fight the infection, a bell toned headache, aching joints.

The desk clerk had come to his room to deliver a message from Comfort Lartey and discovered him, drenched in sweat, shivering from chills, pursued by demons in his fitful naps.

"Oh, sah, you have malaria."

"No shit!"

They taxied him to a small private hospital in Osu, where the arrogant doctor arranged for a saline drip and ignored all of his deliriously slurred questions.

"Doc, you think I'll live? What're my chances? Doc?"

The next few days were days he had labeled "malaria video". He could close his eyes and see scenes, colors, plants, animals, demons, things that he could never have imagined in a clear minded state.

He felt the small bump on the back of his right shoulder. Damn, that's all I need now is a good case of malaria. Mustn't get paranoid.

Wednesday morning in Accra, Ghana, West Africa. He wrapped the sheet he had slept under around his waist and went to the window.

Africa. The swarms of people going and coming made him think of colorful ants. Nothing else would make any sense but technicolor.

He stood there for a few thoughtful minutes, putting story lines and camera angles together. The young woman selling oranges from a tray on her head. The cluster of people surrounding a kiosk across the street.

Two women with babies strapped to their backs, oblivious to the swarms of people who divided around them, like rocks in a shallow river.

Must be a helluva conversation they're having.

Young people everywhere, working. People pushing, pulling, hauling, selling, buying. Old people shuffling through all the activities, seemingly as oblivious to the hustle-bustle as the two conversationalists.

Well, guess it's time to jump down into all of this drippin' drama, find out who has what and what's happenin'...

❖

"Mrs. Chinebuah, please don't worry about me, I'll be o.k. I've been to Ghana, to Accra before, I know my way round....I'll be o.k."

"But we were going to prepare a dinner for you..."

"I will definitely be there Friday evening."

"How will you eat until then?"

"Please don't worry about me, there are some excellent restaurants around..."

"You won't forget, Friday?"

"I promise you, I'll be there."

"One moment, please, my husband wants to speak with you."

Thirty minutes later, after having spoken with Mr. and Mrs. Chinebuah, his designated host/hostess, and several other anonymous voices, he knew that he was not going to spend any more time with them than necessary.

They had mapped out an agenda that he didn't feel the slightest urge to honor, beginning with Sunday church services.

"Yes?"

"Is this the Ministry of Social Welfare?"

"Yes."

"May I speak with Comfort Lartey, please?"

"Who?"

Must be clear, take it slow, remember you have a funny sound here.

"Comfort Lar-tey."

"I'm coming..."

I'm coming, one of my favorites. I'm coming. Does if mean that you're going away, which is usually when someone said. "I'm coming." Or were they actually coming?

"Good morning, Ms. Forson here."

"Good morning, I'm calling Comfort Lartey."

He listened to a flurry of language pass between the woman he had just spoken to and someone else.

He felt something grow calm inside himself. Don't become impatient, there's a different rhythm happening here.

"Lartey here."

The voice was the same but somehow a bit more clipped, more British.

"Kojo Brown here."

"You say...?"

"This is Kojo Bediako Brown."

He didn't know what to make of the sudden silence, has the connection been broken? Did she faint?

"Hello, Kojo..."

"You tripped me out there for a minute. I thought you had forgotten who I was."

"No, no, I have not forgotten."

"Well, look, I just got back yesterday and I would love to see you."

"Long time..."

"Yeah, it has been a long time, about eight years."

Once again the sudden silence.

"Comfort?"

"Yes?"

"I'd like to see you this evening, after work. Is it possible?"

"This evening?"

"Yes, this evening, after work."

It was uncharacteristic of her to be hesitant. This was the fire snorting radical who never took longer than a second to decide anything.

"I cannot stay long."

"Ten minutes?"

He heard the smile in her voice; "Well, it can be a little longer than that."

"Good, shall I pick you up at the entrance to...?"

"O no, no, that won't be necessary, I'm mobile. Why don't I meet you?"

"The Country Kitchen?"

The Country Kitchen, Accra, Osu, Ghana

"Yes, that will be fine."

"See you about 5:30?"

"Yes. I see you have a good memory."

"About some things. See you later."

"O.k."

He hung up feeling uneasy about the situation. She sounded married. O well, let's see what we shall see. Now then, let's see what I can find to eat around here.

The choices remained the same. He could line up ten paces from an open, stinking drainage ditch to eat a hasty bowl of rice and gravy. He could buy an ear of corn, a bag of peanuts or something he hadn't thought about.

Or he could take a taxi to one of the restaurants he knew and trusted. The problem was time. The restaurants opened at 12 noon - closed at 3 pm and re-opened at 7 pm. No one had ever successfully explained to him why it had to be that way.

The alternative was to go to one of the posh hotels where everything was overpriced. He opted for Novotel.

The Novotel dining room faced the swimmin pool and was open for breakfast.

"Good morning, sah."

"Yes, good morning, may I have the breakfast special, please?"

"Yessah."

The sudden downpour startled him. The announcement of rain had been broadly hinted at by a brisk wind blowing, the fresh blowing of a rain storm.

The rainy season.

He started out into a rain blizzard, feeling schizoid. Seems impossible for me not to get wet, with all this rain coming down. He glanced around the dining room, looking for someone to share his feelings with.

No one looked receptive; ... a collection of odd types, Europeans, a couple Indians, six Africans in French cuts suits.

"Your breakfast, sah."

Eggs, toast, sausage, tea, small container of marmalade.

The rain slacked up a bit but remained a constant downpour, as though someone had opened a giant tap.

Breakfast finished, he sat staring at the downpour. The rainy season. He felt the urge to get back out into the streets and vetoed it. I'd be soaking wet by the time I took two steps.

My first day in town and I'm stuck in the dining room of a swank hotel. He signalled for the waiter, remembering to use the palm down, pulling motion.

"Yessah?"

"Can I get a drink?"

"Yessah, would you prefer it here or in the bar?"

"Right here would be fine. Make it Chivas Regal straight, water back, no rocks.

"Beg pardon, sah?"

"Two tots of Chivas Regal, a glass of water and no ice."

He shared a smile with the waiter. Yes, we do talk differently.

Nothing to do at ten a.m. but sit, sip and think. The rain slackened even more than before, for about five minutes, and then a fresh downpour came.

Somebody must be tilting clouds over up there.

CHAPTER 3

"Your drink sah."

"Thank you." Money. Money could buy anything, drinks in the morning, flights to Ghana, things, but it couldn't stop the rain.

He sipped his Scotch and immediately thought of his grandfather. Here's to you, ol' dude. He stared at the rain drops striking the water in the pool.

The rainy season, things have a more natural rhythm here, maybe it's got something to do with the rain. You can put on some heavy shoes and clothes and go out in the snow, but the rain is something else.

Was it raining when I came here the first time? Nawww, I would've remembered that. There's nothing to do when it rains like this but chill out. Or sleep. Or make love.

"Waiter, where's your telephone?"

"Kojo!?"

"Yes, it's me. Damn, I didn't think I was gonna get through to you."

"Well, you know how bad communications are here. Where are you?"

"Novotel."

"How long...?"

"I'm not staying here, I just popped in to have breakfast."

"Where are you staying? How long will you be in Ghana? Did you receive my last letter?"

Kojo felt a sense of hysteria coming over the 'phone.

Was this the slow talking, slow moving Grace Vivian Hlovor, the conservative one, that he had seduced eight years ago?

"Whooaa, Grace, slow down. One question at a time."

"When will I see you?"

"Uhh, how 'bout tomorrow?"

"Why not today?"

"Well....Uhh, I'm busy today, got a lotta runnin' around to do."

"In this rain" You must be meeting someone else..."

"Is that a statement or an accusation?"

"Maybe both. So tomorrow?"

"Yes, tomorrow. Where?"

"Why don't you come here, I'll prepare you dinner."

"Sounds good to me."

He walked away from the 'phone, directions to her apartment, ("it's the first entance before you get to the campus. If you get lost, ask anybody for Grace in apartment 7, they all know me."), feeling ambiguous about making a visit.

She sounds so wired up, so anxious. O well, no one stays the same.

11.30, the lunch hour crowd invaded the dining room disturbing his third Chivas Regal revery. Where did they come from?

He retreated to the bar.

"Yessah?"

"Chivas Regal and water back."

"You say...?"

"A tot of Chivas Regal and a glass of water."

"Yessah."

He was beginning to feel frustrated. The rain showed signs of stopping and then started again.

"How long will this rain last?"

"O, sorry, I don't know, sah, maybe another hour, maybe another week. Only God knows."

A week of rain...a whole week? He did a slow Pan of the bar, fixed his gaze on the beautiful, darkskinned woman sitting at a table with a short, potbellied White man.

They were having an animated conversation, obviously enjoying each others company. Kojo felt an odd twinge of something.

What the hell is she doing with him? Maybe she's his wife. Why would she be married to a male like that?

He noticed that he seemed to be the only one paying the couple any attention. It must be the U.S.A. in me.

"The rain has stopped, Sah."

"Oh, thank you."

So, the rain has stopped, so, what do I do now?

"Uhh, let me have another one of these bad boys."

"Yessah."

The weight was gone, no meetings, no 'phones no frenzied movements from place to place, no crossectional vibes, nothing. He was free to do what he wanted to do, on the "conti'nent", for a solid month.

The thought overwhelmed him for a few seconds.

Maybe it's the rain.

He sipped his drink, working feverishly to put a casual schedule together. He had promised himself that he would come to Ghana without an agenda, that he would take each day as it came.

I have to go to a village for a few days, to really chill out.

12:15, fifteen minutes past noon, the rain has stopped.

He was determined not to put himself on a treadmill, to force himself to go from place to place, just for the sake of saying - I went there.

He stepped to one side at the entrance to the hotel, to allow a wet bedraggled collection of people to slop in.

He recognised the familiar faces of the tour group that he had seen the night before at the airport, as they were coming in.

He took instant photos of the various expressions: I been rained on in Africa, Halleluya!

Damn I'm wet...

Where are we?

It'll be nice to take a shower, have lunch, watch T.V.

It was obvious that they weren't the same group that he had seen last night. Something had happened. They weren't as rambunctious, or as silly acting.

Had they been given a tour of El Mina - the slave warehouse, this soon? No, they would reserve that for the second or third day, but who knows?

Maybe the tour people were going more for instant shock. More quicker.

The rain had left a lot of mud behind, after the paved parking lot of the hotel was left behind. He jumped from one side of the drainage ditch to the other.

This place is filthy. The thought came to him in an uncritical way, simply as an observation.

He made his way for a few blocks before deciding to take a taxi. Why get myself all muddied up?

Three p.m., he mentally ticked off what he had done. A brief, complete tour of the National Cultural Centre - this is where I'll buy my kente cloth for everybody, around Black Star Square, a quick, hot look at the art the architecture of the National Theatre.

He was reluntantly creating a couple films in the back of his head as he was driven from place to place.

This place would be perfect for a <u>real</u> film, one of the-slice-of-life-things with something <u>real</u> happening inside.

"Driver, take me to the Ghana Garden Hotel."

I'll take a shower, nap for a bit, get ready for whatever Miss Comfort is about.

He stared at the scenes passing by; people selling things <u>everywhere</u>, beggars at the traffic lights mingling with teenaged boys selling apples, candy bars, bags of popcorn, girls selling ice water.

Why so many young dudes on the streets?

The woman pushing her face within a few inches of his at a stop light almost caused him to scream.

There was a hole where her nose had been, her lips were rotten and the begging sound she made was like a wounded animal.

Kojo's hand trembled as he placed a five hundred cedi note in her gnarled paw.

O my God...

In a split second he had the feeling being pushed back into a medieval time, filled with cripples, beggars, mad people babbling in Tongues.

Later, he sprawled on his bed, a sheet wrapped around his waist and tried to sort out his emotional state.

It's a poor place but it's rich with resources. Why aren't the people better off? Hardworking folks, hustlers. They deserve a better deal. What keeps them down? Who keeps them down?

He nodded off, slightly boozed from a morning of Chivas Regal sipping. The dream was a recurring theme; he had managed to get ten million dollars, enough money to make the film he wanted to make.

He had written a dynamite script, cast a talented group of people to play challenging roles and was reeking with success.

He woke up and listened to his stomach growling.

Comfort Lartey, twenty four years old, dark chocolate colored, snow white teeth, dimpled in both cheeks, a heart stopping body, the first African woman, (on the "conti-nent"), that he had made love to.

Kojo shifted in his seat, patted the package of Protector condoms in his pocket reassuring himself that they were there.

If my guess is right we'll be twisted around each other's body fifteen minutes after we finish dinner.

"Make a right turn here, driver."

The Country Kitchen, 5:30 p.m., he paid the driver and strolled into one of his favorite restaurants. The Country Kitchen, wonder who in the hell named this place? He liked the design of the place.

Auditorium sized, a high thatched roof, a back entrance and a front entrance on one side, plenty of elbow space betwen tables.

Table fifteen in the rear, my old table. Twelve people scattered around the space, the lunch crowd gone, the seven p.m. dinner crowd on its way.

Good. No audience for my show. Two bumpy hipped young waitresses carried on an animated conversation to his left front, at the far end of the restaurant, flutttering their hands at each other like outgoing ocean waves.

Same glacial service. he was finally able to catch the attention of one of them after ten minutes of waiting.

"Good evening."

"Good evening, I'll have an ABC and order dinner later."

She turned and swivelled away from him. Sisters really got some buttocks on 'em.

Comfort Lartey. He gazed out at the huge ferns and bushes bordering the open sided restaurant. Talk about buttocks. He could clearly visualize Comfort's naked body, the lushness of her hips, the indentation of the waist, the erect, full breasts.

The night we "rented" a prayer mat from the watchman on LaBadi beach to make love on. Starked naked in the moonlight. We were a couple wild young things to be sure.

He sipped his well chilled beer, thinking of the evening ahead. Wonder if she has a place of her own?

The thought of making love with her again, after eight years, make him feel excited. He took a larger sip of his beer, trying to be cool. My first love feast on the "conti-nent". I'll have to write Granddad.

"Hello, Kojo."

He decided to give her his most lascivious up and down look, starting from her low Cuban heels, up to her neatly cropped pixie hairdo. She always enjoyed the way he looked at her.

"Oh, that is such a sexy look in your eyes", she told him on half dozen occasions.

His eyes made it from her shoes to her hips before she abruptly popped into the seat opposite him.

"Please, don't stare at me like that, it makes me feel uncomfortable."

He reached across the table to take both of her hands into his.

"Good evening, Comfort, I'm glad you could make it."

He noticed that her hands were sweating and she was avoiding eye to eye contact. She actually seemed to be squirming in place.

"It's good to see you, Kojo. Long time."

He took her in slowly as she gently pulled her hands out of his. Five or six pounds heavier, a full fledged woman now, gorgeous. But what was all the evasive vibe about?

"Yeah, eight years to be exact."

A pregnant minute passed before anyone spoke again.

"Are you going to be here for awhile?"

"It all depends."

Look into my face, Comfort, share some of these lust-demon memories with me. Let's heat up the pot together.

Dead silence, not a pregnant pause.

"Uhh, as you can see I'm drinking the best beer in the world, would you like one? Oh, sorry, your drink is Guiness. I forgot."

"No, I don't take alcohol any more."

"Since when, if my memory is good, you used to love Guiness Stout."

"I have changed many of my ways."

Kojo felt the urge to reach across the table and shake the woman by the shoulders, to shock her into being herself again.

The waitress holding menus out to them prevented him from following his urge.

"Do you still take food?"

The sly, sexy smile that he loved slid across her mouth.

"Don't be ridiculous."

They ordered food. Sat silently, Kojo was beginning to have second, doubtful thoughts about their meeting.

Worse thing in the world is to get together with someone that you've shared some serious love with, and discovered that it's all gone.

Granddad told me this, "The fire you go back to has usually turned to aches."

He stared at the woman opposite him, recalling the wild moments they had shared.

"Comfort, remember that weekend we spent at Kokrobitey, the first one?"

"Kojo, I'd prefer not to be reminded of my sinful past."

He almost choked on the beer he was swallowing.

"What?!"

"I don't wish to be reminded of the sinful past."

"Heyyy, wait a mintue...let's stop the joking, you're beginning to make me feel weird. Why did you agree to get together with me?"

"I'm not joking and I came because you asked me to come."

"You mean you have no interest in being with me, other than the fact that I called you?"

She was putting him on edge, something about her aloofness, her reluctance to be a little more of what she was.

The waitress placed their food in front of them.

"Will that be all, sah?"

"Yes, for the moment, thank you. Well, how 'bout it, Comfort, what's the deal?"

He was startled to see the feverish look in her eyes as they made eye to eye contact for the first time.

"Kojo, I am now a born again Christian, I found Christ four years ago."

He chewed his chicken carefully and sipped his beer. Best to be cool and thoughtful here. What in the world is THIS?

"So, what're you saying - I'm the Devil?"

She began to eat and talk at the same time. It was the kind of droning monotone he had heard from other religious fanatics. He listened, fascinated.

"Where are the children of the Lord? I am one of them, I know that I am. I know that God loves me. When His only begotten Son, Jesus Christ, came to me I felt healed in every way.

Many are called, few are chosen. When I read my Bible, when I go to Church, when I say my prayers at night, I know that I am one of the few.

God loves me, Kojo. And I love him."

He had placed himself on a mental cherrypicker and was doing a crane shot of their dinner, circling the table.

"Dinner with Andre," that marvelous little two man-film-conversation by Louis Malle came into his mind.

"Dinner, Kojo and Comfort."

"Uhhh, anybody else love you, Comfort?"

"Beg your pardon?"

"I said, does anyone else love you? You know, like a real, flesh and blood man?"

"Kojo, you are mocking my faith."

"No, Comfort, I'm not mocking anything. I'm just asking you a question. Are you in love with anyone besides Jesus?"

She stared at a distant point above his head for a moment.

"Yes, there is someone."

Kojo felt like breathing a sigh of relief. Thank God, I'd hate to have to go through this too many more times.

"Planning to get married?"

"He is already married."

"O, so, you're a married man's girlfriend?"

He regretted asking this question, it sounded unnecessary harsh and mean.

"I am not anyone's girlfriend, I am the mother of his children."

He took a hard look at her face. Damn, she seems normal. This is wild...

"You have children?"

"Yes, a boy and a girl."

"How old are they?"

"The boy is six, the girl is seven."

"You never mentioned anything about children to me in our letters."

"You never asked."

He was dying to ask her a half dozen questions, the first one being - how do you reconcile this born again Christianity with adultery and having children out of wedlock?"

A sober voice counseled him; leave it alone, Kojo. She told you she had changed when she first got here.

He made an instant decision to go with the flow, to enjoy the moment. There was no other way to play it.

If I try to get too logical here I'll wind up beating my head against a wall. Wowww, this is really something.

"Comfort, I have to tell you, you're much prettier than you used to be."

"Oh..."

He wanted to kiss the expression that flitted across her face. Eight years ago she was an innocent secondary school graduate and that was written all over her face.

What is she now? Well, she certainly isn't innocent, not with two kids.

The meal finished, the plates taken away, they sat with their hands folded on the table as she talked to him about her relationship to Almighty God.

"So, you see, Kojo, this is a serious thing with me. I take God seriously, I believe that God loves me...I..."

"Comfort, gimme a break, o.k.?"

"You say...?"

"I said, gimme a break, for God's sake!"

"You shouldn't use the Lord's name in vain."

"I'm not using the Lord's name in vain, I'm imploring His name to try to get you out of this crack in the record. You sound like a broken record.

You've become completely humorless. Did you know that? You used to have such a great sense of humor, what happened?"

"Those of us who are seeking the Kingdom of Heaven have no time for frivolous activities."

Unreal. Here is this gorgeous woman that I used to bankrupt myself with, physically and emotionally, and now look at her, she's become a religious nut.

"Kojo, do you know Jesus?"

"As a matter of fact I do. He lives on 7th and Alvarado, in Los Angeles. His last name is Gonzalez."

The feverish look in her eyes blazed up.

"Hellfire and eternal damnation await those who do not acknowledge the holiness of our Saviour."

"I'm sure. Incidentally, which denomination are you in? Catholic? Methodist? Calvinist?"

"Jesus Christ of Latter Day Saints."

"The Mormons?!"

"Yes, the Mormons."

"Comfort, do you know anything about the history of the Mormons? Did you know that they preached that Black people were inferior, until a few years ago, did you know…?"

"My faith cannot be corrupted by those who doubt the power of Jesus Christ."

She stood up slowly and held her hand out to him….

"Goodby, Kojo, welcome back to Ghana."

He stood as he took her hand and held it. He felt sorry for her, saddened by the circumstances he found her in.

She's as much a cripple as anyone of those beggars working the traffic lights.

"Goodby, Comfort, God bless you."

She cocked her head to one side as though she couldn't believe her ears, performed a neat pivot and marched out of the restaurant.

Kojo lowered himself back into his seat. Wowwww, talk about changes….wowwww.

He felt tempted to order another beer but censored himself. No, no more alcohol or you today, buddy.

❖

The encounter with Comfort could only be balanced off by a trip to the movies. He sat in a small bar across the street from the movie theatre, nursing a bottle of orange drink.

8 p.m. He was a half-hour early for the 8:30 show, time enough to check out the scene again. The same decrepit line of metal chairs, the chickens pecking around, the mosquito loaded drainage ditch, Ghana Films.

Something new had been added, something called "Executive Theatre", featuring mostly American video movies (he had inquired).

Next time for the "Executive Theatre", tonight it had to be Ghana films. Wednesday night, an off night for movie going in Accra. People usually make it out on Friday and Saturday.

8:15 p.m., he joined the thin, scraggly line of people buying tickets to see the latest Ghanaian movie. He was surprised to look behind himself and see a line of people.

Where did they come from?

He had seen enough Ghanaian movies to know what to expect, but he still held out hope that some changes, some progress had been made.

He squirmed in his seat for the first ten minutes of the movie. Don't look at it as a U.S.C. film school graduate, see it for what it is.

It wouldn't work. He couldn't ignore the movie being shown out of focus. He looked around to see if he had any fellow sufferers.

Hmmm....everybody seems to be enjoying the thing.

The projectionist was showing the movie out of focus, the sound was too loaded and mushy, the technicolor was as washed out as a tenth generation bit of zeroxing, the make up was atrocious, (couldn't they see the man's grey beard was unstuck on the side?), but the acting was honest and the story interesting.

He suffered through the convesations that never stopped during the movie, people giving their opinions...

Must be a racial trait, Black people must discuss the movie while it's going on, all over the world.

The conclusion of the movie placed Good in its proper place and Evil in its proper place and that was that. He filed out of the theatre unsatisfied.

It's the kind of movie Comfort would've made, no compromises, no grey areas. He strolled down the side of the street, carefully avoiding puddles of rainwater and patches of mud.

Afrikiko. Why not?

Afrikiko, the acre sized outdoor joint with the tables and the prostitutes. He found a table, ordered a draught beer and Panned the scene.

It all seemed so familiar; the tables with two or three women, the table with three beer swilling Germans and one lonely African whore. A clot of Ghanaians discussing the last soccer game.

"May I join you?"

Kojo stared at the woman and blinked. She could be Comfort's sister.

"Please join me, by all means. Will you take something?"

Ahhhhah, I'm falling into it now - will you "take" something?

"I would like a mineral."

Yes, a mineral, a soft drink. In the 'States it would be iced tea. Or champagne, depending on the level of commerce.

Kojo signalled the waiter and turned his attention to the woman. Yeah, a real person, my kind of person, too bad you're a prostitute.

"What's your name?"

"I am called Patience. And what is your name?"

"I am called Jim."

"You are an American?"

"That's what the passport says."

"You like Ghana?"

"Whoaaa, hold on a minute, sister, I'm supposed to be asking the questions."

"Oh, sorry..."

"I'm just joking."

"Oh, I see."

Pretty woman, no older than twenty. What the hell is she doing here?

"Uhh, tell me something, Patience."

He liked the eager look that lit her features up, she wasn't a jaded old timer.

"Yes?"

"What else do you do, you know, when you're not doing this?"

"I'm a student at the university."

"Run that by me again?"

"I beg your pardon?"

"Explain what you just said."

"That I'm a student at the university."

"Yes, that's what I thought you said. So, this isn't something you do all the time. I mean, this isn't your whole life."

"Oh no, I'm only doing this part time."

He could see the face of the AVENGING ANGEL, Comfort Lartey, above the head of the student-prostitute sitting in front of him.

"Uhh, what about diseases, infections, stuff like that?"

"I always use the condom."

He decided to skip the other questions, the questions that would have carried echoes of Comfort Lartey's judgemental morality.

Questions like: What do you feel, selling your body to strange men? What will you tell your husband about what you did in 2000? What will you say to your daughters? What do your parents think of this?

They matched sips for a few beats, temporarily lost for words.

"Your school fees are pretty high, huh?"

"Yes, it is very difficult."

CHAPTER 4

Kojo had to resist the sudden urge to laugh at the situation. *Am I crazy or what? Here I am, sitting up here in one of the most notorious 'ho gardens in West Africa, listening to some clever stuff that a bonafide 'ho has thought up, about being forced to prostitute helfself part-time, in order to pay school fees.*

There was a time when it was the sick mother, or the father in the cancer ward, now it's - I'm doing it to get through school.

And despite his cynicism, he believed her. The truth was on her face and in her eyes. He followed her eyes as she avoided looking at the large White man who had taken a seat at the next table.

"Somebody you know?" It wasn't necessary to point at the White man, she knew who he was referring to.

"He is one of my regular customers. If you want, I can send him off...

"No need to do that, Patience. Go on and take care of business."

"O.k., come back soon. O.k.?"

"O.k., I'm coming."

What else was there to say? He tried to blot out the sight of the luscious young body going to serve the gross White man.

I should've copped her, just to keep her out of his hands for a few minutes. He felt a moment of intense jealousy.

The slave market is still open, come in and buy anybody you want.

Somehow he wanted to rationlize the situation away. *There ought to be a law against African women selling their bodies to Europeans. No, that wouldn't make sense. How can you legislate an individual's use of herself?*

He winked to her as he walked past their table, she acknowledged his wink with a brief, warm smile.

CHAPTER 5

He sat in his darkened room staring out of the window at the pitch black streets, feeling frustrated because the electricity was off.

He felt Ghana creeping up on him. He was begining, after a day and a half, to expect the unexpected. If the lights are on, the water is off. If one taxi driver tries to overcharge, the other one offers a free ride.

Comfort Lartey, A Mormon. I wouldn't have believed that she would go that route in my wildest dream.

Why?

Pull back that kind of logic, this is Ghana, Accra, West Africa. The why? here operates at a different rhythm, no way I can get into it this soon.

The forms of the few stragglers making their way through the streets, all of them with loads on their heads, gave him a sense of mystery.

Where are they going in the dark? 11:15 p.m. and there is nothing to do but go to bed. He had decided not to go down to the desk to request a candle.

Too much of an effort, just wait 'til tomorrow to write. He sprawled on his bed, laced his hands behind his head and went into a thought mode.

Eight years ago I came here and it blew my mind. I was out of the Diaspora, I was back Home. I didn't see the clogged up stinking drains, the six year olds working eight-ten hours day, the poverty.

I was back Home and that was all that mattered. Being Home meant no White discrimination, being forced to deal with prejudice and racism. I was in a Black place, run by Blacks for Blacks.

I didn't see how well or how badly anything was being run. I was Home and that was all that mattered.

The sounds of distant drums interrupted his back flash thinking. Always some drumming somewhere and usually at night. Wonder what it's for?

The meal he had shared with Comfort was becoming a memory, but he knew he would have to wait until tomorrow for more food.

Who would be open or selling anything to eat this late? He made a mental note to buy something to snack on.

So, Comfort is a Mormon. Why couldn't she have become a Muslim, or a Buddhist or something reasonable? A Mormon.

Sorry, Mom, the percentages have been cut down by a Big One.

Grace Vivian Hlovor, the Ewe queen. I guess I should start praying that she hasn't become some kind of weird something or other.

No, not conservative Grace, it would take tons of magic to turn her around. He had already prepared his mind for a staid, well bred, conservative eveing with his old girlfriend.

He smiled, remembering the two day ordeal he had to go through to get her to kiss him. The kiss led to a month of lovemaking that always ended with Grace silently asking the Lord for forgiveness. And sometimes not so silently.

What a helluva trip the Europeans laid on the heads of our brothers and sisters over here. Crazy madness. They did a number on us too, but that was part of the conditioning process, a way to cool us out.

How could the Africans allow themselves to be taken on the European-religion-trip? And the Muslims. And all the other foreign religions that have come in to create guilt, paranoia, neuroses.

Stop it, Kojo. Leave the brothers and sisters alone, you're being patronizing. If they didn't want it they wouldn't have it.

Yeah, but what the hell do they want it for? A small, persistent voice screamed from the back of his skull.

Patience. I wonder if that's her real name? I wonder if she was tellimg me the truth? Student-sex worker.

Been here, how long? A day and a half? and it seems like layers of stuff is beginning to pile up around me.

Tomorrow, Thursday.

He felt tempted to get up and scribble an agenda. Somethiing he had disciplined himself to do over the years.

47

Nope, no agendas, I'll just let it happen, aside from the pre-set things. Grace. You've been blessed, brother. How many men can say they've had the opportunity to deal with two sisters as fine as Comfort and Grace?

Except for that hair thang. How could they starch and press their hair like that all the time? On the day it's done it looks slick and shiny. Three days later it looks like a rat's nest and they don't seem to notice. He had had a mean spirited argument with Grace about her "rats-nest". She was six days after her latest perm.

"No, Grace, I'm sorry, baby, you can't go out with me with your hair standing all up over your head like that."

"And why not?"

"'Cause it looks like a rat's nest, that's why!"

"You can't tell me how to dress my hair."

"I'm not trying to tell you how to dress your hair, I'm telling you I don't want to go out in the streets with you, with your hair standing all up over your head like that!"

"Oh!"

Morning. He dropped his bath towel around his waist, took up his toy bucket with the soap and net towel in it and took a cold "baff".

They called it, "baffing" and performed the ritual religiously, every evening and every morning and sometimes in between times.

Cleanest people on Earth. The "baffing" finished, he dressed and turned to the next item. What and where do I eat?

The ladies who changed the linen and the men who swept and mopped were always anxious to make a few extra cedis doing errands, but he wasn't enchanted by kenkey, smoked fish and pepper. Or fufu and light soup with goat.

He had forced himself, during his first visit, to be honest about his neutral urge for the ordinary food; the kenkey, the fufu, the stews of various kinds.

They seemed to stress soup-ness, overcooking and lacked greens of any kind.

Strange, with all of these vegetables around here, they're treated like second class citizens.

"'Morning, Sah."

"Good morning." He wanted to ask - when will the lights come back on? - but realized that the question would be wasted on the desk clerk. How would he know?

10 a.m., almost midday for the people who got up at 6 a.m. every day.

Kojo stood on the top step of the hotel entrance, watching the flow of traffic. It's like a river of people; young people, old people, crippled people, determined people, resigned people.

He caried a medium sized shoulder bag with his money, passport and keys inside, along with a clean shirt and a tube of deodorant.

No need to get hot and funky and stay that way. He made his way into the stream of people, arbitrarily going left.

It'll stimulate my appetite to walk a few blocks, I need the exercise. He was beginning to feel the urge for a serious Capoeira workout. Before boarding the 'plane in Los Angeles he had made a conscious decision to give himself a week's holiday from the workout.

After all these years of working out almost every day I can't lose too much of an edge after a week.

The color of the woman and her direct look startled him. It was a face in the crowd going the other way.

A charcoal colored woman, middle aged, sculptured features. Her direct look was not flirtatious, and not obnoxiously curious. It was simply the look of someone who was looking at something she hadn't seen before.

Probably from a village and never seen an African-American before. He had come to grips with being an African-American in Africa during the course of his first visit.

"Got to remember, Kojo, we're a Creole people. That means we have some admixtures that the average African never even thought about. You'll see people on the coast with complexions like ours, 'cause they were the ones who met the ships, remember?

I think the basic difference with us has to do with the Indian connection, with our Cherokee, Choctaw, Creek, Seminole ancestors. Folks in Africa tend to disregard our Indian connection, their focus is on the White boys in our bloodstream."

Kojo paused to stare at himself in a shop window. We are a Creole people. Yeah, Granddad, you're right on the money. As a walnut brown skinned person with semi-kinky hair he had never thought of himself as "fair-skinned" or "red".

But in Ghana he was surprised to hear descriptions of himself as "fairskinned". Grace was the first one to cue him in.

"I knew a girl in secondary school who was fair, like you."

"Fair? like me? You think I'm fairskinned?"

"You are fairer than me, I'm black."

People, as a rule, were generally darker than most African-Americans, but he still had a small problem with being considered "fair".

Well, I guess Adam Clayton Powell, Malcolm X, Lena Horne, Ertha Kitt, Aretha Franklin, Dexter Gordon, Duke Ellington, Billie Holiday, Coretta King, Vonetta McGce, Jasmine Guy, Sinbad, Redd Foxx, Joe Louis, Veronica Porshe and a whole bunch of other people would be considered White folks.

It was a tricky sector of the forest. He had been told that most dark skinned West Africans considered themselves inferior to the Europeans.

The person who explained it, a so called "half caste", put it bluntly; "Well, just look at it, Kojo. The Europeans have all the good stuff. They are obviously living cleaner, healthier, saner lives than the Africans.

The Africans are not stupid. They look around and see how wretched things are here and how good things are there, so they have no choice but to reach the conclusion that the people who are responsible for this better life must be superior people.

It's built into a number of expressions we have. If you want something done properly, you say 'Do it White man!'".

Kojo had fought the idea of the Africans, his people, being addicted to an inferior mindset. He still fought it but found himself surrendering to facets of the accusation.

"Kojo, you don't have to take my word for it, use the evidence of your own eyes."

He had seen it, at 17. It happened graphically one morning at the post office, when a Dutchwoman strolled in with her two little blonde demons and all the people in the post office rushed to admire them, to pat their blonde hair, act adoring in their eyes.

And on the pavement outside, a Black woman selling oranges and bananas had two little dirty children in semi-rags that no one bothered to say anything to. Or to admire.

He had seen it often, at 17, an impressionable age, how one word from one Lebanese was enough to put fifty African bodies into motion.

He had discussed it with his parents when he returned to the states.

"Yeah, we checked that out the first time we went there. I saw some scenes in Cote d'Ivoire that almost turned my stomach. Nzingha, you remember the Uncle Tom in the Hotel Deuville?"

"Never will forget him, the way he used to bow and grin and suck up to the whites. It wasn't about being a servant, it was about being SERVILE. The manager of the hotel used to slap him on his bald head all the time and he'd just grin a little more and say, "oui, m'sieur, oui".

"It's kinda hard to figure Ghana out. I have a suspicion that things would have been a bit different if Nkrumah had lived and remained in power longer.

First off, I don't think the re-colonisation process would have happened; the economic neo-colonisation by the World Bank and the Funny Money Interests."

Dad and Mom, got to scribble them a few lines tonight. The car brushing his right leg told him that he was walking on the wrong side of the street. He crossed over.

I'll, at least, be able to see who is running over my body.

The so called Coffee shop in LaBone.

"Driver, you know the coffee shop in LaBone?"

A casual nod indicated yes, yes, I know the place.

Kojo settled back to look at the people. The whole thing is a giant script. He took mental notes of the hundreds of actions. That he could catalogue. The woman with the baby strapped to her back who was lifting a tray of bananas from her head to sell a few to a nonchalant customer. The man pissing against a wall, ignoring the people all around.

The scene took him back to the first time he had seen a woman lift her skirt and piss. He described what happened to Comfort, who showed him, one evening over a drain in Osu, how it was done.

"It is not unusual, Kojo, we do this from an early age. You pull the crotch of your panties to one side and let fly. What else can we do? There are few public toilets and they are far between."

The swarms of people began to thin out as they left the central section to go to the posh residential area called LaBone.

The contrast was interesting. LaBone wasn't Beverly Hills, but it was a long way from the squalor of Jamestown, Nima and inner Osu.

The LaBone Coffee shop.

"I'll have red red."

"And what will you take to drink?"

"Uhh, make it ABC."

Red red, black-eyed-peas liberally soaked/cooked in palm oil with a few slices of plaintain.

He sipped his beer, waiting for the black-eyed-peas that the Ghanaians called beans.

11:25 and I'm drinking again. Kojo found it hard to put the alcohol consumption into the proper perspective.

Seems like every time I turn around there's a bottle of beer waiting for me. Better watch it, I might begin to like this stuff.

Belly pleasantly full of red red and ABC he settled back for a half hour of people watching.

They came in all shapes, colors and sizes. Six small Japanese men popping out of a Toyota to quickly quench their thirst with draught beers, men and women obviously making rendezvous, two Ghanaian men, comrades, strolling into the collection of outdoor tables, their fingers interlocked.

Interesting, the differences between customs. If two men walked around holding hands in New England or Texas somebody might lock them up, here it doesn't mean anything.

Hmmm......that would make an interesting documentary, an exploration of how the same gestures, body language can be interpreted in a different way, depending on whose border you're within.

More people smoking, buying cigarettes one by one. You brothers are in for some serious cancer in the years to come.

12:30. He paid his bill and wandered away from the coffee shop, wondering what to do with himself until 4:30. He strolled on the side of the road, as far away from traffic as possible.

Somebody ought to put some sidewalks up here, human beings shouldn't have to share the same space with moving automobiles.

What to do 'til 4:30? He began to compare Accra, subconsciously, with few other "foreign" cities he had visited. It ain't Mexico City, by a long shot. Madrid, nothing happening on the café level, thank God it ain't New York.

It's Accra, Ghana, West Africa, that's what it is. I'm feeling a little edgy because there are no neon lights in every block, or fake ways to stimulate jaded appetites.

And no drive by shootings, teen aged gangs, (and middle aged gangs), roaming around, looking for fresh prey. None of the hostility that I've accustomed myself to grin and bear.

The Ghanaian Glance was quick. Men took careful glances at the swaying hips, but didn't go in for the Mexican-sex-lust-demon look.

People are serious here. There is a lot of smiling and joking but the undercurrent is serious. I guess it has to be, if you look at the current cedi times the dollar exchange rate.

People look at me, they give me the Ghanaian Glance, but no one runs up to me with any kind of outrageous games. I like that. I like this place, I'm going to do a film here.

W.E.B. DuBois Memorial Center for Pan-African Culture

The DuBois Centre for Pan-African Culture. Sorry, my brother, you'll have to excuse me for using these grounds that Osagyefo Kwame Nkrumah gave you as a way to kill a little time.

Kojo had been to the DuBois Centre on his previous visit, before he really understood what DuBois had been, what he represented.

Well, he wasn't perfect, that's for sure...

The grounds were peaceful, well laid out, a large dump-grove of bamboo here, great shady trees above, only two commercial outlets; a small gift shop and a restaurant. He strolled the concrete paths, from one section to the other.

"Good afternoon."

"Oh, good afternoon."

Ghanaians were meticulous about their greetings. No one made the mistake of saying "good afternoon" before noon, and "good morning" a minute after twelve. Must be an English hangover.

Too bad they won't buy into the other parts of the time factor, like being on time. They call it "African time," meaning that the meeting scheduled for 11:00 am might not take place before 1 pm. Or later.

Terrible habit to be like that. Three Lebanese and four Japanese could take over the whole country because, if that's what they had decided to do they'd meet on time and do it.

Chill out, Kojo, you're generalizing and you can't generalize about people.

"Oh, pardon me, sah, are you here for the meeting of the African-American Club?"

"No, I'm not. Who are they?"

"The African-American Club is a group of African-Americans who meet here on Thursdays."

"What time?"

The waiter studied his watch as though he were reading the thermometer.

"At 3 O'clock."

Kojo checked his own watch. Two O'clock now. I'd like to see what they're about. I can take a taxi from here to Grace's place.

"3 O'clock? Are you sure?"

O, yes, 3 O'clock."

"I'll take a...uhh...a Guiness Stout. Is it cold?"

"Yessah, very cold."

A table under shady tree, a well chilled brew. No sweat.

"I thank my ancestors and I thank the Orisha for making my return to Africa possible....

I thank my ancestors and I thank the Orisha for giving me a healthy body and a healthy mind...

I thank my ancestors and I thank the Orisha for all the blessings that I receive from now until the day I die...

I beg my ancestors and I beg the Orisha to keep me healthy, make me wealthy and wise..."

Kojo said his personal prayer in a whisper and dribbled a few drops of his beer on the ground.

What better place in the world than this place to say my prayer?

He tried to make himself as inconspicous as possible, to observe the members of the African-American Club as they arrived. The staff of the

DuBois Centre announced the location of the meeting by arranging ten chairs in a circle.

It was ten minutes after 3, early by Ghanaian standards, when the first two members arrived. Two well upholstered, middle aged women, wearing a mix of African and American clothes.

He had to brush aside the idea he had in the back of his head, that this was going to be a collection of fire snorting, rapidly moving younger types.

By 3:20 pm, five of the chairs were filled (well filled, he noticed) by women who could have been called "club women" in the 'States.

He decided to take a chance, find out the rules of the game. What the hell, what can they do but ask me to leave?

"I hope you'll pardon me for interrupting your meeting, but the waiter told me that you all are African-Americans, and that you have this club and you meet every Thursday..."

"You're an African-American, aren't you?" One of the early arrivals asked with a strong hint of the Ghanaian lilt in her voice.

"Uhh, yes, I am..."

"You are welcome, please be seated, we'll speak with you about permission to join the club as soon as we finish dealing with the minutes of our last meeting."

He sat, as directed, and slyly studied the members.

Four decidely middle aged women, and a younger middled aged woman.

They don't look like they're too much into working out and eating 900 calorie salads.

The minutes of the last meeting seemed to go on and on. He made a surreptitious time check. 3:55. What the hell is wrong with me? The woman invited me to her house from 4:30 on, not at 4:30. And what the hell would it matter anyway, I'm in Ghana, how can I be late?

"Now then, Mr....uhh..."

"Kojo Bediako Brown."

"Did you say that you were an African-American?"

"With a Ghanaian name?"

"That's what my parents named me."

Wowww, where are you all coming from? He tried to make it sound as jocular as he could.

"Would it make any difference if I were Ghanaian?"

He followed the exchange of loaded looks, from one woman to the other. Once again, the early arrival with the pseudo-Ghanaian accent spoke.

"No, it wouldn't make any difference if you were a Ghanaian or not, but the rules state that our organisation is only open to African-Americans from North America, specifically."

Kojo felt as though his chair was slipping under him.

"What if I were a Jamaican or a Cuban or a Brazilian?"

He could easily see that he had reached the bristling point with the group. The youngest of the group fixed him in the lower section of her bifocals and ground the words out.

"I believe Mrs. Quartey made it perfectly clear that we are an African-American group."

"But Brazillians are African-Americans...."

A stone curtain fell between them. He waited for someone to say something for a few beats before he stood to leave.

"Thank you for giving me an opportunity to find out what your group is about."

He imagined he heard something close to growling as he walked slowly away.

Unreal. On the grounds of the DuBois Center for Pan-African Culture.... the man must be twisting and tossing with agony every Thursday.

He walked the winding road, bogged down with heavy thoughts about the ladies, the situations, the baggage that many African-Americans carry.

Mrs. Quartey...probably married to a Ghanaian. How could they justify an "African-American only" policy? Specifically African-Americans from North America. It was a denial of the Diaspora.

How in the hell did we wind up in an elite position on the Diaspora totem pole?

Drop it, Kojo, drop it, trying to be logical about illogical stuff is a guaranteed headache.

❖

Kojo exhaled a sigh of relief as Grace opened the door to her apartment and greeted him with a hug and a juicy kiss.

Thank goodness she hasn't become an overweight sister. The overweight sister meant hours of sympathizing with the weight gain, being forced to listen to how it had happened, future plans for future diets. He didn't think that he was an expert but he had been put in the position of counselor to a couple of overweight girlfriends.

She closed the door behind him, they took a few steps into the center of the room and squeezed him to her again.

"Ohhh Kojo, it's been such a long time."

She took his hands and held him at arms length.

"You seem a bit more serious, but you haven't changed much physically."

"I'd say about the same for you. Matter of fact, I'd say you lookin' damn good."

He could recall a time when that kind of language would have been received with a disapproving down turn of the corners of the mouth. Grace glowed with smiles at his compliment.

"You are welcome."

"Thank you."

They held hands and looked into each other's face with open admiration. He could see her lips slowly moving toward his mouth. They kissed again, slowly, more thoughtfully.

What's the deal here? It used to take hours before I could justify my wanting to kiss you, now look at this.

"Kojo, I've missed you."

"I've missed you too, Grace."

"Oh, but I'm not being a gracious hostess, please be seated, make yourself at home. Can I get you a drink? Wine? Scotch? Gin? Beer?"

"Scotch sounds wonderful."

"I have Johnny Walker Red and Black."

"I'll take Black."

He stood in place, watching her walk away from him to the kitchen. Girl, if your body gets much finer I'll scream...

He made a slow move around the room, listening to her pull the ice cube tray out.

"Please, Kojo, play some music. I have record albums, and tapes, they are there, under the book shelves."

"Native Son", "The Fire Next Time", "Malcom X", "Marcus Gavey, Messiah", "The Wretched of the Earth", "Before Columbus", "Before the Mayflower", "Wounded Knee", "Black Indians", "Ebonics", "Master/ Slave", "Mixture or Massacre", "Scars and Memories", "Haiti", "Who Shot Martin?"

"Find anything you like? I was tempted to have music playing for our arrival, but I couldn't think of what would be appropriate."

He liked the sound of her voice. It was a bit crisper than it had been, but the tone was the same and a bit hipper.

"I've found a lot I like."

Coltrane, Ravel, Miles Davis, Stravinsky, Dizzy Gillespre, Alban Berg, Manndite Magic, Mahalia Jackson, Wynton Marsalis, Beethoven's 9 Symphonies, Indonesian Gamelan Orchestra, Sounds of Spain, Billie Holiday In Carnegie Hall, Griots of Mali, Ghana traditional music Cecil Taylor, David Murray, Phavia Kujichagulia, Ghasem Batamuntu, Mozart Hype, De Falla, Rav Shankar, Alla Rhaka, Mongo Santa Maria, Armando Peraza, Francisco Aquabella, Carlos "Patato" Valdez, Muddy Waters, Howlin' Wolf, B.B. King....

"Thought you said you found something?"

"Yeahh, that's the problem. I've found too much I like."

She handed him a tumbler of Scotch with three young ice cubes floating around in the liquor. Wowww....

"To you, health and prosperity."

"And vice versa."

They clicked glasses and took sips.

"Grace, what's happened to you? The last time I saw you you were listening to Gospel music, or country and western, reading the Bible and praying every fifteen minutes and..."

"I've had many changes happen in my life since we were together."

"I don't doubt it." Shades of Comfort Lartey.

Once again they took unison sips.

"How would you like to listen to a little Quartet in F Major, by Ravel?"

"Yes please, it's one of my favourite peices of music. Now I have to finish the groundnut stew. I'll be with you in a little while."

Beautiful woman, ain't no doubt about it. Full up front and ample behind. Gorgeous body, lovely face, full of nuances and animation. Brains. I never realized she had brains. May be I didn't pay that part of her any attention before.

He placed the music on the turntable, adjusted the sound and strolled around. What we would call a one bedroom efficiency deal in California.

After a few minutes he felt he could sum up the scene in a few words - tasteful, clean, African.

He settled himself on the sofa and soaked up the music and the scene.

I'm in Africa I'm in Africa I'm in Grace Vivian Hlovor's apartment. Yeahhh....

The third hard sip of Scotch kicked it in, that mellow buzz. I can see why the old man likes his Chivas Regal.

Kojo's eyes roamed the room and the doors leading from the room. Bedroom, probably. Toilet there, Grace in the kitchen. Hmmmm.... Grace in the kitchen.

He tip toed to the kitchen door. She was seated on a low stool, grinding something in a bowl, sipping from her glass every now and then. An African kitchen; a stalk of plantains in the corner, a large yam, a pestle and a motar, onions and tomatoes on the kitchen sink.

"Hate to disturb you. Where is the little room?"

"Second door on the left."

"Hmmm, smells good."

She turned a dazzling smile up at him...and continued grinding. Kojo deliberately opened the first door on the right, to check it out.

Ahhahh, the bedroom. Furnished in the same lean style, no excessive stuff cluttering up the eyes, a lovely African batik on the bed.

The toilet system didn't work. He was surprised to lift the stool top and discover leavings from other sitttings, as one of his friends in Accra once put it. Experimentally he pushed the flush handle down. Nothing.

O well...

Grace was sitting on the sofa when he made his exit, her glass in her hand, an enraptured look on her face.

"This section right here, this is what I like."

Yeah, Ravel and all those syncopated strings. He sat beside her and listened to the sounds.

"Yes, I like this section too."

The humanities class at Los Angeles City College had opened his head for the European composers one summer. His mother had been a guiding force.

"Don't get into an anti-European bag, Kojo. Try to understand the best parts of everybody's culture. Listen to their music, that's a good place to begin."

His father was less open, less inclined to be tolerant. "No, not the music. I can see myself clear to deal with the sciences may be, but the music, no. Why would I want to suffer through all that white noise when I was raised on William Grant Still and Charlie Parker?"

"I'm glad to see that you've grown to appreciate a variety of music."

"Yes, it's true. I can clearly remember some of the fights we used to have about my love for Hank Snow, Willie Nelson, guys like that. Remember?"

"It wasn't that I didn't think their music was valid, it was just a matter of perspective. How could I listen to the country and western guys, appreciate them, knowing that they had stolen the music from our people."

"Don't worry, Kojo, your argument would be wasted on me now."

She sealed off further discussion with a quick kiss. He was right in tune with her but she was moving so much faster than she had moved, once upon a time.

"Come, I've prepared banku and groundnut stew with fish for you."

Banku and groundnut stew with fish. Delicious idea, wonderful flavors.

They sprawled out on the floor with sofa pillows under their heads after the dinner, fresh glasses of scotch in their hands.

The music was Indian, ragas by Ravi Shankar. He felt at ease, pleased to be back with one of the African loves of his life.

I think I can write Comfort off of the agenda.

"Grace, I don't want to sound like I'm interrogating you or anything, but I'm dying to find out what brought about this change in you. I was thinking that you were going to stay at home until you got married, have four children the first year, you know, become whatever the program called for.

He studied the cleavage that made her breasts resemble two softy welling mountains. They were both feeling warm, and high from their third glasses of scotch.

"So, you want to know what happened? Do you really want to know?"

He leaned up on his left elbow to take a close up of her.

"Are you joking, hell yes I want to know."

"Well, I must confess to you that you were a major element in the process. I know, I can see from the expression on your face that you find that difficult to believe...but it's true.

After you left, I started seriously thinking about what we had done together, what you had done to me, the impact you had made on my life."

"I didn't feel any of that while I was here."

"I concealed a great deal from you, Kojo. While you were smirking at my innocence, I was going home to sleepness nights.

I was thinking of all the things you knew, that I didn't know anything about. I felt very unsophisticated.

I began to look at myself closely. I was "trained" to be a Christian, I didn't become one by inclination. I was sent to Accra Girls Secondary School, I didn't choose to go there.

I was the "well bred" dutiful daughter of a middle class Ghanaian family, my father was respected and my mother was influential. They died three years after you went back to America.

First, mother from a cancer that she never spoke about, she just suffered. And then, my father, from grief. I think when they died a great number of restraints were removed. I couldn't embarrass them if I wore my hair like this...for example."

The short cropped, natural style seemed so right for her that he hadn't bothered to comment on it.

"Or, if I raised my voice in public. The rest of my family tried to rein me in, you know, the way you pull in a wild horse, but it was too late.

I had met a man my own age who knew so much more about the world, someone who was not asking me to wash his clothes or sweep his house. You were a Revolution for me."

Kojo sprawled back on the pillows on the floor, feeling real high, real good, a bit egotistical.

"So, I did that, huh?"

She smiled at his egotistical glow.

"Eh hee; I can't really say that you were the total force, but you see you were certainly an element."

Ravi Shankar and Alla Rhaka grabbed them both for a few moments, the sitar and the tablas creating an intoxication of their own.

"And then, what happened" Please remember, I've been away."

Kojo felt that he was being stared at from a great height.

"I met an older African-American man, who built on the foundation that you had established. You asked me for the truth. Do you wnat to hear it?"

Kojo suddenly remembered a Ravi Shankar Concert, Live! at the Roxy Theatre on Sunset Blud, where the master has asked the alcoholic drinking people to cease and desist. He felt the urge to invoke that kind of feeling, but it was too late.

"I don't think it can hurt me."

"Eh heeee."

He could tell that she was feeling drunker, more freer, her language was slipping into tonal levels that he had to listen harder for....more Ghanaian.

"He worked for an Agency and he was into Ghana. You understand?"

"Yeahh, I know what being into Ghana means."

"What?"

She was shaking him up with her new approach. She didn't go around anymore.

"It means...well, it means....being into...Ghana."

She took a long sip of her scotch, Ravi Shankar had ended, she popped up to put a Horace Silver album on. Horace Silver, damn, where did she get that from?

She gracefully placed herself near him to talk.

"The man was forty years old. He spoke Ga, Ewe, Fanti, Akan and Hausa. He was as close to being a U.S.A. spy as anybody I'd every met but at the same time he was into Ghana. You understand what I'm saying?"

Kojo nodded mechanically, feeling vaguely jealous and drunk. Yes, I understand what you're saying. I think.

"It wasn't so much a love thing as it was an educational thing. Many of the things you hinted at, he established. You had talked to me about jazz, he played the jazz music, from Ragtime to the neo-Moderns."

Ragtime? What the hell is Ragtime?...

"He brought the African-American Civil Rights struggle into focus. He opened my mind to the Diaspora... he... he did so many things."

"What was his name? No! skip that! I don't want to know!"

He thought he detected a malicious shadow of smirking expression.

"You don't want to know his name?"

"No, I feel good about the idea of being the foundation."

He carefully placed his glass off to one side, took her glass from between her splayed fingers, placed it off to another side and pulled her closer to him.

"I feel good about being a foundation."

They kissed a long, down to earth kiss.

He studied the glazed lights on the lake. They weren't far from their destination. Kokrobitey. Another mile or so, a left turn and then the long drive on the rutted red road.

Grace squeezed Kojo's hand in the darkness of the back seat and tilted the glass of sctoch to her lips with her free hand.

Kokrobitey, the beautiful seaside hotel complex where there was singing, drumming and dancing on Sunday afternoon, "cultural things."

He had gone there with Comfort during one of their wilder moments. He could never imagine that he'd be going there with Grace.

He studied her profile. Beautiful African lady. I'm so glad you changed. Whether I had something to do with it, or what's his name? or whoever? Thank God.

The taxi seemed to be wading through a field of tall grass. Grace offered him the glass of scotch and said something to the driver in Twi.

"What did yoiu say to him?"

"I told him to drive faster and more carefully."

He shared smiles with her, sipped the scotch. He felt mellow, romantic. They had made love on the floor of her apartment, a feverish event that barely gave him time to push the condom on.

She had given him the kind of feeling he loved to have a woman give him. She was passionate, skillful in the use of her passion, and responsive. He loved that feeling, of giving and receiving.

They awoke from a deep sexual cat nap, her head deadening the muscles in his right arm. They felt dreamy. He spoke softly in her ear...

"The French call that le petit morte, 'the little death.'"

"I call it the nap after banku and fish stew."

She was so removed from being the still, almost formal person she had been that he found himself staring at her.

Is this the Grace Hlovor that I once knew? The prude, the cold hearted one who said, "I'm only doing this because you insist!"

Kokrobitey had been a word in their joint shower, an idea while they dried off, and a full fledged motion within fifteen minutes of conversation.

"Why not? All I have to do is stop at my hotel for a change of shorts. Tomorrow is Friday, how will you get off?"

"Kojo, I'm the person in charge of my department and I made tentative arrangements to be absent after you called."

"Pretty sure of yourself, huh?

"Pretty sure of you."

❖

Boats on the Beach, Ghana, Atlantic Ocean

They left their bags in the second floor room and immediately strolled out.

"I love this place."

"It really is nice. I think it's one of the loveliest places in Ghana."

They linked their arms, tipsy from the scotch they had brought with them, on each other. A gentle wind swayed the palms and ferns around them as they slow walked down the graveled path toward the restaurant and performance area.

"Looks like it will rain tonight."

"Not before I pee, I hope."

They took a right curve to one of the toilets. He went in to relieve his bladder. Beautiful sister, full of humor, warm, intelligent, sensitive. He was walking out of the toilet and was stopped by the sound of her voice.

"Kojo, don't come out now, wait."

"What?"

The apprehension in her voice didn't make sense. Wait? for what?

The sudden sound of whacking on the concrete steps of the toilet caused him to involuntarily flinch. Wait? for what?

He pushed the door open to find Grace with a short stick in her hand, taking a couple whacks at something that looked like a small black lobster.

"Scorpion. They're dangerous. I was afraid you would come out and step on the bloody thing."

She tossed the stick away, brushed her hands together and nonchalantly linked her arm back through his. They were a few yards from the restaurant.

"Would you like a beer?"

"Yes, why not?"

The restaurant was half filled with white couples. Kojo whispered to Grace as they took a table near the window.

"Looks like we're the only Africans here."

"We're the only ones who can afford to be here."

"Hmmmm...."

They ordered their beers and focused on each other.

"Hey, that was kinda brave of you, you know? I know some sisters in the 'States who would've run away from that thing you killed."

"Really?"

"Take my word or it. They get real squeamish when it fcomes to nasty little things with a lot of legs...."

"We can't afford that luxury here, there are so many nasty little things running around with a lot of legs."

She smiled a lot, he noticed; a kind of punctuation to her way of speaking. They sipped their beers silently for a few beats, looking at each other.

From a distant place they heard the drumming that announces the news about to be broadcast on Ghana Broadcasting.

Kojo, knowing the Ghanaian love of the hourly news reviews; "you want to go watch the news?"

Graced frowned and smiled her little smile.

"They're not giving us any news, they're just videoing people giving great speeches."

He decided to press her a bit, so much was coming out of her that was unexpected. The restaurant slowly ground down to three seriously talkling couples at three separate tables. The waiters looked sleepy.

"Kojo, you must remember, Africa is often a mystery, even to us Africans."

"Run that by me again."

"You say...?"

"Repeat what you just said, I don't know if I understand...."

"Africa is often a mystery, even to us Africans."

"That's what I thought you said. Please explain that, it sounds too mysterious to me."

"Will there be anything else?"

The waiter cut in, yawning.

"No, that's it. Here you go."

"Grace, why don't we give these guys a break? They look like they're ready to fall asleep."

They occupied seats in the area overlooking the outdoor dance floor, beer and glasses in hand. The sky seemed to be brooding.

"It's going to rain."

"You predicted that earlier. Is that part of the mystery?"

"Ahh, I see you haven't changed, you still love to find out what others think. I like that in you."

She leaned over and kissed him.

"Thank you, Madam."

She sipped her beer and tilted her face to the sky.

"I'm not sure I can explain what I mean about the mystery. It's simply something I feel. Here we are on this continent that's three times the size of America, the place where the human being originated, the place where so many different languages are spoken that they've lost count.

In a country as small as Ghana here we speak more than a hundred languages. Why? It's a mystery.

We have life saving medicines that people don't use, and poisons that could kill cities. We have wars on this continent that make no sense."

"Well, wars don't make any sense anyway."

"Don't you think that the people who lived on the continent where the human being originated should know that?"

A jagged flash of lightening many miles in front of them lit up the sky for a moment.

"Yeah, talk about mysteries."

They were silent for moments of serious thinking.

"Are African-Americans a mystery?

"No, African-Americans are familiar strangers, foreigners inside the circle, some more than others."

They were high on the whiskey, the beer, each other. And they had reached into that uncensored place that will allow speech to express the truth.

"I can accept 'familiar strangers,' but foreigners seem a bit much, don't you think?"

Damn, I've been here two days and they've got me saying things like "a bit much".

Grace leaned her head back to stare up at the millions of stars above her.

"Kojo, you are a foreigner, that's what you are. There may be another side of you but the one thing we definitely know about you is that you're a foreigner..."

"Now wait a minute, the Diaspora has to be brought in here somewhere..."

She squeezed her eyes shut, trying to capture the star patterns inside her head.

"Diapora doesn't mean anything to the average Ghanaian, not any more than Ghana means to the average African-American.

We didn't have "Diaspora lessons" in school, we still don't. And I strongly suspect that many Ghanaians, who have no idea of what Diaspora means, have a Japanese attitude toward the whole business."

A stronger breeze was pushing the gentle winds to one side.

"What's that mean?"

"Well, if you know something of the Japanese attitude toward the survivors of Hiroshima and Nagasaki, the problems their descendants have had to face..."

"They were blamed for being in the wrong place at the wrong time."

"Exactly."

"Are you saying that that's the way Ghanaians think about us?"

"I said I strongly suspect many do."

"So, where does that place the White man, the European, in this scheme of things, the mover and the shaker behind the whole business?"

He watched her take a long sip of beer, obviously rolling his question around in her head.

"We adore the Europeans. We idolize them. We beg from them. We copy from them..."

Kojo was beginning to feel slightly put out by the drift of the conversation.

"Grace, you're confusing me somewhat, it seems that the African-American would be the adored one, the idolized figure..."

"O yes, it's true. And we do adore you, but only if you come very close to the European standard. We don't want the confusion that most African-Americans bring us, this overly developed sense of Africaness that you parade around.

The European doesn't create this kind of confusion; he shows no inclination ot assimilate, or to imitate us. He knows that he couldn't do it if he wanted to, anyway.

He is, and always has been, exactly what he is, a bloody, mean, vicious **bahstard** who would sell his own children for a price. They often did that, you know?"

"Yeahh, I read about it. Which makes it still harder to understand why you would admire someone like that."

She turned a wicked little smile in his direction.

"Please don't take what I'm saying literally."

It was his turn to smile at himself. Loosen up, Kojo man, you're behaving like Comfort. Don't you know sarcasm and irony when you hear it? This sister is heavy.

"You know something, Kojo....perhaps we envy our brothers and sisters in the Diaspora. . . .

"Should I take you literally?"

"Yes please. Yes, maybe we envy you in the deepest parts of our psyche."

"But why...?"

"I'm coming."

I love the way those two words are used. "I'm coming" could be the cornerstones of another kind of philosophical thought. It wouldn't be - "I think, therefore I am", but "I'm coming."

"Look at it this way; you've done your slavery, it's a "done deal", as you say in Hollywood. We're still struggling through ours.

We're coping with health care slavery, financial slavery, yes, some of us do know what the World Bank and the International Money Fund, "***I Mess You Funny***" stand for. We're fighting for dignity, self esteem, international respect, trying to deny that we are not divided by tribalism.

Remember the hot little war they had up north a few years ago between the Konkombas, the Dagombas, the Gonjas, the Manprusi?

"Uhhh, vaguely."

"It could have escalated to a Rwanda scenario, if the people hadn't stopped it. The people said "Hell no!" to the whole business and it was all over. But not before hundreds, maybe thousands were killed and displaced.

Your tribalism was nipped in the bud by your enslavement, you were forced to disregard titles like Yoruba, Ga, Akan, Konkomba, wheeever. You became Africans in America. Period.

I am an Ewe. Do you know what that means?"

There was an urgency in her tone that forced him to look at her closely.

"No, I can't really say that I know what that means."

"Well, then, I would never be able to explain it. I'm sure a Ga or an Nzema or a Hausa could say the same thing. It has to do with an accumulation of things, layers of mystery."

They held hands. She made him feel enriched by her presence, the way she spooled things out for him. He liked the way she talked to him. She made him think of his family, the way they were able to say what they wanted to say honestly.

"Granddad, how did you come into this Africentricity, way back then?"

"I don't think I'd ever be able to put my finger on a moment that would say.... yeah! right here! That's when it happened. It wasnt' like that.

My Daddy's parents insisted on him knowing the true role Africa, Africans had played in the context of world history. World history, not African-American slave history, World history!"

The sudden shock of the rain splashing into their faces sent them scurrying to the warmth and dryiness of their room.

CHAPTER 6

Kojo stared at Grace's profile. What was the question she asked before we went to sleep?

"How do you like being back in Africa, in Ghana here?"

He answered her silently....it's much better than it was the first time, much better.

She seemed to stir herself awake, squirming around in place, yawning luxuriously.

"Oh sorry. Good morning."

"Good morning." He leaned over to plant a small kiss on her lips. She turned her head to avoid the kiss and scrambled from under the mosquito net.

"I'm coming."

Yeah, sweetheart, you can say that again.

He listened to her "baffing". Ghanaians, he had discovered, during his first trip were addicted to "baffing", which is what the word sounded like to him.

They took baths at night, before going to bed. In the mornings, in the afternoon and at other times in between. The bath/shower was an event that stood small children in giant wash basins, coated with soap suds, to be scrubbed like living laundry.

He laced his hands behind his head and Panned the room. An old fashioned mosquito net, cane pole chairs, a cabinet for clothes, a bedside table.

The fifth of Johnny Walker Black label was half empty. We put a hurtin' on that bad boy last night. He smiled, feeling pleased with himself, masculine.

The film was in another kind of technicolor, the scene was taking place in a seaside hotel with all the amenities, two lead characters, an African woman and an African-American man.,

He studied her as she emerged from the toilet/bathroom. Gorgeous Black woman, intelligent, lovely attitude... She took a jar of cream from her overnight bag and began to massage it into her face, arms, breast, hips....

"Here, let me help you, I can put some on your back."

She pulled the mosquito net up and sat on the side of the bed with her back to him.

"Thank you, kind sah."

"My pleasure, madam."

Fragrant cream, yellow butter colored. He smeared some on both shoulder blades and gently massaged it into her skin.

"Is this cream responsible for your pretty smooth skin?"

He thought he felt her shiver as he massaged the cream into the two dimples in her lower back.

"I don't really know, I've just been using it all my life. Are you going to take your baff now?"

Kojo make a wry face behind her back, he really hadn't given it much consideration, his mind filled with other thoughts.

"Uhh, yes please..."

An hour later, after the quick cold water shower and a massage with her cream - "I don't know if men use this, normally..."

Grace lay in the pit of his right arm, quietly answering a question he had asked.

"I really don't think that we think of love in quite the same way as you do. I'll have to admit that I've been "westernized" to a great extent, through my relationship with you, trips to England, Charles's influence.

"Charles?"

He was sensitive to the moment she took to consider what she should say.

"Charles was the African-American I spoke about."

"O, I see. O, this is interesting."

Why should I feel jealous? Evidently he didn't make a lasting impression or else I wouldn't be here, she wouldn't be in my arms.

"What I'm doing is generalizing, based on the advice that my mother gave me, my aunts, other women, mostly older women. They never seemed to emphasize the love factor.

It seems, for them, the important thing was that the man would be reasonaly faithful, wouldn't drink too much or spend his money foolishly.

I can't recall anyone talking to me about love.

I think the concept of love, as you know it, is still a sort of movie thing."

They were silent for long moments, unhurried, feeling lovely about their feelings.

"That's interesting, you know? That women would think like that. Where I come from I think everybody is searching for someone to love."

"I don't think it's a bad idea."

She leaned up on her elbow to kiss him.

They told each other silly stories and giggled through a long lunch hour.

"Wonder where our neighbors are?"

"Maybe they haven't gotten out of bed yet."

After lunch they wandered down the rocky path to the large boulders bordering the beach.

"Grace, I have the weirdest feeling that you're not the same woman I knew when I was here before."

"I wasn't a woman at all, not at all. Were you a man?"

"I thought I was."

He spoke so earnestly that it provoked both of them into laughing. A bright, clear day, the air cleansed by the rain, a beautiful woman at my side. I must be in Heaven.

No, you're in Ghana, on the "conti-nent".

They seemed to be doing things telepathically. A second before he unseated himself from the rocks to stroll along the rain soaked beach, she was standing, waiting for him to make his move. When he held out his hand, hers was there for him to hold.

"Grace, let's go back to our room, I have an Ananse story I want to tell you."

"Yes please..."

He woke up from the dream with an enormous appetite. The mosquito net gave the space above their bed an ethereal look. He studied the angles, thinking about the position of the cameras, the need for intimacy in the scene.

"Kojo, what are you doing, shooting a movie?"

"No, baby, I'm designing a film."

"What's the difference?"

"Well, number one, movies are made as assembly line things; a car chase, sixty three bloody numbers, a sexy so-called love scene, a blown up ending. The film is something else. You'll have nuances of feeling in a film that could never be duplicated.

I have the feeling that most movies are zeroxed; a film, never. It wouldn't be possible to duplicate any of the emotional elements that make a film cry."

"Cry?"

"Or moan. Or delight. Or dazzle or whatever. I saw a French film by the French master of comedy/satire, a dude named Jacques Tati, you know him?"

She nodded no.

"Jacques Tati, he may be dead now, but he made a series of satirical films - "Mon Oncle", "M'sieur Hulot takes a Holiday", "Playtime". "Playtime" is the one I've tripped on for years."

"You've done what?"

"Tripped on, you know? Let myself get taken off on."

"Oh."

Hmmmm...this language thing is trippy, have to remember that.

"Tati made a film that satirizes modern life and emotions. I'm sure some New York critic would say something else, but that's what it was about for me. Film, something you may see a dozen times and feel that you're seeing it for the first time every time."

"So you want to do a film in Ghana here?"

"So help me God, if the creek don't rise and the summer don't turn cold."

"Huh?"

"Oh, just something my grandfather says sometimes."

Saturday morning Kojo blinked his eyes open to find Grace staring into his face.

"Well, well, well, what's this?"

"What's what?"

"What're you doing?"

"I'm just looking at you".

"Oh".

It was midday before they unwound themselves from each other as Kojo jackknifed to an awake position.

"Damnit I forgot to call the Chinebuahs!"

She smiled and cooed...

"Don't mind them..."

They sat on the veranda in front of their room, sipping glasses of scotch and watching the misty rain come down.

"I guess this rain will wash out the performances today, huh?"

"It isn't too heavy, it may stop in an hour or so."

"Or a week or so...?

"Only God knows."

It may have started off being just a weekend with an old girlfriend (who had become a new person), but now it was obviously something more.

"Grace, it seems that I've been asking you questions since Thursday evening..."

"I hope I've answered all of them to your satisfaction."

"Except for one, I noticed that you ducked away from that one."

She took a long sip of her drink and turned to face him with a sad look in her eyes.

"Do I want to get married? Yes and no. I'm 24 years old, a good age to get married here. But I don't feel that marriage would be right for me now.

I'm almost too educated and vocal for this place, which would cause me problems with most Ghanaian men..."

"You got other men in the world who are not Ghanaians?"

"And I couldn't imagine myself living anywhere else but Ghana here."

He felt the impulse to argue but censored himself. If I'm not asking her to marry me, what's the point of arguing with her about it. What do we do? Make love, enjoy ourselves, see what tomorrow brings.

"Grace, let's go inside..."

"Yesplease."

A grey toned sun beamed on the people in the triple decked audience, gave the sweating dancers a gleaming look.

Kojo and Grace watched the performances of the dancers, drummers for an hour, drinking and thinking. After an hour, by mutual consent, they threaded their way past the Europeans and wandered down the road leading away from the resort.

"Well, what do you think?" She asked him, "This your first time?"

"No, no I've seen it before. Strange, I wasn't able to put my finger on what disturbed me the first time. Now, I think I can. It's got something to do with things being out of context. You know what I mean?"

"I'm not sure."

They passed thatched huts where people stopped doing what they were doing for a few seconds, to stare at the rich people from the resort down the road.

"The village dances from different places that they're doing don't seem to fit here, making these movements on concrete; White people...."

"They aren't all White."

"Well, people taking pictures of them as though they were animals in zoo."

"People do that everywhere."

"I know, I know they do, but it still bothers me."

"I agree with you. It's good to see the money coming in, but sad to see the decadence that it breeds. Did you notice how sluggish the last group looked?"

Kojo flashbacked on the energetic shoulder/arm movements, the 6/8 pelvic action, the whirling and athletic leaps.

"Sluggish? They didn't look sluggish to me."

"I guess you'd have to know the dance, to know how it should really be done. And that's why I agree with you, about seeing things done out of context. The mood, the feeling, the ambience, if you want to call it that, is missing.

You should see the way the dances, the rituals are done in the villages."

"I'm planning to do that next week."

"Really?"

"Yes, I thought about it, you know, about spending all my time in the big city. That really ain't where it's at in Ghana here."

"You're right. Do you have any specific place in mind?"

"No, not really. I just thought I'd get on a bus and ask them to drop me off somehwere."

She smiled her special little smile at him.

"I have relatives in Tsito, I'll give you a note for my Auntie Eugenia."

Monday morning, 6.00 a.m., on the road back to Accra.

No SEIU for Workers in Ghana

Exterior-Day-interior of taxi taking the honeymooning couple, (who have never been married), back to the humdrum of life in the big city. The woman is making a speech. . .

<u>Grace</u>

"What do people outside care about what happens to us here? All they want to do is come here and take advantage of the exchange rate.

See Ghana, life in the 3rd world on pennies a day. I don't care about the African-American emotional thing. They would probably feel the same if they went to Burkina Faso or Togo. Some of them might feel the same if they went to France or England.

I'm simply annoyed with the arrogance, the ignorance, the assumption that we're happy in our little mudhuts. Bullshit! yes, bullshit! we want the same things other people have, and more, because we've been denied our share longer."

"Kojo?"

"Huh?"

"What're you thinking? You look worried about something."

"No, I'm not worried about anything...just thinking."

"About all of this."

He pointed with his chin at the scenes they were being driven through. Small boys pushing on open cart filled with cement sacks. Small girls balancing trays of different items on their heads, all heavy. Men and women hustling to make their daily bread.

Men taking early morning pisses against piss stained walls, thousands of people trying to figure out a way to get away from the rainy season mud, the mosquitos carrying hallucigenic-deadly malaria, the poverty.

"Yes, it does give one a lot to think about."

"'The Sky Above, Mud Below.'"

"What's that, the title of a song?"

"No, it's the title of a French documentary about the indigenous people of New Guinea, something I saw years ago. This scene brought it back to my mind."

Grace took a pen and a small pad (with her name printed in the upper right hand corner, he noticed) and scribbled a note.

"Kojo, this is for my Aunt Eugenia in the village. When are you planning to go?"

"I don't know, I thought this evening, maybe."

"I would wait until tomorrow, the roads are quite bad in the area you're going to."

"Sounds rough to me."

"Believe me, village living is rough. You'll see. How long are you planning to stay?"

"Oh, I was thinking...about a week or so."

He detected a cynical curl to her smile.

"Give me a ring when you return, I'll be anxious to hear about your experience."

She asked to have the taxi drop her off first...

"I have something to pick up. And I'm not expected in my office before ten o'clock, in any case. Would you care to come in and have breakfast with me?"

"Grace, seriously, if I come inside you wouldn't make it to work today."

"You're right, I wouldn't."

They shared a long winded, delicious kiss under the curious gaze of the taxi driver and parted.

"Don't forget, call me as soon as you get back."

"I will."

He watched her stroll up the muddy path to her apartment entrance. I wonder what's gonna happen to us?

"Driver, I want to go to Tema, here is the address I want to go to. Do you know Tema?"

"I was born in that place."

An hour and forty minutes later they were still trying to locate the Chinebuah family house in the driver's birthplace.

"They have done new buildings here, it is now different when I was small boy."

Finally, after a dozen inquiries they were directed to the proper gate.

"It is just there."

A maid, the kind of maid who gives the occupation a bad reputation, made him undertand that - "They have gone out, Mr. and Mrs. Chinebuah."

"You have any idea when they'll be back?"

"Noplease."

"Do you know where they went?"

"Noplease."

"Can I leave them a note?"

"Yesplease.

SCENE 10/INSERT

"Dear Mr. and Mrs. Chinebuah, please accept my deepest apologies for not being able to come here on Friday.

It seems that Ghana has grabbed me with its own rhythm and I must go with that flow. I'll be in touch.

Sincerely yours,
Kojo B. Brown"

The Chinebuahs, Dad's old friends from his first visit to the "continent". They've probably faxed Mom and Dad to tell them that I've gotten over here and lost my mind.

And I can see both them rolling on the floor, asking each other - "I wonder what's her name?"

11.00 a.m., a fast getaway from Tema. Beautifuly, I've paid my respects, they weren't at home, I'll be back when I get back.

11.00 a.m. Maybe I should've taken Grace up on her offer to have breakfast.

Accra, Ghana, was filled with surprises. Ghana was Accra, Accra was Ghana, a double barrelled load of surprises.

He did "CLOSE-UPS" from his corner table, of the Mercedes hubcaps on the wall in front of him, the photos of Mario Andretti climbing out of the winning race car, spectacular photos of race cars scraping the walls of race tracks, exact drawings of sleekly designed machines.

I can see what Grace means by "African mystery". I ask the driver one simple question - "Where can I get a good breakfast" - and I wind up here.

He could look out of the front door, past a pleasantly designed, fern shadowed veranda, into the heart of a car repair shopyard.

"Well, wot'll it be, mite?"

A short, lumpy Englishman with a bulbous red nose stood at his side with an order pad in his hand. An Englishman?

"Uhh, I don't know, what do you have?"

"Well, all'll sigh this much, we got brek'fast all day long."

He made the statement with a smile and plucked a menu from a nearby table.

Kojo studied the items. He could have been in an English country inn.

"Give me the Scotch sausage, scrambled eggs, rye toast and marmalade."

"Tyke somethin' t'drink wid'at?"

"Uhh, what...?"

"I usually 'ave a beer wid'at."

"Yeah, sure, a beer."

Damn....I haven't had a decent workout in days.

He did a PAN CRANESHOT of the Interior of the restaurant. It was filled with upper class Ghanaians, judging from the U.K. stiffened English they spoke and the large number of old school ties.

The irony of it struck him. I've just left a seaside resort, miles from Accra, filled to the brim with Europeans dying to Experience Ghanaian/African Culture, and here are all the Ghanaians having an English breakfast.

"'Ope the eggs are t'your likin', sah."

Kojo looked at the beautifully scrambled eggs, the crisply tanned sausage, the golden toast, the shimmering marmalade....

"I'm sure they will be. Who does the cooking?"

"O, me missus", the waiter-owner answered quickly and, "'Scuse me, mite, gotta sigh goo'bye to these folks.!"

Kojo forked up his eggs and bit the crisply tanned sausage, watching the waiter-owner bid effusive farewells to a quartet of firmly Anglicized Ghanaians.

"We're gonna do a bar-bee on Sunday, year, plenny f' everybodty, come on, if you can..."

There's logical disorder in the 3rd World, no doubt about it. Well, what are you contributing?

The sausage was a meat eater's dream, filled with a couple spices that talked to the front of the tongue. The eggs were not overfried or greasy and the toast and marmalade were perfectly married.

The well chilled beer was a kind of dessert for all of it. Kojo felt high again, sipping the dregs in his mug.

"Think ya mite like another one o'those?"

"Uhh, no, no thank you, I'm fine. What's the damage?"

"Wots the...? O yea, I thought you was a Yank, but I dinna trust me nose. Hahhahhah."

What the hell was that supposed to mean? O well...

Alfie Snipes, the eastern sector of London... Theres people com' in 'here, wot thinks ah'm Cockney, but ah'm not. Ah'm just me, dinky poo Alfie in Ghana 'here."

Breakfast over, Kojo avoided a prolonged, effusive, farewell scene with the waiter-owner, and made a careful exit.

"Alfie, be cool, see you next time."

"Any tyme, mite, anytyme....we're always 'here!"

Kojo sprawled on his bed in the Ghana Garden, properly, shaved, talc'ed, bellyed up on his English breakfast, daydreaming, one of his favorite pastimes.

Granddad, Momma, Dad, family, I'm here, I'm in Africa, I'm in Ghana here. That's the way everybody says it, "Ghana here".

Even the English teachers, that is to say, the English who brought the English here, say, "in Ghana here". I have the feeling of having returned to the best and worse of all possible worlds. Yeahhh, that's pretty much the vibe, which is one of the basic reasons why I'm moving into/onto the village scene for a moment.

Momma, there's this gorgeous woman; I'm talking about her in the ol' fashioned sense of the word, that I first met when I came here the first time. Now, it's later in the game, maybe the second half, and she has turned me onto her relatives in a village. I can't say what we may mean to each other, but I can assure you that if she winds up being your daughter-in-law, you'll be dealing with a Conscious African Woman. I say ashe.

It cost him twice the amount it would usually cost because; "It is the rainy season, and this place is very difficult to reach. You understand?"

"Where are we going, exactly?"

"This village is in the Volta region."

The Volta region, well that's north of Accra, in any case. One thing is certain, it won't be easy to get to. He's right.

He made a peripheral study of the driver. An older man, forty something, serious looking, doesn't want to do wild things on the road, steady.

7 am.

"Driver, what's your name?"

"I am called Joshua."

Ghanaians have hell of a thing for names. All the women are named Comfort, Mercy, Patience, Mary or Grace, if they don't have something really trippy like Antoinette or Micaela. And all the men seemed to be named after Christian prophets and seers, Ebenezer, Jonah, Immanuel, Peter, Paul, Joshua; no Judas or Jezebel.

"Have you driven to this village before, do you know the area?"

"I am from this area, I know it."

Kojo decided not to question the man's credentials too closely. Give him the benefit of the doubt, don't start lumping people. The Tema driver was a different bird, let it go.

He sucked in a lungful of air and exhaled slowly. They were out of the city, away from the grim scenes that some people thought were "picturesque", the grime of the streets, the people making a bitter struggle for survival.

Ghana was the countryside and he felt himself melting into it. The greenness of it was nourished by the rains, a lush, muddy road took him through it.

Tsito. Tsito was his destination. Tsito, it could be the end of the world. Or the beginning of time. Or nothing.

He resisted staring at the peeled back scenes that popped up in front of his eyes, for a few minutes. The teenaged girls, their pert breasts begging to be touched, walking proudly beside the taxi, carrying loads on their heads that he couldn't even lift.

Middle aged women, bare breasted, pounding, grinding stuff in mortars, totally involved with their work.

Men carrying tree trunks on their heads, walking up steep hills.

"Driver, Joshua! look at that!"

!Eh heeee..."

Kojo settled back in the passenger's seat, trying to cool himself out. No need to be square about things. What the hell am I pointing out to this man? he knows all about it.

There were sections of time when he felt they had entered another time zone, a place so far back that people were still innocent. In the villages they passed through he had the feeling of there being a dream quality to the scene.

No one was rushing to do anything, there was no sense of stress or urgency. Life seemed to be timeless.

"Joshua, let's stop at the bar up ahead and have a beer."

"O, sorry, I never take alcohol while I'm <u>werking</u>."

"Good show."

The brother is a gem, I'll have to figure out a way to stay in touch with him.

The road they were on made him think of a red river of mud.

"How much farther do we have to go?"

"Two hours, maybe three hours.."

"The sky above, mud below". Scenes from the documentary flickered through his consciousness. Men with broad noses, bones stuck through, brooding eyes, magnificent feather headdressers, stomping a dance into the soupy mud.

The river of red mud sequed into a wide trail of lumps, eroded patches of road and what seemed to be no road at all, Kojo made a mental note to "dash" the driver generously.

In the wetness, the mud, people sat at roadside selling fruit, bread, stalks of sugar cane, yams, pineapples, tomatoes and stuff he couldn't identify.

"Joshua, let's stop at the next place they're selling pineapples."

Two pineapples for less than he would pay for a popsicle in America.

The drive continued. He felt nauseous for a few miles, from the jolting of the car over the lumpy roads. The driver noticed; "not far, not far atall."

"Glad to hear that."

It had been on the tip of his tongue a half dozen times - "Turn around, let's go back". Where the hell are we going? Why are we going there?

Around a great green bend in the road, the driver slithered to a stop.

"There, there is Tsito."

Kojo felt himself do a classic double take. Where?! He could only see a muddy path with stategically placed stones lining its length, gently meandering up a small hill.

"It's where?"

"Just there, beyond that rise."

Kojo made a few quick calculations.

"Joshua, I think you ought to come with me, just in case nobody is home, I can go back with you. Or you can translate for me."

"Shall I take your bag?"

"Uhh, let's leave it 'til we find out what the deal is."

Two women with enormous trays of cassava on their heads passed along the road, talking, taking in the sight of the unfamiliar men and taxi as though it were an everyday occurence.

Kojo followed the driver, up the incline, being careful to step on the same rocks he stepped on. On the other side of the slope was the village called Tsito.

Kojo stared at the carefully arranged pattern of thatched homes. Mudwattled walls and thatched roofs. This looks like something out of National Geographic.

Goats and chickens wandered at will. He could immediately see an orderly pattern in the design of the place. A "main street" with Mom and Pop type stores on one side, a drinking bar on the other side, the other structures placed in a wheelike pattern.

Well, ain't nothing gonna happen standing here on this hill, let me dive down into it and locate Aunt Eugenia.

"This Tsito", the driver said as they walked into the heart of the village.

"I believe you."

There was no problem to find Aunt Eugenia. She was delighted to have the note read to her from her niece in the Big City. She was delighted to welcome Kojo to her home for as long as he wanted to stay.

Kojo made a snap decision.

"Joshua, can you pick me up, collect me, next week, on this same day?"

"Yes."

A few minutes later, watching the taxi ooze away on the muddy road, he felt as though he had been left in a small village in the Volta region. He was an immediate celebrity.

Small children followed the two of them through the village, Aunt Eugenia balancing his small, heavily packed suitcase on her head. How did that get there?

The village seemed to be inhabited by women, children and old men. Where are the young men?

Aunt Eugenia stood in front of a red mud wattled hut, with a well thatched roof, that looked like a dozen others nearby, and gestured for him to enter.

Kojo tried not to look like the wonder struck explorer as he entered the hut. Aunt Eugenia came in after him and deposited his bag in another room. He was till standing in the same place when she reappeared with a glass of water and carafe.

"You are welcome", she said.

"Thank you", he answered, and drank the water, remembering to save a few drops to dribble on the floor as he mumbled, "God Bless This House".

She took the glass and carafe, placed them on a nearby table and stood in front of him with shy smile on her face. Beautiful old lady. He thought of his grandfather. I wish he were here with me now.

"Uhh, Aunt Eugenia, I am called Kojo."

"Yes, Kojo, the note tells all."

Yes, Grace had written a comprehensive note, as someone once coined the term.

"This is my good friend Kojo Bediako Brown, he would like to stay with you in the village.

Give him what he wants, love, Grace."

"Uhh, you have a very nice house", he said honestly. He knew the neatly swept hard packed dirt floor, the carefully stashed household items and the dim interior would never find a niché in the pages of "Home Beautiful" but it was exactly right for this place.

After a few moments of shy smiling at each other, she beckoned him to follow her. Hazy sunshine glazed his eyes as he emerged from the hut.

"Come", she gestured with the Ghanaian palm down, finger pulling movement. He followed her slow, steady sway through the village, smiling at the faces that looked at him. A few people returned his smile, shyly, but mostly they simply looked with deadpan expressions.

He followed Aunt Eugenia the length of the village, leaving him to wonder...is she showing me off or what?

They came to a collection of huts with a wall enclosing them. Once again she beckoned for him to follow her. He followed, as she turned the corner of a hut and led him into a courtyard, framed in a circular pattern by grizzled old men sitting on stools.

Where is the camera? Damn, why didn't I bring my Super 8 with me at least?! Look at these dudes! He looked into his grandfather's eyes, his greatgrandfather's eyes.

I'm going to do an Alex Haley number when I get back, I feel like these are my relatives.

A younger man detached himself from the collection of men.

"Good afternoon."

"Good afternoon."

People can be so formal.

"I am called Peter."

"I am called Kojo."

"You are welcome."

"Thank you."

He looked around for Aunt Eugenia. She had done a disappearing act.

The young man led him to the "receiving line", a handshake and a smile for each of the elders and a stool for him.

People can be so formal.

One of the elders stood and spoke for a long five minutes. Kojo found himself feeling sluggish. Stay awake, don't be a poor guest. The sonorous sounds of their Ewe almost made him feel that he was understanding a language that didn't resemble any language he had ever heard before.

Peter gave him a succint translation of the five minute speech - "The elders say you are welcome to Tsito."

"Please tell the elders I said thank you."

Peter, the translator, used the better part of five minutes to say what Kojo had asked him to say.

Thanks, Peter, I didn't have a speech prepared.

The speech making over, it was time for drinking of the local akpeteshie.

Aunti Eugenia led him back through the village, after a couple hours of akpeteshie drinking with the elders.

She had materialized at just the right point, coming back onto the scene to "retrieve" him just as coolly as she had left him there.

"The men like the strong spirits."

"I heard that."

There were younger men in the village now, he noticed.

"Auntie, the young men were not here earlier, they are here now."

"They go to farm, come back now."

He liked the old lady, her spare use of language. Maybe she doesn't speak a lot of English, but whatever she says is right on the money.

He smelled it as he entered the hut, a strong, almost sexy odor. He was tempted to ask what the odor was, decided to be cool.

"Time for food", the old lady spoake in a no nonsense way and brought him a bowl of water with a sliver soap floating in it. After the long taxi ride, the akpeteshie and the new scene he felt tired and hungry.

Yeahhh, some food, that's just what I need.

Fufu, of course, light soup and meat. What kind of meat? Strong scent, strong flavor. This is what I was smelling. Aunt Eugenia had served him a bowl of food and was about to do her disappearing act when he asked her...

"Auntie, what kind of meat is this, goat?"

"This bush meat", she said and eased away.

He stared into the bowl of fufu, soup and small chunks of meat. Rat. Bushmeat. Rat. Bushmeat. Rat. That's what bush meat is, it's a rat.

Suddenly the tiredness that he felt was gone; the sluggishness of travel and drink was pushed to the side.

It was time for decisions to be made. Now what? I'm in the village of Tsito where big rats are a delicacy, if I recall correctly. I'm hungry and, aside from everything else, it would probably be insulting if I refused to eat this.

He ate all of the meat in his bowl first, making a snap decision. If I can't eat all the fufu no one will be insulted.

Aunt Eugenia reappeared at the conclusion of his meal, with another bowl of water and a small cloth to dry his hands.

"Good, you like bush meat, some do not."

Kojo stumbled into the other room and carefully sprawled on a mat that was spread on a low platform of hardened mud.

CHAPTER 7

In his twilight state he felt a soft, lightweight blanket being spread over his body. In his dream he saw them darting out of garbage piles on the westside of Chicago, racing along the edges of deserted buildings ont he southside of Chicago, running through the alleys on both sides of town.

In his dream they screeched, their beady eyes, staring relentlessly at him, their evil mouthes opening and closing, their horrible fangs exposed.

And I ate one of 'em, I ate a rat. O well, when in Rome, eat what the Romans eat.

It was becoming dark when he woke up. He stared at the ceiling as he silently recited his personal prayer. I thank my Ancestors and I thank the Orisha for making my return to Africa possible; I thank my Ancestors and I thank the Orisha for maintaining and preserving my good faith; I thank my Ancestors and I thank the Orisha for all of the Blessings that I receive.

I beg my Ancestors and I beg the Orisha to make it possible for me to become healthy, wealthy and wise.

He sat up on the side of his mud platform/bed, feelling grateful that he didn't have a hangover.

Wowww....that akpeteshie can knock you on your ass.

He stood, feeling the urge to urinate. Where does one go to piss in Tsito?

He walked carefully through the rooms, guided by a flickering light from the front room.

Aunt Eugenia sat near an old fashioned oil lantern, reading her Bible. Kojo placed the cameras in two spots, I would do her from two Angles;

first, the shadows and flickering lights and then the Close-up majesty of her face. That's the only word I can think of that would fit.

She looked up at him, removed her glasses and smiled. He returned her smile. There was no arkwardness now, it was natural with them. She had become his "Auntie" in feeling as well as title.

"Uhh, Auntie....where?"

She pointed him out of the door and around the hut.

"Oh, I see..."

He strolled outside and followed the direction her finger had pointed. Around behind here, where? He followed a clearly defined footpath for twenty or thirty yards and heard the sound of the latrine before he saw it.

Ten yards to one side was well constructed outhouse, and to the other side was a hole in the ground with a grill firmly laid across.

Buzzzzzzz.....what is that noise, bees? O my God! That's the last thing I need is to be stung by some African bees.

Buzzing came from milions of maggots in the hole. This must've been where they had the outhouse...

He pissed on the squirming grubs, inventing all kinds of gruesome scenarios. What if you stumbled through here in the dark? Well, the grill would prevent you from falling in.....but....ugggh.

He walked away from the hole to take a look at the village. He had never lived in an authentic village. It was obviously dinner time. The cooking was done on those ingenious little stoves called coalpots.

He could easily imagine that he could see the whole village from a cherry pickeer. He smiled, once again, at the faces that looked at him. By now they were familiar strangers.

The men who had been working away from the village when he arrived had obviously been informed of his presence.

They waved politely at his smile and continued doing what they were doing. Kojo was taken in by the quietness of the place. A couple radios were on, somewhere to his left, but they weren't blaring. People were having conversations but no one was shouting.

It would seem, at first glance, that the village was in another era. Some of the younger people, men and women, wore clothes that came straight out of the Detroit ghetto or off the racks of a Hollywood hip hop store, but the majority dressed traditionally.

Who straightens the women's hair? That really puzzled him. Way out here in the sticks, O sorry, in the bush, and women are chemicalizing their heads. Strange.

He was drawn to a blueish light at the edge of the village. A television set. Someone is watching T.V.

The television was situated on an in door porch, with people, young an old, occupying chairs and stools inside. One of the elders that he had met earlier in the day gestured for him to come inside.

A path was cleared for him through a forest of legs, women breast feeding babies, and a chair vacated by a younger man.

"You are welcome", the elder spoke gravely and turned his attention back to the television.

Kojo made a surreptitious study of the people on the porch. Several pretty young women caught his eye, their attention focused on the television set.

O, a video. So, we got movies in the village. He stifled the urge to crack up a half dozen times. What in the world are these people watching?

A close, serious study of the film turned his urge to laugh into complete confusion. Why were they watching a Pakistani (or is it Hindu?) movie with Chinese subtitles? And I seem to be the only one confused by it.

Promptly, at seven o'clock, the video was put on PAUSE so that they could watch the news. Kojo stared at the men and women giving speeches to impassive faces, the lack of any real news until it came to foreign affairs.

Places, people and situations he had put on the back burner the minute he strapped himself into his seat, on his way to the Motherland, were suddenly thrown into his face again.

The half hour of news over, they returned to the movie. He didn't feel the urge to laugh anymore. After watching ten minutes of foreign affairs, ten minutes of bloodshed, mean spirited activities by one group of human beings against another group, the Indian movie, where singing and dancing erupted without any conscious motivation, was wonderful alternative.

After the movie he turned to shake hands with the elder and made his way off the porch. It was dark now, the light came mostly from flickering, low flame kerosene lamp.

Now, which way do I go? He made an effort to walk around as though he had a destination, but he was actually lost.

This is funny. How in the hell can I be lost in a place this small? After a half hour of wandering, passing the same people twice, he realized he was walking in the proverbial circle. The young man named Peter, who had created a speech for him, attached himself to his side.

"Come this way with me, please, Auntie has prepared food for you."

It was done very smoothly, the guide coming out of the shadows to take him back to a hut that looked like dozens of other huts. Kojo was grateful.

Auntie Eugenia smiled at him and, as before, brought him a bowl of water to wash his hands. I hope I don't have to eat no mo' rat today.

Blessed Lord in Heaven.... it's fish. She gave him a spoon for the banku and fish stew, and looked pleased when he returned the spoon and began to eat with his right hand.

"Auntie, your chop is delicious."

"You are welcome, she answered him and slipped out into the darkness.

He ate slowly, medidatively, focusing on the things around him. Three rooms. The large one that you entered from outside and two other rooms branching off from the main room.

The flickering lantern made ghostly shadows on the walls, gave the thatch above his head an ominous aura.

Wonder if they have snakes around here? Of course they do, that's dumb question. Snakes. O well...

Auntie Eugenia returned with another bowl of water for him to wash his hands. She must be peeking at me from somewhere.

He had hundreds of questions to ask her, but couldn't bring himself to jump into it.

I'll be here for a week, there's time.

"Thank you, Auntie."

"You are welcome."

You are welcome....you are welcome... She seems to have variety of tones to use for these words.

Once she had taken his bowl and washed it, she returned with a small chamberpot and a bottle of water. She took both of them into "his" bedroom and signaled to him that she was going out.

"Tomorrow morning", she said and eased back into the darkness, closing a flimsy wooden door behind her.

He slumped in his chair. Wonder where she's going? It wasn't late but it was dark. He could hear the voices of men and women, the shrill cry of a baby for a few minutes, odds and ends of sounds that he couldn't decipher.

He remained in his chair, waiting for Auntie Eugenia to return. After a half hour he decided to go to bed. What else is there to do?

He laced his hands behind his head and stared at the thatched roof, imagining all kinds of things in the flickering light from the lantern in the other room.

Wonder where she went?

The thought caused his mouth to drop open. She's gone to spend the night with somebody, she couldn't sleep under the same roof with me, a stranger from a strange land.

He relaxed, knowing that his logic was right on the money. A half hour later he popped up to turn the lantern off. And popped back under the blanket to replay his mental tape.

Tsito. Could be another place in the time, maybe a Shangri-La.

The light in his room came from the moon, through a small window on the opposite side. Feels like I've been here before.

Two hours later he was stunned awake by the sound of someone stomping on the roof. He sat up in his bed, looking around in, the darkness for some place to hide.

An Earthquake!

And thunder and lightening. No, no earthquake, just rain, thunder and lightening. The rain came down vindictively, as though someone were hovering over the hut, dumping tons of water on the thatched roof.

So, this is the rainy season. This is the rainy season,

The rain smashing down on the roof seemed personal, made him feel vulnerable. I'm not enclosed in a stone and steel structure tonight, no Novotel over my head to protect me.

He checked his watch...10:00 p.m. Wowww! Ten O'clock, it's just ten O'clock. What do I do for the rest of the night?

Gradually, he relaxed; there was nothing else to do. The simple things he might've done at home danced through his head. Go down to the 'fridge, make a Gouda cheese on rye and sip a beer. Watch television to find out what's happening all over the world. Call Akosua.

Akosua Ferguson. I'm going to have to do something about that sister when I get back.

The rain suddenly slackened into a steady downpour. You feel closer to stuff here. Damn....wish I could speak a little Ewe.

Thoughts flickered through his mind, ideas for future projects, deals to be made, things to do, a film to be made.

If I could get my hands on five million, that would do it.

He drifted off, dollars gently floating under his dreams.

Roosters crowing and the sounds of people doing things told him it was a new day, Tuesday.

Aunt Eugenia knocked softly before entering....

"Good morning."

"Good morning, Auntie. That was quite a rain we had last night, huh?"

"Eh heeee...."

She moved about, straightening things up. Kojo took note of the fact that her face was bright, she had a chewing stick in her mouth and that she had changed her head wrap.

"You are baffing?"

"Baffing?"

She pantomimed taking a shower, an amused look on her look.

"O, O yes, a bath. Yes, where....?

Once again she did a detailed job of pointing in the right direction.

"I have taken watah there for you"

"Thank you."

Kojo saronged a bath towel around his waist, the way he had always done, carried soap, his toothbrush and toothpaste in the direction she pointed.

Weird, things are standing right in front of me and I can't see 'em. I should've noticed this thing.

The outdoor bathing station was composed of a chest high collection of large bricks, with a run off into a drainage ditch. Aunt Eugenia had bought a pail of water and large tin cup for him to use.

He felt strange to be naked, soaping himself, while watching people pass along the muddy street beside the "bathing booth".

What in the world am I doing...?

Taking an outdoor bath at 6:30 a.m. in the Volta Region.

The "baffing" done, he strolled back to his home. Kojo had never been in love with early mornings, but this felt different.

He was refreshed by the cold water, the brisk morning air and the fact that he was in Tsito. Now, it would be nice to have a workout, but where can I go in this mud to do Capoeira?

Deodorant, cotton jeans and t-shirt. Aunt Eugenia gave him a bowl of something that tasted like rice soup.

He slurped it up, enjoying the elusive flavor. Hmmm, it tasted a little like miso soup. After the soup, she handed him a banana and a handful of peanuts.

"Uhhh, thank you, Auntie."

She must think I eat more because I'm from America.

After the food he was determined to do his exercises.

"Auntie, do you know of any place where I can go to work out?"

It was a stab in the dark that he thought she might be able to understand.

"You want work?"

We are obviously on different wave lengths. He smiled his question into oblivion.

"Uhh, no, no work. It's o.k. Don't worry about it."

She was a shrewd old lady and her lack of full fledged English grammar had nothing to do with her ability to reason, but he realized, immediately, that the concept of a "workout", in a work hardened society, was a bit much.

She was always busy, he noticed. Something always had to be done. She signed to him, with a basket on her arm, that she was going out. He countersigned that he was also going out.

They shared a smile. The smile was worth thousands of words. The smile, coupled to a few pertinent gestures, blazed the trail for an understanding that words would've derailed.

Outside, she made him understand that she would be back later, and he made her understand that he, also, would be back later. The smile, a few gestures, her pointing at her wrist (my watch) and the sky. Later.

He started walking, determined to find a flat surface, dry, workout spot. He felt he knew something about the place after a day and a night.

And now I'm really into the first day. The small market section in the center of the village surprized him. The thing that really surprised him was the attitude that the people in the village had toward him.

They knew he was a Stranger, but that wasn't the signal, as it might've been in some places, for them to leap on him.

The children betrayed their parent's feelings, by doing the things that only children can do. One small boy walked away from his family's kiosk to grab his hand. The parents, like Kojo, didn't know what to make of it, how to handle this natural action.

They exchanged smiles. But the small boy wouldn't release Kojo's hand. He decided to go with the flow and walked the child back and forth for a few yards.

Finally, the boy released his hand and smiled up at him. The mother retrieved her son with a shy explanation.

"He likes you."

Kojo strolled onward, feeling warm about his presence in Tsito. In Accra, even with the "good vibe" people, things cost money.

Here, in Tsito, in Tsito here, they were giving it away. The only price seemed to be involvement.

"I beg your pardon, sah, you are looking for the place to do the workout? Auntie spoke of it."

The young brother named Peter. Hmmm, is he my designated guide or what? 7:30 a.m.

"Yes, Peter." (He liked the appreciative gleam in the young man's eyes. He remembered my name.)

"Please, come."

Kojo followed Peter through what seemed like the backside of the village. A ten minute, mud sloshed walk, brought them to a trio of buildings with the flag of Ghana posted in front.

"Building one and two are being used. You may use building three, that one, to do the workout."

He wanted to hug the man, to let him know how much he appreciated his help, but he was already ten mud clogged steps away, waving good by.

"Thanks Peter," he called to him.

Building one and two were filled with wooden desk-seats, number three was a bare concrete floor and four walls. He took off his shoes and began to warm up.

Twenty minutes later, sweat dripping from his brow, he became aware of hundreds of eyes taking in his every move.

He stopped doing the Capoeira movements, not really knowing how to deal with the attention. The pupils and teachers from buildings one and two were giving him their "undivided attention."

"O, please sah, do go on", one of the teachers spoke to him from the sideline. He took a hard look at her.

O.K., sweetie pie, it that's what you want....

Fifteen minutes later, after linking every movement he could think of into a sequence, he stopped and bowed to the honest applause from the children. And the cutie pie.

She shooed the children back into the other classrooms and marched over to meet him with her right hand stuck out.

"That was quite impressive, Mr...."

"Bediako Brown." Let's see what you make of that.

"O, I see, you are from America?"

"O guess you could say that, in a roundabout way."

"O, I see, and this is kungf fu, is it not?"

He found himself staring past her succulent lips, into her perfectly white teeth. She sounds like somebody out of an English novel. It that not true?

"Uhh, no Miss...?

"Deku, the name is Deku..."

He gave her the brief form of explaination about Capoeira, about how it came from Angola, inadvertently, via the slave trade, and how he got involved with it.

By this time the Ghanaian school children were doing their rote-lesson-recitation and he was feeling the need for another shower - "baff".

"I find all of this perfectly fascinating, Mr. Brown, perfectly fascinating."

"And what do you do here, Mrs. Deku?"

"Miss Deku. I am the Headmistress of Tsito school."

She said it with such an air of self importance that he felt like laughing, but she was obviously not into humor, so he went the straight route.

"Very pleased to meet you, Miss Deku. I hope you'll forgive me for disturbing your classes."

"O, no problem, no problem a'tall, the children need to be exposed to different-new things."

"How about the teachers?"

He found the question irristible, Miss Deku pursed her generous lips in a prissy imitation of an English school marm.

"Similarly. Good day, Mr. Brown."

"Similarly", he replied, repressing a smile.

CHAPTER 8

He wasn't certain that she had gotten the joke of it 'til he saw a gleam come to the corner of her eyes.

"And you will be back, I presume?"

"Presumably tomorrow, a half-hour before classes begin. I don't want our children to be distracted from learning what you have to teach them."

"That's veddy thoughtful of you, Mr. Brown."

"My pleasure, and please, Headmistress Deku, call me Kojo."

9:30 a.m. He strolled back through the village, avoiding the muddiest spots, firmly aware of his visit to Tsito school and his exchange with the Headmistress was being shot ahead of him via village to wireless.

Aunt Eugenia met him in front of the hut with her, by now cool, but amused demeanor.

"There is watah for your baff."

Aunt Eugenia asked few questions, fed him a variety of foods and left him to do whatever he felt like doing.

"Dear Mom, Dad,

I'm spending a week in a village in the Volta Region called Tsito (Chee-to). It's so small that I doubt if it would be on the map. I'm living in the home of my girlfriend's aunt, her name is Eugenia, an she's a real live Person.

I felt the urge to get out of the Big City, to see what was happening in the little places. You know how it is.

It may sound too romantic but life in the village is a groove. It's rainy season now, mud up to your ankles everywhere, but it doesn't create unnatural problems here.

I think, in some ways, that might be considered the key word - natural/ unatural. The naturalness of this scene gives life a certain rhythm, none of it too fast for the human heart.

There is nothing to rush for, or about. There is no hustle for food, it grows everywhere. If you drop a seed from your melon, you might find a melon patch there a week later.

This appears to be a relatively healthy place. I haven't seen any evidence of those horrible tropical diseases that you find in some places. There are a lot of old people around.

Old people, people in their 70's/80's/90's. Please tell Granddad. I'll write him.

I think the natural rhythm that I spoke of has something to do with the age thing. When it gets dark, people go to bed. When it gets light, they get up.

I know this must sound terribly simplistic, but I'm experiencing it for the first time. It seems like my first trip here was a pre-requisite for understanding what is happening to me now.

I wouldn't want to live in Tsito, or any other small place. I think my liking for neon signs and thousands of frantic people would create a problem for me here.

But for now, it's a groove, I'll write more later.

Love, Kojo.
P.S. I've only been here a day and a half.

He finished his brief note, sealed it in an envelope and suddenly thought about how it was going to get to America.

Aunt Eugenia was sewing by the light of her favorite lantern. She had placed a newer one in his room.

"Auntie, I have a letter to send to America. How do I send it?"

She looked at a distant point for a few moments, as though she were trying to remember something.

"O, someone will come here, they will take it to the city for you. Don't worry."

The thought occured to him - I'll probably be the one who gets to the city before anyone else. O well.

"I'm going for a little walk."

"A walk?"

"Uhh, for a stroll around the village."

She looked slightly puzzled but waved him out. Why would anyone want to walk if they didn't have to?

Tuesday, evening, the seven o'clock news on the "T.V. porch."

"You are welcome."

He nodded at the familiar faces and, as before, was given a choice seat. Government T.V., that's what it is....government T.V. A roster of well fed politicians stood behind podiums across the country, telling the assembled audiences, both in the auditoriums they were speaking in, and the bigger ones watching T.V. that "Everything is O.K. or Every THING IS GOING TO BE O.K."

Kojo exchanged cynical glances with the elder. Politicians.

After the news he decided not to run the risk of watching the video-movie. I don't feel like tripping tonight.

He excused himself and wandered off....

People are friendly, but reserved. If I speak, they speak, but there are no welcoming committees. He made a mental note to talk with Auntie, Peter and maybe one of the elders about the African-American thing.

He had to confess, he had no idea about how they thought of him, a brother out of the Diaspora.

People glanced at him but they didn't run up to hail him as a long lost somebody, returned after all these years.

Life seemed so simple, it was almost dull. He stood for a few minutes, watching a man dissect a sheep; others came to his side, to look at what he was looking at.

A sheep being butchered, what's interesting about that? They continued doing what they were doing. He left the scene after a few minutes. Yeahhh, what's so interesting about a sheep being cut up?

He took half a step toward the local drinking bar and censored his urge. I don't want a drink. I don't need a drink. This doesn't even seem like the kind of place where drinking is "necessary".

The fact that there was only one drinking bar seemed to confirm his premise. The old men drink, but I guess that's the prerogative of age.

He strolled slowly, confidently. Once you get to know the signpoints, it's easy. He turned off of the beaten path for a bit, feeling adventurous and, after a few steps, stopped cold.

The girl was rinsing her naked body off in the hazy moonlight. He had seen her on the T.V. porch, staring at the screen with intensity.

Village etiquette, African etiquette, demanded that he not "see" her. He could not simply ignore her, he wouldn't "see" her.

How old? Sixteen, eighteen years old, "baffing" in the bush, charcoal darkskinned, gorgeous figure. He was tempted to speak to her as he passed within half a yard of her bathing place, but cancelled out the urge.

Don't do that, it would square your game. But he could feel her eyes on him as he walked past. Time for the evening meal.

He sat on a bench in front of the hut after eating kenkey, fish and pepper. Hot pepper. Auntie Eugenia was busy, inside, tidying up before making her disappearance.

"Auntie, please come and talk with me."

The old lady came out, sat near him on the bench and turned toward him with her usual look of amusement.

I'm gonna have to introduce you to my grandfather...

"I wanted to ask you about a few things."

The old lady's expression changed from amusement to concern.

"Oh, it's nothing serious. I'm just curious, I want to know about a few things..."

"O, yes please..."

Kojo leaned back against the hut. What do I want to know about? It all seems to be straight up here.

"Uhh, let's say I wanted to marry a woman, somebody here."

"Yesplease?"

"Well, how would I go about it, you know, what would I do?"

The concerned expression gave way to a clear case of pleasure.

"O, no problem, no problem. You tell me the girl..."

"No, no, I don't have a girl in mind. I'm just interested in the procedure, the process, you know; how would I go about it, if I <u>were</u> interested in somebody?"

He could see the gleam in her eyes, fired up by the flickering light from the lantern. Don't try to fool me, boy, I know you've taken a liking to the school madam.

Yes, of course, you'd have all the info on that exchange this morning. By now everybody in town must know that me and Miss Cutie Pie Deku exchanged words. News travels faster than light here.

But no, sorry 'bout that, folks. I got Miss Grace in town and, and sister Ferguson across the water.

"We will have somebody to speak with her father..."

"Is that all? I mean...."

"A bottle of Schnapps or gin. Formerly, they take many things."

"Like what?"

"O, many things. Cows, sheep, goats, yams, corns, chickens, cloth, pots and pans, many things. But now, modern time, they only have permission."

He thought he detected a note of disdain for the "modern time" in her voice.

"Which time do you prefer, now or the old times?"

"Oh, I like modern time. Old time was very, very hard for the woman. The woman work hard all time, take care of children. Sometime the man he may slap the woman..."

"What would happen now, if the man slap the woman?"

"If she does not deserve, she will take him to court."

A feminist movement? Justice, ("if she does not deserve"), of sorts. The mosquitoes came up on them from nowhere. Aunt Eugenia popped up to close the door.

"There is mosquito coil there, they come with rainy season, many."

She was obviously about to make her disappearing act happen.

"Uhh, Auntie, where do you go at night?"

She pointed to a hut, three huts away.

"I go to my sister."

And she was gone.

105

Kojo sat, swatting mosquitoes for a couple minutes and went inside. No win against these rascals.

The air inside the hut was cool, the atmosphere comfortable; Kojo lit the mosquito coil, took off his shirt and sprawled on his mud-platform-bed.

Damn I feel good. A good work out this morning, a short, quick movement in the grim outhouse, only a few yards from the buzzing maggots. Maybe that's the way it's done, when one hole fills up and the maggots take over or start buzzing too loud, they move.

Crazy scenarios swarmed around in his mind. I'm kidding myself, to think that I can be in an atmosphere like this and put my camera-mind on the backburner.

Several stories had grabbed him in middle of the night. The African-American couple, devout Nationalists, who decide to live in an African village - "The way our ancestors did."

The African student who returns to the village with his snooty English wife.

The village elder who gets a scholarship to America and returns as a hippie, almost.

Several of the better ideas had skipped out on him because he couldn't find a pen and paper in the dark.

He had solved that problem by placing a ballpoint and pad on the small table beside his bed.

"Tsito, Where Kojo Stayed For A Few Days." Strange, I don't feel that I'm missing anything. No daily newspapers, no magazines, very few books a, (Aunt Eugenia had proudly handed him four Readers' Digests, when he asked her if she had any books other than the Bible), no rat race, no arbitrary Uzi shootings, no cocaine/heroin/latest drug traffic.

Who am I fooling? I'm missing everything there is to be missed; the espresso in quaint little Italian joints with the sophisticated ladies, the immediate access to any part of the world, the hundreds of vibes that said "Now Dig this!", the colors of all the crazy emotions that go to make up an urbane happening.

I miss filmmaking; yeahh, that's what I really miss. I miss not being able to shoot this scene, to go inside of a character's head with subliminal stuff and bring out what I've been thinking.

I miss the give and take of quick minded people who are into media. The villagers are quick minded, no doubt about it, but their minds are on another set.

They are into another vibe. They can't see themselves as picturesque, film-interesting, exotic or any of that. They're at ease with themselves, Ewes.

The thought crossed his mind for a few minutes...Ewes. It meant that he couldn't understand what other Black people, (in the U.S. Pan-African sense of the word), were saying to each other, they were speaking a "foreign" language. Ewes.

The trippy part of it was that all of them, or most of them, could understand him after they had turned away from their Twi, Ga, Fanti, Gonja, Kokomba, Adangme, Hausa, Ewe, or whatever. That irked him a bit. It was as though his own people had a secret code that he couldn't crack.

But no, his better reasoning gave a more sold foundation to his thoughts; no wonder the European slavemasters wanted us to speak his language, why he only felt comfortable with us after he had turned Kwame into Jacob or George or Joshua.

I got to get into an African language, to recover a serious part of me. He remembered his father talking on the subject, years back...

"Kojo, despite, no matter what these propagandists have tried to promote, we've never been proud of speaking English.

We've done every daggoned thing in the world to retain our speech patterns. If you take the semantical journals seriously, you'll read that Prof. Digembottom has discovered that the people of northeastern Wimmejimmyland have been using a Yoruba grammar, for days.

It took him back to something 'way back when, 'way back when I was in high108 school. I couldn't understand why we had to say 'be' all the time, like 'I be' and 'you be' and 'we be.'

And I'm not gonna jump out of the box and say that I'm on top of the answer now, not even now. But I do know that we've retained a helluva lot more than the usual suspects want to make us believe.

We are the Newest Africans."

"The Newest Africans", Dad, if that ain't the title of/for an Avan' garde film, I'll kiss you all over.

"The Newest Africans". All of what that implied took him off into a hard hour of sleep. The twilight section happened at the end of the sleep, just as he was waking up for midnight piss.

He stumbled-fumbled his way out of the hut, went around back, carefully wrapped in his all-purpose bathtowel, and shot a stream into the mud, away from the hut.

I'm going to have to get a chamber pot in here. What am I? An old man? Running out to pee at night. Maybe there's something wrong with me. Maybe I have a bladder infection.

Suddenly, a hundred hours of paranoid medical wisdom plugged his ears up. "Don't get sick in Ghana, in Africa, the hospitals are cemetaries."

"Don't get sick in Africa, we dump poison-medicine over there."

Even a doctor, one of his father's friends, had suavely warned him - "Uhh, Kojo, I wouldn't fuck without a raincoat, if I were you. Nor would I drink unboiled water, eat unwashed veggies, walk in village rivers, swim anywhere, eat any food from a street stand, have anything to do with anything that didn't look sterile."

What would you say about the language, doc? How do I handle that? If I'm going to learn a few words of Ewe, will I be poisoned?

The Dream that spoke to him was not about disease or cultural paranoias, it was about money. The money came from an unidentifable source, mostly one hundred dollar bills and many, many fifties.

For your film, Kojo, for your film, a subconscious voice whispered to him. For your film, for your film, for your film...

He stared at the sunlight streaming through the window and listened to Aunt Eugenia doing something in the next room.

The rainy season, I thought it rained all the time. No rain. Wednesday...

"Good morning, Auntie."

"Good morning."

"I'm going to the school to do my workout."

"O, but there is no one there at this hour."

Ahhahh, so the word has been put out there about me and Miss Cutie Pie Deku.

"That's the way I like it."

"Will you take food now?"

"No, not now, I'll baff and eat when I return."

Poor sister doesn't have the slightest idea what a workout means. Here, in this place, people eat for the energy to do work. And I'm going to do a workout on an empty stomach so that I won't be bogged down by food. Go figure.

Headmistress Cutie Pie Deku and students, nice timing. He was finishing his last series of kicks when they started filing in.

He exchanged a friendly, but distant wave, with the lady and stepped away cleanly. No need to start getting into scenes that will create problems later on.

Red red with plantain.

"Auntie, your black eyed peas and plantain was delicious."

"Black eye peas?"

"You call them beans, we call them black eyed peas."

"O, I see."

Said the blind man...

"I'm going for a little walk, be back soon."

He couldn't resist giving her a little peck on the cheek. She looked stunned and stared at him curiously as he strolled down the path that would take him into the forest that surrounded the village.

He had paid close attention to the landmarks and felt confident that he could call loud enough, if he got lost, for someone to find him.

One hundred yards on the path, he turned and could only see the steeple of the church, the tallest structure in the village.

That will be my reference point....

Two hundred yards on and the church steeple was blotted out by the tangled web of the forest. He didn't feel nervous, but he wasn't at much at ease as he had been.

The sound of someone singing, mingled with a rhythmic chop chop chop, drew him in that direction. A hacked out path around a half acre of tall corn stalks brought him face to face with a young farmer.

"Good morning."

"Good morning, sah, you are welcome."

"Thank you."

The young man, Kojo estimated that they were about the same age, rushed to get a bottle of water from a makeshift-lean-to-hut.

"Thank you."

He drank. Damn, I didn't realize how thirsty I was. He passed the bottle back to the farmer, who capped it and stood with neutral expression on his face.

"So, this is your farm, huh?"

"O, no, my farm other side," he pointed/jabbed his finger in a distant way, "This my fadder-in-law farm. I work today for him."

Kojo felt like asking a half dozen questions. Do you come to work on your father-in-law's farm every Wednesday? Are you doing this as payment for his daughter's hand in marriage? His daughter's hand in marriage? That really means something here, the way these woman work. Are you a sharecropper? What's the deal?

"Well, take it easy, o.k.?"

He walked in another direction, smiling to himself. The man is out here, trying to chop a tree stump out of the ground and the best I can come up with is, "Take it easy, o.k.?"

O well...

The forest, at midmorning, was damp but not unpleasant. No Tarzans swinging through the trees, no "natives" running around mumbling "Bwana Tuba", or whatever it was that they used to have us saying in those stupid movies.

He walked slowly, meditatively, taking it all in; the unusual formations of tree roots growing above ground, the giant ferns that looked like something from another Age, the Grandness of it.

The only evidence of wild life he could discover on the ground was the quick shake and tremble of leaves as he walked on the spongy ground. Wonder what that was?

Birds with colored patterns that he had never dreamed of danced on branches near him, flew overhead. He could no longer hear the chopping sound.

Does that mean that he's stopped chopping or that I've walked beyond hearing range?

A large log drew him to it. He inspected it carefully, looking for snakes, scorpions, ants. And straddled it to gaze around.

Kojo had been raised on "Wild, Wild World of Animals", "Wild Kingdom" and a few cable stations that focused on life in places where the natural life was still alive.

He didn't fear having giant snakes fall on his body and coil him to death. Or a sneaky leopard prowling up behind him.

They heard me stomping through here and split. Or if they didn't hear me, they smelt me. Smells...

He worried the odor through his nose for a couple beats before turning to his left. A man stood two yards from him, a lean, dark skinned man with dazzling dark eyes and long strips of matted hair running down the sides of his face and back.

The man folded his arms across his chest and leaned against a tree.

Asiafo_Quid pro quo

Kojo filmed the scene immediately and titled it, "Jungle Street Corner."

The odor was coming from the man. Kojo tried to place it, to put it in some kind of perspective.

Never smelled a human being who smelled like that. It wasn't a stink, but rather like a wild perfume, an aroma.

The two men looked at each without malice, without any selfconsciousness, as though they were neutral observers.

This brother has got to be living out here. Talk about Tarzan...

Kojo studied the man's face, his body, the raffia type skirt he wore in a low fringe around his waist. He blinked, thinking of what he should say, and the man disappeared.

The disappearance unsettled him. What? Am I hallucinating or something?

The man reappeared about five yards to his right, his arms still folded, the serene expression undisturbed.

Kojo made a snap decision. Go with the flow, don't freak out. Go with the flow. He also decided to allow the man to speak first.

The split second that it took for him to arrange his thoughts saw the man disappear again. A second later Kojo smelled him from behind his back....hmmmm...well, I didn't see a weapon in his hand.

Kojo slowly twisted around to see the man straddling the log. He stood and turned to face him. Fast as this brother can move I wouldn't be able to do anything to defend myself, in any case.

They straddled the log, facing each other. Maybe he's wild, I don't want to freak him out.

"My brother, don't disappear on me again, o.k.?"

Damn, I said I was going to let him speak first. O well, it's done deal now...

A slow, easy smile spread across the man's mouth, revealing beautifully white teeth.

"O.K."

"You....you speak English?"

"Yes, I speak English."

Kojo tried to place the accent, the tone, the flavor of his speech. It wasn't like anything he'd ever heard. A few words and you realize that you're being taken to another plane.

"How did you learn to speak such excellent English."

"I went to England, America, where they speak it."

"How?" Kojo blurted out.

"I flew", the man said, and disappeared.

Kojo was trying to be cool, but he felt that his heart was making too much noise in this quiet place.

He looked around casually, trying to chill his panic out. The man was sitting on this log with me and now he's gone, disappeared. Or am I losing my marbles?

He stood and yawned, trying to preserve his cool, and began to re-trace his steps back to the village. As an afterthought he announced in a conversational tone...

"Nice meeting you, see you tomorrow...'bout the same time?"

"O.K.", the reply came to him from two directions.

It took all of the composure he could muster to walk through the village on trembling legs. Aunt Eugenia met him ten huts away from her own hut.

"Ahh Kojo, you are here. We thought you were lost in the forest. It is not a good place to be at night."

"O, no, I wasn't lost. I just fell asleep under a tree."

"Ato told us that you stopped to take watah and that you walked into the forest, into the place we will not go."

The place we will not go....uhhh ooohh...

"Come, I have prepared food."

He sat on the bench beside the old lady, his belly plumped out from a dinner of banku and fish stew, trying to put his time elements back together.

"Auntie, you remember what time I left here, when I went for my walk?"

CHAPTER 9

"It was in the morning."

"And I returned at twilight..."

"You slept long in the forest", she said drily.

He couldn't contain himself any longer, he had to tell her, somebody.

"Auntie, I didn't go to sleep in the forest....I met a man there, a very unusual man."

The old lady put her right fist in front of her mouth, a gesture signifying fear, wonder, surprise, excitement. She stared at him as though he had come from a far away place.

"You say...?"

"I met a man in the forest, a very unusual man, and it seems that time stood still..."

"I don't understand..."

"Well, I left in the morning and came back when it was almost dark, and all I did was take a little walk and have a talk with this man, small-small."

"'Heeee..."

"I can't understand where the time went. But that's not important. Who is the man? Do you know him? I think he lives here in the forest..."

"Let's go inside."

He checked his watch.... 8 p.m... she's a half hour late for her disappearing act. This must be about something. He followed her into the hut.

She pulled the curtain that acted as a mosquito net firmly into place, but left the door open. Anyone passing could see that they were talking by lantern light.

114

She went to a large straw purse hanging on the wall and pulled out a bottle of akpeteshie. Kojo looked on in surprise as she poured half full glasses for both of them.

Wordlessly, she gave him his glass and turned hers up to swallow in a few gulps; she sprinkled the dregs on the door sill and mumbled a prayer.

Kojo took a sip and sat down. How can they drink this stuff like that? I'd be knocked out before I finished swallowing.

She gestured for him to sit. He sat and sipped, waiting.

"I will tell you of this man."

Number two cameral Close-Up/Lighting? Just use the the lantern, it has mystery and charm in it. Lights! Camera! Action!

"This man is Asiafo, you understand?"

"No, please understand, I mean, no, I don't understand."

The akpeteshie was shooting through his guts like a toboggan.

"Asiafo is very poisonous spider, very bad. One bite dead. Asiafo, a bad spirit..."

"I understand now."

"Eh heee...evil spirit, Asiafo. This person you speak of is wicked. A wicked man."

"Auntie, I believe what you say. If you say the man is wicked, he's wicked. But what makes him wicked?"

The old lady poured herself another half glass of the akpeteshie, downed it and offered him a hook. He waved it off politely. She sat with her head down for a few moments and finally looked dead into his eyes.

"When I was a girl in this village, this wicked man was banished from the village and cursed for knowing his mother."

Kojo took a hard sip of his drink. People were so into Biblical things. For "knowing" his mother. And thus did Onan "know" his brother's wife.

"Are you sure....he "knew" his mother?"

"They were caught by one of the elders."

Suddenly Kojo felt a warm thud thump him in the stomach.

"So, he was banished to the forest and cursed. How long ago?"

"It was at least forty years now."

"And what happened to the mother?"

"She was a witch and was burned in her hut."

Kojo felt himself trying to shrug it off. The whole business sounded so Medieval.

"How old was this man when he was banished?"

The old lady took a moment to count back, shades of Granddad....

"He was twenty years....eheee....twenty years."

Kojo visualized the man he had seen in the forest, he looked to be about thirty-five, certainly no older than forty.

"Auntie, the man I saw today didn't look like a sixty year old man."

"He has powers, he has learned powers in the forest. There are people in the village who go to him, not now, but formerly."

He held his glass out for another slug. This is interesting.

"Powers you say, like what?"

"Many powers."

"Can you give me an example, some examples?"

He could sense her reluctance to talk about the wizard in the forest, but the akpeteshie had obviously loosened her tongue.

"Eh heeee... this man who lives in our village had a wife. His wife died. The man did not want her to be dead so, he found the wicked one, the bocor, and paid him to have his wife back."

"How much did he pay to have his wife brought back to life?"

"He did not pay money."

There was a short, heavy silence. The sounds of the village seemed deadened.

"Eh heee...this woman was barren fifteen years, no children. She went in secret to Asiafo. Later that year she had twin boys who looked different from any human being...."

"So, what happened?"

"The woman was found hanged. The father and the twins were never seen again."

"Anything else?" Kojo felt greedy for more. How often in my life will I come across something like this?

"There is much but I cannot tell all. This man has become a creature of mystery..."

Go 'head on, girl....a creature of mystery.

"A creature of mystery, huh?"

"Eh heee....there are things of the forest that he has learned that give him the power to disappear.

"To disappear?"

"'Heee, and to fly like a bird. And to become a tree, Or a snake..."

"And you think these things make him wicked?"

"Dabi dabi, o dabi, not these things alone. There is more. He can read the mind and see into tomorrow..."

"Wowwww..."

"And he is wicked because he hates everyone."

"Well, I think that's pretty easy to understand. His mother was burned alive and he was banished to the forest...."

"Eheeee, for doing the greatest sin. Many in the village wanted to kill them and all of the family."

"Are there still family members here?"

"You say...?"

"Does the wicked man have family here?"

"All moved away many years ago."

"So, now, let me get this straight. A man was banished to the forest forty years ago, he's out and develops supernatural powers and all that, and has become wicked."

She stood, swaying a bit, and poured another dollop into her glass, slugged it down.

"Six people of this village have gone to him to ask for something and when they didn't make the proper payment they were never seen again."

Sounds like Chicago to me, or New York. Mafia stuff.

"So, I understand. He is a wicked man."

"Eh heeee, he is wicked. I warn you."

The old lady shuffled out, leaving Kojo perched on the edge of his stool, puzzled and curious.

There's a helluva film in all this, if I can determine which point of view I'd be coming from. And if the seams could be sewn so that the stitching doesn't show.

He undressed and sprawled on his bed, sipping akpeteshie and thinking.

This couldn't be real, it just couldn't be, not in the 21ˢᵗ century.

He forced himself to eat the onion/tomato/fish stew, sprinkled with gari. He felt a need to "line the walls" before he started out this morinig.

"You are taking food before your work/out. why?"

The old girl is sharp, real sharp.

"I think it's the akpeteshie, it made me very hungry."

There was some degree of truth in what he said, he did feel extremely hungry.

After breakfast, he started out.

"Kojo, I warn you", the old woman cautioned him.

"Everything is cool, Auntie, all is cool."

She must know that I'm going back...

No workout for me this morning, I've got to get back out here, into this dripping drama.

He was disappointed when he got to the small farm ("more like a truck garden") and found no one there. Guess Wednesday was the father-in-law's only day.

He hesitated for a few seconds before getting on the path that would take him to "...the place we will not go."

He took careful note of the time - 8:15 a.m. - and looked up at the sky for a long moment. Looks kinda greyish, hope it doesn't rain on me out here.

The trail seemed familiar and longer. Kojo was consciously keeping all of it in perspective. The trail seems longer because I didn't have a good drink of water, the way I did before I started out yesterday.

8:45 a.m. Did I walk this far yesterday? The forest made him feel as though he were in a great, green cathedral.

Yeahh, the log, I'm right on the money. He straddled the log, wishing that he had brought a bottle of water with him.

The hand reaching over his left shoulder, with the top of a coconut lopped off, caused the hair on the back of his head to fright wig up. His hands trembled as he took the coconut and drank the water from it.

Why is he sitting behind me? Maybe he's shy.

"Thank you."

"You are welcome."

Kojo turned to pass the coconut back to the man, to discover that he was now sitting in front of him.

"You really get around, don't you?"

The man nodded pleasantly, took the coconut and smashed it open expertly, scraped two large pieces of meat from the shell, handed Kojo a piece, kept one for himself and threw the rest into the underbrush. They chewed the fresh coconut meat for a few minutes.

"So, now you know all about me."

Once again, Kojo had the fright wig feeling run up the back of his neck. The man had not asked a question, he had made a blunt statement. Now what?

"I know what one person has told me, I don't know your story."

"She told you the correct story."

His expression didn't change, there was no body language to indicate that he felt ashamed, remorseful or evil. Shrill bird cries filled up the word space between them. Kojo decided to be real with the man, there was no other way to go.

"So, you've been living here in the forest since you were banished?"

"Yes."

"I am Kojo Bediako Brown."

"They call me Asiafo."

"Is that your real name?"

"It is the only name I have ever known."

Asiafo, the poisonous spider, the one with evil intentions, the evil spirit. Kojo studied the man's face and form. He's got to be the healthiest man I've ever see in my life. No wrinkles, no bags under this eyes, not an once of fat, all of his teeth, serene looking. This brother knows something.

He gave Kojo the feeling that he could talk, if they talked, or simply sit and look at each other; they were still going to be communicating.

"Asiafo, may I ask you a few questions?"

"Do you want to get wet?"

"Huh?"

"It is going to rain heavily in a few minutes."

"No, no, I don't want to get wet."

Asiafo slipped from the log and beckoned for Kojo to follow him.

Six people of this village have gone to him to ask for something and when they didn't make the proper payment they were never seen again.

I haven't asked him for anything, I don't owe him anything. I'm o.k., I hope.

After a couple minutes of fast walking they came to a small clearing with large hut made of banana leaves.

I've seen this before, what's that book called? The one about the Ituri Forest people, the so called Pygmies...same structure.

Ten seconds after they ducked inside the rain sloshed down.

"Wowww, we made it just in time. How did you know...?"

The man, Asiafo, cut his question to pieces with a look. How could I live in the forest this long and not know when it's going to rain?

The man lit two wicks floating in an oil filled half coconut shell. Kojo didn't conceal his curiosity. He stared at the vine-contraption animal traps, the woven baskets, the hats, the hand fashioned tools.

This brother has everything he needs, well, almost everything.

"Please sit down and relax, this rain won't last long."

Kojo sat on a beautifully carved stool, carved from a tree stump that was still partially attached. It this is an evil man, he certainly has an eye for beautiful things.

Asiafo started a small fire in a deep hole in the center of the hut with flint sparks and dry moss.

Kojo stared at the process, fascinated. No, I don't believe this.

He fed the fire with a few twigs and then, larger sticks of wood. The lamp wick light and the fire gave the interior a bright, warm, hospitable look. Asiafo sat on the other side of the hut, listening to the rain.

Kojo couldn't hold back any longer, there were things he had to know.

"Asiafo, I want to ask you a few questions."

"Yes."

The man gave Kojo his complete attention. The effect was that of a person who could focus immediately.

What do I want to know? Everything!

"Uhhh, what happens when you get sick?"

Asiafo smiled in a patronizing way.

"I don't believe in sickness."

"I don't either, but let's say a mosquito bites you and you get malaria..."

"No, no sickness here, I have medicines."

"You have a medicine for malaria?"

"Yes."

There was a way he said yes that was so definite.

"You have other medicines?"

"Yes."

"You have a medicine for AIDS, cancer, the common cold?"

"We don't have those things here."

"But, do you have medicines for them?"

"Yes."

Kojo gazed into the fire for a thoughtful moment. Where am I? Where is all this? Can I make a film out of it?

"You want to make a film of this?", the man asked sweetly. Kojo stared into the eyes of a man who could read minds and was clairyovant. He felt like a baby just learning how to form words.

"Yes, if not this, then other films, films that would change minds and attitudes, films that would be wonderful, reasonable, sensitive..."

"Why don't you do these films?", the same quiet voice.

Kojo was back on his turf now. You may be able to fly, have medicine for incurable diseases and all that, but there's something quite different when it comes to film making, Mr. Asiafo.

"It takes money that I don't have."

"How much?"

"Lots, like millions. I'm not talking cedis, I'm talking dollars."

The rain seemed to be pounding the leaves like downstroking fufu sticks. They were silent.

"It is possible for you to have the millions to do your film."

Kojo stifled the urge to laugh. A half naked man, making fire with sparks, living in a banana leaf hut in the middle of the Equatorial rainforest, is telling me that it's possible to have millions to do my films, fulfill my vision. Yeahhh...right.

"O yeah, how do I get these millions?"

"Come back to the log on Saturday, I will have your answer. The rain has stopped, I will guide you back to the log."

Kojo stood, feeling lightheaded, carefree. My problems are over, solved, ain't nothing else to worry about.

That was the effect of the man's words on his mind.

The forest was dripping raindrops from its leaves, making a crystalline picture through the huge fern branches, the tangled undergrowth.

Kojo followed the man of the forest, trying to step where he stepped, to bend under branches the way he did it. When they arrived at the log, their departure point, Kojo stuck out his hand to shake Asiafo's hand, to tell him he appreciated his hospitality.

Asiafo was gone. O well, I'll see him Saturday.

"Yes", the voice echoed from above his head, "I'll see you Saturday."

He walked a few hundred yards and held his wrist up to check the time. 9:30 a.m. No, it couldn't be, it's got to be later than that.

He did a clear minded back track. Met the man on the log, it was 8:45 a.m. We talked, we walked to his hut to get out of the rain.

It rained for a long time. We talked some more. We walked back to the log. It's got to be later than 9:30 a.m.

He held his watch to his ear, a fine timepiece it was ticking like a metronome. All this happened in fifteen minutes?

Something real strange going on here.

Kojo spent the rest of the morning and the early afternoon strolling around the village, mentally photographing everybody and their activities.

Children <u>work</u> here. An eight year old girl carrying a bucket of water on her head that is heavier than she is.

The women pounded cassava, washed, carried loads from distant places on their heads, cleaned houses, fed babies, fed their husbands, sewed, ironed, worked.

The younger men farmed. It seemed that the only group in the village who were exempt from labor were the old men, the elders. They played checkers, wari, cards, drank akpeteshie and made decisions.

"Kojo, will you take the evening meal now?"

"Uhh, I'm not really hungry just now, can I take a raincheck?"

"You say...?"

"I'll eat a little later."

I wonder how I'm going to handle this when I leave here? This sister ain't done nothin' but feed me, tell me about things, give me insights. Maybe I can give her 100,000 cedis. Yeahhh, that would make her day.

He stood on the fringe of the crowd, watching the girls in the center dance. They were painted, white-powdered, bare breasted.

I'm sure I must be the only one here who notices stuff like this.

The dance was a part of a puberty rites cycle-ceremony. The girls were almost at the point of being considered women in the community. It would take a husband and a child/or children to give her full validation.

"Auntie, what happens if a woman can't have children, for some reason?"

"Ehhheee, O, that is very bad. The husband will not be pleased, the village will not be pleased. It is bad."

"Where are your children?

"They are scattered like the four winds", she spoke proudly, "I have three sons and one daughter. The oldest boy is a doctor in U.K., the other two are doing business in Accra and the girl is a teacher at Accra Girls Secondary School."

"That's great. Do you see them often?"

"Eh heee, sometimes too often", she smiled warmly. "They come when they have problems or when they want my food."

Friday staggered, shuffled, slugged its way through Kojo's life. He was invited to come to give a little talk at Tsito school by the Headmistress herself.

Kojo felt somewhat flattered, but just a bit annoyed at the same time. He wanted to fix himself in a receptive mode for whatever Asiafo was going to bring him on Saturday.

The invitation to come and give a talk to the children was an excuse Cutie Pie Deku was using to reel him closer.

The girl ain't dumb, I got to give it to her.

"What do you want me to talk about?"

"Why not talk about America? They would like that. We seldom have visitors from abroad come to Tsito, it will be interesting for the children."

"O.K., do you have a map of North America?"

"We have a globe."

"Good."

2:00 p.m.

"We'll have you talk just before they leave for home, it'll give them something to remember."

Kojo made careful preparations for his appearance at Tsito school. He had decided to title his talk - "What is an African-American?"

He started making a few notes and wound up with 8 pages of notes.

CHAPTER 10

The "little talk" had suddenly acquired international implications. This may be the first and only time an Afcican-American will ever speak to some of them, I better get it right the first time.

He was there on time and surprised to see Auntie Eugenia, three other women he didn't know, and four of the men they called "The Elders."

Ms. Deku gave him the sort of introduction that he had always disliked, the barogue, flowery stuff.

"And now, boys and girls, let's put our hands together to welcome Mr. Kojo Bediako Brown, from America."

The applause weas honest and emotional. They really feel something about this.

He took the warmest approach he could take; the touching, joking and repetitions that children all over the world seem to love.

When he finally dug his heels in and announced, "Now I would like to talk to you about what an African-American is."

He held the globe up and pointed his finger at the center of Africa.

"This is where our ancestors were taken from, and this is where they were taken to..."

Fifteen minutes into his carefully structured half hour, he noticed a glaze coming over the eyes of the Elders and many of the students. Miss Deku was carrying on a low profile conversation witha one of the women who had come with Auntie Euginia.

Well, I'll be damned! I'm boring them. Maybe it's my accent. He had noticed that Ghanaians at all levels, loved British accents.

O.K., if that's the way it's gon' be. He made a snap decision to end the talk with iis stagiest England-Lord Cavendish accent.

"And finally, Ah should like to thank yew for your most devoted attention....cheerio."

The students applauded dutifully, came up one by one to bow and shake his hand –boys, and the girls curtsyed.

The Elders, Aunt Eugenia and her friends waved warm smiles at him and moved out sharply. Cutie Pie Deku took his hand and held it.

"That was really quite good, actually."

"Thank you, Miss Deku."

Now what?

"Please, wait a moment. I'll close up. I shan't be long."

He framed her in his view finder as she quick-marched back into the classroom to grab up her purse and to close the schoolroom door.

"Don't you lock it?"

She looked genuinely puzzled.

"Whatever for?"

"I'm sure you must have a thief or two in Tsito."

Lovely smile, lush spirit behind it, obviously. Be careful, Kojo, be careful.

"O, no one would steal from the school."

"Hmmm...."

They strolled in step toward the "Mainstreet" of the village. Ahhhhahhh, I know the game. They see us together, that means we <u>are</u> together. He thought of veering off to his left or right, deserting her on the mainstreet.

"Mr. Brown?"

"You may call me Kojo..."

"O, I see. As an honorarium for your dissertation, may I offer you a drink?"

"A drink?"

"Yes, in the drinking bar just thar."

"Yes, yes I see. Yes please. But I should tell Auntie Eugenia that I'll be a little late for dinner."

"She has been informed."

Yeahh, Kojo, you better pull the cotton out of your mind, this is a slickster.

They were honored guests, the schoolteacher and the stranger, and they were served the coldest beers in town.

It didn't take long, after the second glass, for Miss Cutie Pie Deku to reveal herself as an overeducated member of her society.

"I hate that we are so conservastive, so slow to go with the new ideah."

"Then why do you stay here, why don't you go back to London, or America?"

She slugged half a glass of her beer down, was getting loose. He was becoming conscious about the women, especially. After enough alcohol, they changed, began to be freer.

"They don't need me in London, or America. They need me in Ghana here. And this is where I'm going to stay."

She made her statement with such vehemence that he felt like apologising for asking the question.

"Let's have another drink?"

And hour later, they strolled, a bit tipsy from two beers each.

"Well, Miss Deku, it's been quite enjoyable and I've learned a lot this evening."

"And what have you learned?"

Ahhh hah, so now she's going to play schoolteacher on the village street. O well...

"Well, I've definitely learned something of what it feels like to be a beautiful young schoool teacher, feeling nationalistic, who want's to dedicate her life to upgrading her people's mentalities."

"Is that all you've learned?"

"No, I've also learned that beautiful young school teachers can get a bit horny, every now 'n then."

"Good evening, Mr. Brown."

Damnit where is my cameraman? It's a perfect scene: beautiful young African school teacher gets pissed and flaunces off.

Good evening, Mr. Brown! It was so out of tune with the surroundings that he felt like laughing. Good evening, Mr. Brown! What was that supposed to be? Some kind of final kiss off or something?

O well...

"Auntie, you know something?"

"You say..."

"You know something; I can understand why your children want to come back home to eat all the time."

The old lady smiled proudly and continued washing dishes.

"Now, if you'll excuse me I must go and write a couple letters."

"No problem."

It was his turn to smile. The lady was full of surprises.

He adjusted the lantern to its highest point.

"Dear Granddad,

Peace and greetings from the Motherland. As you always told me, say the important things first. I'm living for a week in a village called Tsito. I'll have to find out what that means.

My ladyfriend gave me a note to her Aunt here, a fine old lady named Eugenia, you would really dig her, I'm sure.

(I've written Mom and Dad already, the letter hasn't been mailed).

Back to the village. I felt the need to get out of Accra. The city was stinking when I was here eight years ago, now it's like a garbage heap. There are no emission controls on vehicles, so all of that noxious black smoke is coming out at you.

The drains are clogged with mosquito larvae, the roads are rudimentary potholes and it's the rainy season, fortunately, beyond all of that, the people are still warm and hospitable.

It's a hard life here. It's painful to see small children working harder than most adults in the U.S., and it's difficult to reconcile so many contradictions. For example, it's hard to figure out how people can take so much pride in their so called history and leave us out.

We "Diasporans" have got to be the proudest beings on the planet, for what we've accomplished, against the odds facing us.

And yet, our brothers and sisters here seem to take no pride in what we've overcome. I'll have to dig into this a little deeper.

Got an appointment with a wizard tomorrow.
That's about all I can say for now, there'll be a lot more when I return.

Stay well, love,
Kojo"

The letter written, he prepared for a restless night. That's always been a problem with me, being anxious the night before any project. O well...

He fell asleep, thinking of what the man in the forest had in store for him. Two hours later he woke up from a strange dream; more like a feeling than a dream.

The feeling was warm and cozy, as though he were floating in a body temperature bath, absorbing vibes from the bath that made him feel strong and wise.

He sat up in bed, pleased and puzzled by the dream. It had been almost a non-representational dream, filled with colors and sliding patterns, beautiful designs.

After a few moments of serious thought, he slid back onto his bed. Hmm.... wonder what that was about?

He fell back into a deeper sleep, listening to the distant sound of owls.

Kojo was awaked by the village sounds; roosters crowing, people talking, a few odd sounds that he couldn't connect to anything.

Saturday. What time did we agree to meet at the log? A surge of panic swept through him. What if I'm late?

A second later the panic striken feeling was replaced with a comic twist.

I must be outta my mind. Here I am, having an anxiety attack about an appointment with a man whose been living in the forest for forty years. A man living in the forest for forty years that I'm meeting with, like a big time producer who is going to finance my film projects.

"How do I get these millions?"

"Come back to the log on Saturday, I will have your answer...."

Yeah, that's what he man said, "Return on Saturday and I will have your answer...."

"Kojo", Auntie Eugenia called to him.

"Yes, Auntie."

"I have taken watah for your baff."

"Thank you, Auntie."

He shook his head, smiling to himself. Ghanaians have to be the "baffingest" people on the planet. Where else in the world do people bath every morning, every night, before they get ready to go out and sometimes in between times.

He saronged his towel around his waist and strolled to the "shower stall". While rinsing the soap from his body he remembered the time of his last meeting with the man he was beginning to call "the wizard".

I can't keep the idea of this being some kind of evil spirit I'm meeting with, the brother's vibe is too positive for that.

9:15 a.m., that's the time we met last. Plenty of time, it's only 7:30 a.m.

Auntie Eugenia seemed to be unusually solemn as she fed him fresh bread, (they bake in the morning), tea and scrambled eggs.

After breakfast Kojo dawdled around, killing time. I don't want to get there too soon, that might show too much anxiety.

8:15 a.m., it was time to move out. Auntie caught him in mid-motion.

"Kojo, you are not going for your work?"

Oh, aren't you the sly one?

"Uhhh, no, not today, Auntie, I thought I'd just kick it around a bit today, you know, get my thoughts together."

He could feel her eyes on his back as he tried to pull off a nonchalant getaway.

"I have warned you," she spoke in a low tone.

He pretended not to hear and kept moving.

No one working on the farm. Hmmm...guess I was right, the brother only works on Wednesday.

Beyond the small, cultivated plot, the forest seemed to swallow him up. He walked at a slow, steady clip, sure of his way.

He was surprised to see his man leaning against the log. It was suddenly time to measure every action, analyze every nuance of what was about to happen.

"Good morning."
"Good morning."

Asiafo, the man in the forest near Tsito

Kojo approached the man, but didn't feel the need to reach out and shake hands in the usual manner, Asiafo just didn't seem to be the type to shake hands.

Kojo leaned against the log, feeling as much at ease, under the circumstances, as he could possibly feel.

An hour seemed to pass before Asiafo turned to face him.

"You will have what you want, your wish has been granted."

Everything in the forest was placed in Freeze Frame as Kojo pulled in the words letter by letter.

"You say...?"

"You will have what you want, your wish has been granted. You will have the millions you need to make your films."

That's what the man said. Why is my heart thumping the way it is?

"You believe me, don't you?"

"Yes, I do believe you."

Am I being hypnotized? No, I feel in control of myself. Now what? Once again the silence rang back in. Kojo could hear his heart beat.

"Tell me something."

"Yes?"

"What do I have to do for this money?"

The hairs on the back of Kojo's neck bristled when the man burst out with the strangest laugh he'd ever heard a human being make.

He sounds like a hyena. I guess that must come from not laughing out loud too often. The laughter jarred to a stop and the man began to speak as though he were reciting a speech or giving a recipe.

"I will arrange for you to have a visitor; the visitor will come 4 times a year and it must be fed. I must warn you that the success or failure of what you want to do will depend on how well it is fed."

"That's no problem, we got lots of food in America, all kinds. There's so much of it in some places that they let it rot."

"Very good. No problem. You will have what you want."

Asiafo started to walk away. Kojo felt a sense of panic.

"Is that all? I mean, that's all I have to do…?"

"Oh, there is one more thing. When you return to your home, you should be married within three months."

"Three months? Married?"

The chess game was on. Which move should I make? What move <u>can</u> I make? Damn….millions and all I have to is get married?

"I accept that condition. One last question. How long can I receive the…..uhhh……money?"

"You will continue to receive as long as you feed your visitor. No feeding and all will be withdrawn."

"One final question, please. What do you get out of this? I mean, why are you making this possible?"

"Because you asked me."

And then he was gone. Kojo suddenly felt that he had been left in a huge, green walled room. The forest seemed to be booming with silence.

He stood in place for a few minutes, feeling emotionally drained, and then dropped to his knees and started praying….

I thank my ancestors and I thank the Orisha for making my return to Africa possible.

I thank my Ancestors and I thank the Orisha for maintaining and protecting my good health.

I beg my Ancestors and I beg the Orisha to help me become healthy, wealthy and wise.

I thank my Ancestors and I thank the Orisha for all the blessings I receive, now and forever.

I ask God to please help me do the right thing, always.

He stood up, brushed his knees off, feeling better but shaky, and began to make his way back to the village, knowing that Asiafo was watching him.

As he reached the path to the village, he turned and waved solemnly; "Goodbye and thank you."

The forest suddenly erupted with Asiafo's hyena laughter. Kojo, extremely puzzled, walked a little faster.

Auntie Eugenia and the rest of the village seemed to be a different place when he returned. Auntie was reserved, aloof, almost cold to him.

The villagers who had formerly been cordial were distant now, some of them frowned when they saw him walking through the village after his evening meal.

Looks like I've blown it here. Wonder what the hell provoked all of this? Even if they know I went to see Asiafo that shouldn't poison their minds against me. What did I do to them?

Kojo returned to Auntie Eugenia's hut just as she was going out.

"Uhh, Auntie, I'd like to talk with you."

The usual look of amusement was replaced by a stern expression. She did acknowledge him; she simply stood in place, allowing him to speak to her.

"Look, I know you told me to be aware...."

She held her hands out to stop him from saying anything more.

"Yes", she spoke in a sharp tone, "Yes, I told you to be aware." And walked away from him.

Kojo entered the hut, searched in the woven basket for the akpeteshie bottle, settled heavily on a stool and took a long swig.

O my God, what have I done? What the hell is this? All of the village sounds that formerly seemed interesting and rustic, had now become ominous. And I can't understand a word they're saying.

He took another swig of akpeteshie and started trying to reason with himself. Be cool, don't panic, you'll be out of here come Monday afternoon. Monday afternoon.

What if the driver, whatshisname? Joshua, doesn't come for me? He broke out in a quick paranoid sweat.

How in the hell could I get out of here? I don't even know where I'm at.

8:30 p.m. The beginning of a long night. Kojo was drunk, the bottle finished. He staggered to his bed and fell into a stupored sleep.

Two hours later he lurched from his bed and stumbled around in the dark.

"Who is that?! Who is it?!"

He grabbed the bottle as a weapon and felt his way to the nearest corner.

The sound was some kind of scraping sound. And it stopped the second he raised his voice.

The interior of the hut had suddenly become too small. He felt cramped and paranoid. What if they decide to fire this place up tonight and roast my ass?

Sweat dribbled down the sides of his face as he stumbled back to his bed, half drunk and exhausted from the tension. He sat on the side of the bed, clutching the bottle, afraid to sleep.

How in the hell did I get myself in a fix like this?

He did a slow Pan of the shapes and sizes of the things in his room. The door! Once again he stumbled away from his bed through the short hallway that led to the front room.

A moonless night, only drifting cloudy shadows passing the the window. He felt his way to the door and frantically placed the small wooden bar in its place.

A lot of good that would do if somebody really wanted to break in here. If not through the door, then through the window.

The hooting of owls, the screaming of something he couldn't figure out, startled him. He stood in place, wishing that he hadn't drank the akpeteshie.

Here I am, half drunk, trying to figure out how I'm going to fend for my life. He found his way back to his bed and sprawled out on it, still holding the bottle in his hand.

Let 'em, come, I'll get one, at least.

The sound of someone knocking on the door and calling his name woke him up.

"Kojo! Kojo!"

It was daylight. He staggered to the door, checking the time en route. Wowwww... 7:30 a.m. I must've knocked myself out with all that booze.

He opened the door and Auntie Eugenia entered.

"Kojo, you locked the door?"

"Uhh, no reason. I guess I just felt like locking it."

She gave him a curious look, sniffed the liquor residue on his breath and began to tidy up her house.

"I have taken watah for your baff."

"Thank you, Auntie."

So, we all play it cool, huh? Let's pretend that everything is the way it was.

He draped himself in his towel and went to the bathing stall. Have to think this one out carefully, keep my wits about me, remember who I am.

He returned to the hut, not really knowing what to do with himself. Sunday, everybody is in town today, no work.

"Kojo, your breakfast!"

"I'm coming!" he called back automatically and checked himself; Poison, that's the way they would do it. Auntie Eugenia?

He was angry at himself for thinking that the kindly old lady would poison him. But he couldn't shake the paranoid driven fear off.

"Oh, Auntie, I'm really not hungry just not, I'll have something later."

She glared at him, both fists mounted on her ample hips.

"But last time, after the akpeteshie you were hungry."

It was close to being an accusation.

"Yeah, you're right, I guess the stuff affects you in a different way each time. Uhh, Auntie, I'm going for a little walk, be back in a while."

He made a smooth move past her, took a hard look at the covered plate on the stool he usually sat on, when he was eating.

Wonder what she cooked? O well...

He made a pitstop at the latrine, trying to make up his mind where he could go to kill a few hours.

The schoolteacher, yeahhh, the schoolteacher, Miss Cutie Pie Deku. Where does she live? He wandered in the general direction of the school buildings, wondering who he could ask.

Sunday morning. The villagers were dressed up; the men in strangely tailored suits, the women in cut down ball gowns, plenty of ruffles, the children scrubbed and polished.

He passed small clots of them and nodded "good morning". They nodded back or made tight salutes. But the smiles were missing.

Well, at least we're still on <u>some</u> kind of terms. May be I went off a little too fast about things, jumped to too many conclusions at once.

The hazy sun and the fresh air perked him up a bit, pulling the residual hangover away from his head.

The sun had half baked the red earth around the school building. Kojo wandered from building to building, pausing to do a few Capoeira movements in his practice space, walked on to Ms. Deku's classroom.

He pushed the door open and strolled around the classroom, thinking. Who could I ask? I don't want to ask Auntie, that might be fuel for all kinds of fires.

He sat on top of one of the small desks and stared at the blackboard. Where are you, Cutie Pie, now that I need you?

The drinking bar! They would know. He hopped off the desk, carefully closed the door and started a quick walk to the bar where they had shared a couple beers.

The owner, evidently not a churchgoer, was absently swatting at errant flies as Kojo walked in. Now, how do I best go about this?

"You are welcome."

"Thank you. Is it too early to get a beer?"

"It is not too early."

Kojo sat, watching stragglers hurry to the church. 9 O'clock. How can I go about this? 9 O'clock, bet she's at church. He decided to cozy up to the owner a bit, the only one who seemed unchanged.

"Uhhh, are you originally from this village, I mean, were you born here?"

The owner, obviously a beer lover, judging from his pregnant look, sprawled in a chair at Kojo's table.

"Oh no, I was born in Accra."

"Well, how did you wind up here?"

"I came to see a girl I knew here, ten years ago, and I stayed."

"So, you got married?"

"Yes, but not to her, to another one."

Kojo shared a laugh with the man and and sipped his beer - now seemed like the best time.

"Tell me, brother...?

"I am called Forson."

"Brother Forson, you remember the lady I was here with, the other night...?"

"The teacher, Deku."

"Yes, how do I get to her place? I have some information I want to give her."

CHAPTER 11

"No problem. She lives on the Eastern Edge."

"Where is that?"

The owner led him to the swinging door of the bar and pointed the directions. "You go right until you come to the well and then go left. She is there, the third house."

"Thank you, Mr. Forson."

Kojo set out to follow directions, aware that the church services were at a peak; he could tell from the sound of the preacher's voice.

Fifteen minutes later he was knocking on the front door of the school Teacher's house in the section called Eastern Edge, acutely aware that he hadn't had anything to eat yet.

Eastern Ridge. He looked up and down a hard packed road that trailed away from the village. The effect was as though twenty or thirty houses with metal roof tops had been designed as a sort of suburb.

Well, I'll be damned. I guess this must be the vilage middle class.

A young girl opened the door, dressed in a formless shift, bare footed. She stood there, looking into his face.

"Miss Deku is home?"

The girl nodded no.

"Is she coming back soon?"

The girl nodded yes.

Well, obviously she speaks English. Guess I'm a little bit of a surprise.

"Can I come inside and wait?"

The girl nodded yes and stood aside for him to enter. The girl faded away like a shadow, leaving him standing in the center of a room that resembled Aunt Eugenia's front room on a much larger scale.

The rooms were large, spacious, tastefully decorated, an honest reflection of the person who lived there. Books. He fingered his way through her library, savoring the titles of old friends; "Malcom X", "The Theory of the Leisure Class", "Class, Caste and Racism", "Tribalism in Ghana", "Ashanti Girls Puberty Rites", "Marcus Garvey", "The Life of Adam Clayton Powell", "Henry Miller"....

Henry Miller, "Quiet days in Clichy", "Black Spring", "Sexus", "Nexus" and "Plexus", Henry Miller.

He pulled the book from the shelf and sat on the wicker woven sofa. Wowww, Henry Miller here, this is a trip.

The girl made an appearance with a glass and carafe of water.

"You are welcome sah", she said shyly and faded away to another part of the house.

Must be about five rooms in here. Kojo poured himself water, sipped and settled into a reading of Miller's "Nexus", one of his favorites, his hunger temporarily forgotten.

"Good morning, Mr. Brown."

Kojo pulled himself up feeling slightly embarrassed to be caught so completely unawares.

"O, uhh, good morning, I hope I'm not intruding, I....uhh....just happened to be strolling in your neighborhood and..."

"You are welcome. Please excuse me, I must change into something more comfortable."

She marched away, a crisp figure in starched white. He could see a metamorphosis that was bound to occur. The slim waist and the neat hips were going to thicken and she was going to become Mistress Deku, an old maid school teacher.

He sat back on the sofa, feverishly trying to put her attitude toward him together. She didn't seem to be too surprised to see me sitting here.

Maybe the bar owner told her I was coming to her place.

Did she really mean it when she said, "You are welcome?" Was it simply a formal statement? I wonder what she thinks of me being here?

She reappeared ten minutes later, dressed in a loose flowing caftan and sandals. She seeemed quite well possessed, he was the one feeling a bit ill at ease, based on the circumstances of their last meeting.

She stood in front of him, the gracious hostess, not interrogating him about his reason for being in her home.

"Can I serve you something stronger than water, Mr. Brown?"

"Please, Kojo."

"Very well, Kojo...."

"Are you having something?"

"I'm having a pink gin."

"That' sounds about right for me too."

Once again she marched away to a room at the rear. The kitchen? He smiled, watching her walk. It was almost a British sergeant's motion, complete with the swinging arms.

A pink gin, Henry Miller, in Tsito?! He glanced at his watch. 11:15. It's going to be a long day.

Subconsiously, he was trying to figure out ways and means to kill off Sunday. Stay away from things.

She re-entered the room, carrying a tray with two generous glasses of gin.

"Sorry, no ice. Our power plant was knocked out a few days before you arrived and it hasn't been repaired yet."

She sat at the opposite end of the sofa, a portrait of a relaxed career woman at home.

"Cheers", he saluted her.

"Cheers", she responded and took a neat sip of her pink gin.

The gin shot down to Kojo's stomach like a bolt of lightening. Hope I don't get sick. What have I had? Two beers already, but that was a couple hours ago. O well...

He decided to break in with a little back spacing, something to justify his visit.

"Uhh, Miss Deku..."

"You needn't be so formal in my home here, Kojo. I am called Cecilia."

"Cecilia, nice name, uhhh; I started thinking about the last time we met, you know, when we parted, and I felt I owed you an apology."

"What on Earth for?"

She was so British, so prissy, in a way.

"Well, if you recall, you seemed to be rather annoyed with me, about a remark I made."

"O, I'm sure I was not annoyed, really. I just felt that the evening had reached its logical conclusion and it was time for me to go home.... silly boy!"

She reached over and spanked his hand playfully. Well, good, I've broken the ice.

"Well, good, I'm glad to hear that. I was a little worried."

"Not too worry, not too worry...."

She smiled her luscious smile at him and took a longer sip of her drink.

"The girl is preparing something, will you stay for lunch?"

"I was hoping you'd ask me."

They shared a laugh and she popped up from the sofa.

"Here, allow me to freshen your drink."

Two pink gins later.

"Cecilia, I have couple serious questions I'd like to ask you."

"Yesplease, you may ask at table. Shall we?" She led him into the room she had brought therir drinks from. The dining room. Almost English, with the sideboard and all. And a nicely stocked liguor cabinet.

Kojo's mouth was almost watering from the sight of the delicious looking food.

"Please be seated."

The girl stood to his left with her hands folded together. Cecilia Deku sat at the head of the table and devoutly blessed the meal. Afterwards she spoke to the girl in Ewe and she faded from the scene.

"Now then, Kojo, I hope you like fish."

"I love fish."

His eyes swept back and forth across the food. I'd shoot straight down on this, the way they shot the huge skillet of beautiful food cooking in "Dona Flor and Her Two Husbands."

One large whole fish that looked like a giant trout, sliced kenkey, a huge salad of different vegetables, smoking soup, several smaller plates with fried things he couldn't recognize.

Hope there's no rat meat here...

She filled his plate, took a smaller portion for herself, and gave him the opportunity to fend off his hunger with a few forks of food before interrupting him.

"Now then, Kojo, you said you had a couple serious questions...?"

He paused, a mouthful of fish, chewed and swallowed.

"Yes, I do. I'm concerned for my safety here and I want to know...?"

She looked at him with shocked surprise. "You are concerned for your safety here, in Tsito? Why?"

"I'm coming. It has to do with me breaking some kind of taboo."

He explained that he had gone to a part of the forest that was considered "off limits", in between bites.

"Oh, don't mind them! How could you take the fears of a collection of superstitious people seriously?

I'm surprised at you, Kojo, I thought you were a modern man... hahhhahhahhhahhh."

She seemed to be putting the whole picture into its proper perspective.

"You're right. I think I've overreacted. But what about this man that lives there...?"

She stopped smiling and stared at him.

"Are you speaking of Asiafo?"

"Yes."

"How do you know of him?"

"I've met him." He was afraid to admit that he had made a deal with the man.

"You...met...him?"

"Yes, the other day, as a matter of fact." He could see the possibility of learning something. His hunger was suddenly appeased.

"Is it true that he has some kind of supernatural powers?"

He could tell that he had touched a sensitive place, from the expression on her face.

"Kojo, if you're finished? Why don't we sit on the veranda?"

"I'm with you, lady."

She led him through a short hallway into the kitchen and onto a beautifully enclosed back porch; trellises of tropical vegetation closing it in, giving off pleasant scents and shade.

He was reminded of the gazebos he had seen in the American South.

They sat on the wicker woven sofa. He could hear the faint sounds of the girl clearing the table.

Cecilia Deku stared through the "picture window" at the tropical growth for a few minutes. Kojo waited patiently.

"This man is a wizard."

"Are you sure?"

He felt ambigious feelings go through him. One was elation because it validated the possibility of him being able to do what he said he could do. On the other hand he felt a kind of dread.

"Yes, I am sure. I have known about this person all my life. I have never seen him, but my father and others that I respect, have told me about his powers.

These are people with good minds and reasonable attitudes."

"What's the source of his power?"

"They say that there are many sources. In the forest he has discovered plants or herbs or something that give him the power to disappear, for example.

Everyone who has seen him gives us the picture of a being who can disapppear. And fly."

"You think he could fly across an ocean?"

She turned to him with an exceptionally serious expression.

"Kojo, as you know, Africa contains many mysteries. Some of them are unknown, some known. Let me give you an example of what I mean. Are you familiar with the Dogon people?"

"I've heard of them."

"Do you know that a French anthropolgist lived with them for many years and discovered that they had a special afffinity for a star, I can't recall its name, that was/is quite near the moon.

They knew as much about this star as most Western astronomers. The anthropologist was determined to find out where their knowledge came from. Finally, after years of gaining their confidence, they told him, confidentially, that in ancient times, what we would call asstronauts, from their tribe traveled to this star."

Kojo did a CLOSE UP of the look on his face, capturing the amazement.

"That's something to really think about."

"Some people think that Asiafo has tapped into that source of energy. Or that he may have been visited in the forest by one of the powerful Gods who rule the Universe."

"Whooaa, wait a minute, Cecilia, aren't you a Christian, didn't you go to church this morning?"

"Kojo, there were forces operating in this land before any church was thought about. yes, I am a Christian, but I also feel deeply about the spirits that were here before Christianity."

It was Kojo's turn to stare out of the "picture window". Hmmmm...

"So, you're saying that this person really does have surpernatural powers?"

"I'm not denying it. I think that's the important point. Are you aware that most human beings only use a tenth of their psychic energy during the course of their lifetimes? And we all have the potential.

Can you imagine what kind of human being you could become, spiritually, if you could focus on that element for many years?

Couple this with other forces and it would be impossible to determine what you could do."

"Would the forces that assisted you in acquiring this power be .... evil."

She hesitated for a few beats.

"Possibly. But they could also be good."

"But the one in the forest, Asiafo, has always been associated with evil."

"Yes, they say it is because the woman he was in love with was killed."

"His mother."

"Yes, Auntie has told you the story."

"He was really in love with his own mother?"

"And his mother was in love with him. One of the elders caught them making love."

"Wowwwww..."

"Can you imagine the impact that had on a community as conservative as this one, forty some years ago?"

"Yes, I can imagine."

They were silent for a few moments. VOICE OVER. Well, Kojo, you do know one thing; if this somewhat Anglicized African woman, with her rational view of life, believes that this man is real, then it looks like everything will be o.k.

"You know, you go through your life thinking, especially if you're a modern man, as you called me, that you know a little bit about life.

And then you come to certain sections and realize that there are huge, empty spaces in your knowledge box."

"I clearly understand what you mean."

Kojo was forced to take a second look at the schoolteacher. I had this sister pegged all wrong. I had written her off as some kind of Englishwoman in disguise.

Well, she has that in her too, no doubt about it, but there's an earthier element there too.

"Kojo, I'm having a small cognac, will you join me?"

"It would be my pleasure."

She turned and called out to the girl, and turned back to Kojo.

"Please don't think I'm a bloody heavy drinker, or anything that sort, it's just so pleasant, especially on Sundays, to "chill out", as you say in America."

"I heard that."

"You say...?"

"I said, I heard that, it's an old African-American expression of affirmation."

"Oh, I see."

The girl padded out onto the veranda with two snifters of cognac on a tray. Kojo performed the cognac ritual of wirling it in his palm for a bit, pausing to sniff the aroma before tasting, a small swallow.

"Mmmm, this is excellent."

"O, good, you like it? I brought it back from France last year, when I went on holiday.

I am saying that to let you know that my sentiments do not belong solely to London."

They smiled at each other over the rims of their glasses.

He wanted to review the Asiafo tape again, go into it a bit deeper, but felt that she had had enough of it; she wanted to talk about what was happening in the "outer world".

"This is quite a lovely place, as you can see...."

"Yes, it is beautiful," he agreed, looking out onto lush stands of trees and ferns.

"But quite boring, unfortunately," she spoke in an off hand way, neither a put down or a criticism, "but it's home and I intend to do what I have to do heah."

"Do you see yourself as a missionary of some sort?"

She laughed. "O heavens no! The pith helmet and all that. O no! I rather think of myself as a young, idealistic African woman, nothing more or less."

"O, I see."

They could hear stray sounds from the village a few thousand yards away. Kojo felt himself becoming noddy; after the beers, the walk to her place, the excellent lunch, the cognac, the release from the tensions of the night before...

He woke up with a start, feeling that he was trapped in a net. The schoolteacher smiled at his reaction and pulled the mosquito net from the top part of his body.

"I left you to go and read for a bit and I didn't want to have the flies chopping on you while you dozed."

"Sorry 'bout that."

"O, no problem. I frequently do the same thing after a meal, 'specially on Sunday."

"Sunday seems to mean a lot to you."

"Yes, I cherish Sundays. That is the one day I can close myself off, after church, that is."

"Yeah, we all need to have private time."

He stood, feeling slightly awkward for the first time. He wanted to go and stay at the same time. He made a broad gesture of checking his watch.

"Hmmm...4:30 p.m. I didn't know it was that late."

She studied him with an amused expression on her face.

"O, I say, are you late for an appointment?"

She had broken through his facade. *And I've been the one who thought I had all the answers.*

He was forced to laugh at the absurdity of it all...

"Well, not really..."

"Good. Now that you're properly rested, let's have a game of chess. You do play, don't you?"

"I'm not in championship form anymore, but I think I can remember what the queen is about."

"Wonderful, let's go inside."

He followed her back through the house, into the front room, where she had set up a chess board on a table and arranged two chairs.

He couldn't help but think....there couldn't that much difference in our ages, but she seems so much older, like a middle aged woman. So mature. Maybe it has something to do with her situation.

They took their seats, she juggled a black pawn and a white pawn behind her back. He got the black and the game was on.

She was an excellent strategist and he had the memory of a solid game from his U.S.C. days. Ten minutes into the game she looked up into his face with a delightful smile.

"It's so good to have you heah. One wishes for a good talk and a challenging game of chess, from time to time."

"You mean there are no chess players in Tsito, no one to talk to?"

"Mr. Brown, may I remind you? I am the Headmistress, I talk to people, no one talks <u>with</u> me. And, insofar as chess players go, there are none. The villagers play other kinds of games."

An hour later, he squeaked through a narrow win because her concentration slipped for two moves. She seemed more pleased than he did about the outcome.

"Well done, Kojo Brown, well done indeed. Shall we go for the best two out of three?"

"I'm game."

"This calls for more cognac."

"I can stand it, I've gotten my second wind now."

She called to the girl, the cognacs were served and they were playing their second game. Kojo sipped his cognac and stared at the intense face across from him as she bent her concentration to the pieces.

What are we really playing for? He was beginning to feel something for the teacher. She was, after all, an attractive lady and by her own admission, lonely for his type of companionship.

"Woman of the Dunes", that's it, the Japanese film where the man winds up in a hole at the beach, helping a woman fill buckets of sand to keep them from drowning in sand.

"Your move, sir."

"Oh, sorry, I was really trying to see too many moves ahead."

"I understand", she said, and took a delicate sip of her cognac.

Wonder how many other men have had the cognac and the chess game?

She called to the girl to bring lanterns. Kojo was surprised to see that twilight had fallen on them.

Chess by kerosine lamp in the Volta region, in Ghana. That ought to be worth some kind of story.

He knew the game was lost from the deadly way she moved her queen and queen's bishop into place. He studied the possibilities for two long minutes before conceding.

"Jolly good show, Cecilia, I must say, jolly good show."

"I'm pleased, but I don't think it would have been as easy if your mind hadn't wandered."

"Oh, was it that noticeable?"

"I'm a school teacher, Kojo, I study faces the day long."

The lantern played lovely lights on the planes of her face, emphasized the prominent cheekbones and the luscious mouth.

They sat, looking at each other for a few moments.

"Cecilia, if you don't mind, I'd rather we not try to break the tie. I'd like keep it at one to one."

She smiled at him and sipped her cognac.

"Interesting, that you should reach that conclusion. I was thinking somewhat the same thing myself."

He stood slowly, not really certain of his next move.

"Well, looks like it's about the Pumpkin Hour for me, Auntie will be sending a posse into the forest to look for me."

He didn't care for the disappointed curl of her mouth.

"O, I thought you would stay for a light supper. I've sent the girl home, I was going to prepare a little something myself."

Kojo felt his brains do fifty emotional flip flops. I can see what's coming. Is it really what I think it is? Supper will take us far into the evening, too far for me to walk. Am I up to a one night stand with a serious woman? Can I go away from here feeling right about myself if I do what I know I shouldn't do.

He held both of her hands in his.

"Cecilia, you've put me at ease about some things that really had me worried. Thanks. Now then, the best way I can repay you for that is to trot back to Auntie's with my new understanding and prepare for my departure tomorrow."

She looked down at their hands and back up into his face.

"Am I that obvious?"

He didn't know what to say for a long moment. He knew it would be emotional fraud to try to pretend that he didn't know what she was talking about.

"I don't think you're being obvious at all, about anything. I just happen to feel that I wouldn't feel right about myself....if I did something that I thought would be wrong for both of us."

O my God, what a situation to be in. I've been fed, cognaced and now the lady wants "dessert" and I don't want to supply it because I think it would do more harm than good.

But what about Grace? Ahhh, Grace is different, Grace is an old friend, she knows what the deal is.

"You're a rare man, Kojo..."

He swept her into his arms and squeezed gently. Her body felt like it was melting in his hands.

"I'm trying to be a good man, Cecilia, a good man...that's as much as I can hope for."

He reluctantly released her.

"Good night, Kojo."

"Good night, Cecilia."

"Will you be able to find our way?"

CHAPTER 12

"No problem."

"What time will you leave tomorrow?"

"Whenever the taxi picks me up."

"I'll see you off, I'll have someone tell me when it's time."

"I'd like that."

"Goodnight."

"'Night."

He turned to stare at her figure in the door, the lantern light giving a full silohuette of her body through the flimsy caftan.

Five hundred yards away, on the path leading "home", he paused to take a piss in the bush, ignoring the cold blooded erection he held in his hand.

He looked up at the stars as he spoke. "Yeah, Mom, you would've been proud of me tonight."

In the middle of the dream he was tempted to call out "cut!" but the scene was going so well he was reluctant to stop the flow.

The leading lady had finally opened up and the leading man had finally pushed the thought of his jealous wife out of his consciousness.

The tenderness that they were showing each other in the love scene was rare. It was a love scene between an older woman (40 years) and a younger man (25 years old). They were African-Americans from the upper middle class, (sorry, Dad, it's what the script calls for), who had discovered a love for each other, almost by accident.

The woman is a close friend of his mothers and this is the first time they've made love.

They were not amateurs; he has been around and she has two divorces behind her. They demonstrate a skillful arkwardnes with each other, neither one wants to do anything phoney, anything that says, this is "old hat" for me.

The only serious problem they face is his mother. But for the moment, she doesn't exist. They are the only two people in the world, and they were creating a gorgeous universe.

He used the cameras like gentle fingers, probing at this point, doing a slow, thoughtful massage at another point.

The erotic and the lascivious were being extended, the pornographic dismissed.

Finally, he was forced to call an end to the scene; it was necessary, if they were going to get the next scene in the can before the end of the day.

"Kojo! Cecilia! cut!"

Kojo opened his eyes and stared up at the dark thatch above his head. A clear night and a full moon gleaming through the window in his room allowed him to see in the dark.

Wonder what she thought about when I left? How could I explain my feelings to her? Would she understand? Did she understand?

He felt frustrated with the way the evening had ended. I should have stayed longer, explained more. Maybe I should have made love to her. And then what? I'd go back to Accra and America, thinking about the little school teacher in Tsito that I had fucked, literally.

Yeah, Mom, you would've been proud of me. I never thought about how deeply your teachings have been dug into me.

"Kojo, don't sleep with a woman that you wouldn't want to have a baby with."

"Kojo, take women seriously, some men don't."

"Kojo, don't let that little worm down there lead you around, if you're going to be a real man you must control it."

He closed his eyes, hoping he would be taken back into his dream.

By 2 p.m., Kojo was feeling a bit antsy. Don't tell me this guy is going to leave me stranded up here.

He had taken an early stroll through the village and was surprised to see that the former cordiality had returned. what a moody bunch this is.

Aunt Eugenia explained the emotional switch to him.

"Reverend Donkor told them to behave themselves. He told them that you are not of our tradition, that you are not bound by our taboos, you could not make a problem for us."

"Problem? What kind of problem."

"O, if you were of the village and went to the place we will not go, we might have to do sacrifice to take the bad spirits away. You understand?"

"I think so."

"Eh heee...."

It was reaching the anti-climatic point when the driver put in his appearance at 3 p.m.

"Sorry."

Kojo quickly reviewed his departure program. He had slipped ¢100,000 into Auntie's basket and hinted broadly that she should buy more akpeteshie.

He knew it would've ben impolite to put money in her hand, as though he were paying for something.

The Headmistress, no longer Cutie Pie, in his mind, made her appearance.

"Cecilia, thank you for everthing, I hope to see you again."

"When you see me again it'll be too late", she said and smiled her luscious smile. Meaning what?

He waved-waved, turned the great green bend and Tsito was gone. Kojo settled himself back in the passenger's seat.

What the hell was that all about? What could I call it? A week in Another Place? Beyond the fringe? What?

The road was not quite so muddy and they were making good time. He felt that he was returning from a very long journey.

It was more than a village visit. There must have been some other reason for me being there, in that particular place. Was I destined to meet Asiafo, the wizard in the forest? Am I actually going to do what he asked me to do?

As the miles sped by and he came closer to Accra, he began to think of it as an experience, something that never happened before, but not something he could really throw himself into.

Ghana Traffic, "Nothing Good Comes Easy"

And yet, there was a nagging edge of feeling that kept whispering...do what you've been told to do and everything will be Beautiful.

Accra slowly opened up in front of him like a dirty rose. How can such beautiful people live in such an ugly city?

"Joshua, take me to the Ghana Garden Hotel."

Nothing new, same old slow moving fans, maurauding mosquitoes, the desk clerk....

"Thank you. Do I have any messages?"

"Ahhh, no sah, no message."

8 p.m., Monday night. The movies, what the hell. I'll get back with Grace tomorrow.

"Ghana films, hurry! I'm trying to make the 8:30 show."

8:15 p.m..... "driver, you ever think about racing for a living?"

"Beg, your pardon?"

"That's o.k., how much do I owe you?"

The Executive Theatre, where they show the American movies. Step up on the stone here, buy your ticket at the kiosk, stumble through the rock strewn packing lot and wait in front of the doors for the 6:30 people to come out.

Why is shit so rough here? Why couldn't they provide a few amenities, like a comfortable lobby for people to sit in while they wait? O well....

What's the movie? He hadn't bothered to check out the marquee. Well, whatever, who knows?

He tried to make some judgement of the movie, based on the expressions of the people who trickled out of the theatre after the first showing. They didn't offer a clue of what they had seen.

It wasn't an American movie audience, erupting from the theatre, spitting and fuming. No, this was a 98% Ghanaian audience, everybody cold blooded about the experience they had shared. The screen might have bled during the time they were inside. The sound might've been muffled for half the movie. The print itself might've been flawed by wavy lines, but no one would have betrayed any of those deficiencies on their way out.

It was clearly a case of - you pays your money and sees what will happen.

Kojo rushed for a good seat in the center of the amphitheatre shaped movie house. He knew enough about the swiftly moving Ghanaians to know that someone would murmur "sorry" as they took a good seat from underneath him.

8:30 p.m., the movies, one of the things in Accra that started when it was announced.

"Paris Blues", Well, I'll be damned! "Paris Blues". He sat up a little straighter in his seat. "Paris Blues", that flawed piece of crap that Hollywood had put together, (one of thousands), trying to sucker Black America into believing that they were going to see racial equality at work, because Sidney Poitier, Paul Newman, Dianne Carrol and Joanne Woodard were going to appear on the same screen together with the Arc d'Triomphe in the background.

Kojo began to squirm, five minutes into the movie. Why don't they put the damned thing in focus? And the couple behind him talking as casually as though they were sitting in their living room disturbed him.

People are watching too much T.V. these days, they come to the movies and can't shut up, they seem to feel they're watching a giant T.V. screen.

But the movie made him squirm more than any of the sideline annoyances. Paul Newman ("Ram"), the jazz musician. Paul Newman, jazz? Why wouldn't it be Sidney? And the casual underlining that made Poitier's involvement with Dianne Carrol less important than Newman's thing with Joanne Woodard.

They could've shot this in New Jersey, why did they have to go all the way to Paris?

He squirmed, watching Poitier belt out his unique brand of fire. It was always a pyrotechnical display that inevitably would up in a neutered state: "Guess Whose Coming To Dinner?", "The Defiant Ones", "Patch of Blue", "Fireball Express", "The Vikings", "Raisin in the Sun", "Island in the Sun...", "Lilies of the Field...".

The brother can smolder, he can simmer, he can boil, he can do a Vesuvius, but it never amounts to anything. He always winds up being just another angry Black man who has figured out a way to cope with his anger.

Kojo studied the credits, looking for familiar names, stood and stretched at the end. O well, it could've been worse.

9:55 p.m. Afrikiko. Monday night. Why not? He crunched up the graveled path, his mind wandering from recent events in the village, to past movies.

Who knows? Maybe the whole thing is a movie. Maybe some great Celestial Force is out there, using us as entertainment. I'm sure we must be a good laugh for somebody.

A Monday night "crowd". Four extravagantly dressed ladies at one table, smoking cigarettes like chimneys, sipping mugs of draugh beer. The usual White man-African woman couple at a few tables, strays going in and out.

"Good evening, Jim."

Jim? Looks like you've got the wrong John, honey. O yes, Jim. I told her my name is Jim. Patience, the school girl-prostitute.

"Well, hello, how is it?"

"Fine. May I sit with you?"

"Please, be my guest. What would you like to drink?"

"I will take a mineral."

"Yes, sah?"

"A mineral and a Guiness Stout."

They sat opposite each other, looking blank for a few beats. What do you ask a whore? How's tricks? Give any good head lately?

"You have come back."

He couldn't put a finger on the tone she used. Was she asking a question or making a statement? Was she saying, you've come back to me?

"Yeah, I just got out of the movies, thought I'd stop here and have a beer."

"O, I see."

Pretty girl, lovely shape, seems to be semi-smart, could be Comfort's sister.

"You have a sister named Comfort?"

"No, my sister is called Rose. And my brother is Ebenezer."

"O, I see."

They sipped their drinks in unison and stared at distant points. The girl looks too innocent to be in this business.

"Jim?"

"Yes?"

"May I ask you a personal question?"

"Sure, why not?"

"Are you gay?"

Kojo felt himself bristling up for a beat. What the hell would make her ask me something like that?

"No, baby, I can assure you that I'm not gay. Why do you ask?"

She pouted her firm young bosom up slightly as she spoke...

"I thought you liked me a little..."

Ahhh...so, it's come to that, huh?

"Patience, I like you a lot. I think you're a fine sister, but I've never been able to go to the supermarket for my loving. You know what I mean?"

She looked puzzled for a few seconds and then stood, clutching her half empty bottle of Sprite.

"Yes, I understand. I must go."

Kojo watched her do a delicate hip swizel to three tables away.

So sorry, baby, I just can't get into the play for pay thing. You are really a sweet looking thing, but I can't run the risk of taking some kind of veneral rabies back with me.

He sipped his Guiness, feeling alternately sad and amused at the scene. Europeans buying African women, and the African men, the waiters, are the connecting links.

There ought to be a movie in here somewhere.... the hyena laugh-sound came from a rear area. Heads turned briefly and then returned to their negotiations.

Kojo suddenly felt chilled, and at the same time experienced a hot flash. Damn, what was that? Hope I'm not coming down with malaria.

The hyena laugh. Who am I fooling? I've never heard anything like that in my life but one place, the forest in Tsito. Asiafo.

He remained in place for long moments after the beer was finished, re-capping the past week, putting together the coming week.

It was a dream. It must've been a dream. That stuff could not have happened. Careful, brother. You're going into a denial mode now.

Yeah, it happened and I have some decisions to make. He strolled out of Afrikiko, past Patience's table; she looked up at him and didn't smile.

"Grace, I'm back."

"Long time."

"Seems that way."

"I expected you yesterday night."

"I thought I would give my mind a chance to settle in place before I got back to you."

"Good, come over at 5-ish, I'll prepare something for you."

"'Til then."

10:30 a.m., what can I do 'til five? Accra is such a funny place. Seems like there's really nothing to do but go from one beer to another. Or wander from one market place to another.

He didn't feel in tune with the normal touristy thing, which was to go from place to place, buying cheap, badly carved mementoes of airport art. Or splashes of the yellow, red and blue that everyone seemed to think that Kente cloth was.

He decided to do all of his thinking in one place; Watos, just around the corner from the post office, the 2ⁿᵈ floor open air veranda that sold mugs of draught beer, a great spot to look down on the business of the roundabout.

Watos. The time was right, the afternoon crowd hadn't come in yet.

"One draught beer, please.

The roundabout below the balcony was Ghana in every detail; the naked woman caulked in white, off on business that had to do with the gods. The swarms of trays with everything on them, being sold by people underneath.

Small stories folded and unfolded, longer stories took shape and were blown away by the passing traffic.

The shapes and evergy of the people fascinated him; for a few seconds everyone seemed to be moving like a school of fish, quickly disrupted by someone swimming cross-stream.

There seemed to be no order about the movement of the people. Sometimes a clot, or a swelling would happen on one corner, dissolve and reassemble on the opposite corner.

It may have been an argument between seller and buyer. Or something he couldn't know about, looking down on things from the veranda.

He isolated a few people for CLOSE UPS: the woman sleeping on the sidewalk in front of the bank of post office boxes. The man and the woman having a passionate discussion in the center of the roundabout.

He looked for evidence of romantic things, the kind of stuff to be found in Paris, Chicago's lakefront or New York's dangerous Central Park, but it was missing.

African men and women didn't slobber all over each other in the middle of the day, or give a lot of overt attention to each other in public. They were somewhat cool.

Gorgeous women in every kind of color he could think of, tropical birds. Counterpointed by women who looked like things that had been flung out to dry. The fright wig, non-hair-dos, disturbed him most.

How can these beautiful sisters walk around here their hair stranding all over their heads like that? Can't they see how tacky they look?

Awwww stop it, Kojo. You're being picayune! Look at for what it is. The Europeans come down here and told the sisters to fry and starch their hair, but they didn't tell them how to handle the steambath that they were going to be walking around in.

Asiafo. Now how am I going to handle that? Talking about people with their hair standing up all over their heads and what not?

"Yes, another one, please."

Yeahhh, how am I supposed to handle that? Here is a man out there in the middle of Nowhere, that I've struck a bargain with, who is going to make my films possible.

He zoomed in on a man who looked like a king. If he's not a king, he should be. There was elegance to the man's step, a measured way of looking at things, glistening cloth draped across his shoulder.

Wonder who he is?

They flickered in and out of his view finder, past his camera lenses; they were tall, lean Northerners with scraped out cheeks, (I don't care how they try to justify it that's some ugly shit to wear on your face for the rest of your life. Somebody could have thought of a better way to say - you belong to us.), circumcised women, he could imagine that condition based on their Muslim clothing arrangement.

Kenkey bellied Ga women, looking full of themselves, pausing to look disdainfully at everything with their fists on their ample hips.

Sliver slim girls carrying loads on their heads that defied descriptions. Jet black, charcoaled colored people, looking like the sun had burned them to a crisp.

"Ethiope, land of the burned faces." Wonder who checked Ghana out when they were concocting that description of Africans?

A dull, rainy season sun burnished, highlighted the rainbow phalanx, stirred his ideas of technicolor around.

There's got to be an Africolor for this, technicolor doesn't come close to dealing with it.

Wonder what Akosua (alias Cynthia) is going to say when I ask her to marry me? Am I going to ask her to marry me?

If you want the money to do your films, you better marry her, or somebody. Less than three months. He looked around at the clusters of people who had suddenly occupied spaces near him.

The trio of postal workers (he could tell from their green and red trimmed uniforms) giggling at a secret joke. Two men in khaki, with berets, talking solemnly, soldier talk. A single man here, a single women there.

He took it all in, mentally stockpiling scenarios. I wonder what the African, the Ghanaian filmmaker sees when he/she sits here of an afternoon?

The movie, "Coming to America" blazed up in his head. God, what an absurd piece of shit. And I think Eddie Murphy actually had something to do with it. Imagine, an African prince going to America, to work in a hamburger joint, of all things, to find himself a bride.

How absurd can you get, with all of these beautiful women walking around?

"I'll have another one here, please."

There seemed to be peak times, when the people in the roundabout were clustered in a confused mass and then it was sorted out. The traffic going around micmicked the people; for long minutes the cars, trucks, tros tros, motorcycles, vehicles of every description, including hand pulled carts, jammed into place and then released.

It was a strangely logical madhouse, almost a silent film. A few arguments happened here and there, but no one pulled out an Uzi or a shotgun to settle the matter.

He couldn't place his finger on any violent element. If this were in "the 'States," with this number of people, all this traffic and everything, somebody would have to die this morning.

The third mug of beer chased him to the men's room. O...ohhh.

The stench of the urine hit him the second he opened the door. A moment later, acclimatized to the ammonia-atmosphere, he stood there, thinking about the contradictions again.

You can go to the swankest joint in town and they expect you to wipe your ass with newspapers. I can sit here all morning, praising the values of social co-operation, and yet when I come into the toilet it's filthy and stinking.

Back to my post, analysis finished.

"Kojo, Africa is a mysterious place, it's even mysterious to us Africans."

Yeah, Grace, you got that right, baby...

A sudden, louder than usual noise drew his attention to two cars. One of them had bumped into the one in front of him, a casual fender bender, nothing unusual.

The man who had been bumped jumped out of his car gesticulating wildly. Kojo heard him scream: "I am quite annoyed with you! Quite annoyed!"

Kojo laughed aloud. Well, I'll be damned. 'I am quite annoyed with you.' That's deep.

CHAPTER 13

He flashed on the number of times he had witnessed similar scenes in his home city, Chicago and New York, Los Angeles and places in between.

Chicago, two men battling in the middle of the street with tire irons. New York, the taxi driver emerging from his vehicle with a police baton. Casual violence on every level.

Five minutes later the argument, the drivers, the situation had dissolved and the normal hum of things had resumed.

The African is not violent, not like us, the way we are in Diaspora. I'm sure, given the right catalyst, you could get your ass snatched off here, but people don't seem to be inherently violent.

He pondered the notion for a few minutes...so many different ways of looking at things.

Kojo strolled towards Osu. What do you do when you have a few hours to kill? You walk. He was startled to a stop by two men strolling out of the Supreme Court building in shoulder length lamb curly wigs.

Wowwwww...look at what the English did to my brothers and sisters, here in our own land. He strolled on, worrying the notion through his head.

How could a small bunch of English men come in here and do what they did? Create a situation that turned the judicial system into an English imitation. Turn the educational system into an imitation. And have such a heavy impact on the social side that a lot of people see the U.K. as their spiritual home.

Well, what the hell look what they did to India, which is much larger than this place. Have to dig into that a bit, at some point in the future, the impact of the little pink guys from Britain, and their disastrous impact on the colored world.

What was the argument the Nigerian brother gave in Chicago? 'They gave us English, man, a unifying language. Think of the what Nigeria would be like if we didn't have English.'

High Street, past the Ministries. Wonder what Comfort is doing?

High Street at 1 p.m. in the afternoon. the street seemed to be about to burst at the seams. People selling everything; dog chains, apples, welcome mats, T-shirts, chocolate bars, ice cream, calculators, toys, flags, hats, purses, bananas, bath towels, peanuts, car accessories, hankerchiefs, soap, chewing gum, everything.

He felt like a stranger in a dream. I guess this is the way the African-American sees this scene; this is my land but it ain't my country. Nkrumah Park, with the giant stone sculpture-gravestone on his re-interred bones.

Kwame Nkrumah. Osagyefo Kwame Nkrumah, a man with vision. Wonder what this place would be like if he had had the chance to fulfill his dreams?

He strolled past the National Cultural Centre and stood looking up at the black star centered on the arch in Black Star Square.

"Soul to Soul", yeahhh, that was the name of the old documentary. Some enterprising producer grabbed Ike and Tina Turner, Les McCann, Wilson Pickett, Roberta Flack, Willie Bobo, the Voices of Harlem and a whole bunch of other people and brought them back Home.

In his mind's eye he could see Tina Turner, in her lioness wig, being greeted at the bottom of the airplane stairs by an old lady doing a little welcoming song and dance.

Damn, Ike, why wouldn't you allow the sister to take her wig off here in Ghana?

Around the roundabout, and on into old Osu. People, people everywhere. He walked the main street for a block and then veered off into the 'hood.

Now this is a neigborhood for real. Men and women were taking "baffs" behind stacked blinds of bricks, women washed clothes and hauled loads, women stirred huge pots of what looked like oat meal.

"Uhh, what're those ladies stirring in the pots?"

"Banku."

He felt completely at ease. People glanced at him, comfirming that he was a foreigner and went on about their business.

He could nod and say "good afternoon" and people would reply. Or he could simply stoll and observe. It didn't seem to make any difference to the people going back and forth.

The crowd surging toward him freaked him out for a moment. The Ghanaian pedestrians, going about their business, had suddenly become an angry mob. They swept past him, beating and kicking a muscular young man in the latest hip hop get up, tearing at his clothes with the kind of impotent rage that makes crowds become mobs.

"Hey Challey! what happened?!"

Memory serves interesting purposes. "Hey Challey," that's the comrade-buddy number.

"He was caught stealing in the market!"

Kojo trailed along for a block, watching the potency of the mob violence disspate. The young man was bleeding from the nose and his clothes had been shredded, but he was a long way from being seriously injured.

Someone would strike out at him with an open palm, sporadically, but there was no hard core viciousness to the blows.

"Where are they taking him?"

"They are taking him to the police station."

Well, that makes sense. Dish out vigilante justice and then turn him over the authorities, that way everybody gets a piece of action.

The vigilantes gone, the narrow streets once again reverted to their normal throb. He walked on, deeper into Osu.

Looks like people have been living in this neck of the woods for centuries. Two little girls stared up at him with large, lustrous eyes. Bet you never seen a brother from the 'States before, huh?

'Brother from Another Planet;' yeah, that was the flick, the one where the Black man comes from somewhere else to Earth.

Joe Whatshisname Morton, a solid actor, no matter whether he was playing the clean cut Black professional, the exaggerated gangster or the scientist who was dealing with how to freeze dry bodies ("forever young"), he was always at the top of his form.

"Brother from Another Planet", yeah, I feel like that. 3 p.m., getting a little snackish here. Kojo by passed the roadside things, the bowls of whatever with soup.

This is the most unappetizing way to eat I've ever seen. He tried not to stare at the people sitting on benches a half step away from stagnant drains, the hub bub and dust of the streets flying around.

No, the brother from the other place will not buy any of that.

The Chinese place on Danquah Circle, a good place to have some hot and sour soup, a first course for whatever Grace was preparing.

Kojo picked a strategic table, a spot to key in on arrivals, departures and the Chinese who owned the place. The African waiter was polite, well trained, and not too subservient.

"Waiter, do you have Chinese hot mustard?"

The man puzzled the question over and went to the kitchen for a small dish of mashed pepper.

"Uhhh, no, this is pepper. I'm asking for hot mustard."

The waiter signalled, "I'm coming", and had an urgent conversation with the young Chinese woman behind the cash register. She strolled over to his table, jean mini-shirt and pony tail announcing her connection to Now.

"Yes?"

"Do you have Chinese hot mustard?"

Kojo almost laughed, listening to the waiter use his version of Chinese pidgin to communicate with the young woman.

"Do you speak English?" He felt compelled to find out.

"Oh, a little," she answered, concealing a shy smile behind her hand, and swivelled back to her post.

Well, that's that. I guess I can forget about the mustard. He spooned his soup, cornstarched to the stretching point, thinking about the Chinese. They all seem to own restaurants, hardly anybody speaks English, or any of the indigenous languages. And there doesn't seem to be any evidence of racial mixing.

I'll bet they arrange marriages between restaurants. He took in the interplay. The cashier took in the money, said hello and goodby to customers, and had conversations with a large Chinese man, (her father?), who came out of the kitchen, from time to time.

I don't think I'd like to be a Chinese in Ghana.

Soup done, now what? Go to the other side of Danquah, sit up at Number One for a bit, check out the scenery. Number One, the place where most of the foreigners in Accra wound up sitting, at one point or another. Number One, large umbrella shading the tables, everything slightly overpriced, service that varied from indifferent to efficient.

Kojo took a side table and waited. And waited, And waited. He tried using some kind of logic to determine why the men/waiters, who earned their living serving the public, were not serving.

Maybe they're on some kind of strike. Or maybe a slowdown for higher wagers. O well...

The waiter blindsided him as he was seriously trying to remember why Tyrone Power and Jack Hawkins had tripped away from England to the Exotic east, including China, in a period flick called "The Black Rose."

And the little French chick, Cecile Aubrey, the ancestor of Brigitte Bardot and the rest of the French "Sex Kittens."

Wonder what happened to her?

"Would you like to order now?"

"Is that why you're here?"

"I don't understand...."

"Never, mind, let me have a draugh beer."

Beer-beer-beer-beer, the only sure way to buy a seat.

He Panned the scene; a trio of Japanese men, taking pictures of Everything. A quartet of White Americans; Momma Bear, Papa Bear, Baby boy Bear and Baby girl Bear.

The mother was reminding everyone to take their pills, the father was inspecting every morsel that went into their mouths and the children were indulging in that spoiled, bratty behavior that he always associated with temperamental actors.

A fleshy White man, obviously a European, with a pony tail, huddled up with a tall, sharp featured, African woman who looked like a well shaved man.

166

A couple African business types, flashing mobile 'phones. Three Ghanaian women, their hands fluttering like birds, having an animated conversation two tables away.

Kojo settled back in his seat, watching the mothers with babies on their backs hustle across the street to avoid being run down. The well dressed chap with the brief case taking a careful piss into the drain fifty yards away, people passing by with trays on things to buy:

I'd need six cameras rolling at the same time to half of this stuff. The mix is almost too rich.

5 pm, time to go to Grace.

He felt that he had sailed into a marina, a well protected cove, as Grace draped her arms around his neck and kissed him.

"You are welcome."

"I thank you. I've missed you."

"And I've missed you too."

They stood in the center of the front room, holding each other, exchanging warm looks and little kisses.

"Oh! Oh! Oh!"

She pulled away from him - "I'm baking something for you!"

Kojo pulled his shoes off, checked the record stack for something special. Let's see here....we've had Ravel and Ravi Shankar and Horace Silvers. How 'bout a little....Charlie Parker?

"Bird with Machito," the Latin-American thing. Wowwww, this sister has some monsters up in here.

"Kojo, have you found something you like?"

He answered by letting the music speak for him.

"Oh yes, the Charlie Parker....I like it."

Kojo froze in place for a minute. The brother she was dealing with turned her on to this. It's just about his generation and everything. Well, what the hell, it's too late to be jealous.

Grace glided back into the room, a jaunty gele on her close cropped natural, a gorgeously flowered gown on.

"Grace, you know something? You are really a beautiful woman, you know that?"

"Thank you, kind sir, I think such remarks should be celebrated. Will you join me?"

Ah yes, the wonderful, smoky taste of Scotch. I better be careful, I'll wind up going Eurocentric...

They sprawled on the carpet, cushioned by large pillows, sipping their scotches, allowing Bird and Machito to set the mood.

"What are you baking?"

"Oh, it's a little Brasilian thing that a girlfriend showed me how to do. Kind of a pie. I've taken it out to cool. Are you hungry?"

"Not for food."

"Oh, I see."

Thirty minutes later, they pulled themselves out of a deep, sexual catnap in her bed.

"What's that sound, like someone tapping on the roof?"

"It's raining."

He stared up at the ceiling, thinking about the thatched roof of Aunt Eugenia's hut. Grace snuggled in the pit of his arm.

"Kojo?"

"Yes?"

"You haven't talked to me about Tsito. I thought you would be bursting to tell me how much you hated the primitive conditions, the mud, the inconveniences and all that."

She smiled as she spoke, letting him know that she was putting him on.

"Yeah, well, you got some of that right. Tell you what, why don 't you feed me and I can tell you everything across the table."

"That's a deal."

He took a deep breath, watching her get out of bed. Baby, you got a body on you....

Splashing water. O course, the "baff".

"Kojo, the water is off, but there's water here in the bucket for your baff."

"I'm coming ."

Manuel De Falla's "Nights in the Gardens of Spain" seemed perfect for the moment. Kojo splashed the cold water on all the important parts of his body, dried off, feeling refreshed.

"There are caftans in the closet, if you don't mind wearing a woman's clothes."

"I won't tell anybody, if you don't tell anybody."

Drizzling rain music, Spanish accented music on the air, chilled white wine, a beautiful Black woman, Africa.

A small salad and a large, golden crusted pie.

"What is this?"

"It's called empadao; got chicken, shrimp, crab meat, hearts of palms, a few other things, and lots of good vibes in it."

"Mmmmmm...tastes like it too."

A few forks of the rich ingredients were enough to satisfy them.

"So, you want to know what happened in the village, huh?

She nodded yes, sipping her wine.

"Well, in some ways, nothing. The village, as you know, is not filled with loads of distractions. I enjoyed being with your Aunt, she's a treasure.

In another kind of way, I could say that I enjoyed life in the village, but I wouldn't want to live there."

Grace laughed, poured more wine into his glass.

"Don't misunderstand, it has nothing to do with the people. The people are beautiful. I met several people I'll never forget."

Asiafo rang a curtain down across his mind, made him frown.

"What is it, Kojo?"

It poured out of him, the meeting in the forest, the deal, the paranoia. Grace looked solemn for a moment and then brightened up.

"Kojo, I'm surprised at you. You go to a small, backwards thinking village for a few days and allow them to turn you around the bend. Come on now, they're just a bunch of superstitous villagers."

"Well, how about the wizard, how do you explain him?"

"Logically speaking, it seems illogical that he would be the same person who was banished forty years ago.

How could he survive in the forest, alone, for forty years?"

"Yeah, how could he?"

He felt a little foolish talking about a half naked man in the forest who had promised him, if he did the right thing, that he would be able to have enough money to make his films.

"Kojo, it's the oldest story in human history, man makes a deal with the supernatural to get what he wants."

"Do you believe it's possible?"

She suddenly became serious.

"The Ashantis are known to make supernatural deals all the time."

Suddenly they were back in mysterious Africa, always the other tribe, the people across the border who were into the murky stuff, not us.

"So, you're saying it's true..."

"Everything is possible, we all know that."

For a moment, there was only the sound of the rain and the dying string section of De Falla's masterpiece.

Kojo decided to lighten the mood...

"Hey, what is this?" What're we doing here?" This is supposed to be some kind of celebration, and we're sitting up here trying to outgloom each other."

"You started it."

"Well, it's ended now, it's all over, o.k.? C'mon over here'n let me feel on your body."

Wednesday morning, roosters crowing, somebody calling out something to somebody. Grace's face, chocolate brown against the white of the pillow held his attention for a long minute.

Good morning, beautiful lady, that was some strong stuff you laid on me last night. What was it? The Brasilian pie, the wine, more music, so much love. So much.

"Good morning."

"Ooooh, Kojo, you are awake..."

"Yeah, I had to wake up and take a good look at you."

"And what do you see?"

"Pure, maximum pleasure."

"Oh, you say the nicest things."

She moved over to him, warm, smooth and firm....

"You're going to be late for work...."

"I made arrangements to be off, I wanted to devote the day to you. There's so liitle time."

They kissed and began to squirm into all the intimate places of each other's bodies. Afterwards, sharing a towel with a giant heart embroidered on it, they talked.

"You know, I was under the impression that African women, Ghanaian women, were sexually repressed."

Grace answered his statement with a shy smile. "It's true, many of us are. But I don't place the blame on the woman. I place the blame on the man. Many African men think that the woman is only there for his pleasure, so he does what he has to do and goes to sleep.

The woman, meanwhile becomes introverted. It doesn't serve any purpse to expose her feelings because they would be ignored. Are you getting me?"

"Yeahhh, I get you."

So little time, only a few days away and I'll be be back in Lala land.

"So, that's how we get this bad reputation. Now, what else do we have to talk about?"

"I'm a man of action, what're we going to do today?"

"I thought it would be interesting to charter a taxi and go to Larteh, have lunch on the terrace at Tamara's."

"Larteh, I've heard of the place. Don't they have a shrine there?"

"The Shrine of Akonedi."

"And the old lady, the priestess who was supposed to have been Kwame Nkrumah's girlfriend?..."

"Her name is Nana Oparebea, but I'm not sure about her being Nkrumah's girlfriend."

"Just a rumor, that's all. When do we leave?"

"Within an hour."

"Good, let me take a quick "baff"; we can run by my place so that I can change clothes and be off."

The desk clerk at the Ghana Garden Hotel looked at Kojo's hurried entrance, puzzled. And looked even more puzzled when he ran out, ten minutes later.

Fifteen minutes later they were on the outskirts of Accra, on the way to Larteh.

The air blowing in on them was clean, fresh, fragrant. Grace closed her eyes and leaned her head back against the seat.

"I love my country, I love this Ghana."

Kojo stared at her, a bit surprised at her gush of patriotism. She opened her eyes and smiled at him.

"Don't you love your country? Don't you love America?"

He stared at the giant anthills on the side of the road, people walking with giant loads on their heads.

"Sorry, Grace, my darling, America has never done anything to earn my love."

"O, I see."

That should go into the book with "I'm coming" and "yesplease." "O, I see."

Kojo felt envious of Grace for a few miles. Maybe it's the Diaspora Blues. Of course we all want to love our country, to feel proud of it, to belong to it.

But here I am, an American who feels no pride in my nationality, no outrageous patriotism for my country's flag, none of that.

I feel more pride in Ghana here, more patriotism, if I could call it that, than I would ever feel for a country that designated my status as "slave". And didn't back away from the designation until it was absolutely forced to do so.

The driver, a large, raw boned man, gave them maximum speed on the open road, virtually crawled through the roadside villages.

"I like this driver", Grace whispered.

"Yeah, I do too." Wonder where Joshua is? I should have made an effort to stay in touch with him.

The roadside villages reminded him of Tsito. People looked up at the passing taxi and returned to chores and business that was hundreds of years old. Kojo and Grace took it in, exchanging significant looks whenever they spotted something that claimed their interest.

The car began a quiet move upward, suddenly giving them a view of the valley below. Five miles later they turned a curve and were driving up the main street to the Shrine of Akonedi.

"Driver, please stop at the drinking bar just there, we want to buy some Schnapps. I thought it would be a good idea to stop at the Shrine before we went on to Tamara's."

Kojo absentmindedly agreed, staring out of the window at a quartet of young women, dressed in white togas, their faces and bodies smeared with white chalk.

"Driver, who are the girls dressed in white?"

"Fetish", he answered, curling the corners of his mouth down with disgust.

The Shrine of Akonedi. Kojo had fixed an idea of what the structure would look like. High walls, armed guards maybe.

"It is here", the driver jabbed his finger at a white washed entrace, off of the mainstreet, a few pennants waving lazily.

"Thank you, driver, I have been here before. Find parking there and wait. Come, Kojo."

No meek, docile African woman here, a take charge girl all the way.

They were welcomed by a young man who led them into the recesses of the Shrine. They have a small village in here. They were led past women cooking, naked children playing, into a large courtyard, with three tiers of stone surrounding it.

Interesting structure. They lead us from the street, inside, to a small stadium that's outside.

The focus was on Nana Oparebea, seated on a carved stool, her right hand propping her chin up, receiving visitors, supplicants.

Kojo zoomed in on the scene. Something ancient about this; people on their knees, asking for something.

The Nana's spokeman, the Okyeame, spoke quietly with Grace, received the bottle of Schnapps and directed them to sit on some folding chairs to the left of the Nana.

Kojo took note of the solemn expression on Grace's face, no sarcastic smiles today, huh?

Couples knelt in front of the old lady, received what they came for and returned to the folding chairs.

"Now, come", the Okyeame beckoned to them.

"Nana has accepted your gift and will pour libation for you."

Kojo found himself kneeling in front of Nana Oparebea, staring into two of the oldest, wisest looking eyes he had ever seen.

She's staring through me...she's staring through me....

He couldn't shake the feeling as the old woman said some words and poured Schnapps on the ground in front of her. He could feel Grace's body tremble slightly.

And then they were ushered back to their seats. Kojo sat with his hands folded in his lap, squeezing his knees together to prevent them from knocking.

She looked right through me...right through.

"Kojo? Kojo?"

"Huh, What?"

"The Okyeame is calling for you."

Kojo stared at the baldheaded man with the Chinese eyes... Come come, the man gestured to him. Kojo stumbled past several pairs of knees to find himself kneeling in front of Nana Oparebea again.

The Okyeame leaned his head in close, to translate the Nana's words.

"She says that you are about to go on a great journey, you will become rich and famous, doing what you love to do. But she warns you to be careful of the forces that you will be dealing with, they can cause you.... difficulties."

When the lady finished speaking she held her hand out to shake. Mindful of the fragility of old bones, Kojo grasped her hand lightly.

CHAPTER 14

He felt a low grade voltage slowly spread from his right hand, to every part of his body. She released his hand and the voltage eased away. He felt cleansed by the experience.

The Okyeame led him back to his seat and whispered, "You may contribute something to the Shrine, if you care to."

Kojo fumbled into his pocket and pulled out ten thousand cedis.

"Thank you," the man bowed elegantly and returned to his duties. The young man who had led them in stood by to take them out.

Kojo turned to take one last look at the scene. The Queenmother on her throne, relaxed, wise, giving advice.

"How long has Nana been doing this?" he asked the young man.

"Oh, many years. Many years."

"How old is she?"

Grace popped into the middle of the young man's hestitation.

"No one really knows. Some say ninety, some say one hundred and ninety. No one really knows."

The young man nooded in agreement. And they were back on the main street, a part of the inevitable stream of people. The car was waiting, the driver trying to disguise his disgust for their visit to a pagan place.

Tamara's, the hotel-restaurant establishment on the gentle slope of a low mountain.

Cold beers at Tamara's, Lartey, Ghana

They sat at a table on the edge of the veranda, overlooking fields and forests.

"Grace, I'm telling you....Nana looked right through me, I felt that I was being x-rayed."

Grace leaned forward with interest.

"Strange, you know, the effect that she has on people. This is the first time I've heard someone speak of being x-rayed. A girlfriend spoke of feeling as though she were floating when Nana shook her hand."

"And electricity shot through me when we shook hands! Did I mention that?! What happened to you?"

"Well, nothing quite as exciting as being x-rayed or electrified. I was told to be calm, to maintain my tranquility."

"What does that mean?"

"It means that I should be calm, maintain my tranquility."

They exchanged silly, loving smiles and stared out at the valley below the, each lost in private thoughts.

Nana Oparebea knows about my thing with Asiafo. She knows. She didn't veto it, she didn't speak against it, she just said "be careful". I **will** be careful.

They had baby barracuda and salad for lunch and kicked back with chilled bottles of beer. A cloudless sky hung overhead.

Kojo felt something of the mood that Visconti had set in "The Garden of the Finzi-Continis", the kind of mood that denied that there was a dirty, rotten world out there, waiting to smear itself all over you.

"Kojo, you ever think of living in Ghana here?"

The question was softly spoken, but intense. He took a long sip of his beer, to gather his thoughts.

"Grace, let me share some thoughts with you. I don't know if they will answer your question, but it'll tell how I feel."

She nodded him on...

"Since my first visit here, at seventeen, when I met you, a part of me has always lived in Ghana here. That's the spiritual section.

Physically, I couldn't actually live in Ghana, or any other developing country. The frustrations are too great, the beauracracy is too burdersome, the technology that I need to work with isn't here.

Honestly, I could see myself going crazy in a week."

"Are those the only considerations?"

"What do you mean? I don't understand...."

"What about your emotions? Don't they play a role in the way you want to live your life?"

"O hell yes! Of course, emotions. I am emotional by nature, but I am also realistic. I know what the emotional binge can lead to....an inevitable let down."

He detected a shadow of disappointment cross her face. Is she asking me to stay in Ghana, without really coming out loud with it?

"So, you're going back to the America you have no patriotism for, to a land that hasn't earned your love..."

Ooo, so... now we're going to play a little hard ball, huh? "You're right on both points. I'm going back to a country I have no patriotism for, not in the sense you feel patriotic about Ghana. And it is a land that hasn't earned by love, but there are other considerations. The first consideration is that I have to get back as much of what America owes me, as I possibly can.

You don't give up hundreds of years of unpaid labor, and forget about it. We could be going into the 90th generation of my grandchildren before America could begin to deal with <u>some</u> of the interest on the principal that's owed us."

He watched her slowly turn her glass around on the coaster, obviously thinking of what he had just said.

"You know, sometimes, I feel that I can come close to understanding how Black Americans, African-Americans feel about some things. But then I find myself totally at sea, like someone who made a wrong turn in the middle of the ocean."

"Grace, there's the difference. We can't afford to feel like that, like we've made a wrong turn in the middle of the ocean.

The minute we fall prey to that kind of thinking, we're lost. We have to keep our compasses firmly focused on the Middle Passage, and what that meant."

"Yes, Kojo, what it meant, not what it means today. There comes a time when we have to forget some things, move on...."

He felt a cold anger swell in his head and subside. This is just a serious conversation, nothing more. Don't get crazy.

"Grace, I know what you're saying. And I know you mean well. But let me lay something on you that my Grandfather, my Grandmother, my Dad and Mom have been laying on me...all my life.

If they've told me this once, they've told me a thousand times; "Kojo, don't listen to the people who tell you - forget about your history, forget about the degradation of slavery and the aftermath, forget about who you are, and what kind of strength it took for you to become what you are.

We African-Americans, are the only people on the planet that they talk that garbage to. They wouldn't dare say anything like that to the Jews, or the Chinese, or the Japanese, or the Russians or anyone else.

It seems to be a piece of advice that's reserved for us. You'll even have some Africans try to fling that garbage at your head. Don't listen to 'em, they're crazy."

Grace stared at him for a few beats, an odd expression on her face.

"Kojo, you know something, you're right. It's true, I've never heard of any other people being asked to forget who they are. I apologize."

"Your apology is duly recorded and accepted. Now then, what's up for tonight?"

"I thought we could go clubbing a bit...."

"Wowww...you're really feeling lively, huh?"

"I think it's you, Kojo, I think it's you."

"I hope so...."

The Balm's Tavern, what a strange name for a bar. He stood in the patio, waiting for Grace to come out of the ladies. Balm Tavern, a series of connected rooms, mirrors here and there, a strobe lit dance floor, blasting music.

He judged the crowd to be upper yuppie, or whatever the Ghanaian version of the animal was. Several men strolled in, holding their mobile phones at the ready.

Kojo smirked at the sight...I don't know who you're planing to talk to in here.

Grace shouted above the noise of the rap music -

"Where do you want to sit?"

He pointed to a corner table, a vantage point to see and be seen.

An exorbitant price for two beers, an effervescent dancing crowd! Kojo led Grace out onto the floor for punishing session of "Shake Your Boody." Fifteen minutes later they left the dance floor, wet with sweat.

"I've needed a workout like that," he shouted into her ear.

They settled back, enjoying the dancers. Funny, when African women do their cultural dances, the tribal things, they seem so free and loose. When they get outside of that, into this other kind of rhythm, they dance like robots.

After a couple more dances, Grace signalled that she wanted to bail out.

"I'm with you, baby, I'm with you."

They were still shouting at each other on the outside before they realized that they had left the music-noise inside. Grace dissolved against him, laughing at the absurdity of it all.

They shared a long, passionate kiss in the taxi on the way to Jimmy's Jazz joint.

"If we're lucky, we'll catch someone good for the last set."

They were in luck. The trio, (piano, bass, wire brushing drummer), was in the middle of a jazz seance when they self-consciously sneaked into a ringside table.

Gin and tonics, a lovely lady, sophisticated music. Kojo leaned into the music, feeling slightly like a traitor to his peer-group. I can blame it on Dad and my uncles, they spoiled me with Miles, Diz, Bird, Lester Young, Lady Day, Erroil Garner, Bud Powell, Monk, Mingus, 'Trane, Horace Silvers, Cecil Taylor, David Murray, Phavia Kujichagulia, Mongo, Armando Peraza, people like that.

The pianist, a sharp featured, brooding giant of an African man, finished off "Night and Day" with a baroque flourish and announced to the half filled room - "We'll be back after a short intermission. Stay with us."

Stay with us. Where else could you go and hear "Oscar Peterson" in Accra, on a Tuesday night. Or is it Wednesday? Or Thursday? Yes, it's Thursday now. 12:15 a.m.

"Grace, did you just hear what I just heard?"

"Yes, he's marvelous, isn't he?"

"Who is he?"

"I don't know, I've never seen him before."

Kojo shook his head with disbelief and glanced around the club. A standard collection of Europeans, most of the men with African women.

They must dream about Black women in Europe and when they get here, this must be a kind of Heaven.

"Grace, tell me something."

She leaned close, a little tipsy, and gave him a sexy stare.

"Tell me what you want to know."

"Why is jazz music so unpopular here, in Ghana here?"

"Well, I wouldn't say its unpopular, but it certainly doesn't compete with Country and Western."

She chucked him under the chin, as though to say....hey, c'mon, guy, let's not take everything too seriously. Kojo caved in immediately. Yeah, why make a federal case out everything?

An hour later they strolled away from the club, bubbling with good vibes.

"I have never heard anybody play like that! That man is a damned genius. Did you hear how he wove slices of Grieg's Piano Concerto into the be bop piece he played?"

"What's be bop?"

He paused to stare at Grace in the light of a full moon. What is/was be bop? We <u>are</u> from different worlds, aren't we?

"Uhhh, be bop.... was a jazz form, way back in my Dad's day."

"O, I see."

They strolled on, casually looking for a taxi, enjoying each other's company.

"Grace, you know something? I'm going to make an honest confession to you..."

She placed her fingers on his lips.... "No please, not now, not tonight. Let's have this moment."

He sprawled in bed, watching every delightfully feminine move she made; stepping into the bubble gum pink panties, fastening the wisp of a bra across her full, firm, uptilted breasts, the lipstick, the tropical cloth wrapped around her body.

"Can I help you do something?"

She sat on the side of the bed and smiled at him.

"If you do one more thing, I won't go to my office this morning."

He mugged a bit and folded his arms across his chest, pantomining a "hands off" stance. She leaned over and kissed him on each eyelid and finally on the mouth.

"I won't be gone all day, it shouldn't take more than four or five hours to do what I have to do. It mostly involves cracking the whip at my staff, making them sit up, as we say in Ghana here."

"Do what you have to do, I'll be here when you get back."

"You will?!" She sounded grateful.

"Yes, you know of a better place to be?"

She winked lascciviously and stood up, ready to go and do battle with her staff.

"There are eggs and a bit of fish, if you'd like something to eat."

"I'll sip a little Scotch, listen to some music and we'll go out somewhere and have something when you get back."

She stunned him by pulling his head between her hands to plant a big kiss on his lips.

"I love you, Kojo," she spoke in a quiet voice and dashed out of the bedroom.

"See you this afternoon", he called to her.

"Eh heeee!"

The apartment was quiet, Grace's perfume lingering on the air. Kojo laced his hands behind his head and stared out of the window at the drifting clouds.

I love you. I wonder if she really meant that or if it was just one of those impulsive things. Do I love her?

The question stirred him out of bed. He saronged a towel around his waist and went to the record shelf. Let's see what we have for a Thursday mood, slightly cloudy.

Miles Davis' "Kind of Blue". Perfect. He placed the disk on the turntable, poured himself three fingers of Scotch, (what the hell, this is my last week in Ghana), and strolled to the window, sipping.

He stared at the passing scene as though it were a film. The women, peddling things, food, whatever, from trays on their heads. Whoever thought of carrying stuff on your head, and strapping babies onto your back?

Muscular young Black men building something across the road, digging into the earth, sweating, laughing and joking with each other.

Why don't they get an earthmover to gouge that out? The haunting music; Coltrane flowing into "Cannonball" Adderley, Wynton Kelly flowing back into Miles, created a mood he felt at ease with.

The scenes from the window made him feel uneasy. The little girls carrying loads on their heads that he wouldn't even think about lifting, the muddy, rutted road, the men laboring across the road. Nobody singing - "lift dat barge, tote dat bail, git a lil' drunk and you land in jail...."

Or any other song. They cracked jokes, he could tell from the explosions of teeth, from time to time. But it was at the survival level, laughing to keep from crying.

He looked around the apartment, studied the convenieces; the telephone, the television, the Grundng Majestic sound system, the hedonistic layout. The place was plush, an asylum from the outside world, the "Third World". Maybe she designed it that way.

He left the window and sprawled on the sofa, slightly high from the Scotch and the music. So, I'm going back to America, to become Kojo Bediako Brown, big time producer-writer-director, master of my destiny and captain of my soul.

All I have to do is marry Akosua Ferguson and feed a visitor when "it" comes. What could be simpler than that?

He replaced "Kind of Blue" with Dizzy's "Night in Tunisia". The sister has really got a helluva collection here, and I was trying to rag her bout how unpopular jazz is in Ghana.

He dolloped a couple more fingers of Scotch in his glass and wandered through the apartment. It could be any apartment anywhere, except that it's not. There is only a cold water tap, and it's not flowing. And the people all around me are speaking Ewe, Twi or Ga or whatever, and I am an African-American.

He saw it as a glittering veil, slowly settling into place, back lit by a phosphorescent light, laced through with a desperately lonely music. The Blues; that's what I'll use for my silent film.

A silent film, the idea had grabbed him years before, during his undergraduate time at U.S.C., when he realized that the Hollywood movie industry had by passed serious African-American films during their "Silent Era".

Chaplin, yes; "Birth of a Nation" and all the rest of the garbage, but no authentic silent African-American themes.

I'm going to do an African-American silent film. I'll dedicate it to the memory of Oscar Michaux, an African-American film-maker, who was before his/their time.

It was time to eat something.

"Kojo, I must warn you, these are a bunch of very conservative Ghanaians. Don't get your hopes up."

He nodded, a mellow high in his guts from a morning of Scotch sipping, kenkey-fish-pepper eating and serious thinking.

Grace had come home with an invitation to an afternoon party.

"It's almost an obligatory thing. You know what I mean? She did it for me, now I've got to do it for her...a pain in the ass, if you ask me!"

Kojo in his relaxed state of mind, cooled his lady out.

"Grace, come on now, baby, let's be real about things. A social obligation is a social obligation."

He could tell, from the way she was re-dressing, that it was going to be a special occasion, whatever it was.

"Grace, gotta stop at my place for a sec, I feel the urge for a suit for this one."

The desk clerk simply lowered his lower jaw and let it hang there. Whoever paid money for a room and didn't live in it?

Kojo dressed quickly and carefully; black leather Morrocan loafers, sea blue socks, egg yellow "political suit", collarless.

"Kojo, you look very nice."

"Thank you, sweetthing."

He felt himself falling into a groove with Grace. She was an honest woman who knew how to cover his back. And his front.

An afternoon party. Ghanaian style, some place deep in LaBone.

"Charity, this is my friend, Kojo."

"You are welcome, please come in."

Kojo placed one camera at the indoor - second floor level, to Pan-scan the sparkling, glittering crowd. And another camera in a corner, like a burglar camera, stealing shots at people who wandered within range.

"Grace, please introduce your friend around, I must see to the food."

That was one of the things he truly liked about the Ghanaian way of hospitality, the introductions. No matter if there were twenty people or two hundred, each person was introduced to the others as he/she came in.

Kojo contrasted that way of doing things with the number of times he had been invited to sets, in the 'States, where he came, not knowing anyone but the hosts and left, not knowing anyone else.

The obligatory handshake, the men doing the middle finger pop that he loved, the women, mostly, holding their hands out like dead fish.

"Grace, what's the occasion?"

"O, nothing special, Charity and Veronica like to give these little get togethers, from time to time."

"Veronica? Did I meet her?"

"Yes; there, the tall, one."

Kojo lifted a glass of wine from a passing tray and checked the situation out closely.

"Grace", he whispered, "Are these two lesbians?"

She looked genuinely puzzled.

"I really can't say. I know they've been roommates since Secondary School, and as you can see, they're quite successful."

Quite successful. The two storey house with the winding staircase, (I can just see Rhett Butter carrying Scarlett O'hara up that staircase), the expensive, clean limbed Scandinavian furniture, the clean cut, expensively dressed party goers.

Kojo wandered away from Grace as she held an animated conversation with a large woman wearing an enormous turban.

I'll have to ask somebody about the sexual thing here, especially the lesbian number. He meandered out into the back patio, more glamorously dressed people.

Talk about colors, and beautiful people.

He got the impression that they all knew each other, that they were a social set.

"Oh, there you are. I can't afford to let you out of my sight, there are some absolutely rapacious women here."

"Oh yeah, where?"

"Here's one right here," Grace spoke in a low voice, before greeting the Halle Berry type swimming through the mix.

"Grace, how nice to see you."

He watched them perform their cheeky-cheeky-kissy ritual.

"And who is this lovely boy?" The lady had an upper crust British accent and the bold eyes to go with it.

"This is my very close friend, Kojo Brown, from America."

"Ohh, America, I was just thar last month, in Chiicargo, as a matter of fact."

"Kojo, this is Selena Acheampong."

"How do you do? And how did you like Chicago, your first time there?"

Selena Acheampong was half high from something other than liquor. Marijuana maybe. Or cocaine. Or maybe just simply uppers. He could tell from the jerky way she talked.

And the sister is fine, too, one of these dull yellow women with all the tits and ass they'll ever see. Yeah, stay close to me, Grace.

"Chiicargo, yes, I go thar quite often. I have friends on the Gold Coast, on the Near Northside, in Chiicargo."

"I'm familiar with the place, I was born there."

She linked her arm through his left arm and tried to steer him away, but Grace counterattached with a firm grip around his waist. Kojo felt that he was being fought over, a flattering feeling.

When she realized that she wasn't going to be able to steer him away, she dug down in her camera sized purse and pulled out a card.

"Here is my card, do call me anytime, I should so much like to talk to with you about Chiicargo. Grace, see you latah."

Grace waved her away with a frozen smile. Kojo, feeling devilish, decided to egg the situation on.

"She seems like a nice person..."

"She's a fucking nymphomaniac, that's what she is. She has probably slept with half of the men here."

Kojo took a closer look at the beautiful woman doing a social butterfly number through the crowd.

"The Three Faces of Eve." Hard to tell about a woman. they can look one way and be the complete opposite. A nymphomaniac....hmmmm.

The music was low keyed and rhythmic, just dynamic enough to add a little spice to the mix.

"Oh, Kojo, you haven't had any food. Let me get you something. If Selena comes back, don't go with her."

Kojo laughed at the serious expression on Grace's face.

"Don't worry, Grace, I can only handle one nympho at a time." She pouted a kiss at him and eased away to the buffet.

He held his ground, sipping his white wine, studying the mix.

It could be a gathering of Black folks in California, or Hyde Park, Chicago. Or New York. Except for the real dark ones who are obviously Africans, the rest of us have what Granddad calls, "that Creole look."

There wasn't as much dipping in the knees, the men didn't assume the kind of hip postures that the brothers would've fallen into, and there was definitely a more English air about the people.

But for all that, he still saw more in common than the opposite.

That's got to be a film too, someday, the Pan-African Connection.

"Here, sir, food for the starving man."

"I thank you, sweethang."

They occupied two garden chairs.

"My God, what is all this on this plate?"

"I didn't know what you'd like, so I put a little of everything..."

Succulent salmon patties, jollof rice, black eyed peas, cucumber and tomato salad.

"This is delicious..."

"Charity and Veronica have a woman cooking for them, for years now."

Dinner done, they stacked their half emply plates on a passing tray, pulled glasses of wine from another tray and sat looking at the thinnning crowd.

"Kojo, you know I'm beginning to feel guilty about monopolizing your time.."

"You couldn't do it if I didn't want you to do it."

"I'm glad you said that."

CHAPTER 15

"And besides, I didn't come here to run all over the place. I've seen people do that. They come to Accra, trip up to Tamale or Kumasi and then to Cape Coast, and run through a few slave warehouses and jump back on the 'plane.

I'm satisfied by being in the Africa I've been in."

She smiled at his double entendre and squeezed his hand. He felt turned on.

❖

The Corner Salon de Beauté

Well, I thought, since we're all dressed up and everything that we would go to the National Theatre, to see the Ghana National Dance Ensemble."

Grace, you're wonderful, you know that?"

"If you say so...."

The mood was mellow. After the party, the good food, the vibes, a well mixed drink in the Novotel bar, a performance by the Ghana National Dance Ensemble, what could be better?

He had the feeling that he was seeing a number of the same people in the National Theatre, that he had seen at the party.

"Grace, is this my imagination?"

She glanced around.... "no, not really. There is a sort of elite in Accra here, the middle class people who can afford to have expensive parties and go to performances at the National Theatre. Someone has to do it."

The performance started a half hour late, early by Ghanaian time/ standards.

Sections of the dance pieces made him laugh out loud; enjoying the dilemma of the village dandy who has dug himself a hole that he can't crawl out of.

Which of the three maidens that he has seduced will he marry? Solution. Marry all three!

The outrageous energy of the Ensemble made him feel that they were bankrupting themselves with every movement, every gesture.

He whispered in Grace's ear... "I'd be tired for a week if I did any of this."

"They can't afford to be tired, some of them work during the day, others at night, I suspect that there are some of them going to work after this is over."

Kojo looked at the Ensemble with new found respect. And the artist thinks he's got it rough in the 'States..

They strolled along the beach in front of the Rivera Hotel, shoes in hand, enjoying the cool night washed ocean air. It was time to go behind the scenery.

"Grace, I started to tell you something earlier but you cut me off...."

The ocean flushed white caps at them from far out. This is where they loaded us on/into sardine cans, tightened the screws and shipped us off into Nowhere.

"I'm sorry, I just had a feeling, from the way you were looking, that it just wasn 't something I wanted to hear at the moment...."

"Should I cancel out again?"

"No, please say what's on your mind."

So many stars, so black, so big. What did they think when they had a chance to look up at the sky in the middle of the Middle Passage?

"Today, just before you dashed off to work, you said – 'I love you.' Do you remember?"

She nodded yes, scuffing grooves in the tightly packed sand.

"I thought about that, all day. I've been thinking about a lot of things, about us. That's why I started off saying I wanted to make an honest confession to you."

She stopped, looked at him with a calm expression on her face, calm but expectant.

"Grace, I already have someone in my life, back in the 'States. That's what I wanted to tell you."

She strolled on, gazing out to sea.

"So, I can't love you because you love someone else?"

He had to sift the words through his mind, to make certain that he really understood what she was saying.

"That does complicate things a bit, doesn't it?"

Grace sank down on the sand and patted the place beside her for him to sit.

When she spoke, it sounded like a low pitched drone.

"Kojo, do you know for most of my life I have been directed? I was told to do this and I was told to do that. And I did what I was told, because it was expected of me.

When we first met I was close to being a religious fanatic, because those were my instructions.

I don't have to tell you what I was like, I'm sure you remember."

They traded smiles.

"Yeah, I remember well."

"You were a liberating force for me and I didn't truly understand that until you went back. I loved you for what you had done with me.

Yes, I said I love you and I mean it. I'm not saying I love you because I need you to return this love. Are you getting me?

I love you for the way you are with me, for the way you've been with me. I would be a fool to think that you were in America, with all of the beautiful women there, and that you didn't have someone.

I don't feel that has anything to do with me. Please give me, but I want my happiness with you. I don't want to think of others. When I received your letter saying that you were returning, I started "cleaning up my act", as you say in America.

I sat down in front of my mirror and talked to myself. I wanted to have you, I wanted you to have me, the <u>New</u> me. And I didn't want big, heavy strings attached to any of it.

I prayed, when you came, whether you spent an hour, a week or a month with me, I was going to try to do everything in my power to please you, to have a time that I could always remember."

They didn't see the jagged flashes of lightening far at sea as they smothered each other in their arms.

Ghana Transportation

An outdooring? No, baby, I think I'll have to take a raincheck on that one, 6 a.m. is a bit too early for me to be saluting newcomers."

"Have you been to an outdooring?"

"Grace, I was outdoored, my grandfather was outdoored, my uncles were outdoored..."

"That's unusual for Americans, isn't it?"

"Yeah, you got that right. But you have to keep in mind, I come from an unusual family."

"O, I see."

They sat up in bed, eating cookies and drinking beer, finding out more about each other every minute.

"So, you go to welcome the newborn baby into the community, everybody gets a chance to say I was there when you came into the world, a lot of drinks are served and everybody goes away happy."

She laughed at his version of an outdooring.

"Well, there's a bit more to it than that, but I guess you could say that's basically it."

Roberta Flack was singing, "The First Time Ever I Saw Your Face...."

They were silent, sipping their beers and listening to the words of the song. Kojo reached over to take Grace's glass, placed both of their glasses on the bedside table, and gently pulled her down under the covers.

"I love you too, Grace."

An hour later Kojo was awakened by the feeling of someone else in the room. He opened his eyes without moving his head.

Grace slept with her head against his left shoulder. He slowly swept his eyes from right to left, looking hard into the shadowed spaces. Nothing. What's the matter with me?

Juliet of the Spirits/8½ = Federico Fellini, that man could make a film. The way he used Marcello Mastroanni to say what he wanted to say.

That's what I need, I need an actor, an actress with a lot of depth and ingenuity. Why can't I sleep any more? Why are the sounds or things or whatever the hell it is waking me up?

Beautiful beautiful Grace. Maybe she's the one I should be marrying. No, not Grace, Grace wants to remain in her country and do something. It will have to be Akosua.

What if she says no? No, she couldn't say no. What have we been edging up to for the last two years anyway?

Get married and feed a visitor and wait for the goodies to drop into my lap. It sounds too simple. What's the angle? What's the catch?

I'll have to put a tight organisation together, no pootbutts, flash men, coke heads or crazies.

Names and telephone numbers whizzed through his head. Be cool. There's time to put it altogether...be cool.

He closed his eyes and tried to dream his way into the future.

"Kojo, I'm off."

"Off? Off what?"

"I'm off to the outdooring."

"Oh, yeah, I forgot. Have fun."

"Well, it won't be that exactly, it's more like a social obligation."

"Lot's of social obligations in Ghana here."

"It's true. O, mentioning social obligations. My senior uncle is having a memorial service for his wife tomorrow afternoon."

"Memorial service for his wife?"

"Yes, they were married for 25 years and she died two years ago. The memorial service commemorates her death."

"Wakekeepings, funerals, outdoorings, memorial services....wow! You could get fat going to celebrate everything, huh?"

"Some people overdo it. I must dash. What're you going to do today?"

"I haven't made up my mind yet."

"How about a movie and dinner this evening?"

"You're on!"

Friday morning, the weekend is here. And Monday is on its way. He checked the bedside clock. 5:30 a.m... and fell back into an untroubled sleep, punctuated by random scenarios.

Was the girl in "Ramparts of Clay" a slave? a member of a lower caste in the village? What?

Beautifully photographed. How did they get those Berbers to act so natural? I'd like to go to Tsito and do something like that.

I'll bet "Cool Hand Luke" was really a Black screenplay, originally. All the elements are there; a rebellious Black man who decides to defy the natural order of things just because he's got the devil in him.

I can just see it now, the meeting the producers had, to make the Decision.

"We gotta make this fuckin' thing White. First off, we don't have a Black guy who could pull this off. Diesel wouldn't be believable, he's too hung up on being cute. McCoy is up to his ass in scripts and Sidney, I don't know, Sidney can't rebel so well. Whaddaya think, Phill?"

Yeah, "Cool Hand Luke" was a Black man's film until they turned it into a White movie.

I wonder how many Black screenplays have been turned into White movies?

"Raging Bull" could've been, should've been the "Sugar Ray Robinson Story."

"Easy Rider" was a Black movie, Peter Fonda, with his connections and his father's profile, carried it off as a "hippie" movie. O well...

Donald Bogle's "Mammies, Coons and Darkies" or was it "Coons, Mammies and Something Else?" caused his limbs to twitch.

All of the shit I forced the U.S.C. film department to watch when I did my "Review of African-Americans in American movies." I know they hated me after that.

Even a couple of the brothers and sisters were upset. "Awww c'mon, Kojo, what's the point, man?"

"The point is history, brother, the point is history. Don't you understand what happens when your history is stolen, or degraded."

"But history is yesterday..."

"No! No! history is today! you fool! history is Now! History lives!"

He woke himself up, clenching and unclenching his fists, alternately punching and strangling imaginary opponents.

9 a.m. O well, guess it's time to get up anyway.

He "baffed." The water is on. Made tea and toast. Stood at the window. The workers across the road were gradually erecting a building, he could determine the outline of the structure.

The women selling things from the trays on their heads were still there, passing in solitary review. The shoe shine boys made their shoeshine/repair kits.

It's timeless. I'll bet some of these things have been happening since the Beginning of the Beyond.

"Dear Akosua, I'll probably be back before you receive this letter, but no matter, the important thing is the writing of it.

As you know, I'm not a great one for social letter writing but I feel compelled to do this one.

I almost feel that I should apologize for not overwhelming you with mail. Why? Well, because if there is anyone I have overloaded with my pet dreams and schemes, it's been you. And, in some way, I feel you should be rewarded for your fortitude.

I've done a lot of thinking about us since I've been over here; what we've done and what we haven't done.

One of the things I know we'll have to do is "tighten" it up. For many months you've given me enough rope to hang myself but I've only succeeded in bungling the job.

I'm going to use the rope to better advantage when I return. I hope all of this doesn't sound too far out to you.

It's like I know what I'm talking about, and I feel that you're on the same wave length."

A noise outside the apartment door. Grace coming in? Kojo covered up the letter he was writing with a book. No, no danger, false alarm, someone stumbling upstairs with a load of something.

Three months. Does that mean three months from the day we made the deal? When I get back I'll have less than three months.

Why did I tell Grace I had another woman in my life, back in the 'States? Akosua Ferguson, the other woman, the woman "back home."

He could think of three women that he felt close to, but Akosua Ferguson was his main draw. He folded up the half written letter and stuffed it into his pants pocket.

How can I lay up here in one woman's house and write to another woman? Easy...

He thumbed through the cassettes.., something for a Friday...

"Bolero." Why not? Just the right piece. He adjusted the system and sprawled out on the sofa, listening to the intensity of the music building.

Akosua Ferguson. The sister has a lot of heart, a lot of heart. How do you go about bucking against the wishes of a couple right wing thinking Negrocentric parents, all the way to changing her name from Cynthia to Akosua, and telling them to stick the inheritance, the house and all the rest of it up their asses, if they didn't like what she was about.

Akosua Ferguson, novelist, lovely woman, full of good vibes, independent thinking.

He squeezed his eyes shut and held his hands to the sides of his face. What have I been doing?

We've had a thing going on for almost two years and I've never even introduced her to my folks.

He quickly slipped past Marvina and Jackie; beautiful but basically empty. Marvina wants a new car every year, someone to fund her expensive habits and Jackie lives in a dream world.

Akosua, I owe you an apology. Here I am, thousands of miles away, and I suddenly realize I've been taking you for granted. I need to have my ass kicked.

He felt pin pricks of anxiety. How is she going to take it when I propose to her, when I ask her to marry me? Am I going to ask her to marry me?

He stood and slowly paced around the room. I can just see the expression on her face and the question she'll ask; "Isn't this awfully sudden, Kojo?"

Three fingers of Scotch and more thoughtful pacing, "Bolero" was building to a crescendo.

Should I tell the truth? Should I tell her the whole thing?

No, don't tell anybody else. It was a mistake to tell Grace. You'll have people thinking you've lost your mind, no one will ever take you seriously again.

I'll call her...yeahhh, I'll call her...

After five minutes of Transatlantic negotiations Akosua Ferguson was on the line...

"Kojo, what a nice surprise! I'm sorry that I wasn't in town when you left... I had this conference..."

"I know, I know, you told me about it. Look, Akos', I'll be getting back on Tuesday, I need to get together with you, we need to talk..."

"Kojo...bleep bleep bleep...Kojo?!"

"I'm here."

"Is everything o.k.? you sound a little disturbed..."

"O, I'm alright, I think it's the 'phone."

"Well, look, let's not spend a lot of money with AT&T. You want me to pick you up Tuesday? Give me the flight number and time of arrival."

He gave her the information and settled back on the sofa.

"Akosua, I've missed you."

"I've missed you too, Kojo."

"See you Tuesday."

"Yes, Tuesday, byyy."

He placed the 'phone in its cradle and felt a film of perspiration under his arms.

Well, there's the opening pitch, let's see how the game goes.

They decided to go to the movies first.

"I go to sleep if I go to the movies on a full stomach."

"I heard that. Well, let's make the 6:30 p.m. show and go Chinese after that."

In the taxi to Ghana Films, Kojo could feel himself slipping away from Ghana, from the mood it had laid on him, from Grace.

He studied her profile, tried to read her -mind. *The sister laid some dynamite stuff on me last night. I wonder if she meant it.*

She turned toward him suddenly and flashed a big smile

"Hello, beautiful."

"Hi, handsome."

Ghana Films, Friday evening, 6:15 p.m., the couples had already formed a line. The choice was between Ghana Films and the Executive Theatre.

Grace offered the first veto of the Ghanaian movie; "I don't think I could stand a Ghanaian movie tonight, with the terrible sound and all that."

"Well, let's see what's playing at the Executive."

"Cooley High."

"Grace, you're in luck. "Cooley High" is what we call "a sleeper.""

"A sleeper, that doesn't sound promising."

"Bear with me, "a sleeper" is one of those better than average films that a lot of people overlooked. I think you'll enjoy this."

Glynn Turman was the star of "Cooley High," a rite of African-American passage that made "American Graffiti" look like phoney money.

They scrambled for the good seats in the center of the stadium shaped theatre. Kojo held Grace's hand, clearly excited by the idea of seeing an African-American film that he had studied, and enjoyed a half dozen times.

Michael Schultz, the director, Glynn Turman, the actor, and the other young Black men and women in the film had opened themselves up for this one. The director hadn't asked them to dance out of church, ("The Color Purple"), and prance down the road, waving their fingers like idiots, or do anything that wasn't them.

And it showed in the finished work. Norman Lear liked the Eric Monte film so much he "borrowed" it for a stupid T.V. series.

Kojo leaned back, fixing his director's cap on as the film started.

He blinked at the wide, watery line that floated across the screen. What the hell is that? Dirt on the projector lens? A scratch on the film? A damaged print? What the hell is that?

And then the people behind him began to talk. It was a conversation that only dealt with the movie in a side view light. Grace squeezed his hand, cooling him out. Kojo looked at the floor for a couple beats, cooling himself out.

How can people sit up here and watch a damaged print? And talk like they're sitting in front of their T.V. sets?

The film came to the inconclusive ending that he didn't care for. The young blood who kills the other dude, down under the "EL", goes into the Army and that's the end of that. Flaw, serious flaw.

He stood at the end of the film and turned to glare at the man and woman who had carried on the marathon conversation.

"Why are you guys so quiet now? The movie is over."

The couple and several others within hearing distance looked at him, puzzled expressions riddling their faces.

Grace tugged gently at his fingers as they joined the exiting crowd. They didn't speak until they reached the main road, started looking for a taxi.

"Grace, you've got to explain it to me before I go nuts..."

Her signal pulled the taxi over to them, they hopped in.

"Let's go to Hinlones, in LaBone. Now, you say I should explain something to you?"

Kojo stared out of the window at the kerosene lamps marking the places where people were selling, selling, selling.

He wasn't sure if he could phrase the question properly, without making it sound as though he were condemning a whole nation. He decided to go at it in a circular way.

"Black people in the U.S. are just like the Black people here when it comes to talking in the theatre. Except that there's a difference.

When you get to the upper crust theatre goers, the "sophisticated" people, they go to see the movie and it isn't likely that they would have a running monologue with the screen.

The people in the Executive Theatre, who've paid twice the price that they would pay for a Ghana Film ticket, shouldn't be doing a running commentary.

It just doesn't add up. In addition to that big blue stripe. Did you see that? How could you show a film with a blue stripe slicing across it?"

He thought he could detect a slight air of disgust in the down- turned corners of her mouth.

"So, what's your question? Are you asking me why people talk through the movie? Or why there was a blue stripe on the screen?"

Yes, the tone indicated a defensive posture. He decided to try to defuse the situation.

"I guess I don't really have questions, I'm just thinking out loud."

"Don't worry, I understand. It's not the first time I've heard foreigners express frustration with us.

If you listen closely, you will hear us do the same thing. My father used to write letters to the newspapers about different things, all the time.

It's just a theory, mind you, just a theory, but I have this notion in my head abut us, about Ghanaians.

We are really and truly a developing nation, what Mao Tse Tung called "Third World."

That means that many things have not reached a certain level here. It means that we don't have very high standards, yet. When people come here, who can compare their excellent stuff to our mediocre stuff, then of course, we suffer by comparison.

I would wager that there were people in the theatre tonight who were not terribly put off by the blue stripe."

"Really?"

"Remember, I'm just being theoretical. I can't say for sure. But I think we have a much more stoical, maybe fatalistic attitude toward things.

Some people might think - ha! a blue stripe? So what? At least we have the rest of the movie.

So, the water is off. The electricity if still on. God is Great.

Today is hot, tomorrow it will be cool. Amen.

I am poor today, tomorrow I will win the National Lottery. Halleluya.

Five of my children have died, we will have a sixth who will live. We cannot afford to become bogged down by what we don't have, or what is not working.

We are a very young nation, less than fifty years old, and there is much to be done. And we are going to do it.

Hopefully, when you return to Ghana, there will no longer be blue stripes in the films."

"But people will still be talking..."

CHAPTER 16

She shrugged eloquently and gave him the palms waving out motion that spoke volumes.

Kojo was paying close attention to the order of things; first we were served water, then corn wine, now beer and soft drinks, and here comes Uncle Henry with a fifth of Scotch.

In between times, little cakes, slices of this and that, chunks of dough that he didn't have time to ask Grace the names for.

''You are welcome.''

"Thank you."

They were seated under a broad awning, a privileged place to be, with the fifty closest family members.

An hour went by; more beers, more Scotch, a giant bottle of Beefeaters made an appearance. The men poured the gin down their gullets like water.

Kojo grimaced, watching it happen. Grace laughed at his frowns.

"If I tried to drink gin like that it would knock me flat on my ass."

A collection of young men, all dressed in the latest African-American teenaged garb, got up and started doing their versions of hip hop, pop lock, breaking and the latest Fifty-Cents movements.

Kojo stared, fascinated by the African adaptations. Yeahhh, we are One.

A memorial service that was a party, the way it should be. Nothing draggy and blue. Remember the good times.

Kojo felt high, not so much from the booze, but from the good vibes. He leaned over to Grace...

"You know we've really been burning the candle, haven't we?"

She nodded in agreement. The movie, Hinlone's 'til closing, a nightcap at Attohs in Osu, music and a love feast...

The scene had become extremely loose. A couple of the older women were doing a sedate version of something that resembled the Hoochie Koochie. Or the Atomic Dog.

No tribal music today. I wonder why. Guess that would put another vibe on things.

Conversations ebbed and flowed, people moved from one place to another, all the evidence pointed to a sign that said - Good Times.

Hours later, after the water, the corn wine, the beer and Scotch, with munchies in between, Kojo and Grace made their exit with a scattershot round of handshakes and goodbyes.

"Grace, you must bring your young man again."

"I will, Uncle, I will, but we must go now, 'by 'by.'"

"Have another drink before you leave...."

They had to pull themselves away from the expressions of goodwill, one last drink, a final round of handshakes.

Once outside the large metal gate, Kojo took a deep breath and started walking down the rutted road, holding Grace's arm.

"Now that's what I call a Party. A memorial service, huh?"

"Yes, a memorial service."

"You got that right."

He felt satiated, full of everything. I feel like I've been everywhere and done everything. What else is there to do?

"Kojo?"

"Huh?"

"I've really enjoyed having you here."

They flagged a taxi and headed for home, both of them looking forward to some mellow music and a late afternoon nap.

Sunday morning...he felt her empty space next to him. O no, don't tell me she's gone to a funeral or something.

A few minutes later he heard her struggling back into the apartment. What's going on?

He slipped out of bed and draped the sheet around himself. Grace was placing a VCR on top of her television set. She caught sight of him peeking around the corner at her.

"Good morning, sleepyhead. Come, help me put this machine together."

"What have you got here?"

"I've borrowed my girlfriend's VCR, she won't be in today. I thought it would be nice to have a quiet Sunday watching films.. .with no blue lines and only the two of us talking."

He hugged her and kissed her.

"Grace, you're too much, you know that."

It took him a minute to attach the VCR to the television.

"O.K., what's first?"

"We'll have to go for films. There's a video shop in Roman Ridge where they have foreign films."

"Be with you soon as I brush my teeth."

He prowled the aisles, finding it ironic that he would be looking at American titles in the foreign film section.

"One Flew Over the Cuckoo's Nest." Jack Nicholson played his ass off in that one, him and Nurse Rached, Louise Fletcher.

"The Rose Tattoo." Burt Lancaster and all his teeth, nawww.

"The Day The Earth Stood Still." Michael Rennie as the man from outer space, the creature who made the Earth stop trying to kill itself

"A Fine Madness." Sean Connery as Samson Shillitoe, the crazed poet, and Joanne Woodward as his unintellectually inclined-waitress woman.

"The Lion in Winter." Peter O'Toole and Katherine Hepburn chewing up the scenery.

"Lolita." Ahhhh, James Mason playing himself Peter Sellers playing everybody else.

"Dr. Strangelove..." Peter Sellers really playing somebody else.

"On the Waterfront," Brando before he got fat. Yeah he coulda been a contenduh...

"Streetcar Named Desire." Tennessee Williams probably wrote this as an African-American play. In the back of his old sick Southern mind anyway.

"Bonjour Tristesse." That was an interesting moment. The little French girlwriter, what was her name? Francoise Sagan, came up with a kind of rich/romantic whimsy.

"Goodfellas." Robert DeNiro and the Mafia. How do they manage to get away with making so many movies about themselves?

"Coming to America." Eddie Murphy showing about as much consciousness as a box of rocks. Why would you have to leave all of the beautiful women in Africa to go find one in America?

"Hollywood Shuffle." More power to you, Robert Townsend. Once they saw where your head was they tried to bury you, but you wouldn't let 'em do it.

"She's Gotta Have It." Well, I'll be damned. Spike Lee's maiden voyage. Except for "Malcolm X" and "Mo Better Blues," I have philosophical problems with the brother.

I can't believe that three bona fide brothers would knowingly share the same woman... "She's Gotta Have It."

"School Daze." Yeahhh, it did the Butt. Such an outmoded piece of nonsense.

The wannabees and the Blacks, or something like that. Do we need that?

"Do the Right Thing." Seems like Italians were the only ones doing the right thing in that one.

"Jungle Fever." Pleezzzz. What a waste of talent. How can you make me believe that a Bensonhurst-Italian-Catholic-girl with a racist father and two racist brothers would screw Wesley Snipes on a drawing board in an office? That one was to stir up White blood. Crossover time.

"Kojo, you find anything you like?"

"I'm coming."

"Dona Flor and Her Two Husbands." Sonia Braga, Brasil, do el Brasil Brasil Brasil Brasil.

"Seven Beauties." Giancarlo Giannini's eyes and Lina Wertmuller's direction. Got it!

"A Man and A Woman." Give me the sound track.

"A Taste of Honey." Hmmm...that was a moment.

"Darling." Julie Christie and freaky ol' Laurence Harvey tearing at each other.

India. "Distant Thunder," the caste-starvation-revolution-nightmare. Worth seeing again.

"Ran." "Chushingura." "Realm of the Senses." Wowww. I wonder if they know what they have here? Oshima freaked out on this one. I wouldn't want to check this out with Grace, we'd wear ourselves out talking about it.

"Sugar Cane Alley." Nice touch. A taste of Martinique.

Bergman/Swedish Angst. "Wild Strawberries." "The Virgin Spring." "Cries and Whispers."

Spain. Carlos Saura. "Carmen." "Blood Wedding," Gypsy passion.

"Uhh, Kojo, I don't want to rush you or anything but we've been here for an hour."

"I'm coming. I just need one.. .more. . .and. ..here it is. "Black Girl," from Senegal, Osmene Sembene's beautiful thing. Let's go, I got all the goodies."

They decided to do it "proper," to use Grace's term.

"I'll collect your fare at the ticket window, you'll go into the darkened theatre, there you'll find small sandwiches and other snacks. A cold beer, or a glass of Scotch if you choose. And a willing female at your side when you take your seat."

"That sounds quite "proper" to me."

He decided to start them off with the two heavies; "Black Girl" and "Distant Thunder" and gradually lighten the mix by going from "Seven Beauties" to "Dona Flor and Her Two Husbands."

They sprawled on the floor, their backs cushioned by pillows, Grace's snack-smorgasbord off to one side. Kojo decided to sip Scotch rather than drink beer.

"I don't want to have to pee at the wrong time."

"We can always place it on hold."

"Never. A fine film should never be put on hold."

"Black Girl" put Grace on the verge of tears.

"How could they treat that poor girl so badly?"

"That's the colonial mentality. They thought they were treating her quite well."

"The bahstards!"

"Now, now, Grace..."

"Distant Thunder," a classic Indian story of caste-starvation and the eventual revolution that forces changes to occur.

"Whenever I've gotten into a discussion with an Indian, and they've tried to talk to me about the glories of Indian civilization, the Taj Mahal and all that, I'm always forced to remind them that they have the caste system...."

"And how do they respond to that?"

"They usually brush me off with some kind of comment, like, O well, you wouldn't understand, you're not an Indian. Rubbish! It's a foul system, no matter how you look at it."

"Kojo, you really love films, don't you?"

"Grace, I live, eat and sleep films. That's one of the reasons why I'm here."

"Oh, I thought you came back to see me."

"Like I said, one of the reasons why I'm here."

"Seven Beauties," the Lina Wertmuller-Giancarlo Giannini film had them thinking-laughing-questioning.

"Kojo, do you really believe that a man would make love to a woman who looked like a pig, for a bowl of macaroni and sausage?"

"Like the lady said,..'The Nazis forced some Greek intellectuals to fuck ducks in order to avoid the firing squad.' It's amazing what the human animal will do to survive."

He was tempted to take her through a few of the stories he had collected from the Jewish Holocaust, but stopped himself.

What purpose would it serve to use ten examples of how inhumane people can become, under the pressure of the need to survive?

"Dona Flor and Her Two Husbands" supplied the right kind of twilight to a beautiful day. Sonia Braga, the Afro-Brasilian love of color, emotion, music and drama flooded the film, flowed out from each frame.

"Oh, that was gorgeous, delicious. I will always remember that film."

"And be sure and remember who you saw it with."

Kojo wrapped her in his arms, lured into reminding her of the afternoon by the example he had just watched. No need to have any ghosts here, pal.

INT. - GRACE'S BEDROOM - MORNING

Grace snuggles into Kojo's armpit, looking dreamy, blissed out. Kojo gently strokes the side of her face and back, stares out at a distant point.

We hear Miles Davis' "Green Dolphin Street" in the **b.g.**

The scene is loving, sweet, but tinged with melancholia.

Grace disengages herself, walks from the bedroom naked, unself-consciously. Kojo stares at her back with obvious appreciation.

He listens to her speak on the telephone. He doesn't understand what she's saying. She returns to the bed, to her place in his arm.

Kojo

What was that all about? What language was that?

Grace

I was speaking to my office manager in Ewe. I told him that I wouldn't be coming in today.

Kojo
(smiling)

I'll bet they will be happy to see me get outta here, so that they can get some work outta you.

Grace smiles and snuggles closer to him. He cups her chin in his hand and kisses her gently, and then with more intensity. She responds. Her hand roams from his hairless chest to the navel and from there to his manhood.

They caress each other unhurriedly, enjoying the pleasure that they release in each other. Grace slyly turns her back to Kojo, he is now kissing her. (Camera ANGLE over her left shoulder.)

FADE OUT

"So, what do you have to do?"

"Well, basically nothing. My bags are packed, except for a few things. I'm sure they'll be amazed at the hotel to see me."

"They will probably want to know if there are others coming, like yourself people who rent rooms that they don't sleep in."

They sat on the floor, half lotused, sipping Scotch. I'll have to go on the wagon when I get back, and double up on my Capoeira too, but for right now...to Hell with everything.

He stared at Grace, sitting across from him. Something white-gauzy, showing the succulent outline of her full breasts, the curve of her thighs.

Ahhh Grace, what a beautiful-wonderful surprise you've been, what a helluva turn about. I never would've dreamed that you would become what you are.

"I'll give you a hundred cedis for your thoughts."

"I'll give them to you for nothing. Can you stand to hear what I have to say, what I've been thinking, honestly?"

"I asked, remember?"

Kojo took a long sip of his drink, channeling his thoughts.

"I was just thinking of what a gorgeous woman you are, in every way, inside and out, and what a fool I am to be leaving you."

Grace sipped her drink and tried not to stare into Kojo's face.

"I was thinking of how many days and nights I'm going to be thinking and dreaming of all the love we've made, the sweet times we've shared.

I was thinking of how right my decision is, to go back to America to do what I have to do. I know that this may sound like a contradiction but bear with me.

I know that it's a mistake to be leaving you, but it's the right thing to do. You have some things to do here and I have some things to do there.

I couldn't stay here and do what I have to do, and you couldn't go there and do what you have to do.

I was thinking of the letters we'll exchange. I know that I'll receive one that tells me you've met somebody. I'm already prepared to deal with that.

Sometimes, in the very best films, we'll have what is called 'A Moment.' 'That Moment' will almost be incandescent. Are you getting me?"

She nodded sadly.

"We've had many moments, from the first time and definitely from this time.

Nothing, nor anyone can take that away from us."

I was thinking that I'll always love what we've shared...."

"And so will I, Kojo, so will I," she vowed.

The desk clerk at the Ghana Garden Hotel blinked with surprise to see Kojo stroll into the lobby with a woman, a very pretty woman.

"Good evening, sah."

"Good evening. I'll be checking out shortly, please prepare my bill."

"I will do it."

Number 206, a glorified storage locker. He clicked on the overhead fan and made quick work of stuffing his shirts, socks, shoes and other stray items into his suitcases.

"There, I'm all set."

Grace laughed. "Now that's what I would call serious packing."

"I like to keep things in perspective. What sense does it make to spend hours packing when I'm going to dump it all out the minute I land. Come over here and sit beside me."

They sat side by side on the battered bed and laid back to stare at the fan.

"I wonder if the fan is symbolic?"

"I don't think so, I'll be flying in a jet. No propellers anywhere."

"No, I wasn't thinking of your journey, I was thinking of how the fan whirls the air around, of how it never strikes the same air twice."

"Never thought of it that way."

A few moments later, as though mutual telepathy had informed them, they began a wordless ballet of taking off each other's clothes.

"Kojo, I may never see you again..."

The tears started simultaneously, making their kisses salty, turned their love making into a bitter-sweet moment.

Afterwards, holding each other, they were silent for long minutes.

"You know it makes me think of a ceremony I went to in San Francisco; it was what you would call Juju here. In the U.S., we call it The Religion, or Santeria, or sometimes, simply Yoruba.

During the course of the ceremony, one of the priests who had been mounted by Oshun, began to cry. The sight of this woman weeping, with her eyes closed as tight as fists, was a sight I'll never forget.

Later, when I asked the senior priest why Oshun, the deity, was crying he said; "I think she was so hurt by the ugliness of the slave trade, the brutality of it all, that she sheds cosmic tears, tears that come from behind the beyond."

I felt some of that kind of feeling with you, a little while ago. I didn't want to cry, I was determined not to cry but something pushed it out."

"I know. I understand. We have a proverb, 'Tears are not needed at the funeral.'

Are you getting me?"

"Yeah, baby, I get you."

He woke up from a small-small sexual catnap, taking quick note of the fact that it was twilight and that Grace was "baffing."

Gotta wash that body, huh? Just gotta wash that body.

He gave her a quick peck on the lips, passing into the bathroom. Yeah, I better do this, your crotch can get kinda raunchy, sitting for fourteen hours, or is it sixteen?

Showered, dressed, they stood in the center of the room, holding each other.

"Grace," he whispered, "There is another proverb, it says, 'We should be strong until our dying day because we have no idea what is going to kill us....' You get me?"

She nodded numbly and tried to smile.

The airport was as chaotic as he remembered it to be.

"O.K., that's done, baggage checked in. That leaves us forty five minutes to drink and be merry!"

They made their way upstream through the arrivals and departures... to the airport lounge.

"Double Johnnie Walkers here."

"Yessah."

They stared at each other over their drinks. So much to be said, no way to say it.

"Grace, I want it to be good between us, I want to fly away from here with the best vibes in the world happening."

"You won't get an argument from me."

"Let's write each other once a month..."

"Agreed."

"And let's be brutally honest with each other...."

"Agreed."

"I can't say when I'll be back, like the day and month, but I know that I will be coming back. What I'm trying to say...."

"Kojo, I understand. I'm not going to put myself on a shelf and wait for you, or anything like that. If I had nothing but the memory we've shared I'd be a happy woman for a long time."

"Grace, you make me feel blessed."

They held each other for five minutes after the announcement had been made to board Flight J-514 for Los Angeles, North America, U.S.A.

"Kojo, it's been good. You get me? It's been good!"

He kissed her one last time and stumbled away, afraid to look back. He wanted to carry a perfect memory away.

In mid Atlantic he could feel another kind of energy beginning to flow through him. *The party is over now, it's time to re-focus, pull my act together.*

"Would you care for a cocktail, sir?"

"Do you have orange juice?"

It won't be a problem to pull my crew together, they all know me and I know them. That crazy Pilipino-Thai-Japanese woman who has memorized everybody's bad habits and telephone numbers - Thelma Nagata.

I'll get her to set up my office. Everything goes more smoothly when you've got the right person running your office.

D.J. Ross, my camera man. Hope they haven't dragged him off to Tibet somewhere, to shoot that Hollywood crap that he hates.

Lights - Philip Charles, a lighting magician. He thought back to a film they had worked on, where Charles had lit the inside of a barrel so cleverly that it seemed natural for a person to be able to see, inside of a dark barrel.

Sid Burns for the sound. He has ears like a bat, and knows how to edit like nobody else.

I'll need assistant directors. Ed Burris and Mac Weaver. I'll go for P.R. with Jackie F. Muhammad and use Michael Ross for my stills.

Akosua Ferguson, writer. He sat up straighter in his seat. Akosua can write her ass off. Where has my head been? Akosua can write her ass off.

The thought of the woman cancelled out the grocery list he was mentally putting together. Akosua....

He slipped into the twilight sleep that always happened to him during long 'plane trips. What's the matter with you, man? Are you out of your mind?

Have you forgotten the process you have to go through to get money to do a film? What do you think is going to happen when you get back, you think somebody is going to stuff a few mil in your pocket and say - "Get busy!"

He tiptoed up to the thought, timidly. If I do what Asiafo told me to do, everything will be alright. He wanted to laugh at himself for believing such a thing could happen, but he couldn't find the humor in it.

The drone of the airplane narcotized him into a numb state.

This is going to be a helluva weight to walk around with. I hadn't seriously thought about getting married until I was thirty, at least.

What would Akosua think if I told her that I wanted to marry her, as a part of a deal, an agreement that I made with a half-naked man in the forest?

No, I can't tell her that. I'll never be able to tell her that, or anyone else.

He tried to focus on Akosua, and his relationship to her, but Grace kept blotting out the idea.

Don't worry, there's time. Don't worry, there's time. There's not a lot of time, but there's time. He told himself not to worry, but he worried anyway. Worry, brother....

Let's see...it's July now. I have two months to get it together.

The inflight movie helped ease him away from his worries... "Under Milkwood," the Dylan Thomas epic. The English really know how to do their thing. He put the earphones on and allowed the mellifluous flow of Peter O'Toole's English, and the lush technicolor highlighting a Welsh town, to lull him back into his own world, the world of film.

Days and nights, after the movie, seemed to pass. He lost track of the snacks, of the neatly arranged meals on the plastic trays, the number of times he fell asleep.

And finally, when he felt that he was about ready to scream, a suave female voice announced, "We are preparing to land at Los Angeles's International Airport, please fasten your seat belts…."

Flying into the City of Angels

Yeahhh, there it is. He found real pleasure coming into Los Angeles at night. He often fantasized that he was landing in a horizontal Christmas tree.

So many lights. They could use the lights from a couple blocks in Inglewood to light up the city of Accra.

The daytime was a different story. In the daytime you can see that sulphur-killer-haze that they call smog, the open air crematorium.

Well, I'm back, it's time to put my stuff in gear and start running for the goal.

He took advantage of the argument between an irate airport cop and a motorist who had lingered too long in the no parking zone, to study Akosua Ferguson.

Tallish, but not really tall, about 5'6 or so, but it's the way she carries herself. A designer body, not the natural fullness of Comfort or Grace, but something else, an athlete's body that called out, "I am a woman, full up front and ample behind."

A couple shades lighter than Grace, a higher set of cheekbones and small, cat like eyes. Wonder which tribe her people come from?

CHAPTER 17

After two years they had evolved into something that could almost be called "comfortable." She knew a lot about him, his work, his dreams. And he was in tune with where she was coming from.

She had spent a number of weekends in his apartment in Los Feliz, and he had spent a few weekends in her Echo Park house. From time to time, under the spell "of a full moon." Or after a good Italian pasta and a few glasses of red wine, they would become more passionate than usual. But what did that mean?

He came up on her blindside-thinking, she's a fine sister, she's my "girlfriend," but am I in love with her?

"Good evening, Akos'."

"Oooh, Kojo, I thought I had missed you."

They embraced, held on to each other for a few hot minutes.

"C'mon, let's get away from this crazy place."

Getting away from the Los Angeles Airport was always a trip. He thought about the number of times he had picked someone up and spooled back into the circuit.

Night drive through Los Angeles

You have to be positive about where you're going when you pick someone up from L.A.X.

Kojo watched Akosua's handling of the traffic; she's heading toward my place.

O.K., let's get ready for that. Capoeira. She tripped him out with a tape of Mestre Moraes...Berimbau, Berimbau, soiel, soiel, soiel, soiel, ellll.

"Akos', thanks, that's a nice sound to come back to."

"I thought you'd enjoy it."

She drove fast, and skillfully, thrusting herself into quickly closing spaces.

The San Diego Freeway into the Santa Monica, to the Hollywood, off at Vermont.

The familiar seemed unfamiliar.

"Kojo, guess what?"

Slow down for the exit, lights twinkling everywhere....

"What?"

"I've just sold a book. Remember the monster I've been working on for the past year?"

"How could I forget it?"

"Well, I sold it to KOSMIC Muffin Publishing House, got a decent advance for it. They promised to give me the T.V. show interview, the prestigious news-book review, the whole banana...."

"That's great, Akos', really great. It'll be a treat to read about something serious for a change. How many is that?"

"My fourth. It looks like I'll go with Kosmic Muffin, they're talking about a three book contract. I like that. In addition, I'm dealing with a sister there who makes a lotta sense to me."

"I'm happy for you, Akos', really happy for you."

He placed his hand on her thigh and kissed her on the cheek, she stroked the side of his face. He settled back, enjoying the sensation of being on familiar turf. Los Angeles City College on the left. The Thai restaurant and the Jack in the Box on the right.

Santa Monica Boulevard. Santa Monica Place, across the small street that bordered Master Yong Kil Kim's Tae Kwon Do studio. Had a lot of weird fun in there, no doubt about it.

He felt he was photocopying years of sidekicks, hours of stretching and sit ups. Thank you, Master Kim.

Akosua stabbed affectionate glances at him, from time to time.

Kojo has returned, Kojo has come back to me. She didn't feel that it was something she wanted to shout to the world, but she felt it. As a writer, as a novelist, she felt that she could see into the future of their relationship.

I've given everything and demanded nothing. I've been his sounding board, and yes, his "whipping boy," when the occasion demanded.

I haven't been given the future-in-laws bit because I don't really think you've known what to do with a woman like me. It's a new ball game now, I think, let's see what the deal is.

Kojo was jolted and delighted to discover that he was in the perimeters of his own neighborhood. The car wash, where the Mexican dude made the best cheese tortas in the world.

Luigi's, the Italian restaurant with the Belizean woman who managed the place, and the singing waiters who could've been candidates for the Met, or LaScala.

The movie theatre, where the films, the real films, "Koyanisquatsi", and stuff like that shown, next to the bookstore and then the Skylight Theatre.

The Hiroshima Cafe next door to the bookstore and the theatre. The bigger Italian restaurant across the street, that specialized in big pizzas. **Biggg.**

The post office across the street.

"Akos', let's stop and have a glass of wine." A glass of wine, (and maybe a bite of Tiramizu), was always "Papa Milano." They could never figure out why "Papa" served these minestrone sized glasses of excellent San Antonio Burgundy.

And after the second one it didn't matter.

"Well, how do you feel. Are you glad to be back home, or what?"

Kojo stared at her for a speechless moment. Back home; coming back to America never meant coming back home.

It was more like a starting point than anything else.

"Hard to answer that, Akos'; in a way I don't feel that I was ever away from here. I think that's the effect you have when you realize you're surrounded by miles and miles of Black people.

On the other hand, you know you're somewhere else by the way people do things."

"Like what? I haven't been to the conti-nent yet..."

"Well, like...like the service we've received here, the minute we sat down; we may or may not have been served as quickly in Accra."

He could tell that his comparison story was registering, "proper" service be so quick in L.A., and so slow in Accra?

"But, hey, let's put the negatives on the back burner. There is no major league drug problem at the street level, yet. Babies are not being Uzi-ed to death in their cribs, extended family will support a *drone* for years, just because he's a member of the family.

People are polite, on a whole, the art is what African has always been. Young people do not go around dissin' their elders.

The society is serious. They're having problems putting it together, but they will overcome, I'm confident of that."

Papa Milano's was filling up, the after theatre crowd.

"I think it's time for us to go," she whispered in a low sexy voice.

4616 Rodney Drive. Akosua parked in a convenient space two houses away. Beautiful summer night, crickets chirping, the sound of Armenian music down low.

"Wowww, this is really what I call traveling light."

"That's the way I like it. Four pieces and a carry on bag."

They made their way up to his second floor apartment, feeling loose and tipsy from the wine.

"Enter, my lady, home sweet home…."

Kojo liked his apartment, the polished floors, the Persian carpets, the small, workable fireplace. He had furnished it very carefully over a period of years.

Two bedrooms; one for sleeping-dreaming, the other for work-study. Books on film, books about screenplays, books of screenplays, authorities on the media were arranged on wall book shelves.

Akosua browsed, Kojo dumped his baggage in his "study-bedroom" and returned from the fridge with a half gallon of San Antonio Burgundy and two glasses.

"You see, 'Papa Milano' ain't the only one with winery connections."

He flicked the draughtman's light down, made quick work of choosing, "Africa Brass," the Coltrane classic, and led Akosua by the hand to his low Danish-Modern sofa.

They sipped their wine, absorbing the music for a few beats.

"Kojo, have you contacted your folks?"

"Nope, not yet. But they know I'm here. They usually give me a couple days to settle back in before they start pulling at me.

If my guess is right, I probably have a couple messages on the machine now."

A few wine sips later Kojo stood and announced, with mock seriousness, "Akos', I haven't had a shower in a number of hours, I would deem it my very great pleasure if you would consent to join me. It'll conserve water, if you know what I mean?"

"Yes, I do know what you mean…"

She went into the bedroom to undress, Kojo left a trail of clothes leading to the shower.

He turned his back to her, pretending to be asleep. Of all things! Why me?!

"Kojo, listen to me, I know you're not asleep. Don't be depressed. Heyy, this is Akosua Ferguson, remember? Formerly Cynthia Ferguson, daughter of Negrocentric parents, etc.

You've just flown across the Atlantic Ocean, we've had a little too much vino, and there's no doubt in my mind that you have a lot on your mind. Plus jet lag... correct?"

He nodded, still unwilling to face her.

"O.K., let's cuddle up here and get a good night's sleep, for a change."

He turned to face her hesitantly... "Akos', I love you, do you know that?"

She looked stunned for a second, and pleased.

"You've told me a lot of things but you never told me that before. I love you too, Kojo."

They wrapped their arms around each other and, within minutes, had drifted off into a dreamless sleep.

He woke up and stared at the note pinned to the pillow next to him.

Dear Kojo, welcome home. I can't tell you how great it is to have someone I can talk with, joke with, make love to again.

Concerning the last mentioned; it happens to every man at some point in time, that's what my conservative papa once told me.

In any case, I don't believe in obligatory love making. We'll talk more about this at a later date.

Sorry I had to leave so early, but you know how it is when you have a day full of appointments, plus "lunch."

I'll hook up with you tomorrow, about six. If that isn't cool, call and leave a message on my machine.

Love, Akosua"

Kojo sat up slowly on the side of the bed, gathering his business together. Check the telephone messages, check my fax, start talking to the people I want to be in my company.

How am I going to handle Akosua? He didn't want to appear to be manipulative. Well, asking her to join my crew will place us on another level anyway.

Ten a.m. He brushed his teeth, made a pot of Jasmin Tea and sat at his kitchen table feeling powerful, sensitive, able.

Yeahhh, I'm going to put this bad boy together and fly. But first, I have to get back on my track.

He changed into his workout clothes and started out. What sense does it make if I have a million dollars and a bad heart?

"Morning, Kojo, I told Julia that I heard you come in last night. How was your trip?"

Frederick and Julia Chan, two of the best apartment house managers in the city. He had the feeling that his back was covered whenever he had to make a trip somewhere.

"It was stimulating, provocative, interesting, enlightening..."

"All of that, huh?"

"And more, I'll talk to you about it later, I'm on my way to do my workout."

"O.K., o.k., o.k., I checked the garage yesterday morning, to make sure your car was still there...hah hahhhah."

He waved him on and started his ten minute walk to Barnsdall Park. Walk west for ten houses and turn left onto Vermont.

The Los Feliz Theatre. Hmmm, a Norwegian film, that oughta be interesting. Luigi's across the street. The Thai restaurant next door. The espresso-Bohemian-Ancient Hippie-hangout.

The bank and across the street, the shopping mall.

This little neck of the woods has damned near everything. Up the hill to the park.

Barnsdall Park, with the art gallery and the Children's Art Center, the park placed on a hillside like a Roman villa.

A small field that he used for his Capoeira exercises, being careful of the dog shit that some of the park-dog-walking lovers left behind.

"Morning, Kojo, haven't seen you up here in a spell."

"Morning, Harry, I can't talk with you now, I got work to do."

"I understand... coff coff coff. . .I understand. Well, see you tomorrow."

"Yeah, take it easy, Harry."

Kojo smiled at his morning-park-acquaintance; Harry Hessler, with his wire-whiskered Schnauzers and a smoking habit that made him coff-coff-coff as though he were going to die any minute.

The others knew better than to disturb him, or they were so intent on their own thing that they didn't need to disturb him.

Harry, the gay couple who liked to stroll in the mornings, arms linked. The Yoga woman, who was apt to be found on the front lawn of the art gallery with her heels behind her head.

The bookworm who read as he walked his floppy eared Beagle. The joggers. The old Armenians who assembled on a picnic bench under an olive tree, looking dark and solemn. The artists, the man-woman combinations, the man-man combinations, the woman-woman combinations.

Rendezvous time. The Tai Chi guys. The beauty of a place that was in the city, but seemed to be in a different setting.

An hour later, sweating, he made a brisk walk back home, feeling loose and flexible.

Shower, shave and go into my business mode. It's all over for playtime.

"Playtime," that beautiful, almost silent film by the fantastic French comedian-Jacques Tati. The satirical things he did in that film, the sight gags, the timing, the sense of pace, the diversity of approaches to familiar happenings.

The man was a genius. I wonder if he's dead?

The 'phone was ringing as he entered his apartment. Well, here we go....

"'Morning, sleepyhead...."

"Oh, Akos', how is it, baby?"

"I'm fine, how 'bout yourself?"

"Well, so far so good. I just had a heavy workout, feels like I sweated out about ten quarts of toxins."

"I heard that. I gotta run now, just wanted to check with you..."

"Akos', about last night...?"

"We'll deal with that some other time. Are we on for tomorrow evening?"

"By all means!"

"Good, see you around six. Why don't you come to my place?"

"See you tomorrow."

"'Bye...."

O.K., got that settled, now...get down to business.

Dressed in T-shirt and tennis shorts, sipping orange juice, Kojo sat in his converted-bedroom-office. Computer, word processor, scanner, fax machine, VCR, DVD, cell phone on the table, all of the office gadgetry he needed surrounding him.

Messages on the phone, predictably from Mom and Dad.

"We know it'll take you a couple days to get your wind back, so...we've scheduled the family get together for Friday evening. Hope you had a wonderful trip."

He laughed aloud at the idea of "the family get together". That meant the Uncles, Aunts, Cousins, Granddad, extended family.

The other messages were not as joy provoking.

Producer's secretary: "Mr. Dryson would like you to contact him, concerning the possibility of doing a script for UTD, International, upon your return from Africa. Thank you.

"Sheila Buttram here, we've carefully studied your treatment and find it intriguing. Upon your return, please call me. I think we might be able to come to some sort of deal over lunch."

"Charley Bascom calling. Look, Kojo, I know this may seem to come at you from out of the blue but that's the way it happens.

We're very interested, here at Bascom Studios, in the possibility of you doing a six part series on the jazz greats of the forties, fifties and sixties.

If we like what you come up with, we can extend the thing into the nineties and beyond. O.K.? Gimme a jingle."

"Hello, my name is Jan Alborg of the film department of Copenhagen University. We are quite interested in doing a show of your twelve documentaries, beginning with "The African Influence in Polynesia.

We are prepared, of course, to make the necessary compensation for the exhibition of your works. In addition, if possible, we would like very much to have you present during the series to answer a few questions about the works.

We are willing to underwrite your expenses for the trip to Denmark and subsequent accommodations. Please contact us as soon as possible. Thank you."

"O.K., Kojo, time for you to go back to work, no sense running away to Africa, thinking you can avoid the inevitable.

Looks like we got a slot open for you, as assistant director for this feature that we're going to shoot in Brazil, starting... ohhh. . . about September-early October.

Beautiful story, boy and girl get lost in the jungle, raised by Indians, etc., etc.

According to your machine you'll be back in town by the latter part of June. Let's make contact and do lunch.

You got my number here at Paramount. O.K.? O.K.? Frank Goldstone here."

The racist bastard - "Beautiful story, boy and girl get lost in the jungle, raised by Indians, etc., etc., Tarzan again?

The boy and girl are obviously White and the Indians are just background material. They want to play "Tarzan" in as many forms as they can manage, 'til the end of time.

Like that horrible thing - "Dancing With Wolves" - the Kevin Costner monstrosity, with him as "Tarzan" on the Western plains. Where he becomes more of an advocate for Indian rights than the Indians.

He even found a White woman in the heart of Sioux land to be "Jane" to his "Tarzan." And many Indians loved it.

O well, I guess when you've been treated as badly as they've been, cinematically, anything that doesn't show them being shot down circling a wagon train seems like an advance.

Kojo tilted himself back in his chair, propped his feet on his desk, and sank into deep thought about the substance of the messages.

The Danish call was one that he could easily give himself over to. All of the others, including the treatment that he had submitted to the Sheila Buttram Organization, were going to blur his focus.

A script for Dryson. I would belong to Dryson, to UTD, International, for at least six months of outlines, treatments, first drafts, second drafts, third drafts. No, I won't touch that.

Sheila Buttram and company are going to think that I'm playing a little game for more money when I ask to have my treatment pulled out of the running.

Bascom Studios, Charley Bascom. Well, I know what that means. It would be a fight for artistic integrity from beginning to end.

He had had to deal with Charley Bascom in the past; once concerning a treatment that validated the continued existence of racism in the movie industry.

"C'mon, Kojo, you gotta be kiddin', that stuff went outta here in the sixties."

"No, it didn't."

And the second time dealt with Kojo's insistence that the late genius of the trumpet, Dizzy Gillespie, was not a clown, had not been a clown.

"Kojo, I don't fuckin' believe this! You're trying to tell me this guy was more than a fun thing?"

"I'm telling you that he was one the modern masters of what is called Jazz; a composer of immense depth, an incredible trumpet player."

"He was a clown, a jokester!"

"No, he wasn't!"

So now he calls me to do a six part series on the jazz greats of the forties, fifties and sixties and maybe up to the nineties.

I can just see us having fist fights now over the points of view...

He would say, "Bird was just a common junkie." "Diz was a "fun thing." "Monk was mad."

"Lester Young was a drunk." "Billy Eckstine wasn't a bandleader, he was a pimp." "Bud Powell was a schizo." "Coltrane was blinded by his own outrageous playing." "Miles Davis was a warped personality." "Billie Holiday was just a hooker."

No, I better leave this one alone. I don't want or need the headache, no amount of money is worth it.

That was the biggest consideration he had to make, whether the money would be worth his time. None of the gigs promised more than thousands. I need millions, not thousands, **millions**.

He laced his hands behind his head and stared out of the window. Just look at this, here I am, being offered deals that a lot of brothers would kill to get, and I'm saying no because I want to do my own thing.

He did a quick financial inventory; $18,000 in the bank, savings; $3,000 left in the checking account, $ 1,500 on hand, left over from his trip.

He had to smile at himself, for the nickname that a few close friends had laid on him, "Tight Wallet."

Well, I guess I'm not a typical 25-year-old, out to toot as much coke as possible, or see how many women I can impress. No, my thing is films, that's what I want to spend my money on.

$22,500. I can hang tough for a few months and, O what the hell am I worried about? My family would never let me starve, bottom-line.

But, would they be willing to support a man and his wife? No, I wouldn't want to ask them to do that.

CHAPTER 18

He unpropped his feet from his desk, grabbed a legal pad and ballpoint and began to put his organization together.

The first thing I need to do is write each one a personal letter, explaining what I want to do. And we'll go from there.

A mid-afternoon siesta had given him the extra energy to continue his organizational work.

It was 11:30 p.m time to study a movie before wrapping it up. He went to his video shelves.

Letssee here, what do I need?

"Dinner with Andre"? Brilliant piece for another night. "Moby Dick"? Whose joke were they playing? "From Russia, With Love"? Naw, too much glitz. "Blood and Sand"? Old freaky Tyrone Power...

"Gone With the Wind". When did I buy that? Why? 'I don't know nothin bout havin babies Miss. Scarlet.'

"Papillion". Dustin Hoffman, Steve McQueen...hmmm....

"Casablanca". Love you, Ingrid, but not tonight.

"Key Largo". Edward G. Robinson as Capone, Bogart.

"Treasure of the Sierra Madre". Bogart at his best.

"The Outlaw". That ol' big busted Jane Russell in Howard Hughes' western bra ad.

"Saturday Night Uptown". Shit with Travolta on it.

"Cotton Comes to Harlem". More shit with Redd Foxx to be in it.

"Harlem Nights". Even more shit.

"The Toy". Richard Pryor, how could you stoop so low? Well, I'm sure cocaine helped a lot.

"The Godfather". Vavavoom. Siciliano Negro.

"Five on the Black Hand Side". More shit than before.

"Suddenly Last Summer". Uh huh.

"Hud". Patricia Neal forcing Newman to sit up.

"Sweet Sweet Backs Baddd Ass Song". You killed 'em Van Peebles, you slick ass you.

"The Sun Also Rises". Errol Flynn playing himself

"Buffalo Soldiers". Yeah. Stiff stuff

"Pixote". Why couldn't they find a Black boy?

"Quilombo". Tudu Bem.

"Lambada". Floor sex, standing up.

"The Red Lantern." Polysex, Chinese style.

"Xica". Black Brasilian sex, from a White P.O.V.

"Mambo". Silvana Magano when she was the finest Italian actress on the scene, with Katherine Dunham furnishing the steps.

"La Strada". Poor Julieta Massina.

"Seven Beauties". Giancarlo GiannIni, the man with the most expressive eyes in the world, directed by Lina Wertmuller, one of the best.

"Mon Uncle". Jacque Tati. Merci Beaucoup.

"Under Milkwood". Saw that coming back from Home.

"Nothing but a Man". Ah hah, just right for me right now, a man doing what he has to do. Thank you Ivan Dixon!

He set himself up with a medium sized goblet of San Antonio Burgundy and settled in his favorite chair to watch what Ivan Dixon and Abbey Lincoln had to go through to remain together.

A real film about authentic African-Americans in 1945(?), in deepest Alabama, or is it Mis'ssippi?

After the Fade Out, he stared at the screen for a few long moments, feeling once again, gratified by the acting, dissatisfied with the length.

That movie should've been two hours long. We should see him go back with his son, to his wife, to racism, to see him become Medgar Evers the First.

He yawned and stretched. What am I doing? Taking their movie and making it my movie. Time to go dream a bit.

Kojo took pride in knowing how to care for himself, it was one of the things his Dad had always stressed while he was growing up.

"Kojo, treat yourself good. If you decide you want to drink Scotch, drink the best in the world. If you're going to be involved with a lot of stress, learn how to de-stress yourself in the wisest, healthiest way possible.

Always go for the gold, kid, anything less is second best."

A quick hot bath in a tub saturated with "Skin-So-Soft" and the beautifully cool white cotton pajamas.

Lights Out moonlight in. He folded his hands across his stomach and stared at a laughing quarter moon. The Dogon had astronauts in ancient times. No doubt about it. And what about the Tibetan walking monasteries — where they taught people how to walk across thousands of miles in a day? And the Peruvian landing strips that received extraterrestrial visitors, external planetary travelers. Who knows what the indigenous people of Brasil are doing, have been buried with..?...Asiafo?

The Aztecs, the Dogon, the Melanesians, people who could communicate with sharks. Polynesians, people who could move volcanoes from island to island, or insist that they not erupt before time…Pelé.

The Esquimo supermen, living on ice, eating snow, creating babies with "ice-picks." The Kalahari guys wandering around in two thousand mile circles, picking up ostrich eggshells of water that they had buried two years before.

The incredible Africans, who used to upset the world's financial patterns when they went on pilgrimages and decided to take some of their gold with them. What was his name? Musa Mansa?

Africa, I was just there, less than three days ago. He sat up in his bed, aroused by the thought, and slowly re-settled himself. I was on the "continent", the place where it all started, where the "First Family" kicked off, the place where **Everything** was first understood and overstood (as my Rastafari brothers would say it).

Ignore the personal stuff, so, Comfort became Comfort and Grace became Grace. Nothing important about that.

Well, what is?

Kojo squeezed his eyes shut and tried to see what was important.

Asiafo lit his darkness up like a candle, munching on a banana.

When he opened his eyes again, it was tomorrow. He blinked through the filmy veil that the Japanese call "eye cum", and stared at the sky. Bright, sunny morning. My second morning back in America. Time to do the Routine.

The Routine gave him a balance for the rest of the day. After the Capoeira in Barnsdall, the shower and breakfast, life was apt to be hectic, if not chaotic.

The thing to do is grab control of the tiger's tail at the top of the day. Is that an ancient proverb?

The first call of the day to Mom and Dad was loose, almost jolly. They were busy and he was busy and they had been to Africa several times.

"Kojo, save it 'til Friday, son, 'cause you know you gonna have to repeat yourself a half dozen times."

"You o.k.?"

"I'm fine Mom, everything is on track."

"Good, we'll see you tomorrow night."

How in the Blessed World could I have been gifted with a set of parents like that?

Round about Oludumare….

He sipped his orange juice and took a deep breath, exhaled slowly. 9:45 a.m., time to deal with the mo-ghouls.

"The name is Kojo Bediako Brown, yes, I'd like to speak to Mr. Dryson."

"Mr. Dryson is in a meeting right now, can I have him call you back?"

The Drysons were always in a meeting...

"Yes, please have him call me back as soon as possible. He has my number."

Meeting my ass, it's just purely a method of screening calls. O.K., who's next?

"Mrs. Sheila Buttram, please, Kojo Bediako Brown calling...."

He loved to use all of his names when he called the studios and production companies, they seemed to attach more importance to the call when they heard "Bediako".

Or is that purely my imagination?

"Kojo! Great to hear from you! When did you get back?!"

"Yesterday."

"Great! Great! Lessin! read your thing-wanna-do-lunch-with-you hows about tomorrow?"

"Tomorrow is good for me."

"Great! Mustache on Melrose? One thirty? After the Holly-Hollywood guys have done their thing."

"One thirty tomorrow is fine."

"Terrr-rific! See you then!"

He caught the beginning sentence of her next deal/involvement before her phone hit the cradle. That's the way it was. The Deal was the thing, nothing else matters.

Great! Great! Great! Terrr-rific! Terrr-rific! Everything was done in superlatives. Everything. If there was the slightest opportunity of Anything making money, it was Great! Terrr-riflc!

U.S.C. had been an invaluable university, in terms of understanding the Hollywood Mentality. Kojo felt capable, after his four year stint there, of dealing with all. Everything.

Goldstone. Forgot Goldstone.

"Frank Goldstone, please, Kojo Bediako Brown calling."

"One moment, please."

Wowww, I must be calling during a break in his sex life or something. Seconds later, Goldstone entered.

Kojo was tempted to laugh at the ultra cultivated mellifluous tone of voice, the fake atmosphere of quietude.

"Hi Kojo, great to have you back, guy. So, how was it over there?"

You couldn't sound more enthusiastic if you were asking about the quality of a pound of monkey shit.

"What can I say, Frank? Africa."

"Yeah, I know what you mean. Hold on a sec, gotta get this guy before he runs down to Palm Springs."

Kojo felt like hanging up on his interrupted call but had to cancel out the emotion. These are the assholes I'll have to deal with, in some form or fashion, in the future, can't afford to alienate anybody.

Eight and a half minutes later, Frank Goldstone's suave tones re-insinuated themselves back on the line. "Sorry, Kojo, just had to talk to one of those guys who doesn't wanna understand anything.... Now, then, we're talking about you doing a little assistant directing on "Emerald Jungle". Love that title. I think I pretty much gave you the complete scenario when I called..., couple kids lost in the vastness of the Brazilian jungle, raised by savage Jivaro Indians, you know, the babies who used to take heads...."

"Sorry, Frank, I'm not going to be available for this one...."

Kojo could hear the machinery of Frank Goldstone's mental factory shut down for five hard seconds.

"Other commitments, huh?"

"Wellyes, I guess you could say that."

"Oookay. . .but, look, if it's a matter of money..."

"No, Frank, not that, I know you're a generous guy. This just simply conflicts with another project."

"You don't have to explain, Kojo, I understand. So, we'll keep in touch. O.K.?"

"Yeah, Frank, we'll keep in touch."

Kojo knew that that was the last time he'd ever hear from Frank Goldstone. He had turned down the opportunity to participate in a Goldstone project. That was a no-no, a serious ticket to the minor-minor leagues.

He's probably passing the word now, don't have anything else to do with Kojo Brown, he's gotten to be a bit full of himself. The darker parts of his scenario were interrupted by his 'phone ringing.

"Mr. Brown?"

"Yes."

"One moment, please, Mr. Dryson calling."

A ten second pause for Dryson to slice through another call before getting to Kojo.

He took careful note of the measured tones, the deliberate effort to seem cool. Evidently they had all been counseled by the same P.R./psycho-speech teacher.

"Kojo, great to have you back. Now then, we're talking about a baby for UTD..."

"Sorry, Henry...looks like I'll have to pass on this one."

Once again, Kojo heard the machinery shut down for five hard seconds.

"Think we're gonna try to feed you peanuts, huh?"

"Uhh, no, it's not that..."

"Look, Kojo, I've got a meeting thirty minutes ago, why don't we take another look at this... say...Monday?"

"What I'm trying to tell you is...."

"Monday, say about ten-ish? Look, really great to chat with you. Looking forward to hearing about how many lions you killed 'n all of that. Take care."

"Yeah."

Click up!

Who did I miss? O yes, Bascom and the Danish deal.

"Mr. Bascom, please, Kojo Bediako Brown here."

"O, Mr. Brown, Mr. Bascom has been waiting for your call. One moment, please."

Been waiting for my call? Do I believe that I can fly? Do squirrels love bananas?

Bascom's voice, heavy grained from a past addiction to Camel cigarettes and shouting at people.

"Where in hell have you been, Kojo? I mean why in the hell would you wanna go over there? Who the hell do you know in Africa? That's o.k., don't tell me.

Look, lemme tell you why I called. Hold on a sec..."

Kojo leaned back in his chair, visualizing Charley Bascom, head of Bascom Studios, chomping on a Romeo y Julieta, growling like a Rottweiler at people, being tyrannical.

"Sorry, Kojo, just had to hand a sonavabitch his head to him. You know what I mean?"

"I have some idea."

"Now then, I'd like to arrange a get together to rap with you about the jazz series, my girl will give you a clear hour on my schedule..."

"Sorry, Charley, I'll have to pass on this one."

"What? What the fuck are you talking about?! We're talking about doing a six-parter on jazz greats of the forties, fifties, sixties, maybe the nineties!

What's with you, guy, you contact a little fever over there in the jungle?"

Kojo could feel the red anger rise in him, the kind of anger that made him feel as though his eyeballs were burning. This racist bastard....

"I wasn't in the jungle, Charley."

"Well, whatever. Look, I got a meeting. If you come back to your senses by tomorrow, gimme a jingle. Otherwise we'll have to go to Spike or maybe Johnny with this one. O.K.? O.K.?"

Kojo deliberately, gently replaced the phone in its cradle. Thank God I don't have to work with assholes like that anymore.

The letter to Jan Alborg, film department of the University of Copenhagen, was a pleasure to write.

"I'm available during the course of the coming month, August; after August I will no longer be available.

Many thanks to the film department of the University of Copenhagen for making the decision to deal with my documentaries.

I'm sure that our mutual experience will be extremely rewarding."

Now, onward to the hard letter writing. What the hell can I possibly say to a profoundly talented group of African-American professionals plus one Asian organization freak?

Dear Thelma, Dear D.J., Dear Phillip, Dear Sid, Dear Akosua (I don't have to worry my way through a letter to you. We'll talk...), *Dear Jackie, Dear Michael, Dear Ed, Dear Mac....*

Dear every damned body...I want you to be a part of a dream I've had for years. The idea is to come together and create an authentic African-American film era. We've come close, from time to time; I think Oscar Micheaux was the pioneer figure in that direction.

What I'm proposing that we do is start off with our own "Birth of a Nation;" yes, a silent film from our own perspective, and go from there.

We can bring it all the way down to the "Red Herring" days in Hollywood/ Washington, when Dalton Trumbo and the "Hollywood Ten", (or was it fifteen?), were hounded out of an industry where brothers and sisters hadn't even been thought of.

I was invited to a panel discussion, during my U.S.C. film school days, to deal with the effect of the loss of a number of very talented scriptwriters in the movie industry.

I almost caused a riot by "suggesting" that it would be ludicrous for me to be up in arms over the plight of some White people, (men, women), who had decided to defy McCarthy and the red baiters.

"Why should I feel anything for them, when my own people haven't been given the opportunity to write screenplays? During the era under discussion, ALL African-American writers were considered "communists" or "outcasts", or just simply "niggers".

As you know, we really haven't stepped too far from that kettle of fish. I'm not writing you in an egotistical way, the great Kojo trying to gather up his troops and all that.

I think you all know me well enough, (and we've worked with each other long enough), to know where my head is.

Someone has to do it. I'm doing it and I invite you to do it with me. I'd like to get together with you on the third Sunday in September, about 1 p.m. in the afternoon.

Looking forward to seeing you,

Bravely, Kojo."

He flirted with the idea of re-re-writing the note, cancelled it. What the hell, I'm not going to be able to say it any better.

Now, hope I've got everybody on the ol' Rolodex here.

Akosua flitted about the house, fluffing pillows, double checking her Brasilian stew, the Vatapá. Vatapá: chicken, shrimp, garlic, onions, olives, pimentos, coconut milk, love. She tasted a tablespoon of the seasoned liquid...

Akosua at home

Ahhhh, yes... and with this good French bread and this white wine.., amen.

5:45 p.m. Time to do a quick shower and put on something sexy. She literally danced through her house, tripping on Alice Coltrane's "Oludumare". The sister is baaddd. . .too bad they didn't really have the opportunity to righteously get it together, she and John.

The phone buzzing caught her off balance. Wonder who that could be? O well, they're calling at the wrong time, this evening belongs to Kojo, every minute of it.

She listened to the voice being fed into the message unit.

"Cyn. . . Akosua, this is your Mom. I'm just calling to remind you of our shopping date, Saturday. It looks like I'll be able to drag your father out of his easy chair to buy a new pair of shorts. He promised, at any rate.

We haven't seen you or heard from you in the past few days. Hope everything is alright. As you know, crime has reached epidemic proportions.

Your father and I were discussing the problem last night, and it's especially rough over there where you are, with those Latino gangs and all.

Well, that's it for now. Please don't forget Saturday, I'm looking forward to it. By' now...your Mother."

Akosua stood in place, allowing the message unit to click back into a receiving mode.

She hated her mother's voice, the nasalized whine of it. She had used that whine very effectively, for years.

She whined her husband into submission and tried to do the same with Akosua, and failed.

"Cynthia?"

"I'm not going to answer to that name again, Mom. My name is Akosua, and that's what I want you to call me."

"Well, awright, if you insist. But that doesn't have anything to do with you rejecting membership in the Young Republicans Club. It's prestigious, the connections you make will be invaluable and...."

"Mom, I do not want to join the Young Republicans Club. I don't want to have anything to do with those people, they're all crazy."

"Are you implying that your father and I are 'crazy'?"

"Of course not."

"Ako', I just don't understand you. We've given you the benefit of a superior education, travel, whatever you've wanted, and now you're turning your back on all of it. I don't understand."

"Maybe, someday you will. Or maybe you never will. I gotta run, got a date with a couple radical magazine editors."

Shower, splash the "Heavenly Skin Tonic" everywhere. Now, let me see here.., she pushed the mirrored door of her closet open and studied the contents. The red and black striped Harem pajamas. Yeahhh...

6 p.m., she carefully arranged herself on the wrap around Swedish sofa, sipping a chilled glass of Vouray, thumbing idly through Essence.

Her heart did a quick double thump, listening to him pull into her driveway. The chimes told her that he was on the front porch.

"Hello, Lover."

"Hi, Kojo."

He placed the bottle of Vouray that he had bought on the coffee table and folded her into his arms.

Groovy woman. That was one of the adjectives that sprang up in his head. Groovy, lush with her feelings.

"Mmm, what's that I smell?"

"Vatapá."

"O yeahh, the Brasilian thing. I love that...."

"Take the weight off your feet, I'll get you a glass of wine. O, I see you brought Vouray too."

"You know how it is, when Trader Joe's comes up with something good, you better grab it. Have you had the 'Shaw's Chardonnay'?"

He slouched on the sofa, feeling expansive, relaxed. A well chilled glass of white wine, a wonderful Brasiian meal, a beautiful woman...

The music changed from Alice to John and Johnny Hartman.

"You know something? That is really a treasure those two men put together. It has to be some of the most romantic music on earth."

"I must agree. C'mon, let's sit out back. The food will be ready in about fifteen minutes."

Kojo walked through the house, admiring the taste and elegance of the decor. The polished, hard wood floors, her bed-room/writing asylum.

"I stole that directly from you, Kojo."

"I'm glad."

The "out back" was ten-yards of sloping green lawn that made it seem as though the city's lights were twinkling at their feet. They had spent midnights and dawns "out back".

They sprawled on the round sofa-bed-deck chair, using the pillows to obtain better perspectives.

"Akos', this is beautiful."

"Yeah, it's what sold me on the house."

They sipped their wine and stared at distant points, thinking creatively.

"Kojo, you want to eat out here?"

"That'll be fine. Let me help you bring the table and chairs out."

Dining in the open, a sophisticated picnic. A bowl of mixed salad, a bowl of Vatapá, fragrant French bread. They ate like hungry people for a few minutes...

"Baby, you really put your little pinkie in this one."

The first edge of the appetite bitten off, they settled back to sip and dine at leisure.

"Kojo, I've been dying to ask you...what did you find that was most negative about being in Africa, in Ghana? Now please, don't get me wrong, I'm not after the negative, I'm after the balanced look."

"I know what you mean...."

He chewed thoughtfully for a few beats, sipped his wine.

"I think the most negative thing I can think of is the fact that our brothers and sisters over there don't know us. And they don't seem compelled to know us.

Ghanaian school children can give you the names of the House of Windsor, and the descendents. And what happened in 1066, in Britain.

But they are not taught anything about their, our Holocaust. It's as though there is a Black Hole that they can't see through.

When people my color are called 'White', you know something is wrong."

"They called you 'White?!'"

"I remember it from the first trip, but I was moving so fast, it didn't make any impression on me. This time it did.

It's when you find out that culture means more than color. We don't speak Ewe, Ga, Twi or one of the other hundreds of languages, we come from America, we have money, we must be 'White', that's our culture."

"Wowwwww."

"Yeah, that's what I said too. The thing that's scary about the whole thing is that the African is doing a crippling psycho number on his head, in order to dismiss the Diaspora, the genocide.

I can think of Africans, male and female, who are in such a denial mode that they are actually Eurocentric.

Believe me, I hate being forced to say something like that, but it's true. It's hard to say why it's true, so many factors involved.

Let me give you one example; all the women, even in rural villages, straighten and perm their hair. If you suggest that there's an element of self-hate involved with doing your hair like that, they'll deny it.

They don't really know what to make of us. I mean, in the African mind, the conquered/enslaved person is meek, subservient, docile. You see a lot of that kind of behavior especially around Lebanese.

Don't go to Ghana looking for your pride, there's a 90% chance you'll be taking more of it over there than you'll find there."

He paused to fork in a few mouthfuls of Vatapá. Akosua sipped her wine and looked pensive.

"You know, that's a far different picture than the one a lot of people paint."

"I know. A lot of the sisters and brothers get over there and begin to over-appreciate everything. If the lights go out for three days, that's romantic.

If the water stops flowing for a couple days, they excuse it by saying - well, too much efficiency is Eurocentric. Or some such crap.

I don't know about West Africa, as a whole, but Ghana could definitely benefit from our expertise. It's a hard thing to say to the people of your ancestral land, — hey, we've been in the belly of the beast, let us share what we've learned. I won't say all, but many Ghanaians would prefer being bullshitted by one Englishman, rather than have a dozen brothers show him the way."

"Are you bitter?"

"No, not really. I just feel it's an absurd situation and I wish they would come to themselves. You ever noticed the travel ads from Ghana? They never focus on African-Americans because they feel it will alienate the English, the Europeans.

Even the Jamaicans say - "come home, mon"... - the Africans never. That is, unless something has changed in the last three days."

Kojo paused to take a sip of wine, charged up. Akosua was the only person he knew who could clearly understand what he was saying.

"It doesn't sound promising."

"No, I guess not. Any time we have to line up behind Germans, Japanese, Lebanese and I don't know what else, as though we have no ancestral gene pool on the conti-nent...well, you know something is messed up."

"I never really thought about it like that."

She re-filled their glasses and stared up at the stars. Kojo, a little of the heat siphoned from his mind, stared at Akosua.

CHAPTER 19

"Akos', before it skips my mind, I'd like to invite you to a family gathering tomorrow evening."

She turned to him, fully aware of the implications connected with being invited to a "family gathering."

"Should I wear something special?"

"You could wear what you got on, if you want to."

They made simultaneous moves toward each other, their urges fueled by good vibes and Vouray.

"Ooh oh, let's take these things in first...."

"No problem. What's for dessert?"

"It all depends on you," she answered with a provocative smile.

Later that night, after having massaged each other with fragrant oils and made slow motion love for long minutes, they curled up in each other's arms.

"Akos', I want you to be my wife."

He felt her body stiffen as though an electric shock had passed through her system.

"Say that again."

"I said...I want you to be my wife, I want us to get married."

She was silent, hardly breathing for a few beats. "Don't you think this is a bit sudden?"

He stroked the side of her face and laughed aloud. "Hahhh hahha. . .I knew you would say that, I knew it!"

"And did you prepare an answer?"

"Yes, I did. My answer is...what've these past two years been leading to?"

He suddenly felt nervous, a bit uncomfortable with the idea of trying to "pitch" the idea of marriage.

"Kojo please don't misunderstand me. I do love you, you know that, but marriage is a Big step."

"I know, I know..."

The silence rang back in, thoughts trip hammering through their heads.

"Kojo, are you sure this is the time for us?"

"It's now or never." Was I a little too strong with that? Should I have softened it a bit?

"You sound pretty definite about this."

"I've never been more definite about anything in my whole life."

"Let me think for a couple days. O.K.?"

"It's the lady's choice."

They folded themselves together and gently slid off to sleep, each lulled by different thought patterns.

What if she turns me down, what if she says "No"? Who will I turn to?

I must not have a case of high self-esteem to think that he wouldn't want to marry me. Marriage? Mrs. Kojo Bediako Brown. No, Mrs. Akosua Ferguson-Brown.

So sudden. Maybe he found himself in Ghana.

We'd be a dynamite couple; hip, into all the scenes, creative, strong. Yeah, it's got to be Akos', ain't nobody else on the scene.

The lush Technicolor dream cued him into the tropical scene; he was back in "Sugar Cane Alley", on the island of Martinique, floating from one dream scene to another; absorbing the frank aromas of ripe fruit and under-odorized bodies. "Kric?" "Krac!"

He was the boy who sat in front of the old man, getting history lessons - "Kric!" "Krac!"

He was the singer of satirical songs, "What more does a stinking nigger need but more low paid work?"

He was the revolutionary plotting to free the island from the aftermath of French colonization.

He stretched and slowly opened his eyes. A bright, beautiful, wonderful, gorgeous day. Wish I could film the day, from opening yawn to closing yawn.

"Kojo, want some herb tea?" Akosua called from her kitchen.

"Let me have the rose-hips, that's what I'm in the mood for."

He smiled at her liquid laughter. What the hell am I talking about, getting married? Hell, we're already married.

He studied her approach to the bed with a tray of tea and toast. Akosua would not be the woman I'd have to hide from every morning. The thought came to him, midway through his second cup of tea.

"Ooohh, I blew it!"

"What?!"

"I had a date to "do lunch" with Sheila Buttram..."

"Buttram Enterprises?"

"One and the same. We were scheduled to meet at 1:30 yesterday but it completely skipped my mind."

"Maybe you can sew it back up."

"Nawww, I was going to get together with her to back out of a deal anyway. So, thus be it. I got another deal to back out of, come Monday, a thing with Henry Dryson."

"Wowww, you pick on the big guys, huh? And why, may I ask, are you backing away from the 'Gravy trains?'"

He took a long sip of his tea before answering...

"I'm backing away from their thing to do my very own thing."

She carefully placed her cup on the tray, placed the tray on the bedside table and crawled up into his arms.

"And I'm going to help you."

Kojo carefully wrapped each one of the small gifts in a piece of bright colored gift wrap, sealed them with scotch tape and artfully-draped a bit of colored string around the packages.

Five wari-boards for the math types, dozens of wrought metal figurines, a few gold rings, lots of earrings, Kente cloth scarves for the Uncles, a couple well done carvings for Mom and Dad.

Damn, glad that's finished, now let me check out the messages.

"Sheila Buttram here, what's the deal, Ko-jo, haven't you heard that it's impolite to stand a lady up?" Click.

The words were jocular but the tone was steel flaked. O well...too late to do anything about it now.

Click. "Charley Bascom on the horn. Say look, Kojo, it seems to me that we oughta start looking at the future here. If you turn away from doing this jazz series, a six-parter, what the hell are people going to think? Think about that!"

Yeahhh, Charley, I hear and understand your threat. If I don't come in under your wings, you can make things awfully cold for me. O.K., I understand.

Look at this, I haven't been home a full week yet and I'm on the threadmill.

"The Threadmillers," a play a friend had written ten years ago. "The Threadmillers" were anonymously garbed, shadowy figures who walked on conveyor-belt sidewalks, stage left and right.

There were short hoses sticking out from T.V.. sets placed at the head levels of "The Threadmillers," the White House was placed squarely at center stage and off to stage left was unmistakably an outhouse.

Periodically, the occupant of the White House walked the few steps to the outhouse. The minute the plumbing-flush was heard, the conveyor-sidewalks stopped and "The Threadmillers" rushed to suck on the hoses attached to the television sets.

"The Threadmillers" was never seen beyond ten rehearsals. Noplease, they'll never put me on "The Threadmill," not while I'm alive and kicking.

The morning Capoeira workout done, the beginning outline for the first film started, a pause for a glass of mango juice.

Akosua has decided to come in. Wonderful. Now, all we have to do is tie it up within the next few weeks, to honor my agreement, my obligation. My agreement with Asiafo. My obligation to Asiafo. If I want to get what I want. One of the oldest stories in the world, the man who sells his soul to the Devil in order to get what he wants.

Kojo shook his head no, no, I haven't sold my soul to anybody. I've simply made an agreement to get married, feed a stranger when "it" comes, (that means a lot of strangers are going to be well fed around here), and do my thing.

Maybe Asiafo is a film lover. Seems that he would be.

What do I say to the people I'm trying to pull into my club? They've heard it all, all of it, from A to Z.

I won't bullshit them, I'll just tell them straight up, here's the deal. Someone is bound to ask where the funds are coming from. I'll have to get there when we get there.

He went to the fridge for another glass of mango juice.

Akosua stepped away from her computer. No sense trying to be logical and sensible right now, I'm too excited for all that.

Kojo asked me to marry him and it took me less that a day to say yes. A nagging thought kept insisting that she should have prolonged the suspense.

No, that's something my mother would've done. O my God, mother...!

She strolled through her house and sat on the back porch steps. Look at the smog. We'll be wearing gas masks in a few years. Lovers will be committing suicide by leaving their masks off and standing up straight.

"But, Akoosu', we don't even know this young man. How could you even consider marrying him and your parents don't even know him, we haven't granted approval or anything."

The whining tone grated her nerves. Yeah, I can see it now. I guess I'll have to be the villain they think me to be, by telling everybody, as usual, kiss my ass, it's my life.

Why do I have to continue to fight for my independence from the very people who should be the first in line to grant me independence?

It's always a fight. Always.

"Akusa?"

"The name is Akosua, Dad, Akosua."

"Yes, of course. In any case, your mother and I are quite distressed at this move you're making."

"I'm buying a house in Echo Park, what's distressing about that?"

"Well, think about it. You're only twenty two years old, you're attractive, you'll be having visitors...."

"Male and female!"

"Please let me finish. I don't think you've considered all the ramifications...."

"Mom, Dad, look, I've considered all the ramifications I need to consider. I've managed, through a friend in a real estate office, to get my hands on a choice piece of property, dirt cheap, and I'm going for it."

"But what's going to happen to us? We'll be worried sick about you."

"You'll have my 'phone number. And remember, Leimert Park isn't thousands of miles from Echo Park. We'll visit each other when we have the time and energy."

Ms. Akosua Ferguson-Brown. Somewhat aristocratic I would say.

So, after two years, the brother is taking me to meet the family. I wonder what took him so long? I guess he wanted to be certain that I was "The One." Well, let there be no doubt about it...I am "The One."

A gush of egotism pulled her up from the porch steps. Guess it's time to get back in here and put this outline together for my next masterpiece.

"Well, how do I look?"

"Akos', you look absolutely gorgeous."

"You don't think this outfit is too...too colorful?"

Kojo smiled, watching Akosua whirl around nervously.

Sweetheart, you have no idea where you're going, do you?

The Friday night streets of Los Angeles, 8:30 p.m., passing by "downtown."

"You know something about EL-A? I'm always thinking that it's a collection of villages and shopping malls looking for a place to call itself a city."

She laughed, feeling gay, loose.

"For me, it has something to do with the lack of city "patriotism." There's no 'I left my heart in San Francisco,' or 'Chicago, Chicago' or even 'New York, New York.' It all seems to be about freeways."

"Yeahhh, that's about the size of it."

Kojo had written a treatment for a film about "EL-A,"... it's lack of cohesion, while he was in film school. He had placed the city in a surrealistic state, a place used as a dumping ground by other planets. Anthropologists of the future made frequent trips to study the monumental strips of concrete that stretched from here to there. The film review committee rejected it. He pressed for a reason for the rejection, as usual, and was told; "the project is too pessimistic."

A hip Capoeira tape to listen to, miles to go to get to Mom and Dad in Watts/Compton. . .South Los Angeles.

"Kojo, I didn't know your folks lived in Watts."

"O yeah, always, since we moved out here from Chicago. It's hard to tell if it's Watts or Compton, there's like a thin border here."

140th and Stanford, off of Avalon. . . South Central Los Angeles.

Kojo drove cautiously through the streets, making certain that he was within the speed limits. . . racial profiling

"You can't be too careful in this neck of the woods, you still have some maddog cops around who have Rodney King on the backs of their minds."

A short street, curving at the end, the family house tucked into the middle of the curve. They had to park on the next street.

"Looks like everybody's here. Akos', can you carry this small box for me?"

He reached into the trunk of his car and unloaded two fairsized boxes and a small one. They struggled with the awkward boxes up to the front lawn of the family house, when it seemed that the whole family rushed out to meet them.

"Kojo is here! Kojo is here!"

"Here, gimme that I can carry it!"

"Come on in! Come in!"

Akosua stood in the doorway for a few seconds, dazzled by the brightness of the scene. The huge front room was filled with relatives and everyone was dressed in one African fashion or another.

And I thought my light green and yellow was going to be too.. .too colorful.

Kojo smiled at her reaction to the scene.

There was African music backing the dancing, drinks passed around to the adults, warmth, joking, laughing, cheerfulness, good vibes.

Akosua turned from the scene to see a distinguished man who looked like Kojo's older brother embracing Kojo, and after his embrace, a statuesque, dark skinned woman with almond eyes.

"Akosua, I'd like you to meet my Mom and Dad, Mr. Kofi Brown and Mrs. Nzingha Brown."

"Welcome, Akosua, welcome. Please feel at home."

From that point, Akosua felt that she was about to be overwhelmed by the hospitality. First, she had to be introduced to every person in the house, beginning with Granddad Kwame.

"I'm very pleased to meet you, sir...."

"I'm even more pleased to meet you," the old man responded with a twinkle in his eye, and abroad wink to Kojo.

"Uncle Amen, Aunt Deborah."

"Uncle Kwabena, Aunt Rose."

"Uncle Kalo, Auntie Afiya."

"Cousin John."

"Cousin Ernest."

"Cousin Freda."

"Cousin Pokua."

"Cousin Asavia."

"Cousin Ewe."

"Cousin Fatima."

"Cousin Kwasi."

"Cousin Kalo."

"And there are a few cousins missing, they'll show before it's all over."

The flavor of the gathering became solemn for a few minutes when Kojo's father, acting as Granddad's okyeame, asked, "I'd like to have your attention for a few minutes."

The old man stepped lively into the center of the main room.

"I want us to form a circle here, around me, a big circle. Y'all know how to do it."

The circle was formed quickly, the music clicked off

"Now I want all in the circle to hold hands, I would like to say a few words and offer a prayer."

Akosua felt herself on the verge of tears. It wasn't Christmas, New Year's, nor were they in church, but the feeling was definitely sacred.

She found the contrast with her own family gatherings pale, distant affairs, in comparison to the togetherness she felt happening.

"I will make my remarks brief because I know how impatient younger people are these days. Impatient to do what I-don't-know. But that's the prevailing vibe."

Members of the circle smiled broadly as the old man slowly walked a slow, tight circle within the circle, seeming to direct his remarks to each member of the circle.

Kojo smiled and shook his head from side to side with good feeling. Granddad was so hip.

"I, as the oldest living member of this clan, would like to say...welcome home, Kojo..."

The relatives sang it out as a chorus - "Welcome home, Kojo."

"Now, I don't want anybody to misunderstand me, I'm not saying – 'Welcome back to America' - Kojo. I'm saying...welcome home, Kojo..."

Once again, the chorus sang out - "Welcome home, Kojo."

"I want us all to bow our heads in prayerful respect for those great spirits who are responsible for us being alive today, those wonderful men and women who refused to break under the cruelest whippings and the greatest tortures ever invented to crush the human spirit. I want us to remember the spiritual possibilities they left for us to feed on, the incredible reservoir of strength and determination they left for us to drink from.

I want us to repeat after me...we thank our Ancestors."

"We thank our ancestors."

"We beg our ancestors to hear our thanks."

"We beg our ancestors to hear our thanks."

"We praise our ancestors for having the determination to break **Out of slavery.**"

"We praise our ancestors for having the determination to break **Out of slavery.**"

"We beg our ancestors to continue to give **their spiritual strength** to our struggles, to cope with life in this foreign land."

"We beg our ancestors to continue to give **their spiritual strength** to our struggles, to cope with life in this foreign land."

"We promise to carry on and sacrifice for those yet unborn."

"We promise to carry on and sacrifice for those yet unborn."

"Now don't repeat this...think the most positive thought you can think for a minute."

For one minute there was only the distant sound of an airplane, the honking of a car horn, a dog barking.

"Now," the old man spoke again, "repeat after me... **Ashayyyyy**."

"**Ashayyyyy**."

Quietly and smoothly the music sequed in, the solemnity went to another level, the circle became pairs, duos, trios, people partying.

Akosua remained in place, looking stunned.

"Heyyy, what's happening, sweet thang?"

"Kojo, do you know how deep, how beautiful that was?"

"O yeah, Granddad can lay it on you. Come on, let's get something to eat."

Midway around the buffet table, father Kofi eased up to them, Holding Akosua's three published books. Akosua almost dropped her plate from surprise.

"Oh! my books?! Where did you get them from?!"

"Akosua, I'm a book store owner. I'd suspect that half the people in this house have your books. We're all readers."

"Sorry, I didn't mean to…."

"No problem. I'd just like to have you autograph these before Kojo sneaks you out of here."

"It'll be my pleasure."

The father slipped away as easily as he had eased up to them. Akosua suddenly had enough food on her plate, Kojo took note and nodded for her to join him on the patio.

"You see, we have an outback too."

A few people were strolling around, having quiet talks, a few of the cousins, male and female were there with boyfriends and girlfriends. One of the cousins came over to them, took their plates and led them to a small picnic table.

"Kalo, you're beginning to look more and more like Uncle Kalo every day."

"Yeah, that's what people tell me. What would you all like to drink?"

"Bring us a couple glasses of white wine."

"Hey, that's a good choice, Uncle Kofi just copped a case of Vouray from Trader Joe's."

Kojo and Akosua laughed with delight.

Akosua looked across the table into Kojo's eyes, feeling pure pleasure with the atmosphere.

"Kojo, I love your family. I adore your family."

"I thank you for that, me lady."

"Your wine, madam, sir."

"Thanks, Kalo."

"If you need anything else, just call."

"Hmmm, this is delicious, what is it?"

"Ground nut stew with fish. It is good, huh? One of Auntie Afiya's specialties."

CHAPTER 20

"Ground nut stew and white wine from France. Here's to your health."

Round about midnight, half the family gone, the other half sitting on the patio, enjoying stimulating conversation.

"The visual media will give us the final turning point in this country, and a deeper commitment to our own sense of spirituality."

"Kalo, I'd love to agree with you on both points, but I can only go half way. I agree with you about the spiritual thing, but not about the media. The media is only a facet of it.

What we have to do is create foundations loaded with money, organizations that fund, grant, fellowship for those of us who've been caught in the 'culture of poverty,' as one sociologist put it."

"But don't you see, Amen? The media blitz could open the door to that... what we have to do...."

"Schwarzenegger...."

Nzingha Brown signaled to Kojo and Akosua to follow her back into the house. The heat of the conversation, with partisan participation, waxed warm enough for them not to be missed.

She led them into the library.

"Hope you guys don't mind, but I felt like having a little non-family conversation..."

Akosua wandered around the large room, staring at the titles of books, six tiers of titles mounting three walls.

"See something you like?" Kojo asked her facetiously.

"I like it all. You must have the best collection of African-American literature, studies, whatever you want to call it, in the country."

"Well, you know how it is, if you own a bookstore, you have access to more stuff."

"I'm sure that's true, but do you know that this is the first time in my life that I've ever been in an African-American home with a library.

Don't misunderstand me, I've been in homes where there were books, but not a library, fancy homes too.

In most of the homes I can think of, the large, oak paneled bar was the centerpiece."

Mrs. Brown smiled, liking Kojo's lady.

"Well, we have one of those too. Can I offer you a little something? Cognac?

Don't worry, Kojo, I got you covered. A little Bristol...we have Milk, the Cream and the Directors Bin."

"The Bristol Cream is my favorite."

Akosua watched her future mother-in-law sweep past, a gold and sea gold and sea green caftan swaying majestically on her body, to open a corner liquor cabinet.

"Kojo, your mother is like a queen," Akosua whispered.

"Yeah, I know," he whispered back.

She poured cognacs for Kojo and herself, a Bristol Cream for Akosua, served them from a silver tray. They sipped their drinks in unison.

The room was walnut paneled, filled with strategically placed lamps, a sofa along one wall, four comfortable reading chairs, a desk and chair behind it.

Kojo Panned the room and sighed.

"I've spent a lot of time in this room, lots of time."

"It's a good room to spend a lot of time."

A polite triple knock drew their attention to the door. Kofi Brown peeked around the corner with a mischievous look in his eyes.

"I knew Nzingha had brought you two in here. The minute I looked around and didn't see the three of you, I knew. May I join the party?"

Mrs. Brown patted the cushion beside her on the sofa.

"I'm coming, let me pour myself a couple of tots."

He sprawled beside his wife, gave her an affectionate peck on the cheek.

"I hope y'all are not talking about the same things they're talking about on the patio."

"No, Dad, we were just about to talk about me and Akosua."

Mrs. Brown leaned over and playfully pinched her son's cheek.

"You rascal you!"

Kojo smiled, fending off her attack. "Well, isn't that why you invited us in here?"

Akosua loved the interplay, the naturalness of the mood within the family.

"Now, c'mon, Kojo, you know your mother wouldn't do no such thing as that...."

"O.K., guys, o.k., so, I'm a manipulator, huh?"

"O Mom, don't take it like that."

"Yeah, Nzingha, don't take it like that, just come on out and say - I've got to get to know this charming, beautiful young woman that Kojo has brought home. And a writer to boot."

They laughed at father Brown's gentle sarcasm.

"Well, what's your excuse for being in here?"

"I wanted to get to know this charming, beautiful young woman that Kojo has brought home. Who's also a writer."

The vibe was loose, warm, loving. Akosua laughed harder than the other three.

So, this is what the Brown family is like....

"What's your family like, Akosua?" Mrs. Brown slid in on a light tone with a heavy question. Akosua looked at the couple in front of her, reached over to hold Kojo's hand.

She suddenly felt a bit shy. It was an honest question that demanded an honest answer.

"Well..." she smiled at their open expressions. They were obviously saying - speak, if you like. Or don't speak.

"Well, to begin with, coincidentally, we have a nuclear family just like this — father, mother, me. And there is the end of any other kind of resemblance.

O, I have relatives out there. An aunt on my mother's side that I talk to about once a year. She's in New Orleans.

And my father's oldest brother in New York and cousins scattered here and there. But I couldn't really call us the Ferguson family, not in the sense that you guys are family.

I don't want to make it sound as though I'm running anybody down, but I have to be honest about this.

We have collections of individuals and they're not warm to each other, they're not...."

Mrs. Brown reached for her sherry glass.

"Kojo is driving, so I can top you off O.K.?"

Akosua nodded thank you and wanted to continue, to unburden herself

"My family isn't supportive, spiritually. Yes, I have to say that I've been well taken care of, materially. Dad's an architect and Mom owns four boutiques. Two of them are in Beverly Hills."

Mrs. Brown raised her eyebrows. Beverly Hills....

"But they haven't been supportive of the inner me, the creative me. Mom has been after me to join the Young Republicans organization...."

Father Brown whistled through his teeth. Kojo's jaw dropped and Mother Brown took a healthy swig of cognac.

"But what about your writing? You're one of the finest in the country. And I'm not just saying that because you're here either."

"Thank you, Mr. Brown, I really appreciate that. But we've always had a snag there too. Mom has always felt that my books were too much involved with people "living sinful lives." And Dad felt uncomfortable about a girl calling that much attention to herself. It's been, as the saying goes, an uphill struggle. But, above and beyond everything I know they love me and I love them too."

A silently collective sigh seemed to be released in the room.

"Now then, if nobody has any objections, I'd. like to switch the subject to something a little more romantic...."

Three curious faces turned to Kojo. He played with their attention artfully for a full ten seconds.

"Akosua and I are going to be married. She is going to be my wife."

Kofi and Nzingha Brown turned to each other and embraced, and then exchanged hugs with Kojo and Akosua.

Father Brown jumped up and started out of the room to shout the news.

"Dad! Dad! no, no, not yet, they'll know soon enough. I just want to keep this with us for the time being."

"Whatever you say, son."

He freshened his drink, reseated himself next to his wife. The air of the room was suddenly glowing with electrical feelings.

Akosua looked stunned by the announcement.

So, this is what it feels like when the favorite son tells his mother and father that he's going to marry you. Woww...

"You two set a date yet?"

"Not yet, Mom, but it'll be soon."

"I'm very, very pleased with your choice, Kojo, I'm sure you know that, or else I would say so."

"I know you would, Mom, I know you would."

"And I'm glad to be able to say we can look forward to some grandchildren before we get too old to enjoy 'em."

There was a sudden, awkward, pregnant pause, as though nothing else could be said. Kojo decided to work them through it.

"Mom, Dad, I think the fat lady has sang...."

They stood and did another round of embracing.

"It's getting late and...uhh...."

"My goodness, it's 1:30. I didn't know it was that late."

They strolled out of the library to find a deserted house, save for a few cousins doing after party tidying up.

A few last embraces and Kojo had artfully steered them to the front door.

"Kojo, keep us up to date on things. O.K.?"

"Yeah, Mom, will do."

"Remind him, Akosua, you know how we men can be at times."

"Don't worry, Mr. Brown, I'll do my job...."

"Hahhh hahh that's the spirit, sweetheart, that's the spirit."

"'Bye now."

"'Bye."

Kojo and Akosua linked arms and strolled to his car, each humming a nonsensical little tune.

They sat in the sand near the Hermosa Beach Pier, staring at the great black horizon, punctuated by single spots of light.

"See, that's what's been bugging me for a long time, the media emphasis, the racist emphasis on the dysfunctional African-American family. They almost never popularize my type of family."

"You got that right. That was one of the sore points we had, this first publisher I had for "Stolen Souls.""

"That was your first one, right?"

"And then, "The Newest Tribe," "The Chosen Folks" and now "Outlaws." O Kojo…"

"What is it? What?"

"I forgot to autograph your father's books."

"Awww, don't worry about it, you can drop into the bookstore any time. You were saying…?"

"Yeah, about my problems with my first publisher. He tried to get me to slant things that way, you know, make it seem like the dysfunctional African-American family, the aberrant relationships some African-American men and women have with each other is just simply an element that's always been there.

There's supposed to be no pre-life, no catalysts, no motivating factors, nothing. It was just in us to be messed up."

"Yeah, they never want to deal with how much they messed us up."

"I guess that would force them to deal with how much they messed themselves up; men having babies with their daughters, raping their mothers, selling their sons, having babies with babies."

"I read that book too. It was some sick shit happening back then, no doubt about it."

The glitter of the moon on the water's surface, a shimmering dance took him back to Africa for a minute.

If I were in Ghana I could marry Akosua and Grace. The thought held him captive, made him smile.

"That nice, huh?"

He moved closer to her and wrapped his arms around her shoulders. "Yeahhh, that's nice."

They kissed, tuned to the soft lapping of the ocean against the pier pilings.

"I think it's time for us to go home."

They stood and brushed the sand from their bottoms, started plodding through the sand. Kojo turned to stare at the face of the moon. It seemed to have a sardonic look on its face.

Am I marrying this woman because I really love her, or is it because of something I want?

Am I marrying her just because of the agreement I made?

Before they reached the car he was reluctantly forced to admit, to himself, that he wouldn't have asked her to marry him, had it not been for the agreement.

I'm sure I would've asked her to marry me, eventually. The thought that he was, to some extent, using her to further his own ends, made him feel vaguely ashamed.

10 a.m., Saturday. The lushness of the film's multiplied looks at the human psyche swirled around in his head, made him blink in his sleep.

Some would prefer Bergman, I know, with his Swedish angst, but I'll take Fellini and his "Juliet of the Spirits," "La Dolce Vita" and "8 1/2" any day.

Julieta Massina, Marcello Mastroanni, the incredible faces that he used to make his points, the fearless ways he had of probing through the emotional layers, of making people reveal their inner selves.

I bet Sophia Loren probably became an actress under Vittorio de Sica's direction. Interesting thing about the Italians, their movies, when they're good, are as complex as their food, filled with different spices and flavors.

I wonder if there is a Northern style of Italian film making and what might be considered a Southern style? And who would be most representative of each region? Wonder what Roberto Rossellini would be doing if he were alive now? "Paisan" and "Open City" gave us something to really feast on, but mainly because of Anna Magnani; I think he slipped badly with "Stromboli."

Maybe it had something to do with the number he played with Ingrid Bergman, getting her pregnant and all. That must've really been a Biggie back then, the crystal clean Swedish actress who had played a nun in "Bells of St. Mary's" getting pregnant by a greasy headed wop.

I think she had twins too. Or was that the second time around? Have to check out my film history book for that one.

"Oh! I almost forgot!"

Akosua popped up to a sifting position startling Kojo from his film revelry.

"Hey! What's wrong? What happened?!"

She was already reaching for the bedside phone.

"Just remembered...gotta date to go shopping with my mother this morning. She probably started calling my house at 8 o'clock this morning to remind me.

I can just imagine the conversation she's having with my father now..."I've just called Cynthia"...I'm sure that they use that name when I'm not around, "and she's not at home. She must have stayed out overnight somewhere."

"Mom, this is Akosua, what time are we getting together?.... Yes, I know you called. I have the message on my machine. I had some errands to do this morning...I thought it would be a good idea to get that out of the way before we got together.

Well, mother, you didn't actually set a time, we agreed on Saturday. Yes, mother, I understand all of that, but we didn't set a time frame. I'll be there at 11:30. No, I can't make it before then. No, mother, I can't...it's 10:15 now. Mother? Are we going to talk all morning or what? Good. See you in a few minutes. 'Bye!'"

She hung up and looked at Kojo with a sad expression in her eyes, as though to say - see what I have to go through. Kojo smothered her in his arms and trickled little kisses from her ear to her neck.

"Heyyy, you better stop that or else there will be no shopping done on this particular Saturday.

Kojo reluctantly released her, feeling for her. Damn, what a bitch it must be to have parents like that.

He listened to Akosua hurriedly prepare herself for her ordeal; toothbrushing, quick shower, makeup, dressing.

"Kojo, think I could persuade you to run me over to my place to pick up my car?"

He was already sifting on the side of the bed, waiting for her summons.

"Why don't I just drive you straight over to your parents?"

"If you did I would be in my mother's tender talons all day long. In my car I'll be able to call the shots. You know what I mean?"

"Yeah, I guess so," he mumbled and shuffled off for a quick shower.

They traded a quick set of kisses in her driveway. And then another quick set.

"Kojo I had a beautiful time last night, thank you."

"I'm sure that we'll have many, many more of them."

"I'm looking forward to it. When will I see you again?"

"Any time, I'm going to be dealing from my own turf for the next few weeks, with little ends and outs, from time to time."

"Call you tomorrow."

"Good. Akos', one last question before you go. You know I've been hearing you talk about your parents, your mother and father, for two years and I've never heard their names."

"Harvey and Minerva."

"O, I see."

He watched her race up the steps, dash into the house to change her dress into purple slacks and dash back out, waving to him as he backed out of her driveway.

Poor baby. Imagine, being obligated to go shopping with your Mummy and your Dada. And all the rest of the stuff she's been trying to break away from.

And these are going to be my in-laws? The idea jarred him for a moment. Looks like I got work to do.

Saturday morning, I got my tennies and sweats on, think I'll jog the track up in Griffith Park a couple times.

Yeahhh, bro' Kojo, looks like you have work to do.

Akosua turned up the street leading to her parents' palatial home, feeling irritable.

Why should I have to go shopping today? I could've spent the day with my man, doing a picnic in the park or something.

O well...guess I owe them a little time, I haven't been over here since last week. If only my mother weren't so...so manipulative.

"Cynn...Akosha! come on around, we're having coffee on the patio."

Akosua started up the long driveway that fed into a three car garage, gritting her teeth.

"Akosha." Why can't they learn how to say my name correctly? They can pronounce every Polish name, every Greek name, every foreign name in the book, but they don't seem to be able to manage "Akosua."

She turned the corners and took in the yards and yards of rolling green back lawn, her mother and father seated at their filigreed-iron breakfast table, being served by Dolores, the Mexican maid.

She strolled onto the patio, dutifully pecked her mother's cheek, her father's cheek and sprawled in a chair opposite them.

The very picture of a successful, urbane couple. Dad, with just the right amount of grey at the temples, in good golf shape, rather handsome in a rough cut way.

Mom, neatly built, always immaculately curled and manicured.

"So, you finally made it," her mother spoke sweetly, but the undertone was accusing.

"Yes, I finally made it."

Mr. Ferguson smiled benevolently and sipped his coffee.

"Coffee smells good. Ola, Dolores, un taza de cafe, por favor?"

"Si, Senorita." The maid beamed at her. She was obviously her favorite Ferguson.

Mr. and Mrs. Ferguson frowned.

"Sweetheart, why must you insist on speaking to the help in such a familiar way?"

"Mom, Dolores has been in this house for ten years. Don't you think we should be somewhat familiar with each other by now? I don't think it hurts to speak a little of her own language to her...."

"Now, now, you two, let's not start off our Saturday with an argument," Harvey Ferguson broke in with an attempt at gruff humor. His wife cut a sharp eye in his direction.

"Gracias."

Akosua sipped her coffee, mentally measuring and comparing the differences between her parents and the scene she had been a part of, the night before, with Kojo and his family.

I don't think I've ever had a good time with my mother and father. Maybe it's my fault, maybe I've always expected too much, or I was asking for something they didn't have?

What are they going to say when I tell them about Kojo? The thought made her smile.

"So, when are we going shopping and for what?"

Akosua felt like withdrawing the question. It seemed to convey the feeling that there was no need to go shopping. For what? They had everything they needed already.

Her father answered, "Well, your mother and I have decided to do a little cruise to the Caribbean next month...thought we'd pick up a few cruise things."

"That's great, you guys deserve a break. The Caribbean? That ought to be fun."

"It will be," her mother said, grimly, and stood. It was Time.

"Mom, Dad, I'll drive. It'll give you guys a better opportunity to focus on what you want."

Mrs. Ferguson saw through her daughter's ploy immediately. If you drive, we'll have to measure our time by your clock. And you'll leave us as soon as we return home.

"Sounds great to me. Minerva, you ready?"

"Let me get a scarf."

Crenshaw north to Wilshire, (because Mrs. Ferguson hated being on the freeways), west on Wilshire into Beverly Hills.

"Akosha, first thing I have to do is stop at the boutiques for a moment or two. Sylvia wants to talk to me about this new line that the Japanese want to bring in."

"Akosha." I'm going to have to straighten her out before the day is over, again.

She looked up into the rear view mirror at the aristocratic looking brown skinned woman, pointing out people, places and things to her indulgent spouse.

"Which shop do you want to stop at first?"

"We're closest to "The Latest," let's go there."

This was the one area that Akosua felt thoroughly impressed by her mother. A Black woman who owned two successful boutiques in Beverly Hills, one in the Valley and one in Malibu.

"I've always wanted to deal in fabrics, hats, jewelry, that sort of thing...."

The sore point between them is that most of the employees in all four shops were White.

"Akosha, there's nothing personal in this, I just try to get the best qualified people to run the places. Which makes my job so much easier, don't you see?"

"The Latest."

"Ahhh madam, you are here."

Akosua followed her mother and father into the glass panelled shop, ("women like to look at themselves"), concealing the urge to sneer at the manager.

The manager, a middle aged, very svelte Jewish woman from Cincinnati, pouted a French accent that was obviously gleaned from French movies.

Akosua idly fingered her way through a rack of dressing gowns, peripherally studying her father, who had settled into "the waiting chair", as her mother and the manager huddled over a sheaf of papers.

The old girl must know how to do something right. She's worked out a situation that allows her to do a round robin of her shops once a week and, so far as I know, she isn't losing any money.

Forty-five minutes later they made a similar entrance at "The Place." A carefully developed operation, managed by a woman who resembled a sophisticated mannequin.

"Mom, did you say something about shopping?" Akosua whispered in her mother's ear after thirty minutes of going over figures, costs, outlay, overhead and a dozen other items with her manager.

Once again, Akosua studied her father's actions. He must be one of the world's most patient people. Over the years she had watched him wait.

Wait while her mother, his wife, tried on shoes, wait for his wife to get home from a meeting. Wait...wait.

Well, I guess that's what you do if you're a wealthy, semi-retired architect with an ambitious wife.

"Harvey, Akosha... shall we? Monique, I'll call you tomorrow to give my final word on this matter."

"Yes, Mrs. Ferguson."

Akosua had to smile, following in her mother's wake. What a dictatorial ol' bitch she is.

After an exhausting three hours of watching her mother try on dozens of exotically shaped straw hats, sunglasses, beach jackets and sandals, Akosua was beginning to feel a deadly sense of boredom.

Guess I must've taken after my Dad. Look at him, he's bought himself two pairs of gaudy shorts and a pair of Mexican sandals and he's ready to go back home.

"Mom, you think you have everything you need for your Caribbean holiday?"

"I think so, for the moment. Harvey, you promised us lunch, remember?"

"I did?"

CHAPTER 21

"Yes, you did, darling. Don't you recall?"

"Oh, yes...I did promise you that, didn't I?"

Akosua concealed a grim frown. So, you've done it again. Shopping all morning and then you grab me up for most of the afternoon, knowing that I would rather be at home working. Or sleeping. Or doing anything rather than this.

Ma Maison. Yes, of course, <u>she would</u> want to come here.

"Table for three, please."

"Yes, Madam."

Akosua felt uncomfortable in Ma Maison, all of the Ma Maisons. A lot of pretentious crap. Women, in large floppy hats, seated behind tall stands of ferns, everything white and glistening, expensive.

"Order whatever you like Akosha, it's on your father...hah hah hah."

Akosua slammed the oversized menu closed, placed it carefully on the table and stared daggers into her mother's face.

"Mom, I don't know why I have to continue to tell you how to pronounce my name, it's Ah-ko-su-ah. Now please repeat it after me... Ah-ko-su-ah."

Minerva Ferguson looked as though she wanted to slip under the table.

"Akosua, please, you're embarrassing me, people are listening," she whispered.

"Good, then they'll know how to pronounce my name too. What're we having here? I think I'd like to start with a glass of the overpriced white wine. Garcon!"

Harvey Ferguson had, as usual, concealed himself behind his menu during the exchange between his wife and daughter.

Akosua felt the neat little thrill of knowing that she had pulled the right card to trump on her mother. She loves to be seen in the White places, to pretend that she's White and she wants me to play the little game with her. Bullshit.

I wonder what the hell happened to her, to make her the way she is? Look how intimidated she is by the waiter.

She can employ White people, tell them what to do and how to do it, but the minute she goes social she begins to kiss their asses.

"Harvey?"

"Yes, Minerva?"

"You're not saying anything, how is your steak?"

"It's delicious."

"Good. Ah-ko-su-ah?"

"The shrimp is wonderful, Mom, wonderful, just the way I like it, hard and rubbery, with just a dash of stale mayonnaise...."

Mrs. Ferguson stared at her daughter, wondering for the umpteenth time, what in the world happened to her? Maybe it was a mistake to allow her to go away to school.

Maybe if we had kept her closer to us, instead of allowing her to go down south to school, to be amongst all of those radical Blacks.

"Oh, I can see that you're joking."

"Yes, I'm just joking, Mom, just joking."

They shuttled their forks of exquisitely prepared goodies into their mouths, each of them absorbed by a different vibe.

Mrs. Ferguson nodded super-pleasantly to the people at the next table, seemingly to assure them that they were well mannered colored people who knew how to act in Ma Maison.

Akosua sipped her second glass of Pinot Chardonnay, wondering why her mother felt compelled to be liked by Whites.

Harvey Ferguson made long work of a palm sized piece of half done meat, trying to avoid everything.

"Someone you know, Mom?"

"Who?"

"The people at the next table."

Mrs. Ferguson pursed her lips at her daughter, clearly on the verge of saying something sharp, but was blindsided by the arrogant waiter.

"I trust everything is satisfactory, Madam."

"Oh, it's wonderful. I love dining at Ma Maison, the food is always superb and the service. There is such an ambience..."

Akosua studied the man's impatient expression. C'mon, Mom, give the guy a break.

"Ahhh yes, of course, madam...please excuse me."

Look at her beaming, as though she has just finished talking with a Biggie or something. In this day and age...unreal. My own mother, coming off like a high tech Aunt Jemima.

"Minerva, wonderful idea to come here. What're we having for dessert?"

"They have these marvelous little tarts, remember? You had two of them the last time we were here."

Akosua frowned as her mother turned a super-pleasant smile on a super-sophisticated looking couple passing their table. The couple looked at her with jaded blue eyes and didn't return her ingratiating smile. Good. Maybe you'll stop trying to make White people like you.

God, what the hell is it going to take to jar you out of this White love bag?

Who knows? Maybe it's terminal.

Why not now? What the hell!!

"Mom, Dad, I'm getting married."

She almost laughed aloud, watching their jaws drop in tandem. They were silent for a long beat. Surprisingly, she thought, her father started the questioning.

"Anyone we know, dear?"

"No, not really. You've heard me talk about him I'm sure, brilliant filmmaker-director...."

"What's his name?"

"Kojo Bediako Brown."

"Oh, an African."

"No, Mom, an African-American like me."

They diced through their tarts, completely upset and distressed by the news.

"How long have you known this person, Ah-ko-su-ah?"

"A little over two years.

"And you've never brought him home, never given your parents the opportunity to know him. Does he come from a good family?"

"The best."

Harvey Ferguson finished his tart and settled back in his seat, stared at a point above Akosua's head. Mrs. Ferguson couldn't finish her tart. She didn't know whether she wanted to slap her daughter's face or throw her tart at her.

"Well, I assume we'll have the opportunity of meeting the young man before you two elope. Have you set a date yet?"

"It'll be soon."

"Does that mean...it'll have to be soon or just soon?"

"What're you asking me, Mom?"

"Are you... are you pregnant?"

"I don't think so, but I won't know 'til next month."

She was amused by the drained expression on her father's face.

"Harvey, why don't you pay the check?, I don't think Ma Maison is the proper place to discuss our daughter's affairs. Why don't we go home and...?"

"Sorry, Mom, not today. I'm going to drop you guys off and go on back to the drawing board. I have a book to write."

Once again Akosua took note of her mother's pursed, disapproving mouthset. The woman ought to be an actress, she knows how to form expressions.

"Well, when would you suggest we get together to discuss this matter? You are, after all, still our daughter."

"I know, I know. Why not Monday or Tuesday? Tuesday is best."

"Perhaps you could persuade the husband-to-be to come with you."

"I'll try, Dad, I'll try...."

She watched her father spool out two one hundred bills and receive five dollars change.

Bullshit. Pretentious bullshit.

Kojo stared at the screen, watching the credits roll past. "Guess Who's Coming to Dinner?" God, what a joke. It would be comical, if it weren't so sad to think that a beautiful brother like Poitier had to wade through all of that crap.

Imagine, they had to give the brother international credentials just to have a relationship with an ordinary White girl, who seemed to have no credentials at all, beyond being the daughter of Katherine Hepburn and Spencer Tracy.

O well....

He took the salad bowl and orange juice glass to the kitchen, placed them in the sink, slowly revving his mind up for the evening's work.

The phone buzzing startled him.

"Kojo, this is Thelma."

"Thelma, you got my note..."

"Got your note, will be there on the third Sunday in September. O.K.? So, how've you been?"

"Great, just got back from Africa."

"O.K., see you on the third Sunday. 'Bye!"

He smiled, placing the receiver back in the cradle.

Thelma Nagata, pure business, a real no nonsense type. That's exactly what I need for an office manager, an unemotional straight shooter.

He returned to his office-bedroom, huddled over the legal pad on his desk.

"A silent film, Mr. Brown...?"

"An African-American silent film, there's a difference."

"I'm sure there is, but don't you think it's a bit retrogressive to think?..."

"No, I don't think that at all. I think that the American film/movie industry overlooked us, except in the most negative, stereotypical, during the White silent film era.

I want to do a series of films, starting during the silent era, that will take us through the years, utilizing an Africentric P.O.V."

"Sorry, Mr. Brown, I'm afraid the committee will have to veto this one."

"Just like you vetoed the last one, and the one before that...."

"Mr. Brown, perhaps the committee could see its way clear to fund one of your projects if they were less esoteric, more mainstream, you might say...."

"You mean - Whiter."

"Good day, Mr. Brown."

Kojo leaned back in his chair and smiled at the memory.

I bet they were glad to see me get out of there, the "troublesome Mr. Brown."

The buzzing phone stirred him away from his revelry.

"Hello."

"Kojo, my brother, my brother, my brother...yes, I received your note this morning and I'm down for all the action. All of it."

"I'm glad, D.J., I'm glad. You know we can't pull it off without the camera man."

"I know I know I know. So, third Sunday in September, at one o'clock, huh?"

"On the dot."

"Cool, I'll be there."

"Later, D.J."

"Yeahhh."

Good...they were coming in, the cream of the crop that Hollywood neglected or treated so shabbily that they never felt any loyalty to the mega-studios.

Our own "Birth of A Nation", four films, five films that would take us through the film eras that the Whites went through, dealing with African-Americans from our own perspective, if we had had control of our image during those years.

From African slave (a rebellious, hard headed, clear minded lot, who understood what they were up against, and bit the bullet. The Denmark Veseys and Nat Turners and Sojourner Truths. Why have we never had films about these heroic figures?...Henry "Box" Brown, others).

To Colored - to Negro - to Black - to African-American. FADE IN.

The series would be honest, stimulating, thought provoking, **edu-taining**. The key word is **edu-taining**, a word I've coined to indicate that we are not simply about the business of brow-beating a film going public with loads of historical facts. The facts will be there, as a seminal element of the exciting stories that will be told.

Kojo dropped the ballpoint and massaged his knuckles. This is the hard part, laying it out so that everyone will be able to see it and understand it. African-American satire. Authentic African-American comedy, not the canned stuff they put behind some cardboard figures.

271

Drama, real drama, not "Raisin in the Sun" forever. As good as it was, we've passed the era long ago, of wanting to move into somebody's White neighborhood.

A facsimile of a few of our geniuses. The Real McCoy, the doctor who first did the heart operation, the woman who owned a good piece of San Francisco at one time.

Marie LeVeau.

Kojo stared out of the window at two children skipping down the streets. Innocent, virginal, new. They haven't even scratched the surface of African-American history or life, and we've been sluggish about doing what we should've done a long time ago.

Bessie Smith, Monk, Dr. George Washington Carver, the space shuttle guys, Duke Ellington, Malcolm X, (well got to give Spike a pat on the back for that one), all kinds of people, places, events. "My Grandfather's Eyes".

He paused to reflect on what he had seen in his Grandfather's eyes, and began to scribble furiously.

No one will be able to say that we didn't start out with an arsenal.

Joe Louis, Sugar Ray Robinson, Muhammad Ali, thousands of incredible people of African descent. Hell, we'd need a thousand film crews, working night and day, to film a tenth of what we're about. Well, what is it they say? A journey of a thousand miles begins with that first step.

The phone again.

"Yeah?"

"Kojo, is that you, man?"

"Oh, sorry, Phillip, I was kinda in another world there...."

"Writing, huh?"

"Like a fiend."

"O.K., I won't hold you. Just thought I'd let you know I might be out of town, on the third Sunday in September, but if I'm not, I'll be there. Looks like you got your finger on something, huh?"

"I hope so, Phil, I hope so."

"O.K., check with you later."

"Yeah, later."

Phillip Charles, the best lighting technician in the world. Hope he can make it. He continued writing....

We want to use a character, I'm calling him "Chester L. Simmons," as an alter ego for dozens of types of African-American men; he can be tender, cruel, merciful, merciless, sharp, dull, up, down, completely sane, completely insane, (depending on the circumstances), witty, solemn, full of devil-may-care, very conservative. In a few words he is a reflection of the many moods and emotions that have been a part of the African-American psyche since the Beginning.

"Ed Burns here, hey Kojo, what's this shit about a meeting on the third Sunday in September, at 1 p.m.

What're we getting together to do, plot a robbery of Wells Fargo. Include me in, as Sam Goldwyn was supposed to have said."

"Thanks, Ed, I needed that. I'll fill you in when we all come together."

"Gotcha! See you on the 3rd. Bye!"

Ed Burris, assistant director, Mac Weaver, assistant director, guys who understood the importance of timing and cohesion.

Kojo stood up to stretch. Incredible how much energy you can put into your own thing, here I've been at it for hours and I still feel fresh.

Wonder how Akosua made out with her parents? They are really a drag.

The Pan-African fringe will be a frame of reference for what goes on in these films. There will be people with "West Indian" accents, people with Cuban, Brasilian, Venezuelan accents, people with no accents at all.

Ten thirty. Ten thirty?! Time to take a break. No wonder my stomach is growling.

Cheese, bread, wine. Terrible diet. I love the combination.

So, I gather up the people, put a broad outline together that will offer us the guidelines for five, six, maybe ten films.

And where will the money come from? He sipped his wine meditatively. I'll get the money, he thought grimly, I'll get the money doing what I'm supposed to do.

Twelve fifteen, time to call an end to it, check out a movie before the end of the day.

"Scent of a Woman". Yeahhh, something, lush, something Italian, Vitorio Gassman. I wonder how the moguls pulled it off. They took the same movie, altered it slightly, and gave it to Al Pacino.

They didn't even change the name - "Scent of a Woman". If they really did rip off, it was a colossal ripoff

"Scent of a Woman", the story of a blinded officer who doesn't see his blindness as a handicap, refuses to be just another man with a cane.

Beautifully photographed, well designed, art in every frame.

Twelve thirty a.m. Kojo took a quick shower, wrapped himself in a bath towel and sprawled across his bed.

Something is driving me to do this. The face of the moon glared at him, hypnotizing him with the faces that he found on its surface.

Well, we know it ain't made out of green cheese now, not after all those people have trampled around up there.

The phone buzzing startled him. Akosua?

"The Bediako Brown residence."

"Kojo, this is Juna. I got your note."

Juna, the wayward genius who is going to give us the music for the first film, at any rate. The woman was known to be notoriously "difficult" to deal with, full of off rhythms and attitudes.

"I'm glad you called. I won't be able to give you the full run down until we meet. There are some things that I have to put in place before our meeting."

The sudden, loud crashing of a piano blasted his ear drum.

"Sorry 'bout that. This crazy cat of mine likes to slam the piano key cover down. I think it freaks him out or something. Now, what were you saying?"

"I was saying that I can't really give you the complete picture until we meet."

"Why not?"

He detected a hostile tone in her voice.

"Juna, you know how this business is, if I started painting rosy pictures in the sky, someone would be terribly disappointed. I have to deal with things as I get to them."

"So, what do you want me to do?"

"I want you to do the music for the film. I hope it might be films, and not necessarily sequels."

"Why did you choose me to do the music?"

"Because you're the most imaginative, the most sensitive, the best musician in the world."

Juna's manic laughter shook him for a moment. Well, half dozen people had already expressed their opinion about Juna's state of mind.

Of course, she's a musical genius, no doubt about that, but the sister don't have both oars in the water.

"Kojo, what kind of film is this going to be?"

Kojo took a deep breath and swallowed hard.

"It's going to be so close to being a silent film, that we may as well call it that."

"Silent film, huh? With special effects and a musical score that won't quit."

"You got it!"

"Yeahh, yes, yeahh, I can see it in the back of my mind right now. We're talking about an African-American thang, right?"

"From Fade in to Fade out."

"Kojo, I have to go, I'll see you!"

"'Bye Juna."

He replaced the phone, sprawled back on his bed and laced his hands behind his head. I think I'm gonna put Akosua on Juna, she would run me nuts in a week.

"Harvey, please put your newspaper down, we have to talk?"

Harvey Ferguson reluctantly lowered the paper. One of his real pleasures in life was to wade through the Sunday edition of the L.A. Times.

"What is it, Minerva? What're you upset about?"

"Do I need to tell you? You should be upset as well. Aren't you concerned about the announcement our daughter made at lunch yesterday, about getting married to somebody we've never heard of?"

"Well, I'll have to admit that was a bit unsettling, but what can we do about it? After all, she's an adult."

"She may be an adult, but she's still our daughter and we can't allow her to go off and make a mistake like that."

Harvey Ferguson, semi-retired architect, golfer, easy going guy, Minerva's husband for twenty-six long years, sighed.

It was going to be one of those days...

"Sweetheart, how do you know it's going to be a mistake?"

Minerva Ferguson, Nee-Jackson, of the Jacksons of Evanston, glared at her husband.

"Any man that Cynthia chose without consulting us would be a mistake."

"Oh, without a doubt, I agree with you, but once again, I have to ask you...what can we do about it?"

She was silent and thoughtful for a few moments.

"I don't know, offhand, but we'll certainly have to think of something, won't we?"

Harvey Ferguson, anxious to get back into reading the Sunday Times, nodded in agreement.

"They'll be coming here on Tuesday. We'll have an opportunity to take a good look at this rascal."

"Yes, Minerva."

Monday, bright and clear in Los Angeles for a change. Kojo went through the automatic motions of starting his daily routine.

Brush teeth, comb hair, go to the park for the Capoeira workout.

"Morning, Kojo, looks like you're dragging it a little bit."

"Oh, 'morning, Fred...you know how it is when you don't have a day off it begins to catch up with you after awhile."

CHAPTER 22

"Yeah, I know what you mean. You sorta got off the plane, back onto the ol' threadmill, huh?"

"Yeah, guess you say that. Well, gotta get the workout. Talk to you later."

"O.K., don't forget, Julia and myself, we want to hear about your trip to Africa."

"We'll get together."

Nice people. Too bad we don't have a whole world with Fredrick and Julia Chans in it.

The ol' threadmill. Maybe it seems like that to him, but it's the new threadmill for me. My own threadmill.

It had been a busy weekend; putting a treatment-outline together for his project, answering the phone on and off, Akosua's problems with her family.

Damn, she wants me to go with her to see them on Tuesday. Well, I guess I have to pay my dues like everybody else.

"Morning, Kojo...coff-coff-coff...up here for your daily dozen, huh?"

"That's a good way to put it, Harry."

They waved to him from the paved street that circled the park, and he waved back.

The last thing I want them to think is that I'm homophobic.

The Yoga woman had wrapped herself around herself and gone into what seemed like a trance.

The bookworm was walking his sad eared Beagle, reading a newspaper for a change. The Tai Chi guys were doing their thing and the old Armenian men were assembling for a morning of card playing, doing surreptitious

277

vodka drinking and having sad discussions about their Holocaust, the one that the Turks were responsible for, in 1915.

This place would make a helluva film, just going from scene to scene. And me and my thang.

An hour later, sweating, he made a brisk walk home, feeling loose and flexible. He walked in to the phone buzzing. Well, here goes my day.

"Hello."

"Hello, this is Mr. Dryson's office. Mr. Dryson would like to speak to Ko-jo Bediako Brown."

"Speaking."

"One moment please."

"Kojo, Dryson here. Let's rap, I gotta meeting a half hour ago. Now give it to me straight, what's this business about turning away from making an honest buck...hahhahhah."

The mirthless laughter informed Kojo that the daisy chain had connected. The word was out over the course of a couple days. Goldstone had talked to Bascom at a swank Beverly Hills party Friday night. Buttram had a business call to Dryson and "The Kojo Syndrome" was discussed. Or a number of other scenarios could be imagined.

In any case, the word had gotten around.. .Kojo Bediako Brown was committing Hollywood suicide. It had to be for a reason. Dan Dryson wanted to know what that reason was.

"I'll have to give it to you straight. I won't be available to do a script for UTD, International."

"I'm just curious, mind if I ask why?"

"I'm not at liberty to say, just now."

"Well, o.k., pal, keep in touch...'Bye."

There, now it's done, I've burned all my bridges, there's nothing to do but move forward and upward.

He headed for a hot shower and cold glass of orange juice.

"Nzingha, what're your feelings about Akosua?"

Mrs. Brown placed the book she was reading on her lap and removed her reading glasses.

"I like her. That's my gut feeling. She strikes me as being assertive, but not aggressive. She's obviously intelligent, being a writer and all. I feel that she's a good match for Kojo."

"Yeah, looks like the boy really got lucky, wonder why he never introduced her to us before now?"

"You know how Kojo is. He reminds me of your father in lots of ways, the way he has to reflect on things before he'll give you an answer.

I suspect he had to be 100% sure that this was The One."

"Yeah, no doubt about that. Wonder how they met?"

"Film maker-writer-director meets writer-novelist on the street, recognize each other."

"Hahh hah hah. . .that's the most unlikely scenario I could imagine."

"Me too."

She shared smiles from the depths of their library-reading chairs.

"You know, the thing that disturbs me the most is what she had to say the other night, about her family not being spiritually supportive, that sorta eats at me."

"Yeah, I feel that too. I think she was really brave and honest to come out with a statement like that."

"And the other things she said, the mother who wants her daughter to join the Young Republican Organization, the mother who feels that her daughter's books are too much involved with 'people living sinful lives,' stuff like that."

"The father who feels uncomfortable about his daughter 'calling that much attention to herself' I don't have the feeling that we're going to be compatible in-laws."

"Well, let's see, we may be able to shift them around a bit, make them look at life from another perspective."

"I hope so."

Mrs. Brown replaced her glasses, took up her book and started reading again. Mr. Brown took a sip of sherry and returned to his task of compiling new titles to order from the latest book catalogue.

Tuesday morning. Kojo felt a healthy glow from his workout. This would be a great day to do a little picnic in Griffith Park.

He frowned. Nawww, dammit, I'm committed to a lunch with my future in-laws.

"Kojo, believe me, I hate putting you through this as much as I hate going through it."

"C'mon, it can't be that bad. I mean, let's face it, nobody's perfect. What time are we scheduled to be there?"

"Lunch time, about 12:30 - 1 o'clock."

"No problem. We'll go and play the game."

Damm-iit! I got stuff that I could be doing today. I could put a few hours in on this treatment-outline. I could start compiling a list of the actors and actresses that I might want to use.

I could think of a hundred other things to do, rather than go and try to impress a couple fuddy duddies. O well...guess I gotta do what I gotta do.

Messages on the machine. "Kojo, this is your father, but I guess you would know that from the sound of my voice...hahhahhah.

Anyway, just calling to thank you for the carvings you gave us. Also, to let you know that all the relatives have called in their thanks for the things you gave them. Thought you should know that.

O.K., ol' man, that's it for the moment. Oh, one last thing...your grandfather was quite taken with Akosua, his only regret is that she didn't have an older sister.

That's it for now, talk to you later."

Click.

"Good morning, Kojo Bediako Brown, my name is Felicia Davenport. I'm an actress and I've received information from a reliable source that you are casting for an avant garde production."

"I will, of course, submit my resume and portfolio of composites, but I can assure you that I'm capable of handling tragedy, comedy and all of the nuances in between. Please contact me - my number is 483-6220."

Kojo slumped into his desk chair, feeling a bit sad. Damn, it's started already. The hungriest, most talented people in town have picked up the scent.

No need to try to determine the source of her information, it doesn't take but a minute for news about anything to spread in this town.

The fax. "Mr. Kojo Bediako Brown, we have received your letter, indicating that you would be available for the exhibition of your works, here at the University of Copenhagen.

If it is convenient for you, we would like to have you come here August 10th to August 15th.

If this is convenient for you, please let us know as soon as possible and we will send you a round trip ticket, and commence to design our program around your arrival. Peace, Jan Alborg"

O yeah, I'm damned sure going to Denmark on August 10th. Wowww, wait 'til I tell Akos', she'll really trip out.

August 10th? Today is July 25th, I got a couple weeks to get all my balls rolling here, and then I'll break out for a few days of Scandinavian fun and games. I'll drop them a yes tomorrow.

Meanwhile, let me see what I can put on here that won't distress the fuddy duddies. Akos' wants me to trip with her from her place. Guess she needs the morale boost.

He laid an ivory white linen suit on his bed, a manila woven cotton shirt and a dull pink tie with small black dots.

Now then, with these Italian pimp shoes on I'll look elegant and cool. He began to strip off his sweaty workout clothes to take a shower.

So, they want to "do" lunch. O.K. then, lets "do" lunch.

Akosua blinked involuntarily as she opened the front door and took in the picture of her man, decked out in ivory white.

The bright sunlight behind him seemed to halo his presence on her front porch.

"Well, should I come in or do you just want me to stand here while you admire me?"

"Please! please! by all means, come in! come in! come in! My goodness! What fashion magazine did you step out of?!"

"Nice, huh? I had this suit made a couple years ago, right after I picked up a little change as the assistant director on that forgettable feature, the last one, I did.

My grandfather is the one responsible for me having it. He's always saying - "a man needs to have a white suit in his closet.""

Akosua draped her arms around his neck and kissed him.

"Well, you can definitely say you've got your white suit. You look good enough to eat."

"I thought you said we were going to your parents' house?"

She tweeked his nose...you're a naughty one, you know that?"

Kojo smiled, denying nothing... "Sorry, baby, that line was just too juicy not to play on."

"I heard that. Gimme a sec to freshen up my makeup... and put on something white too. Maybe that'll shake 'em up...to see two angels floating up the driveway...."

"Hah hahhh hahhah..."

Kojo didn't feel intimidated by the prospect of dealing with his future in-laws, he felt vaguely pissed at the idea of being forced to cope with a couple fuddy duddies on such a beautiful day.

Dolores, the maid, escorted them through the house, out onto the all purpose terrace. Kojo carefully noted and catalogued the plastic covered sofas, the fireplace that was never used, the sterility of the place.

They must spend most of their time "out back." He was beginning to feel a deeper sense of compassion toward Akosua than ever before.

"Mom, Dad, I'd like you to meet Kojo Bediako Brown, my husband-to-be."

That's the spirit, girl, rub their noses in it. Kojo, the director, did a Freeze Frame of Mr. and Mrs. Ferguson.

"Kojo, my parents, Mr. Harvey Ferguson, Mrs. Minerva Ferguson."

They both stared at him as though he were a creature from another planet. It must be this white suit that's bedazzled them.

"How do you do?" He shook their limp hands politely and leaned back to look down on them. If you think you've got a pootbutt out here on your veranda, you're going to be in for some rude surprises.

Kojo had made an early decision to go with the flow, if it were flowing forward. If they decided to play hardball, he was ready to go to bat with the first pitch.

Mr. Ferguson recovered first.

"Uhh, please sit down, uhhh, Mr. Brown."

Akosua pulled up her chair beside him as he occupied a seat opposite her parents.

O.K., the perimeters have been set, let the games begin.

"Mr. Brown," Minerva purred in that phoney tone that Akosua hated, "Would you care for something? We'll be having lunch shortly."

Akosua popped in to take up the slack.

"Yes, that's a wonderful idea, Mom. Dolores, tragamelos dos bottellas de Bohemia. Hay Bohemia?"

"Si, senorita, pronto," came the answer from the kitchen. Kojo smiled at the frown that ceased Mrs. Ferguson's brow.

"Ako-su-ah insists on speaking to the servants in their own language."

"Doesn't sound like a bad idea to me, after all we are in California, which used to be a part of Mexico. And depending on demographics, it may be Mexican again."

There, that did it, the battle lines were drawn. An icy curtain settled across the table as the maid delivered two frosty cold bottles of Bohemia beer.

Harvey Ferguson signalled to the maid....

"Bring me one of those too. Minerva, are you having something?"

"I don't drink beer," she snapped, with a disdainful curl of her lips, "Dolores, bring me an iced tea."

Akosua pinched Kojo's thigh under the table, he stifled a sarcastic smile. The beer was deliciously chilled.

A few pregnant moments passed, Kojo and Akosua sipping their Bohemias, Mr. and Mrs. Ferguson looking uncomfortable.

"Uhhh, Mr. Brown?"

"Please call me Kojo, Mr. Ferguson. And you too, Mrs. Ferguson."

"Yes, of course, Ko-jo. So, our daughter tells us that you two want to get married..."

"Dad," Akosua broke in, "I told you that we were going to get married, not wanted to...."

"Cyn. . .Ako-Su-ah, must you interrupt your father like that?"

"Yes, I must interrupt my father like that, because he needs to be corrected."

Once again the icy curtain dropped. Mrs. Ferguson decided to do a flanking movement.

"Ako-su-ah has told us that you're a brilliant writer-director-film maker...."

"Yes, it's true, I am."

Akosua threw her head back and slugged half her beer down. My man, brother Kojo Bediako Brown.

The sour expression that sucked Mrs. Ferguson's cheeks in made Kojo smile.

"Well, I must say...you're quite modest. Have you done anything noteworthy?"

Five minutes later he let them off the hook, after a monotonic recitation of his credentials, with his latest.... "I'll be going to Copenhagen, Denmark August 10th. The University is giving screenings of my work for five days."

Akosua beamed at him.

"Dolores, dos mas, por favor?"

"Si, Senorita!"

The Fergusons were beginning to slump a bit. Kojo and Akosua drank their beers nonchalantly.

"Kojo, I hope you don't think I'm being intrusive, but I'd like to know one thing."

"What's that, Mr. Ferguson?"

"Why do you want to marry our daughter?"

Kojo hesitated for a split second, on the verge of laughing, decided to go straight in.

"Akosua is a treasure. She has brains, she knows how the world works, she's beautiful and she's a luscious sister. What more could a man ask for?"

Mrs. Ferguson coughed into a napkin and was about to go on a tirade when the maid announced, "Lonch, she is ready."

Tamales, enchiladas, refried beans, salad and more Bohemias later.

"Ko-jo, I'm sure you come from a good family...."

"The Best!" he snapped in on the old lady. The time for bullshit was totally over.

"Yes, of course. I was about to say...in good families, the business of marriage is taken quite seriously."

"Oh, Mom, please, give us a break."

"No, go on, Mrs. Ferguson..."

"It seems to me that a suitable period of time should have been set aside for an engagement...."

"Mrs. Ferguson, I can assure you we have been firmly engaged for the past two years." He gave Akosua a sly wink.

"But we weren't informed, where is the ring?"

"You weren't informed because our engagement concerned us, period. And so far as rings and all the rest of that Eurocentric nonsense, who needs it? I mean, what does putting a ring on a woman's finger mean? The important thing is a heart to heart commitment, not a ring commitment."

The Fergusons stared at him as though he had just slapped them in the mouth.

"Are you saying that it's Eurocentric to have an engagement ring?" Mr. Ferguson rumbled a bit.

"Yessir, yes, it is. As well as this charade that we're going through right now. If matters were really going to be handled in a proper way, members of my family would have contacted members of Akosua's family, gifts would have been exchanged and so on.

But this is America and, for better or worse, we are African-Americans and things are different for us here. Akosua has accepted my proposal and we're going to be married. There really is no need for us to sit out here on such a lovely day seeking to antagonize each other over a done deal."

Akosua noticed an odd gleam creeping into her mother's eyes. She likes him... she likes him....

"Well, I must say, Ko-jo, you do give the appearance of knowing what you're about."

"Yes, Mrs. Ferguson, I do know what I'm about."

"Well, fine, I'm glad to hear that. It really puts my mind at ease to know that we can give our approval for your marriage to Ah-ko-sua without reservations."

Mr. Ferguson did a double take. Akosua laughed aloud, unable to contain herself. Kojo smiled slyly at the old lady.

You ol' fox you....

"Mrs. Ferguson, I can't begin to tell you how happy it makes both of us to know that you and Mr. Ferguson approve of what we're doing."

Mr. Ferguson looked slightly bewildered.

"Now then, have you set a date?"

"No, Mom, not yet."

"Don't worry, Mrs. Ferguson, you'll be the first to know what we're going to do and when we're going to do it."

"Well, that takes a load off my mind. Ah-ko, how do you say...bring more beer?"

"Mas cervesas, por favor."

"Dolores, mos sir-vases, por fa-vour."

"Si, Senora," the maid answered, giggling.

A half-hour later, after the cheek to cheek kisses and half hearted handshakes, Kojo and Akosua drove off, trying to maintain straight faces. They both exploded with laughter at the first intersection.

"Kojo, did you see the flip flop that lady did?"

"Your mother is a very clever woman. If you can't beat 'em, join'"

Akosua shook her head with wonder...well I'll be damned...

"Kojo, I gotta tell you, son, you really know how to pick 'em."

"Yeah, Akosua is really a fine lady, no doubt about it."

"Whatever happened to those two African girls you had in the deep freeze?"

"Granddad, you don't forget anything, do you?"

"Well, I guess when you get to be my age there's less time for forgetting."

"Oh, I see..."

"Said the blind man...."

They clinked their glasses of Chivas Regal and sipped. The old man settled back in his chair and waited....

"It was the most incredible thing. Remember me telling you about Comfort the Passionflower and Grace, the Conservative's conservative?"

"I fixed them in my brain. In literature, they would call them a juxtaposition of opposites."

"Uhhh, yeah, that's right."

This old man is so full of surprises it's frightening.

"Opposites they were and opposites they've become. Comfort, the Passionflower, has become a humorless, straight laced Jesus freak. I can't say she's become a humorless, straight laced, sexless Jesus freak because she has two children by a married man."

"Evidently she's found a way to rationalize some wayward conduct."

"So it seems, so it seems. Meanwhile, Grace, the former Miss Goody two shoes, has become a fresh spring of groovy thinking, of sensitivity, the whole thang.

I was really tripped out by the change. If she hadn't let me off the hook, emotionally, it would've been real hard to come back here to Akosua.

I'll never be able to tell you exactly what she said to me, but it was made clear that we had shared something special and there was no need to have regrets about anything."

"I love that type of woman, they make you feel that emotional involvements are really worthwhile."

"Hmmm. . .I never thought about it like that."

"So, you're getting ready to take a trip to Viking country, huh?"

"Yeah, I told you they're giving me a free ride, round trip, accommodations, a week's screening of my work, questions/answers, all that."

"That's wonderful, Kojo, really wonderful. I was just thinking... when you first told me about this; ain't it a shame that we always have to go to some other country to achieve recognition for what we do here?"

"Yeah, well, that seems to be the way the cookie crumbles. I'm sorta glad it's the Danes because I've always thought well of their social attitudes.

I'm sure there must be prejudiced, racist Danes running around, as well as Swedes, Norwegians and Finns, but the Scandinavians have never seemed to give the racist ethic enough soil to take root in. You know what I mean?"

"That's true, that's true. I remember, during the Second World War, when Germany took over Denmark and passed a decree or something that was supposed to force the Danish Jews to wear the Star of David on their clothes.

The king was the first one to have a Star of David on his chest and rode through the streets on a white horse, the day after the order was given. In addition, when things really tightened up, they loaded hundreds, maybe thousands of Jews on boats and ferried them over to neutral Sweden."

"I didn't know that."

"Yeah, it's a fact. Got to be some nice people to do something like that."

"I would think so."

"When're you leaving?"

"About two weeks from now."

"That oughta be a blast!...Going somewhere to have people appreciate what you've been doing with your life."

"Come to think of it, that will be a blast."

"You know you have my blessings, Kojo."

"Thanks, Granddad."

Kojo left his Grandfather's house, slightly buzzed after sipping four fingers of Scotch, and drove aimlessly...for a few minutes.

Think I'll trip up to the park. Griffith Park, with all of the crooks and crannies he had explored over the years. He decided to go to the planetarium and look out over the city.

Los Angeles sprawled beneath him, hazed by late afternoon smog.

I wonder if I should have talked with him about Asiafo, about the deal I made. No, I did the right thing, don't talk with anybody about it. It sounds tooo crazy.

People will be running around here screaming that I'm into "Voodoo" or something. As though they really knew what Voodoo was.

How much time do I have to do the first thing I'm supposed to do? He felt the edge of panic creep up his back for a moment. Three months. I got less than a month. No, more than that.

He suddenly felt too nervous to try to count backwards to the time he had met the man in the forest.

September. It's got to be September, before the second week in September. I'll return from Denmark on the 16th, we'll get married then.

What if she wants to wait 'til spring or something? No, we'll have to do it in September.

Kojo started to turn away from looking at the hazy smog, but was drawn back to stare at a collection of clouds that seemed to form the face of Asiafo, the wizard.

Well, I'll be damned...

Kojo hurriedly adjusted his earphones to catch the opening music of "Citizen Kane." "Citizen Kane," I'm going to write somebody a letter of appreciation.

"Citizen Kane," one of Orson Welle's best. The larger than life story of William Randolph Hearst, a mogul who really knew how to be a mogul, him and his Xanadu.

Kojo soaked in the story for ninety minutes, checking out, (for its time), Orson Welle's radical use of lights, shadows, plays within the play, unusual camera angles, serious acting.

He felt drained at the conclusion of the film. Yeah, now that was a film.

"Care for a cocktail or a glass of wine, sir?"

"An orange juice would be fine."

He stared out at the clouds surrounding the 'plane. Europe, Denmark. Never thought about going to Europe. Just goes to show how little control you have over your own destiny.

He reached down into his briefcase and pulled out a letter from Grace Vivian Hlovor. He glanced at the strong, but spidery lines of her handwriting, and re-folded the letter.

A beautiful sister, by anybody's standard. *"Yes, of course, I miss you, Kojo, but that's normal. I don't miss any of what we shared because I wear the memory of those moments like a glove."*

How long can we keep this up? I'll write her, she'll write me, we'll tell each other the honest truth and one day soon, for me it'll be as soon as Akosua and I are married, we'll have to cancel the letters.

He stared out of the window...life is a real motherfucker, at times.

"Kojo, I think this thing in your honor, in Denmark, is a very good sign. You know what I mean?"

"I hope it's a very good sign..."

Akosua had almost squeezed him to death at the airport.

"Think about it! They're pulling the kind of rabbits out of the hat for you that they usually reserve for ol' gray men. I'm so proud of you I don't know what to do!"

"Well, look at you...getting ready to do a cross country P.R. thing for your book."

"Yeah, we do seem to be trippin', huh?"

"And loving every minute of it. I'll call you from Copenhagen."

"I love you, Kojo."

"Love you too, Akos'."

"Ladies and gent'men, please fasten your seat belts, we will be landing in approximately 15 minutes...."

Kojo looked down at neatly squared fields and farm houses as they lowered the flaps for a landing.

He was impressed by the courtesy and efficiency of airport people. No fuss, no problems, come on in.

It wasn't difficult to spot his reception committee either, they were holding up a large, well designed banner — **"Mr. Kojo Bediako Brown, Welcome to Denmark, University of Copenhagen."**

"You must be Mr. Alborg."

"And you are Mr. Brown."

"Yes, pleased to meet you."

Alborg turned to introduce him to the other three members of the welcoming committee.

"Teresa Arbus, who will be your day to day coordinator. She will be responsible for you to make the screenings, workshops, question and answer sessions, etc."

"Harold Andersen will be your driver and as you say in America, your 'gopher'."

They shared a laugh.

"And finally, Fred Helsinger, who will help you arrange a social schedule."

CHAPTER 23

Fred Helsinger, a large ruddy young man with a flaming beard, gave Kojo a broad wink.

He scanned them quickly, completely. A young set, the oldest couldn't've been older than thirty.

Alborg was already a professorial type with black horn rims and a mop of uncombed hair.

Teresa Arbus took his breath away. She was almost a duplication of Ingrid Bergman with raven colored hair. And I thought all Scandinavians were blonde.

Harold Andersen gently tugged his bags from his hands as they strolled from the terminal.

By the time they reached the exit they were chatting as though they had known each other for years.

He was given an apartment near the University campus.

"We hope you don't mind, the apartment belongs to Professor Stein, the head of our philosophy department, who is currently lecturing in Switzerland."

We had thought to place you with one of our faculty families...."

"But I vetoed that suggestion," Teresa Arbus slipped in coolly, "because it would have meant that you would not have a moment to yourself.

The professor would be asking questions all the time, the children would be all over you and the wife would be stuffing you with Danish pastries."

They laughed. Kojo took note of how easily they related to him. There was none of the usual American White/Black reserve. Maybe it's because we don't share the same horrible history.

"I must honestly say that I'm grateful you've made these arrangements, it is good to have time alone."

Teresa Arbus pushed her chin in the air, as though to say... see, I told you I was right.

Alborg studied his watch as though he were checking a compass.

"It is now two o'clock. We have placed a few provisions for you in the 'fridge, but we would like to come for you to take dinner at...say five o'clock?"

"Sounds fine. That'll give me time to unpack and shower."

"Good, Teresa and Harold will collect you at five. And I have no doubt that Fred will find ways and means to help you occupy your evening."

Once again, the ruddy faced man winked at Kojo. What's that mean?

"One question?"

"Yes?"

"When do I go to work?"

"When do you go? ...Oooh, I understand. We have scheduled the first screening of two of your short films - "Good Times" and "Mambo Baby" for ten a.m. You will find a complete schedule of the program on the desk there. We thank you very much for coming, Mr. Brown."

"Please call me Kojo, and the pleasure is all mine."

They marched out like a small army unit.

So orderly, so precise. Maybe that's the Northern way.

Kojo wandered around the spacious apartment for a few minutes. Books, books, books. A few provisions in the 'fridge? He opened the door to stare at a ham, sausages, fish, eggs, cheeses, milk, orange juice, fruit, pastries, champagne.

O my God...he closed the refrigerator door with a smile on his face. These people know how to treat a brother.

Ten a.m. Lights! Camera! Action!

Kojo looked over both shoulders at the tiers of people in the auditorium. There must be at least a thousand people in here.

"Teresa, are all of these people film students?"

"No, there are many from related disciplines: philosophy, art, theatre, the humanities in general."

Kojo leaned back in his seat. "Related disciplines." I can just see the looks on the faces of people like Sheila Buttram, Dan Dryson, Frank Goldstone, Charley Bascom and all the rest. They think money is the "related discipline" to films.

It had been a full night. After a smorgasbord, (the five yard long table loaded with food), at a swank restaurant, Fred Helsinger and Teresa Arbus had given him a taste of Copenhagen's night life.

A taste of Tivoli Gardens..."One could spend days in this place. I know, I often did that when I was younger."

The Club Six, six different styles of music on six different levels: Jazz at the top, Blues at the bottom, Country and Western, Latin, "ethnic Danish" and an avant garde mish mash in between.

"Now that's what I call having something for everybody."

Fred was obviously a good timer and, after a couple aquavits, Teresa Arbus revealed a dry wit.

"As you can see, we Danes are the Italians of the North. Or perhaps the Italians are the Danes of the South."

They had taken him to a few high spots and a few low spots.

"Don't worry, there is much more in the days and nights ahead...hah hah hah...."

The lights were dimmed and the first film, a ten minute short from his U.S.C. student days was off and running.

"Good Times?" was a wide rimmed satire on a Norman Lear produced television program of the same name.

Kojo had written a series of catastrophes into the piece and, in the middle of each catastrophe, the family hemmed into the hell of life in the Chicago projects, rejoices at the latest layer of misery heaped on them.

The ending finds them rejoicing because there is no hope. The underlined sentiment is bitterness.

"Mambo Daddy" traced the life of an African-Cuban dancer who finds himself working as a messenger in New York City. He did a lot of intercutting and subliminals to show where the man had been and where his head was now.

Kojo was honestly shocked, pleased and surprised at the sustained applause at the conclusion.

Jan Alborg took the podium....

"And now, ladies and gentleman, it is my privilege and honor to introduce you to the man who is responsible for the two works you have just seen.

We will be showing more of his works this afternoon. The series will continue, mornings at 10 a.m. and afternoons at 2 p.m., until Friday.

Now then, without further interruptions, Mr. Kojo Bediako Brown."

Kojo strode to the podium, feeling like an authentic celebrity. There wasn't a great deal he had to say about himself, Alborg and company had done a complete bio on him, on the back of the program for all to read.

The questions came in an orderly manner, but rapidly.

"Would you say that your being an African-American has been the biggest influence on your work?"

"Unavoidably, that's a given for any African-American artist working in America. Some would deny this, but I would vehemently disagree with them."

"In the two short films we've seen you limit yourself to concerns about the Black experience, do you intend to remain in that particular groove?"

"First, I would like to say that delving into the African-American experience offers unlimited possibilities, and if I should choose to remain in that particular groove, I would have enough work for ten lifetimes."

"Is there a universal message, or messages, in the two short films?"

"Yes, one film is worth a billion words."

"Are you married?"

Jan Alborg called a halt to the questions after an hour with a curt - "Thank you, ladies and gentleman, our series will continue at two p.m. today and ten a.m. tomorrow."

It took another half hour of handshaking and exchanging pleasantries with students who couldn't resist a parting shot.

"I love your "Mambo Daddy", it is an important work. Thank you."

Kojo was exhilarated by the reception. Wowww. .wait 'til I tell Akosua about this. Unreal.

"Mr. Brown, Kojo, come...we are having smorgasbord with the faculty."

Once again he was led the length of a five yard table, with Teresa Arbus suggesting bits of this and bits of that.

"One must pick and choose carefully here, or else you will lose your appetite. We Danes eat too much."

Fifteen faculty members welcomed him to their round table with more questions.

Teresa Arbus whispered, "sorry."

Kojo floated on the exchange. He could not ever recall having such a free flowing conversation with men and women who were twice his age, except for his parents and grandfather.

They wanted to have answers to serious question; and, if the question happened to be rooted in racial soil, no one tried to avoid the question because of that.

It's like just talking with people, for a change. Yes, they are White people, I can see that.

And they can see that I'm an African-American, but the tension is missing. He mentally analogized the setting; just think of the crap I'd be dealing with if this were the U.S.C. faculty cafeteria. We'd probably be at the fisticuffs level about now.

"Kojo, it's one o'clock, I think it would be a good idea to rest for a bit before the next session. Do you agree?"

He nodded in agreement, not feeling the least bit tired of the exchanges. Fifteen faculty members had to shake his hand before he departed.

Harold Andersen, the driver, whipped him to his flat in five minutes.

"I will come for you at ten minutes of two."

"I'll be ready."

Kojo entered the apartment, stripped to his shorts, opened a well chilled champagne and sprawled in a well upholstered chair.

Damn, this is great!

Two o'clock. The short films were "Black Indian Cowboys" and "Bluessingers."

"Black Indian Cowboys" was his homage to the thousands of men and women of African-Native American descent who herded cows in the west. The men and women who were responsible for so much of the Western Mystique that they were never given proper credit for.

"Bluessingers" offered insights to the Blues tradition; he focused on the work of Howlin' Wolf, Muddy Waters, Lightenin' Hopkins, Taj Mahal and Baba Alade Olamina.

Once again the auditorium erupted with sustained applause at the conclusion.

Hmmm... I could begin to like this.

He was pleasantly surprised to discover that there were people in the audience who knew a great deal about the American West.

"At some point," one of them explained, "We all wanted to play cowboys and Indians. Here, in Denmark, of course, everyone wanted to be an Indian."

He assured them that he was not a sociologist, but that the logical amalgamation/integration of the Native American and the African was a natural mating.

"We had so much in common with each other that they never detail, (like when they detail a car), in our history books; common ideas concerning the nature of the universe, and the supernatural.

The biggest distinction is that the West African was coming from a more agriculturalized society and the Native American, on his horse was more of a gatherer-hunter.

But aside from that, we clicked. As a matter of fact, you don't have to scratch too far beneath the surface to find a Native American ancestor in most African-American families."

He felt a bit sad trying to explain why young African-Americans turned their backs, on the Blues. And why so many young American Whites adopted it.

"There are many things about America that I couldn't possibly begin to try to explain to you."

The auditorium bubbled with seriously good vibes at the end of the presentation.

"You are a smash hit," Teresa Arbus whispered to him as he signed autographs and answered last minute, off the cuff questions.

He was able to break free after forty five minutes.

"Kojo, it is 4:30 now. Would you perhaps like to have an early dinner, before Fred scoops you up for his "Night in Copenhagen" or...?"

"I'd like to go see a good Danish film."

No sooner said than done. Fifteen minutes later they were strolling down the aisle of a plush theatre in downtown Copenhagen.

He took careful note of the reactions of the people who looked at them. The women simply smiled and gave the kind of look that asked.... where can I get one?

The men made a surreptitious study of the woman's beautiful body, her shining black hair and her Ingrid Bergman profile and seemed to say... you lucky dog you.

He couldn't detect any of the customarily bad vibes he would've felt in the 'States. It might be a different scene if there were some sisters lurking around here.

Kojo found himself drawn to colored faces. The Africans he could spot in a second. A few fast moving African-Americans.

"Teresa, who are the Chinese people? They from China?"

"No, not China, they are Greenlanders, Esquimo people from our island-colony."

"I didn't know Denmark had a colony."

"Of course, all European countries have their colonies. Come, the film is about to begin."

A Danish film. Three men and six women in the forest, searching for the true nature of meaning. Or something close to that. Which seemed to involve a lot of sexual exploration. A lot.

Kojo took note of the audience, a real cross section of Danish life — men, women, children.

Children watching a film that would have been considered artistic porno in the U.S. Artistic porno, but still porno.

They strolled through the "walking streets," no cars allowed,.

"Well, what do you think?" she asked, with a curious gleam in her eye.

"I must say, it was certainly explicit, no punches pulled."

"Ah yes, Danish films are like that."

A pleasantly warm summer evening in Copenhagen. He admired the stylishness of the people. They dressed well and they looked healthy.

"So, now, you have seen the film. Shall I return you to your place and offer you to the tender mercies of Mr. Helsinger?"

Kojo made a snap decision.

"No 'Copenhagen Tonight' for me. I would like nothing better than to have a well made sandwich and a bottle of Tuborg dark."

"Come, I know just the place."

A sandwich house, nothing but sandwiches, beer, and coffee. The menu listed one hundred sandwiches and their contents.

"Wowww. . .this is what I call serious sandwiches." Sandwiches and beer. After the second beer he became aware of her looking at him in a curious way.

"Kojo, yesterday, one of the questions was whether or not you were married?

You answered "Not yet."

Does that mean that you're engaged, or that you're thinking about it?"

"Both. I'm engaged and I'm thinking about it." She laughed at his answer. Lovely lady, maybe beautiful would be a better description. So free and easy.

"Teresa, you ever been to America?"

"Never had the slightest urge. I'm satisfied with what I see on CNN and in the films. The place strikes me as being rather violent, the gangs, the police, the general make-up of the place.

I like the atmosphere of my country, of Denmark. We make mistakes, of course, but we don't attempt to cover the mistakes up with violent actions.

Someday I would like to go to the U.S., but it isn't high on my list of priorities."

"Oh, I see."

No Ghanaian taxi driver here, begging for help to secure a visa.

Three beers and two sandwiches later they stutter stepped out of the Sandwich House.

"Now what?"

"Teresa, I would like nothing better than to take a hot shower and curl up with a good book. I think I'm beginning to feel a little jet lag."

"I understand."

She gave him a little kiss on both cheeks as he was about to exit the taxi.

"Teresa, thank you for everything."

"My pleasure. Rest well, there is tomorrow."

"I'll be ready."

He stared at the taxi as it pulled away, Teresa waving from the rear window.

That's a groovy lady, quite groovy...

10 a.m. Wednesday morning. Fred and Harold were standing at attention by the side of the car.

"Ahhh, Kojo, Teresa told me that you wanted to rest last evening, so I did not collect you. I wanted to take you to an authentic Danish nightclub."

"Maybe this evening, after dinner."

"Very good."

One thirty minute film in the morning, a documentary that he fought for; "The African Presence in Ancient Polynesia/Melanesia." And "Capoeira in Brasil, the Dancing Martial Art," in the afternoon.

"The African Presence in Ancient Polynesial/Melanesia" stimulated an hour of discussions.

Most of the students had heard of or had read about Thor Hyerdahl's sailing to the South Seas on a balsa raft. They were also unresistant to the idea that African adventurers had visited the islands.

"One only has to look at the faces of the inhabitants of those places. They certainly didn't emigrate from Switzerland."

Kojo was forced to take them through the racism at U.S.C. He could see skepticism on many faces.

"I am telling you the truth. Right now, in the United States of America, it is very difficult in many institutions, to receive funding for projects that are not considered Eurocentric."

"Capoeira in Brasil, the Dancing Martial Art" was pure pleasure, offering the students a look at a facet of Brasilian culture that they knew nothing about.

"I thought those guys were simply soccer players."

Kojo was persuaded to do a few Capoeira movements after he confessed that he was a student of Capoeira.

The applause rang in his ears at the conclusion of his mini-demonstration. Have to call Akosua this afternoon, tell her how well things are going.

Back to the apartment for a brief rest and a small dinner party in his honor at the home of one of the faculty members.

He couldn't remember when he had been surrounded by so many men with full fledged beards, and provocative questions.

"I've often asked myself why the African-American didn't emigrate to a more hospitable environment."

"Professor, what you have to remember is that we built America; four hundred years of our blood, sweat and tears made it the great power that it is today. We couldn't turn our backs on what we've done."

The beer, the Aquavit, the wine flowed, the conversations went 'round and 'round.

"Please tell us, Mr. Brown, what are your plans upon your return?"

"I will be forming a production company, to produce Africentrically oriented films."

Teresa Arbus rescued him from another hour of honest curiosity by simply announcing in Danish, "Mr. Brown has had a busy day, and will have a busy tomorrow. Good evening!"

Fred Helsinger was waiting.

"What do you say? A night cap at the Danish Club?"

Kojo couldn't resist the man's urge to show him a good time. Teresa Arbus gave Fred Helsinger and Harold Andersen pointed looks and tapped her wrist watch.

"Only a night cap, Teresa, only a night cap."

The Danish Club, on the second floor level, overlooking the river. Danes were having full throated conversations, fueled by steins of Tuborg beer. He did a double take on the two beautiful blondes smoking cigarillos.

"Teresa, you smoke cigars?," he whispered.

"No, I don't smoke anything. It's a stupid habit, sucking smoke into your body."

They occupied a wall table and ordered steins of beer. The atmosphere was lively.

"Fred, what makes this a Danish night club?"

Helsinger buried his moustache in his beer before answering... "Well, if you are unlucky or lucky, as the case may be, you will have the opportunity to find out."

Kojo, a people watcher from 'way back, did a slow Pan of the room. Huge space, maybe fifty yards by a hundred.

His eyes swept back to a trio of men who were crying at a table a few yards away. Crying? What the hell were they crying for?

"Yes, Kojo, I see them. Now, perhaps Mr. Helsinger can enlighten us."

Fred Helsinger took another full swallow of his beer.

"They are feeling what you would call 'the blues.'"

Kojo was honestly puzzled.

"The blues? About what? It's a beautiful summer evening, the beer...."

Harold Andersen popped in.

"That's it, that's the problem. They know it is a beautiful summer evening now, but it will become winter next month.

It will be cold here, we will be closed in. We will have everything we want; our taxes will be paid, our national health service will take care of us, we will not have any of the concerns that you have in your country."

"So, that causes people to have the blues?"

"Yes." Teresa Arbus answered sharply, "Yes, that is one of the reasons for the blues. Personal initiative is last. We know that we are going to be taken care of and it's somewhat distressing. We know that the huge sums that are deducted from our pay checks will be used to take care of us."

"Ahhh, Kojo, my friend, you look quite puzzled. Think of it, think of what it would be like to have the government treat you like a baby. All your life."

"I can think of some people in America who would like nothing better."

"So, they think."

A half-hour later Kojo signalled that it was time for him to call it a night.

"Fred, Harold, Teresa, I thank you for taking me to this authentic Danish night club, I'm sure I'll be depressed for days."

They shared a big laugh on the way out.

"Sounds like you're having a wonderful time, Kojo."

"I am, I really am. In some ways it seems unbelievable. Here I am, in this Nordic country, surrounded by White people and I can't think of one bad vibe, not one.

I don't quite know how to put it, but the clearest thing that I feel is that we, the Danes and us, don't share a common, horrible history.

You don't see people trying to avoid looking you in the eye, for example. Or coming off with stupid stereotypical thinking."

"I can see how that would make a lot of things seem more positive."

"Well, that's enough from this side. What's happenin' over there?"

"Well, two biggies off hand. My publisher decided to cancel out on the cross country P.R. thing, they seemed to think the money would be better spent on T.V. ads, newspaper ads."

"That doesn't sound too bad."

"As a matter of fact, I like the idea, it keeps me away from other folks' germs."

"Hahh hahh, now, what's the other thing?"

"My mother has been running all over town telling people about this incredible young man she found for her daughter...."

"Your mother is a politician, no doubt about it."

CHAPTER 24

Pregnant pause....

"Kojo, I'm missing you."

"And I'm missing you too, baby."

"When will you be coming back?"

"I'll leave here Saturday night. I'll arrive in L.A. Monday morning."

"I'll be waiting."

"You better be...."

"'Bye now...."

"'Bye."

The film was called "Body and Soul," starring John Garfield and Lili Palmer, an interesting story of the fight game, of how corruption disfigures the psyche.

Kojo laced his hands behind his head and stared at the film he was seeing in his mind's eye.

Wonderful lighting in that film, the shadows, the harsh black and whites of the fighters in the dressing rooms, under the evil glance of evil men.

Canada Lee was in that movie. Wonder what happened to him? And to James Edwards? — who was supposed to have been the first Sidney Poitier. Last time I saw him he was George C. Scott's valet in "Patton."

How many of us have been wasted like that? How many of us have been shuttled through the little door labeled oblivion.

The face appeared on the ceiling as though it were a giant photograph. Asiafo.

He didn't laugh, smile or make any sign to Kojo, he simply appeared for a moment and then the image blurred into thin air.

He stared into the space where the face had appeared, undisturbed by the appearance. It seemed natural that his patron would look in on him. Strange, here I am, the brother who has always questioned everything..., and I don't question this.

He snuggled under the cover and fell into a sound sleep.

Thursday, ten a.m. It was working like a well made Swiss watch. It was ten a.m., he was surrounded by his trio of handlers and they were showing two documentaries; "The Life of a Homeboy," the story of a gang leader and a hard look at the drug traffic in Chicago, "Crack Crack Crack."

The questions were becoming more precise, more articulate. He noticed that the same people were returning, day after day.

"We think of this as a master class in African-American film philosophy."

"Why were my works chosen for this exposition? I'll have to let Mr. Alborg answer that."

"Ah yes, very good question. We made the choice of Mr. Kojo Bediako Brown because, number one, he has quite a substantial body of work for a filmmaker of his age.

Secondly, the committee felt that the quality of his work was superior, and that is what we were looking for.

Thirdly, we wanted to have our film students here at the University exposed to the work of an African-American filmmaker-director-writer.

And, finally, we felt, by selecting Mr. Kojo Bediako Brown, we would be giving ourselves a look at the future. Mr. Brown, would you care to add something more?"

"Mr. Alborg, you have said it all. And I thank you."

The applause, the river of students who wanted to shake his hand, chat for a moment, made him feel honored, strengthened.

"Are you not paid similar respect in the U.S., Mr. Brown?"

"Unfortunately, I must say, no."

Damn, you mean to tell me I had to come all the way to Reindeer land, to the heartland of Eurocentrism, to have my work validated.

God does indeed work in mysterious ways.

"Kojo, we have a bit of a treat for you this evening, I hope you are not feeling too exhausted."

"Fred, Harold, Teresa, I'm ready to go anywhere with you, except another 'authentic Danish night club,' I'm not in a mood to be depressed."

"We promise you, you won't be depressed."

They made a "rum quartet," as a friend of his once defined it. Fred Helsinger obviously knew all of the high and low spots in Copenhagen; Harold Andersen was a loyal camp follower, Teresa Arbus reeked of class and culture.

And then there's me, the *melanin element.*

The taxi deposited them in front of a nondescript nightclub, entitled "Montmartre."

Up some badly carpeted steps, past a velvet curtain, into a spaciously designed room. The stage was elevated to the level of the generously scattered tables, which gave everyone a decent seat.

"Ah hah, good, we are just in time for the second set."

Kojo took a hard look at the customers — raggedy faced Danes, dreadlocked brothers and sisters, a few Asians scattered here and there, a mix.

Fred, the good timer, was obviously a favored patron. He shook hands, laughed, told little jokes to the waitress as they were led to the best table in the house.

"Ahhh hah, my favorite table. Now, what shall we have to drink."

Kojo checked Helsinger out with an amused look in his eyes. This guy really has Gusto. He never seems depressed and he's always willing to have a good time. A true hedonist.

"Think I'll go with a little white wine tonight, Fred. That Aquavit kicks my butt."

"Make that two white wines, and you two will, of course have the beer."

Harold and Fred reached across the table to give each other high fives.

Kojo was still trying to get a fix on the place. They were obviously in a musical establishment of some kind. But what kind?

Ten minutes after their drinks were served, the house lights were dimmed and the players took the stage.

Kojo felt himself sliding off his seat.

"That's Don Cherry, one of the most avant garde musicians in the world," he almost yelled to his table mates.

"No," Teresa Arbus whispered back, "That is Don Cherry's son. And that is NaNa Mayato playing the Berimbau, the pandiero, chekere and all those other percussions. The Indian man seating himself behind the tablas is the son of the late Chatur Lal."

"Do you know him?"

"Strangely, I do. I've been an Indian music freak all my life. There are two Indian percussionists you would have to know, if you liked Indian music at all, Alla Rakha and Chatur Lal."

"And finally, the bass player, Mr. Otis Blackwell."

"Wowww."

Don Cherry the second made a brief announcement...

"We're glad you're here. We call this 'One Earth Music' and our first piece, written by my father, is called 'Moon Fruit.'"

Forty five minutes later "Moon Fruit" faded out. The combination of musical elements that seemed so incompatible; Cherry's pocket trumpet, Mayato's Berimbau, pandiero and agogo, Chatur Lal's tablas and Otis Blackwell's Latin bass style, blended into something that Kojo could only call Ethereal.

The audience was seriously appreciative, no footstomping or wild cowboy yells. They knew why they were there and they were almost cultish about it.

Kojo solemnly shook hands around the table... "Teresa, Fred, Harold, I thank you guys for sharing this experience with me."

"Oh, there is more...."

An hour later they, literally floated out of the club..., the "more" had been a small, finely shaped African-American woman who sang in six languages.

The songs, like the instrumental music that filled them with ethereal feelings was haunting. Kojo was especially drawn to a song she called "Steps to Alabama"

"What is her name?"

"She is called Kanda." 1•

Kojo wanted to ask hundreds of questions about the quintet. How did they get together? How did two sons of two famous musicians (Don Cherry and Chatur Lal) meet? Who writes Kanda's music?

The questions seemed irrelevant. They were there, the music was being presented to the world, why question anything? Why question such an experience?

I'll certainly have something to lay on Juna's head when we start talking about musical ideas.

Friday morning, 8:30 a.m. Kojo had decided to do a little Capoeira in the park a half block from his apartment. One thing he had noticed is that the Danes were into physical fitness. And beer.

Five minutes into his workout a dozen people had paused to take a closer look at the "strange" movements he was making.

By the time he had worked up a sweat, there were at least a hundred people checking him out. They didn't interrupt his flow, they didn't ask questions.

They simply observed and passed quiet comments amongst themselves. When he finished, they gave him a polite round of applause, which he responded to, and kept on about their business.

I like this, people who know how to appreciate what you're doing, but no need to bug you about it. I like this.

Shower-shave-ready for the last day. The last day... It's been an interesting time, very, very interesting.

He was stunned to see four of his "industrial training" films, shorts made for various organizations.

"What is the difference between a disabled person and a handicapped person?"

"He can't see but he can feel."

"Brother, can you spare a moment?"

"We need sympathy, not ignorance."

"Teresa, where...how did you get these...?"

"We began to assemble your works months ago, we felt certain that you would accept our invitation."

The afternoon session ended too soon, he felt, the questions never stopped.

"Why did they stop making the Hollywood-Extravaganza musicals?"

"What happened to the Cowboy/Wild West genre?"

"Are African-American actors and actresses paid the same as Whites?"

"Would it be possible for a White man to make an African-American film?"

"What roles are given to African-American women?"

"What motivates your art?"

"Have you enjoyed Denmark?"

And to conclude, Jan Alborg stood to announce that the film committee of the University had voted to give Mr. Kojo Bediako Brown a $3,500 dollar honorarium for being willing to come and answer so many questions.

Kojo caused a lot of jaws to drop when he counter-announced that he was returning the honorarium to the committee "for future artistic endeavors."

He thought they were going to shout the roof off.

"This is good what you have done," Jan Alborg informed him in the midst of the bedlam.

And finally - finally it was over, time to go for the lobster dinner, the Australian Riesling and later, more of Fred Helsinger's Copenhagen.

He made a firm commitment to stick it out, no matter what.

In the quaint Danish styled chalet/restaurant, nibbling on the biggest lobster tail he'd ever seen, he casually questioned Fred about the night's activities.

"Oh, there are a few places. I think you will like. Yes, I think you will like. Teresa will not accompany us this evening."

"I see."

The Danish sky was opening up with a lovely blue-yellow as Kojo staggered out of Harold Andersen's car.

"Oh, Kojo, what time is your flight?"

"I think it's one thirty."

"Good, that will give you time to rest, we will collect you about noon."

"Yeahhh, o.k., whatever..."

He staggered into his apartment, took a hot shower, drank a cold glass of butter rich Danish milk (someone had told him that it prevented hangovers) and sprawled under the covers, trying to piece it together before he fell asleep.

The Transvestite Theatre. I never would have known they were men if somebody hadn't told me.

The Jam Session. How long did we stay there? Heavy jazz sounds by visiting brothers from the U.S. and Danes who could hold their own, everything from post-Be-Bop to ultra-future.

And finally - "to top the evening off" - a visit to an exclusive whore house.

"It isn't necessary to do anything, Kojo. You might like to drink a little champagne and have a little conversation with one of the girls, eh?"

An interesting two hours. Fred Helsingor and Harold Andersen were barely inside the beautifully designed "day room" before they were led away by designing females.

"Don't worry, Kojo, we'll be back."

He took a glass of champagne from a passing tray and settled back on a low slung Danish sofa.

He liked the way it was done. Every five minutes or so a woman would wander through the room, nod politely in his direction and move on.

It wasn't a hard sell establishment, obviously. Kojo hadn't felt the need or the urge to have sex, but it felt good to sit around in a swank whore house, sipping champagne.

The look of the woman startled him. She looked familiar.

He prevented her from continuing her stroll through the room.

"Uhh, pardon me, but don't I know you from somewhere?"

"You ever lived in Oakland, California?"

"Not really. I know the place. I'm from L.A."

"Ohh, Los Angeles. I have some cousins in L.A."

The conversation had been smooth and casual; a mutual liking, things, places in common, no real need to go into why he was there or why she was there.

"Oh, incidentally, my name is Arlene."

"Mine is Kojo."

The lustful Danes, Helsinger and Andersen, joined them after a bit.

"Hah, aren't you the sly one?"

They shared a couple bottles of champagne, laughs, jokes, and it was time to move on.

There were no professional expressions of regret, nothing maudlin.

They smiled into each others face, shook hands and that was that.

Wonder how a twenty year old sister from Oakland, California winds up in a Danish whore house? Yeahhh, truth is trying to figure odd things out. O well...

He forced himself to wake up at 11:15 a.m. Have to get packed, scribble a few thank you notes.

"Kojo, always try to thank people for kindnesses shown you, it will earn you friends for life."

Jan Alborg, Teresa Arbus, Fred Helsinger, Harold Andersen, the host and hostess of the faculty party.

The notes finished, he began dumping dirty shirts, socks and shorts into his suitcase. It definitely pays to travel light.

They literally poured him on the 'plane after a final round of drinks in the airport bar.

The goodbyes were properly given, reassurances made that they would definitely see each other again.

And he was away in the big bird. Wowww... That was a blast. Remembered incidents forced smiles from him during the course of the marathon naps that he took during the flight.

Conversations, real and imaginary, flitted through his consciousness. The possibility of doing a West African version of "Dinner With Andre." I would use three people, instead of two.

FADE IN

SCENE I

INT. - Shalizar Drinking Bar - NIGHT

The conversation takes place over the course of a few hours. The fuel for the talk is well chilled bottles of A.B.C. Lager.

The conversationalists are Kojo, Adule and Kalo.

KALO

I saw a television program last evening where a number of African
American youths were being interviewed on what they know about
Africa, in general, and Ghana in particular.

Their ignorance was appalling.

KOJO

Why would you react with such surprise? Think about how African
Americans are educated. The majority of us tend to think that
"education" is supposed to circumnavigate the idea of racial identity,
especially for Africans in America.

We are the only racial group in America that is consistently asked
to forget who we are — that is a deliberate ploy to push us away from
identification with Africa, African causes and aspirations.

What I'm saying is that we're dealing with a four-hundred old
disinformation campaign.

Most of us, incredibly, have managed to retain some knowledge of self
despite the Euro-blitzkrieg.

What I'd like to know is, what is your excuse for not knowing more
about us?"

CAMERA ANGLE I CLOSE

ADULE
(innocent expression)

I don't know what you are asking, my brother.

KOJO

I'm asking you why Africans don't know more about Africans in the
Diaspora. You make a big thing about us knowing a lot about Ghana,
but how many Ghanaians know much about us?

KALO

Well, you must remember, my brother, what the colonialists did to us. They didn't want us to have proper knowledge of Africans on the outside.

KOJO

What do you think you're hearing/seeing when, they interview young African-Americans who say stupid things, like, "I'm not an African, I'm an American." Can't you see the effects of a harsher, more brutal colonialization?

ADULE

Hmmm. . .I can see that. But how do you explain the ignorance of Diaspora Africans concerning us? The computer, all of the technology and information is at your fingertips.

KOJO

Ahh, yes, my sister, at our fingertips, but who controls the button that releases the information?

ADULE

What does that mean?

KOJO

It means that those who have a vested interest in keeping a veil of ignorance over our heads can do that as long as we allow them to do it.

KALO

Now then, let me ask you this, my brother."

KOJO

Go for it...

KALO

You are an American, are you not?

CAMERA ANGLE

KOJO
(defensively)

I am an African-American.

ADULE

We know that you are an African-American. You've told us that often enough... (They trade smiles)... But do you consider yourself an American?

KOJO
(pregnant pause)

Adule, Kalo, as weird as this may sound to you, I have to say it... I am an African in the Diaspora...

KALO

Does that mean that you're not proud to be an American?

KOJO

No, I'm not proud to be an American, not in the sense that you're proud to be a Ghanaian."

KALO

Why not?

KOJO

Kalo, my brother, I'm proud of what our people managed to do in America, in the Caribbean, wherever, but I can't start waving the flag around.

You have to keep in mind, both of you, that the kind of background that may breed patriotism, pride and all those other abstract tidbits are missing from our experience.

It would be extremely difficult for me, for any conscious African American, to say that he was "proud" of America.

I have met African-Americans who talked about America with great pride, in Ghana here. But 99% of them were government employees. They wouldn't trust the average brother or sister to come over here because they'd be too likely to say what I'm saying.

ADULE

You sound like someone who is out of sync with his country.

KOJO

I am, definitely. And I think most African-Americans are, to some extent. Look, let's face it, we have peeked the suckers hole card and we know what the deal is.

CHAPTER 25

ADULE

(puzzled expression)

What does that mean in plain English?

KOJO

It means that we know the character of this
snake and what kind of venom he has.

KALO

Ahhh, Kojo, my brother, you see, that's where you leave me cold.
I can't make myself believe that White people are inherently evil...or
any different from any other people, actually.

KOJO

That's what makes y'all perpetually naive Africans... Now please be
clear about what I'm saying. I'm saying that we have had, are having an
experience with the snake that you brothers and sisters know nothing
about.

I'm saying, for better or worse, we have been out, forced to live in his
world, and beat him at his own game, in order to survive.

KALO

Kojo, I have some notion of what you're talking about, but it always makes me feel uncomfortable when you block it off into Black/White us and them terms.

KOJO

Sorry, man, but that's the way it is. Look, right now, at this moment, the Eurocentrists... you like that better?

ADULE

I know what you mean by the term...

CAMERA ANGLE CHANGES

KOJO

Good. The Eurocentrists are waging all out war on our people here in Ghana, and elsewhere, and I don't see any effort being made to counterattack or even to defend...

ADULE

Of course we know about the World Bank scheme to indebt us back into colonial times and all that...

KOJO

I'm going beyond that, Madam, way beyond that.

KALO

O.K., go! Let's have another round. Hey Cholly, three more of the same here.

Kojo squirmed around in his seat, feeling restless after so many hours of being confined to one space. Despite the discomfort he felt it was ideal for his twilight thinking of his Ghanaian-trio-version of "Dinner With Andre."

KOJO

O.K., I'm going to go, to start from the top and go down. Here we are in Ghana here, in the middle of the rainforest and every woman I see has her hair starched, ironed, fried...

ADULE
(defensively)

And what's so wrong with straightening one's hair?

KOJO

Adule, I don't want to get into the right or wrong of it, on a personal level, we're talking about the war, remember?

ADULE

So, what's hair got to do with it?

KOJO

On some levels, everything. That's the basis of my argument. We start off, when I say "we," I'm talking about the Eurocentric bad guys; we start off convincing the African woman that her own naturally kinky hair should be straightened.

In a very symbolic sense that act of treachery causes the African woman to open up a jar labeled "self hatred"...the self hatred comes from trying to take a comb, that wasn't designed for your hair, in the first place - we went through those changes in America, for many years - now here we are in Africa, where the first Natural combs were carved and what's happening? All the women are frying, starching and ironing their hair.

KALO SIPS HIS BEER,
A NEUTRAL, AMUSED EXPRESSION BLANKING HIS FACE

ADULE
(trying to be cool)

Kojo, I think we have to see hair straightening as a personal matter, not an element of this so-called war, you're trying to make us see.

KOJO

Adule, I would love to agree with you, but I can't. You know why?

ADULE
(pissed)

So why?

KOJO

Simple, we convince the beautiful African woman that her hair is ugly. We go from there to the skin, to the face, with skin bleaches and chemicals designed to lighten the skin to go along with the pressed hair. You see it on the billboards and in commercials, they're constantly pushing the idea that lighter skinned women have more "fun", drive fancier cars, are better cared for.

Don't you see?! It's called Cultural Imperialism. The Eurocentrists have walked in here and convinced you that they are superior. What do the blonde, blue eyed Jesus representations really mean?

KALO

I say, Kojo, ol' sock, aren't we going a bit off the track here?

KOJO

No, I'm not. I'm right on the track. Can't you see what will happen in a few years? Can't you see what has already happened?

Once your children have been saturated by ads glorifying Eurocentric values, your crime rate is going to go up because the poor people who can't afford to do anything but watch American re-runs are going to start to thirst for some of what they see?

Drugs are coming. Different, strange, crazy new drugs that will have people throwing their babies in the ocean, killing their mothers....

ADULE

And you're saying all of this is a spin off from the Eurocentric syndrome?

KOJO

Well, I can't honestly say that I see a collection of Europeans sifting around a table somewhere saying, "Lets destabilize Ghana by stuffing the country full of false values.

No, I can't honestly say that. I think it's a bigger game than that.

I think the Eurocentrics are so self centered that they don't even concern themselves with all of the elements as weapons in their war. They just simply fire their weapons and hope to kill as many Africans as possible, either spiritually, mentally, physically, however.

ADULE
(sarcastically)

And could you give us some justification for this war being waged?

KOJO

That's a naive question. It's to prevent us from forming the kind of link up that would make us the most powerful people on the planet.

FADE OUT

Time to eat. He stared at the tray, with its neatly arranged bites of this and that.

Is it breakfast? Lunch? Dinner?

It must be dinner, they're serving wine with the food. On the way back now, the funny time is over, the serious stuff is about to begin. He sketched and erased, drew and smudged out pages of sketches and ideas.

Maybe I should wait until I touch a solid surface before I try to put this together.

A few times, staring at the frosted clouds in mid-Atlantic, he put the whole puzzle together (the script, the production company, people, places, all of it) in an instant, only to have it slip away from him.

Better get off this McDonald fast food-image-kick and do it the way it's supposed to be done, inch by bitter inch.

He felt anxious, but determined as the 'plane circled for landing at LAX. Akosua was there with smiles and kisses.

"Well, so how was it?"

"Akos', I got some stuff to lay on you."

Back in the city, back in the smog.

"Kojo, roll up your window, unless you want to drop dead."

"Yeahhh, you can say that again."

She drove expertly, casting flirtatious looks at him from time-to-time.

"Well, come on out with it, man, I've been dying to get the whole story since your phone call."

"Patience, love, patience. Why don't we go somewhere for a chilled glass of white wine?"

"Milanos?"

"Our spot."

Milanos at 11 a.m. on Monday morning looked like an overdressed woman without her make up.

Papa Milano himself led them to their favorite table.

"Nothing done yet, you wanna little garlic bread or somethin'?"

"Just a couple chilled glasses of your white San Antonio."

"No problem."

They sipped as Kojo began to spool it out; the reception, the receptivity, the lack of racism, the intellectual openness.

"I'm not going to say that these are the perfect White folks, or nothing like that, but I have to admit that I was impressed by their appreciation of my work.

I could kick myself for not checking into the publishing angle for you, I'm sure they would be interested in your work."

"We'll get to that, I'm sure. I'm just glad it was such a positive experience for you."

"It was, baby, believe me, it was."

Thirty minutes later they were cinched in each others arms, trying to make up for a week's absence. Afterwards, Kojo nodded off into a deep, sexual cat nap...it gets sweeter and sweeter and sweeter....

He woke up to the smell of something delicious....

"Akos', what is that?"

"Nothing special, egg plant fried in olive oil, Parmesan cheese, a little salad."

"Think we could sip a little vino with that?"

"That's the way we started our day."

They sat across from each other in his "breakfast nook," enjoying the taste of the good food, each other's good vibes.

"Akos', we're at the serious part of the story now."

"I know, I could tell from the expression on your face when I picked you up this morning."

"That obvious, huh?"

"To anyone who knows what a determined look looks like."

"I guess that's good. In any case, after the Danish pastries and the late nights and the applause, it's time for me to get back into putting the kind of program I need to put together to hold the dyno group that I've asked to join me."

Akosua circled the table and sat on his lap...

"When do you want me to start?"

"Glad you asked that. I got this crazy idea in my head of us taking a working vacation in Mexico for, let's say...a week."

Akosua kissed him solidly on the nose....

"God! You don't know how wonderful it is to have a man who can dream...."

"And, hopefully, make the dream come true."

"Don't worry about that, <u>we're</u> on the job. When do you want to leave?"

"Well, I thought I'd get stuff squared away here, give you a chance to tidy up your desk and we could leave this weekend."

"Where to?"

"Just meander down Highway 15 on the east side, the Gulf side, 'til we find a little town we like, stay a couple days and meander on back."

She surprised him by popping off of his lap and dancing around.

"O yes! I'd love that! The last trip I made to Mexico was with my parents, to Mexico City, about five years ago. And my mother being my mother, wasn't satisfied until she had shopped at every exclusive shop in the city, 'dined' at every posh restaurant in the city and bored the hell out of me."

"Now, now, Akos', we mustn't be too hard on our parents. Remember, she's the lady who brought us together."

"How can I ever forget it? Hahhh hahh hah....

The following days slipped by, punctuated by odd snags and obstacles. Juna, the genius musician, the designated film scorer, called to express pessimism.

"I don't think it's going to work, Kojo. I just don't see how...."

"Juna, rest your worries. And besides, we haven't even gotten into a script yet, let alone pre-production. Give it a chance, o.k.?"

"So, you're really feeling that definite, huh?"

"More than definite, confident! Talk with you on the third Sunday, next month."

"Yeahhh, hope I can make it."

I'll definitely have to have Akosua walk her around.

"Patterns" / "The Man in the Grey Flannel Suit," "business" movies... he replaced the 'phone in its cradle and stared out of the window at the two movies strolling side by side; Van Heflin, the bright new man replacing the old warhorse, Ed Begley, in the corporate structure. Gregory Peck, the fledgling executive, out to make his corporate mark.

Wonder what that's got to do with me? O well...a letter from Grace.

"Dear Kojo,

Just a page, a note really. I know you're probably up to your neck with projects, things to do. More power to you.

Ghana hasn't been the same since you left. I'm saying that for many reasons, the main one being the fact that I miss you a great deal.

That may come as a big surprise from someone who is supposed to have an upper lip as stiff as mine.

Onward. My office staff has shown a greater appreciation of my presence since your departure (smile) and life continues.

I hope you had a pleasant trip back and that you'll remember to drop a few lines, now and then.

Love faithfully,
Grace

P.S. Went to visit my Auntie Eugenia in Tsito last weekend and she told me to tell you to be aware, to be careful. Sounds a bit mysterious to me."

Kojo folded the letter in half, unfolded it and stared at the gracefully slanting curves of Grace's handwriting...*Dear Dear Grace.*

A bit of touchie-feelie with Mom and Dad...

"We thought the Vikings had captured you." A bit of reaffirmation with Grandfather Kwame.

"You were right on the money, Granddad, some pretty nice people over there."

An obligatory Thursday afternoon visit with his prospective in-laws.

"I didn't tell them that we were going out of town together, I just thought I'd let them do their own arithmetic...so, when Mom makes her frantic call on Saturday morning she should be able to figure out – 'the last person I saw her with was him.'"

Friday morning... "C'mon, let's get outta here." They kept a conspiratorial silence from the far flung suburbs of Los Angeles to within sight of the San Bernardino mountains. Akosua broke the silence with a loud sigh... "Thank God we're out of that place for a few minutes."

"Yeah, EL-A can attack your last nerve, and lots of people don't even know it's happening until they've shot somebody or driven into a crowd of school children."

The car was loaded with the bare necessities, a few sandwiches, water, changes of clothes.

"A lot of people trip off to Mexico like they're on safari in the Sahara. Whatever we don't have we can buy en route."

"I'm in your corner, Mr. Brown. I wish you had been able to convince my mother of that."

The High Desert and Mountains

San Bernardino, straight through the Imperial Valley, kicking off into Yuma, Arizona for the first leg. Arizona sprawled in front of them, a spread out adobe platter.

They were going to cross-over into Nogales, Mexico from Nogales, Arizona.

The air was dry, the sky blue with flecks of clouds, the way clear for good traveling.

"I'm glad we left in the morning, the evening traffic makes me feel mentally ill at times.

"Yeah, I know the feeling."

They traveled without making unnecessary commentary, a casual point with the chin at some unusual rock formation. Or a full fledged, "Look at that!" — as a coyote chased a rabbit across the road at twilight.

"Time to ease up, we've done a good day's journey."

"Where in the world are we?"

"This is the fantastic little place called Gila Bend."

Arizona Desert

The Gila Bend Motel was dusty but clean and they had showers in each cabin.

"Jest put 'em in a week ago, good clean water. Enjoy your stay."

They showered, changed clothes and strolled out into the desert night.

"Kojo, you know this is the first time we've traveled together."

"Yeah, I was thinking about that myself."

And how compatible we are. You don't find the need to fill up every moment with a lot of words and we communicate on another level. What was that woman's name that I took to the bullfights in Tijuana, the one who never stopped running her mouth?

"Have you taken this trip often?"

"About six or seven times over the years. When we first moved to L.A. my Dad used to do a lot of "exploring." We'd pile into our V.W. and drive to Tepic and back. Once we made it to Guadalajara and almost had to walk back."

The distant howl of a coyote startled them.

"You kinda forget that there are still wild things in the world. Why don't we go back to the motel?"

"Scared?"

"Not at all. I just feel the urge to tell you a bedtime story."

"As they say in Ghana...yesplease."

EXTERIOR - DAWN IN THE DESERT

The morning-cool-desert-wind whispered into the open windows of the car. Kojo hated air conditioning, it made him feel like he was living in an artificial environment.

Akosua looked cool and glamorous behind her shades, just the right shade of lipstick glossing her lips.

The road ribboned ahead, seeming to flow gently up and down, but in reality, only led to Tucson.

West 60_Arizona to Mexico

KOJO

We make a right turn at Tucson and head south to Nogales....

AKOSUA

You know, I've been taking casual notes of all the Indian reservations we've passed, beginning in California...the Santa Rosa Indian Reservation, the Fort Yumal, the Colorado Reservation, the Gila Bend/Gila River Reservation and we'll be passing the San Xavier Reservation just past Tucson.

And that's just a few. I never knew there were so many reservations in this area.

KOJO

Yeah, the Indians are really America's Invisible People. They settled back on the thought, there was nothing else to say.

FADE OUT

"Kojo, you want me to drive for awhile? You've had it since this morning."

"I'm o.k., I enjoy driving, makes me feel like I'm involved."

"Good. I enjoy being driven, it makes me feel uninvolved."

The casual, brief conversations were dwarfed by the spectacle of the country swallowing them. The glazed distances slowly dissolved into hazy lakes, mirages that promised cool dips and delivered hot desert winds and parched throats.

"Let's stop for a cold draught beer."

A right turn at Tucson and southward to Nogales.

They hadn't talked about Kojo's film idea or the outline for Akosua's next book, they felt the urge to drift at sixty miles an hour, shaking off the frenzied tempo of the place they had left the day before.

A few times during the course of a long stretch of highway Kojo felt the whole of his film project bloom in front of him, how all the pieces would fit, how the piece would be written, how the actors would play it, the music that would space it out, the whole thing.

It was there for a few seconds and then it faded, leaving him with only one or two sections to think on.

"What're you smiling about?"

"Oh, just tripping on what the creative surge can do with your head."

"I know, I've re-written the ending of my book about four times, in four different ways, in the past hour."

He surreptitiously studied her profile. Thank God I love the woman. It would really be a drag to have to marry someone you didn't love.

The thought of what he had to do made him tighten his grip on the steering wheel. Time is running out for me. We have to get married down here. Nogales straight ahead and then the other side... "El Norte" slid through his consciousness as Akosua dealt with the surprised customs people in her academic, but correct Spanish.

U.S. Border, Inspection Station, Mexico

"El Norte," the Mexican quest to go north to get to where the goodies are. The tortured couple crawl through a drain pipe full of rats, the human blood hounds sniffing around for a scent that would send them back.

And now, here we are, heading to "El Sur," for another kind of goodie. What a crazy world.

"O.K., Senor Brown, we can go now."

"That didn't take long."

"A little honest corruption goes a long way. That gentleman over there, the one with the cigar and the pregnant looking belly, is a professional fixer. I gave him twenty dollars and he walked the whole thing through.

We have insurance coverage, which means practically nothing. We have visitor's permits, the whole thing. Let's go."

"I'm impressed, my lady."

"All it takes is a bit of rudimentary Spanish."

The great Sonoran desert opened up in front of them; hot, dry and windless.

"Wowww, coming through Arizona is like heading into the mouth of the furnace...this is the furnace."

"You got that right. We'll have to go through here for a stretch before we can get over to the ocean at Guaymas, that'll be after we pass Hermosillo."

The plots of a dozen ocean-desert survival tales swam through the back of Akosua's brain. "The three men who find themselves stranded in the desert...Kojo would know the movie?...one of the few John Wayne movies I ever saw."

"'Three Godfathers,' that's the one, with that gorgeous Pedro Armendariz, with his beautiful almond eyes and lovely brush mustache. The 'Three Godfathers' who discover a woman about to give birth.

The baby is born and they struggle to walk it through the desert. Of course, the gringos find a way for Pedro to commit suicide so that he won't clutter things up in the end.

And, of course, John Wayne makes it to the town of New Jerusalem, conveniently on Christmas Day."

Miles of sandy earth, relieved by splashy green splotches of desert blooms, and other, more unbelievable sights.

"Kojo, did you see those children? Where can they possibly be going out here...?"

He stopped the car and backed up a couple hundred yards. Four boys and three girls, the oldest about ten years old. The children stared at the couple in the car.

Akosua asked them if they could give them a lift. She wasn't sure that, "Queres Ustedes un viaje?" conveyed the proper message but their mimicking was unmistakable.

They smiled shyly. The oldest boy announced gravely that they were only going - "there." He flopped his arms at some indiscriminate point away from the road.

Kojo offered them water and each one took two tiny sips.

"Gracias," the oldest-spokesman said and tipped the brim of his small sombrero.

"De Nada," Kojo resp onded and slowly geared up again.

"Where do you think they were going?"

"Where do you think they were coming from? That's the question."

Miles of beautiful, sandy yellow, deathly dry desert. They sipped water to relieve the idea of thirst. Occasionally they passed another car going in the opposite direction.

"Kojo, did you say this was a well traveled road."

"O yeah, this is Highway 15, a main artery. We'll be in Hermosillo in a few hours."

After a brief stop in Hermosillo to do a little supermarketing - "Kojo, how about a bottle of this?" They found themselves eagerly sniffing the fragrant breezes coming from the Gulf of California.

CHAPTER 26

"We made it to the sea."

Kojo in Mexico

Guaymas... "they made "Catch-22" down here, that mad thing with that crazy guy, ahhh, whatshisname? Alan Arkin…anyway, the last time I was here a lot of people were complaining about how the film company inflated local prices.

Lemonade went from a dime to twenty cents, that kind of thing."

He drove up and down a few of the main streets, to give Akosua a feel of the place.

"Hasn't changed much, a little more touristy than it was a few years ago. Let's hope they have a vacancy in "La Mar.""

#102, "La Mar." They showered in water that mingled with the salt of the ocean on their front door step.

"Akos', shall we dress for dinner?"

"Of course.

They had the "La Mar" dining room to themselves, dressed in their wrinkled, but spotless white outfits.

"Huachinango a la Vera Cruzano for two."

"Si, Senor."

"Kojo, I thought you couldn't speak Spanish."

"I know how to ask for food in about six languages...."

The large, firm fleshed fish, drizzled with succulently fried onions, pimientos, olives and spices tasted as though it had been plucked out of the sea minutes before.

"Mmmm...I'd forgotten what fresh fish tastes like...mmm."

Fresh fish, chilled bottles of Carta Blanca. They strolled out onto the pier in front of the Hotel, taking in the sight of the low skimming pelicans, the far flung sparkle of stars.

He stood behind her, his arms circling her waist, nuzzling her neck.

"Akos', I love you, do you know that?"

She made a slow, wordless turn, held his face in her hands and kissed him. There was nothing to say.

They sang wordless songs driving south, a few miles from the sea coast. They paused to have finger sized tacos and cold bottles of beer in towns that seemed too small to have a name.

"What do they call this place?"

"If they called it anything other than 'this place,' it would be too much."

Kojo was delighted to discover a sense of humor in Akosua that he hadn't been exposed to before. It was dry and sharp, but not acidic.

"It's too bad more of our people don't travel to Mexico, the way we're traveling, they might not miss the concrete slave ships as much as they think."

Akosua admired Kojo's way of coping. It was always a positive vibe happening.

The car won't start? It must be out of gas, that's all.

We're stranded in the middle of nowhere? No problem, someone will be passing soon.

"Nothing is a real problem if your mindset can find the proper frequency."

"What's our destination? Or do we have one?"

"Interesting, that you should ask that. I wanted to surprise you by just coming to a dead stop in the town of Huatabampo."

"Sounds like a beautiful place to stop...Huatabampo."

Huatabampo, population a few thousands, Spanish and Toltec spoken. They drove slowly through the town, circling the miniature plaza and the town's police officer, who smiled and waved at them, and then exited the town to rent a room at the Huatabampito Hotel.

It was midmorning when they arrived and there was no sign of a desk clerk or anyone who could register them.

Kojo signed the register, decided that they should occupy "Suite #6" and settled in.

"Eventually someone will show up to collect our money. Count on it."

They unloaded the car and settled into a sparsely furnished, but neat little room, the Gulf of Mexico a hundred yards to their direct front.

Huatabampito - the beach at Huatabampo - curved gently for two miles. The water was warm as blood and filled with shrimp, porpoises, Portuguese Men of War, large and small sting rays, and thousands of other types of sea animals.

Kojo and Akosua sat in the shallows, gazing out onto a horizon that was so blue it looked like a painting.

"Akos', I want you to help me put a script together."

"That's why we're here."

It was the beginning of a creative surge, they both felt it.

"I don't want this to interfere with your work."

"It will, but don't let that bother you, I think the dividends will be worth it."

"O.K., here's what I have in mind." They strolled the curving beach, tossing thoughts back and forth.

"I'm calling it a silent film, but it won't be silent in the old fashioned sense of the word. The tentative title is "My Grandfather's Eyes.""

"Mmm... I like that."

"I haven't worked the complete story out in my head yet but I know what the elements are. I want African-American satire, the stuff we hear in some of the old blues singers, serious realism, history, edu-tainment, a cross sectioned look at what we're about.

I want to peel back some layers and take a look at some stuff that hasn't been considered before. When I say it won't be a silent film, per se, but I want to use a lot of the elements that were used in the White silent film era — subtitles, transitional music, stuff like that. The problem I'm dealing with is what kind of story can I tell that will be strong enough to hold up under these elements?"

"I see your problem. Let me think on it."

"Camarones! Camarones! Camarones!"

The sight and sound of the little man with a huge sack draped across his back startled them.

"Wow! Where did he come from?"

"This is Mexico, wherever there's a customer you'll have someone selling something."

They bought a pound of the finger sized shrimp for a dollar. The vendor explained that they would go well with "cervesa frias."

"Akos', he's right. I'm going to run in town for a minute to pick up some beer, and a few other items. You want anything?"

"Sounds like we're going to need some note pads and a few more ballpoints."

"Be back in a bit."

She watched him jog away, feeling suddenly lonely. We haven't been out of each other's sight in days...she strolled, nibbled on a few shrimp, thought about the proposed script.

"My Grandfather's Eyes." Yeahhh, I can get into that, we can take a serious look at perspectives that most American movies ignore. Even now, whenever there are older African-Americans in movies, they're either treated like antiques or off brand jokes.

I can see ways to bring in the African-American woman's points of view. He talks about the silent film era and how it missed Black men. We weren't even thought about.

The beach scene was hypnotic, a school of porpoises, behaving like children out of school, leapt from the water, chased each other in turbulent circles, had fun.

A distant ship that looked like a Chinese junk edged close enough for her to see that they had huge lights fore and aft, a shrimp boat that used the lamps to attract their catch.

She sat at the shore line, thinking. Strange, I've known this man for two years and now, after a few days of driving through Mexico, I have the feeling that I'm meeting him for the First Time, for real.

She smiled at the idea. Me, the romantic novelist, him, the visionary film maker. We ought to be able to stir a few fires around.

After an hour and a half of serious thinking and digging her toes into the warm sand, she strolled back to "Suite #6" of the Huatabampito Hotel.

Mr. and Mrs. Ferdinan Chavez and the six stair-step-children of the Chavez' greeted her as she walked into the hotel lobby.

"Welcome, Senora, welcome. We were not here to greet you and your husband, we were attending a birthday party for my sister in town.

Please, whatever you need, please call upon us. This is my wife Anna, my son Juan, my son, Felipe, my daughter Carlota, my daughter Juanita, my son, Jose and my latest daughter, Carmen...."

She liked them. The wife was Mexican-woman shy, the man was macho-proud and the children resembled black eyed cherubs.

They stared into her mouth as though she had released a stream of gold when she greeted them in Spanish. And all but performed a little dance around her.

"The gringa speaks our language hurray! hurray!"

"And your husband, he also speaks Spanish?"

"Only when necessary."

"My wife will prepare your dinner this evening. It will be our welcome to you."

Kojo returned an hour later, two six-packs of beer in hand, looking amused and distracted.

Akosua introduced him to the Chavez family. The amenities over, everyone seemed to melt into their own niche.

The children went up and down the beach capturing crabs and doing the simple things children do. Papa Ferdinan dozed away in a hammock and Mama Chavez quietly began to assemble a collection of seafoods and spices that drifted through "Suite #6" like a seductive perfume.

The beer was cold and the shrimps were warm and crunchy, a perfect first course.

"I don't know what the sister is cooking but I think I'm going to eat a lot of it."

They sprawled on deck chairs in front of the Hotel, the sole tenants, note pads at the ready, enjoying the lush afternoon.

"What took you so long, Kojo, I thought they had deported you or something?"

She detected an elfin, mischievous gleam in his eyes, "Just trying to find the coldest beer in town, that's all."

An hour later, the youngest Chavez came to tug gently at Akosua's hand.

"She's telling me dinner is ready."

They raced to their room for a quick shower and a change of shirts.

"As good as it smells, it's got to deserve a change of shirts."

The five-table sized dining room was opened to them. Papa Ferdinan wished them "buen provecho!" on his way down to the beach with a long fishing rod.

And, as soon as they were seated, Mama Chavez marched in with a beautifully formed clay pot, steaming with seafood.

"What is it called, Senora?" Akosua asked.

"It is called Sopa de Huatabampito."

Sopa de Huatabampito steak firm cutlets of red snapper, slices of squid, chunks of turtle meat, stewed tomatoes, olives, onions, shrimps, small corn tortillas and bottles of chilled Bohemia.

"Kojo, you ever tasted anything this good in your whole life?"

"Only one thing," he replied, dead pan.

The stew was served in soup bowls and the small tortillas were replaced as soon as the stack was decimated.

They swallowed the cold beer, washing down the soup-stew and bit chunks from the tortillas.

Mama Chavez glanced from the kitchen from time to time, to make certain that they were enjoying her food. She was not disappointed.

Thirty minutes later they surrendered to drum tight stomachs...and sat smiling at each other.

"Akos', tell me how to say that was a hell of a meal."

"Gracias, Senora, un buen provecho!"

"Gracias, Senora, un buen provecho!"

"De Nada, Senor, de nada."

The Chavez children cleared their bowls from the table as they waddled out of the dining room.

"Kojo, let's take a little walk."

"Good idea."

The sky at twilight was rainbowing a collection of purples, blood reds, orange, blues and umber. They strolled the beach, their arms around each other's waists.

"I want to get some of this in the first film, especially the first film, this sense of the romantic that we are never given credit for having. It's always hump-thump-sex-next with us."

"You're right. I'd love to see this kind of scene in an African-American film."

"We'll put it in."

They passed Ferdinan Chavez casting his line far out into the waves. He held up two small dolphin sized fish for them to admire.

"Un buen provecho!" Kojo called out. Papa Chavez laughed.

A soft blooming night, the gentle lapping of the Gulf against the shore lured them back to their sanctuary. The lamp in their room was dim but serviceable.

"How about the ending of the film? How do you see that?"

"I see the ending as a beginning."

They were beginning to work out an intellectual shorthand, the result of imaginative minds in sync. Kojo was going to supply the bulk of the substance and Akosua was going to add to that, as well as create the form.

They exchanged ideas and made future plans before falling into dreamless sleeps.

❖

"Akos'! Akos'! Wake up! Wake up!"

"What?! What's wrong?!"

"It's almost nine o'clock!"

She gave him a curious look and snuggled back under the sheet. What's with my man? Doesn't he know we're on a vacation?

Kojo went into a different mode. He shook her gently by the shoulder and kissed her in her right ear.

"Akos', please wake up, baby...I need your help with something."

She responded, as he knew she would, sympathetically. "What is it, Kojo?"

"C'mon, I can tell you on the way to town."

A puzzled frown covered her face watching him go into the shower. What's going on here?

She popped into the shower just as he was toweling off, a half dozen questions on the tip of her tongue.

"Don't worry, baby, I'll answer all your questions, just hurry up, please."

He had laid her pearl white skirt and pink short sleeved blouse across the bed.

"I didn't know what color panties you were planning to wear today."

He cut her puzzled frown in half with a seriously probing kiss, and whispered... "Please hurry, we don't want to be late."

The sea breeze and inland desert wind splashing in her face pushed her into a fully awake state.

Kojo was driving a bit faster than usual, focusing on a distant thought. He wants me to help him do something? Oh, something he's come across in Spanish? But what's the rush?

He slipped into a parking space in front of the most imposing building in town, the City Hall. What?!

"Come on, we're on time!"

He held her hand tightly as they raced up the five steps into the city hall. He seemed to relax, once they were inside the building.

"Where to, now?"

He pointed at a door at the end of the corridor. The Mayor's Office....

She could see the outlines of a number of people through the opaque glass as she approached the door, Kojo's hand gripping hers.

He opened the door and an animated group of people burst into smiles and applause.

"Kojo," Akosua spoke in a small voice, "What is this?"

He held both of her hands and stared in her eyes. "If you consent to be my wife, this morning, the Mayor is going to say the words, these gentlemen are going to Mariachi us and we're going to the Floridita Cafe down the street and have a wedding breakfast with champagne."

Akosua burst into tears.

"Does that mean yes?"

The words were said, in Spanish, Akosua translating tearfully, the Mariachis crooning soulfully in the background.

"With this ring I thee wed...."

Akosua stared at the beautifully designed, double tiered gold band he placed on her finger, and the one he gave her to put on his finger.

"I've always thought it should go both ways," he whispered.

After the final words, the kiss, a discreet distribution of pesos to the Mayor and the Mariachis, they floated out of the office with a license that certified that they were husband and wife.

Three doors away from City Hall they entered La Floridita Cafe. The owner, a golden skinned, plump woman with thickly coiled braids, smiled them to a corner table where two bottles of Piper Heidseck were plunged into a zinc bucket and covered with chunks of ice.

"The breakfast is now, Senor Koho?"

"Si, senora, now."

Akosua kept dabbing at her eyes, trying not to cry.

"Kojo, when did you do all this?"

"Yesterday, when I came to get the beer."

"But, but how?...I mean, your Spanish is...."

"My Spanish is subnormal, but this makes up the difference."

He held a thick wad of peso notes under the table. Akosua laughed.

"Yeah, I guess you got a point."

Huevos Rancheros, refried beans and spinach.

"I had to convince her that we didn't want the sausage. She struggled with that for a few minutes."

"The spinach is delicious with the eggs and beans."

Customers wandered in and out, were informed of the reason for the celebration at the corner table, and smiled in their direction.

Midway into the second bottle of champagne. "Kojo, burp! where did you find Piper Heidseck burp! 'scuse me! in Huata-bimpa burp!"

"The Mayor's brother is the 'fixit man' in town. See him and you can get anything."

An hour later, they made a clever stagger back to the car, supporting each other, waving to a cafe full of well wishing Mexicans.

"Kojo, can you drive? You o.k.?"

"Never felt better. If this were EL-A, I'd say lets take a taxi, but once we get to the end of the street there's nothing to hit but open road."

"Let's hit it!"

They made a shaky start from the curb but leveled out just past a donkey loaded with tree branches.

They drove slowly, carefully, feeding on each other's good vibes.

"Kojo, you've just given me one of the most beautiful mornings of my life."

"Let's try to see if we can extend it to the rest of the day."

He stopped the car in the middle of the road to kiss her.

By the time they arrived at their hotel, the Chavez' had been informed, via the small town gossip system that is more effective than the telegraph, that they had just been married.

The Chavez' were obviously pleased with their guests and with the fact that they were now renting a room to an authentically married couple.

But they were discreet. Mrs. Chavez announced, "I will bake a small cake for Mr. and Mrs. Koho."

"Gracias, Senora."

It was close to high noon before they found themselves in bed together, again. Akosua draped her arms around Kojo's neck and squeezed him.

"Kojo, you've made me a happy woman, a truly happy woman."

They made carefree, champagne soaked love and settled into a world of dreams....

The film was lushly photographed, the characters memorable, the music haunting... "Courtesans of Bombay" out of the Merchant House of Indian movies. And the other one that the Frenchman made before he was snared by Jane Fonda, the thing about the Kathakali Dancers.

Something about the superior Indian films, maybe it's the music...

Kojo felt himself drifting on waves of sound, the sitar, the sarod, the shanai...

The sixth sense that sometimes warns us of danger, or that someone is staring at you in your sleep woke him up. He opened his eyes to see Akosua staring at him with an amused glint in her eyes.

"Quick, tell me, what was that dream about?"

He laughed and scooped her up in his arms..."I was thinking about you, baby, I was dreaming about you."

It was dawn and they had made the decision the night before to begin their day with a walk on the beach, prior to beginning the drive back to Los Angeles.

"Akos', I see the first film as a collage, almost, which is one of the reasons why I want it to be relatively silent.

I've always been impressed by how well the Japanese, especially, use the silence in their movies.

The collage will give us a chance to weave in a number of themes. You ever listen to Indian music?"

"I have, with you."

"Well, o.k., think about the big sound you hear coming from the sitar, and then those sympathetic sounds...."

"The sounds that shimmer."

"Exactly, shimmering sound is a damn good description. I see the film, I see 'Grandfather's Eyes' in that way.

Sometimes I think dialogue is over used in many American films simply because some people need to hear noise. For example, if we were shooting this scene, I would only want to hear natural sounds. I'd like you to keep that in mind when you start writing.

In some ways it'll make our job harder...."

"Because the economy of word usage will entail greater need for selectivity."

He hugged her to his chest.... "I couldn't've said it better."

They strolled, pausing to watch porpoises at play, to pick up interesting stones, to envelope each other with wordless hugs, strolled....

"Akos', just think, this time yesterday morning I was Kojo Bediako Brown, friend-lover-single guy. And today I am Kojo Bediako Brown, husband. I feel proud."

She held her ring up to the light.... "Yesterday, about this time I was Akosua Ferguson. Today I'm Akosua Ferguson-Brown, wife. And I'm proud."

They made a gentle right turn and started back, each of them swamped by a barrage of feelings.

"I'll have to break the news gently to my Mom and Dad, she'll be close to a heart attack, no matter what."

"I'll have to figure out a way to prevent **my Mom and Dad** from giving us a Big Celebration. It'll be hard to make them understand that this trip to Mexico put us on the work bench."

What a beautifully creative mind he has. The whole concept that he's talking about may be twenty years old but he makes it sound fresh, new.

Now then, I've done the first thing, I've made the first step. But I don't have to feel that I did it as an obligation. I think I would've probably married Akosua anyway. I think.

Mama Chavez welcomed them with a lush fish roe and egg breakfast.

"We'd be fat if we stayed here longer than a week."

After the breakfast and heartfelt handshakes with all the Chavez', it was time to head "back into the storm."

"Well, are you ready to go 'back into the storm?'"

"Frankly no, but we can't stay down here living like fat cats either."

Akosua took the wheel for the first lap... "We've got about three days to get back, let's make every hour count."

❖

343

CHAPTER 27

Guaymas came too soon.

"Weird, isn't it? It seemed that we were traveling in slow motion on the way down here..."

"Let's try to re-capture the motion."

A late lunch at La Mar's, a small nap on the beach.

"Kojo, I hate to talk in cliche's, but this whole thing seems like a dream."

"I was thinking that too. I think it's what we need, from time to time. Reality can be sickening."

"Yeah, that's true."

Hermosillo gave them the opportunity to buy a small bucket, fill it with a bag of ice cubes and six bottles of Carta Blanca. They dipped cups of iced beer out of the bucket whizzing through the blast furnace air of the Sonoran desert.

"We're back to the serious part of the heat again."

The glare of the sun and the dry heat kept them in a state of thirst. They stopped for more ice and beer.

"I can think of a time when I would have thought this was quite... quite gauche."

"My, my, Mrs. Ferguson-Brown, what language! Gauche."

It was too hot to laugh, they simply smiled.

"Yes, gauche, a perfectly legitimate way to say in French, wrong. I can think of a time when I would've thought it was wrong to be drinking an excellent beer with ice in it...."

"Just goes to show you how relative things are."

Ten minutes down the road, in a gleaming sandy place, speckled with hard scrub desert vegetation, Kojo gently tapped Akosua on the shoulder.

"Please pull over, the iced beer wants out...."

"You got to pee?"

"Well, if you want to be gauche about it."

She slowed to a stop, stretched and got out to flex her legs. The moan of the motor was off, the desert air locked into a bright stillness.

Kojo waved and walked fifty yards away from the road. He smiled at himself, a bit tipsy from a full afternoon of iced beer drinking. Stupid how fastidious people can be. Why would I have to walk this far from the road, from Akosua, to take a leak?

The figure sitting on the low growing cactus looked like a strange animal. The figure grew to full size as he walked closer.

Asiafo!

Kojo stood in place, absently urinating as they stared at each other. The urination finished, he zipped his pants. The man's strangely unaccented English immediately took him back to the rainforest.

"Good, Kojo, good. You have done exactly what you agreed to do. And she is a lovely girl."

Kojo nodded numbly. It didn't seem possible that this half-naked man from Africa could be sitting in the middle of the desert, talking to him. No, I'm hallucinating. He rubbed his eyes carefully, trying to blot out the figure in front of him, and when he removed his hands the figure was gone.

Yeah, just what I thought, too much heat and beer. He turned with a smile on his face, to find Asiafo leaning against a cactus plant.

"The marriage was done within the proper time, good. Things will go well from this point, but you must remember to feed the stranger who will come."

Kojo's mouth was dry, his tongue felt heavy, thick, and he was feeling the beginning of a headache.

"Feed a stranger? How will I know...?"

"Don't worry, Kojo. . .you will know the stranger when it comes. It will come four times within a year and it must be fed, if things are to continue to go well for you.

Do you understand, Kojo?, the stranger must be fed, to continue to have things go smoothly."

Kojo nodded, feeling suddenly drained of energy.

"Do you understand, Kojo? The stranger must be fed...."

"Yes, yes, I understand."

And Asiafo was gone. Kojo stood in place for a few minutes, his sight fixed on the place where the man had stood a moment before. He was here and now he's gone.

He bent over to look at the naked foot-prints in the sand. He was here. He was definitely here.

He looked around and walked back to the car. Akosua was swabbing her face with a wet terry cloth towel.

"Kojo, I've heard of constipation...but not for someone taking a pee. What's that called?"

"That's called a very full bladder. Here, let me share that with you...."

He got behind the wheel, joking with Akosua, pretending a humor he didn't really feel. He looked up into the rear view mirror as they pulled away, to see Asiafo standing in the middle of the road, offering him a military salute.

Akosua was sleeping lightly in the passenger's seat, tired from a day of glaring at sunblanched landscapes. The evening breeze was a merciful hand fanning cool air in on them.

Kojo drove by instinct, his mind wandering from subject to subject, trying to be rational. A half naked man in the forest promises me that I will be able to make the films I want to make, the money will be there.

Why does he do it? He says he is doing it because I asked him for help and he has the power. And I get on my horse and charge into the sunset, primed by the promise.

The only thing I have to do is get married. He smiled at Akosua's sleeping profile.

And feed a stranger four times a year. Four times a year for how long? Well, what the hell difference does it matter? If I feed a stranger four times a year for four years that would only be sixteen meals.

Asiafo <u>does</u> have supernatural powers, no doubt about that. Anybody who can disappear, who can trip from continent to continent, must have some kind of super power.

He felt the urge to wake Akosua up. My lawful wedded wife... and talk with her about the whole thing, but censored the urge.

No, this is between me and my patron. My patron, yes, I guess that's the best description I could use.

Carlos Saura's "Blood Wedding" and "Carmen" swept through his view finder. Films within films. I have a lot to do before the third Sunday in September.

When the brothers and sisters come to this meeting I want to lay something on them that will be so heavy that they'll want to stick with me until the bitter end.

Too bad I can't invite Asiafo to the meeting.

"Blood Wedding" I "Carmen," Spain's Gypsy passion, what happens when people want to find out if blood is truly thicker than water.

What makes me think of stuff like this? A lot of subliminal stuff that's what it is, that's what my subconscious is saying to me...daydream.

The scattered lights ahead indicated a town, a village or a city was ahead of them.

Akosua yawned herself awake, feeling the car slow down...

"Yawnnnn. . .want me to drive for awhile?"

"Naww, I'm cool, we seem to be in the middle of a small town here, you want to get a bite to eat?"

"That doesn't sound like a bad idea."

It was a restaurant called "Panama," open on four sides, with a thatched roof. They were welcomed with smiles and smudged, fly specked menus.

"Think carefully, what could we have in here that we could eat that wouldn't give us a case of heebie jeebies?"

"Well, the beer is pasteurized and the soup is boiled. Let's have soup, beer and tortillas."

"Excellent idea."

They ordered and sat back to watch the evening scene in a small Mexican town.

"You know, Mexico reminds me of Ghana in a lot of ways. It has that same timeless quality about it. You get the impression that people have been doing the same thing for ages."

The restaurant faced a plaza, one of those affairs with a dry fountain in the center, where the flirtatious young people strolled, the men clockwise, the women counter clockwise.

Kojo and Akosua sipped their beers, spooned in their soup "albondigas, delicious" and made casual matchups between the perambulating couples.

"Look at that, the skinny guy winking at that fat girl. Does he really know what he's getting into?"

"He'll soon find out, won't he?"

A half-hour later a collection of mariachis wandered onto the set....

"Wowww, this is the real thing!"

Soup finished, they sprawled in place, sipping Moctezuma and nodding in time to the romantic drenched strings and voices of the Mariachis.

"Kojo," Akosua whispered in his ear, "Let's spend the night here."

"I was just about to whisper the same thing to you...."

The Hotel California, two avenues east of the "Panama," offered them a shabby, but clean, second floor room - with a shower that sprinkled drips of water.

"Hotel California? There's irony in here somewhere."

"Or maybe sarcasm."

A drippy shower, clean sheets, pillow talk.

"Kojo, we haven't talked about a lot of things..."

"Let's talk."

"Well, we haven't talked about babies, about children...."

"I love 'em."

"You mean that? You want to have babies?"

"Only one at a time, please. Why do you ask me that?"

"Because I flushed my birth control pills down the toilet yesterday morning...."

They were driving through Nogales, Arizona at ten a.m. the following day, feeling a bit solemn because the holiday was over, they were back in America.

"You know I always have the feeling that a weight of some kind has been lowered on me when I come back to America.

I remember the first time Mom and Dad took me to Europe..."

"I didn't know you'd been to Europe?"

"Three times, to be exact. But it wasn't your Europe, it wasn't your Copenhagen. This was my Mom's Europe - Luxembourg, Paris, Belgium, Amsterdam, Holland, and London, England and back home in nine days."

"Oh, one of those – 'if-it's-Friday-we-must-be-in-Brussels-things.'"

"Exactly that. I was sixteen the first time we went and my mother's rationale for taking me was to experience 'civilized, Western Culture.'"

"Your Mom is kinda big on the Eurocentric, huh?"

"You've met her...."

"Don't worry, she'll be alright. You'll see."

They put a working schedule together driving through Arizona.

"We may not have a final draft on tap when we have our meeting, but it'll impress them if we have something in hand. You know how skeptical the Hollywood crowd can be."

They put a living pattern together at the same time...

"Well, the obvious move is to my place, I have the house."

"It makes sense. But let me suggest this, why don't we phase me out of my apartment over the course of the next three months? My lease has six months to go but I'm sure my landlord will allow me to break it. They're really sweet people."

"I know, I've met them. O.K., that'll work. As a matter of fact that's a good idea. It'll give me time to have a couple walls knocked out to give us more working space.

I think I'll extend back to the back porch, that'll give us all the space we need to work in."

Plans, Plans, Plans.., plans for a script, for a home life, for future dinners, for trips to Mexico again, for a series of books, movies, for a future.

"Kojo, how do you want to do this?"

"Do what?"

"Break the news to our parents."

He was forced to laugh.

"Well, for mine, it'll be very simple. I'll stick my head in the door, announce that we're new husband and wife, and run before they start having an ALL-FAMILY CELEBRATION."

Akosua looked glum.

"I wish I could say it was going to be that way with my people. I can almost hear the screams of anguish right now. And my Dad grumbling... betrayal of trust or something.

"Don't worry about anything, I'm on your side. Don't look now but we just crossed the border into LaLaLand."

The familiar landmarks and freeways began to appear.

"Kojo, there's just one important item we haven't discussed...

Concerning the production, to begin with. Where's the money coming from to set up an office, get the 'phones in, the office equipment, stuff like that...?"

"That's the one big hurdle I have to jump over...."

"Well, I've got about $38,000 in savings' and the equity in the house...."

"Akos', I love you for even making the suggestion but that's not the way. One of the things that they taught us at U.S.C., which made lots of sense. Never use your own money to finance a project.

Don't worry about the funds, I got irons in the fire...."

She smiled at the confident thrust of his chin. My husband.

Bumper to bumper traffic / Friday evening from San Bernardino to L.A.

"Welcome back to the parking lot."

They had decided to give themselves the weekend to be together a little longer, to map out the future....

"Wouldn't it be wonderful if this weekend never ended?"

"We can try to keep it going as long as possible. Why don't you come to my place? It'll keep you away from your mother's messages for a few hours longer."

Saturday morning.

"Oh, you coming with me to the park?"

"May I?"

"Of course you can, Mrs. Ferguson-Brown."

Kojo had an odd, almost self-conscious feeling strolling to his workout area with Akosua. My wife. I better get used to the idea, I think she's going to be on the set for quite awhile.

Akosua made a fast walk around the avenue circling the park, while Kojo sweated a few bottles of beer out his system.

"'Morning Kojo, — *coffi coffi coffi*, nice looking lady I saw you with."

"Yeahh, yeahh, I'll talk to you about her tomorrow, after my workout."

"You promise? *Coffi, Coffi.*"

"Cross my heart!"

"Okey-dokey."

Kojo smiled to himself through fifty push ups. The park telegraph system was clicking. Of course they would see me as the latest news, after all this time.

"Woww, how many, you really work up a sweat, don't you?"

"It's not usually this much, this is mostly holiday in Mexico coming out. Nice little walk here, huh?"

"Yeah, love the hills...."

They strolled back to his apartment, feeling loose, pleased with each other.

Cold, fresh orange juice, a hot shower, a mid morning nap.

"Kojo, don't you have some work to do?"

"I'll get to it in a little while...."

Forty-five minutes later, Kojo felt himseif being pulled upwards by his shoulders, by a lightening series of brain storms. He slid out of bed, draped a bath towel around his hips and disappeared into his office-workshop.

Twenty minutes later, Akosua, curious, peeked in on him, scribbling furiously on a yellow legal pad.

"Akos', come over here, baby. Here, sit here, in the chair of honor."

"Thank you...what's the excitement about?"

"I've just hit on something, or rather something just hit on me. This film script has been on my mind..."

"I know, I know...."

"Well, anyway, I've been thinking about it as a collage in film, but I was stumbling around, searching for a theme. Or some themes. And what I've come up with is a theme. It'll still be a collage but with subliminals that will show the disharmony of African-American life, part one.

We'll get heavily into the reasons why, but subliminally, which means it's going to be very, very important to have the right ideas and images running side by side."

"And the music...?"

"And the music. Which reminds me.. .I'm really going to need your help dealing with Juna."

"No problem. She's an old friend...."

"You know her?"

"Been knowing her. She's a little flaky and has to be coddled a little but she's basically cool."

"Wonderful, it's on you. Now then, in a very subtle way, we'll have a transition to part two that shows how we've been able to use some psychic superglue to smooth out the rough spots that <u>our</u> Holocaust put in front of us. I don't want to put out some kind of "And-they-lived-Happily-ever-after" bullshit. But I think it's important to show how far we've come. What do you think?"

"Let me make us some tea and we can get started on part one...."

Sunday bloomed sunny and humid, Harvey Ferguson felt cool and collected, starting from the front page of the Los Angeles Times.

"Harvey, aren't you going to put something on? They said they'd be here about two."

"Minerva, it's only 11:30."

"Yes, I know, but don't you want to make a good impression?"

"Oh, the Browns, they don't strike me as the kind of people you'd like to make a 'good impression' on."

"Oh please, Harvey, don't be so... so snobbish, those are the parents of this young man that Ah-ko-su-a has fallen in love with."

"So,what should I do?"

"Change into something, why not your blue blazer?"

"Minerva, it's a bit warm for that, don't you think?"

"Perhaps. At any rate, you can't sit there in your golf shorts, reading the newspaper, expecting guests."

"And why not?"

Minerva Ferguson cocked her head to one side, her serious listening mode posture. O... So what the hell is this?

The Browns strode up the driveway, laughing, bringing gay vibes all the way....

"Welcome, you must be Mr. and Mrs. Brown."

Kofi and Nzingha Brown looked at each other with mock surprise....

"We must be," they chorused. And then introduced themselves. "Kofi Brown - Nzingha Brown..."

"I'm Minerva and this is my husband Harvey."

They stood looking at each other awkwardly for a moment, before shaking hands.

"Uhh, please, please have a seat. Would you care for something? tea? fruit juice? Beer?"

"Fruit juice sounds fine."

"Dolores!"

They sat on the terrace/veranda, the Fergusons looking uncomfortable, the Browns amused.

The car braking in the driveway announced Kojo and Akosua's arrival.

"Ah hah, the love birds are here."

They rushed onto the veranda, kissing and hugging their parents... "Sorry, we're late, guys."

"No big thing."

"Fruit juice? I think we'd like something a little spicier. Dolores, hay cervesa?"

"Si, Senorita."

"Dos botellas, por favor."

Mrs. Ferguson spotted the gold band on Akosua's ring finger, took a deep breath and leaned back in her chair. There was something so theatrical about the motion that it focused attention on what she had noticed.

Akosua decided not to play past the moment.

"Well, I guess we may as well come on out with it. Mom, Dad, Mr. Brown, Mrs. Brown, Kojo and I got married last week."

The Browns embraced them and offered congratulations...

"I knew you two were up to something."

Minerva and Harvey Ferguson stared at each other, trying to figure out what to say and who should say it. Harvey Ferguson cleared his throat. "Akosua, Kojo, we wish you two young people all the happiness in the world."

Akosua hugged her father and stared a question mark at her mother...

"And I want to second that motion. I knew I had made the right choice the minute I met your son. Where did you get married?"

"In Mexico, in a little town called Huatabampo."

"Sounds so romantic. This calls for a celebration of some sort. Dolores, por fa-vour, bring the two bottles of champagne here. They're in the bottom of the 'fridge."

"Si, Senôra.

Kojo and Akosua stared at her mother, shocked to see her reaction.

"So, now, we're all one big happy family. When do we get our first grandchild?"

Nzingha Brown initiated the laughter, and it became contagious. Kojo and Akosua laughed with relief, their parents with joy.

"So, what've you got?"

"About five hundred pages of script, in my head, and about ten pages written. How about you?"

"Well, I'm a little bit beyond that, but only slightly. What's your biggest problem?"

"Juxtapositions, how to put the right images next to the right images. Without using a narrator or some kind of traditional transitional device, it's rough...."

"You tellin' me."

"Is it wearing you out?"

"It's challenging me to the max."

"How is the house work going?"

"Right now it's a mess, but the contractor promises me that they'll be finished by the second week of October."

"I can't wait."

"Me too. Kojo, do you miss me?"

"Desperately. You know of any other married couple that took their honeymoon together and came back home to live apart."

"Yeah, that is kind of hysterical. But don't worry, it won't be that way for long."

"It better not be...hahhahhah."

"Don't worry, Mr. Brown, it won't. I'm barking at the contractor like a maddog."

"Good. Well, that's it for now. Will I see you tomorrow?"

"Let's 'do lunch' and compare a few notes, say about one?"

"See you then, nite."

"Goodnight, Akos'."

He replaced the phone in its cradle and leaned back in his desk chair. This sister is a gem, an absolute gem.

They had split the script into two parts. He was dealing with the disharmony, the grief of part one, the African Holocaust/Diaspora, as a series of small stories within the big story.

"The scope of the thing is too big for a two hour film, I'm trying to scale it down to human terms, to make it understandable for people who couldn't imagine the genocide of millions over a four hundred year period. And yet, somehow, maintain the enormous scope of the madness."

Akosua was working on part two, showing how a kind of super psychic glue was used to prevent the complete disintegration of the Africans who were exported.

"What forces can you identify that would serve the purpose of preventing total disintegration of the African psyche, of the Africanity in us?

Well, spirituality is one of the major factors. I'm speaking of African spirituality, not Christianity or Islam or any of those other foreign religions.

I'm having my eyes opened by studies that pinpoint the vitality of an African spiritual systems. It's called Vodun in Haiti, Candomble in Brasil, Santeria in Cuba, Shango in Trinidad, Obeah in Jamaica, The Religion or Yoruba in the U.S., that exists wherever there are African people.

I'm putting an emphasis on our spiritual thing…. And, of course, the role that women have played in helping us retain our souls….we got work to do."

The days galloped past, the telephones were seldom silent during the course of the day.

"Kojo, we've got about a week. What do you think?"

"We have enough between us to light a few fires. I feel confident."

"I'm glad to hear that, I was feeling a little down."

"Don't be down, sweetheart, whatever you do, don't be down."

They paid Grandfather Kwame a two hour visit to discuss the African-American genius for pushing Nihilism into a corner.

"Now don't get me wrong, you two. I'm not going to come right out and say that we were spiritually stronger in the old days. I can't honestly say that.

What I can say is that the floods that cause erosion are deeper now. I can see it in the way a lot of young people have just given themselves up to substances and garments, that is to say...'pleasure' and 'adornments.'

They block out matters that they think will cause them any kind of deep thought. Even when they riot, it's almost with a sense of 'pleasure.'

I don't know, it may have something to do with how cleverly the White men who run America have manipulated obstacles in front of them. And behind them. And around them.

Years back, in ancient times, in my day...ha ha ha. . .we knew exactly what the deal was. We had two simple choices to make — either survive and thrive, or lay down and die.

As I see things now, there are so many distractions on the way to the Real Deal, so many strange con games being played.

For example, to use a blatant example, I could never imagine a Michael Jackson being a heroic figure to the members of my generation, even minus the glove, the stringy hair and the facial altering.

The basic reason we wouldn't've dug him, I think is because we were into the Real Deal.

The Real Deal meant seeing things in their real light. This was during the time of Mahalia Jackson, Muddy Waters, Charlie Parker, Billie Holiday, Little Esther, Dinah Washington, Marcus Garvey, Little Willie John ha ha ha, I've mixed the pot up on you, but I think you get the idea of what I'm talking about.

The distinction between something Authentic and something Cosmetic is the difference between a woman's face and a woman's face Made Up."

"Ooooh Granddad..."

"But it's true, Kojo, it's true. A lot of men like to pretend that they like the Cosmetic woman, but they really yearn for the Authentic woman. I'm using that analogy in relation to what we're talking about.

Early in the game we were exposed to the raw face of reality, in the South especially, but in the North too. There was no make up on the face, which meant that we knew what we were looking at, straight up.

The pity of the situation is in the disguises, what may seem to be Black Nationalism may actually be a programmed note from the C.I.A.

What may seem to be a closer connection to Afrikan values may be simply a backward look at the 15th century, and so on. Am I going too fast?"

Akosua and Kojo blinked, their eyes glazed by the old man's reasoning.

"You're here to talk with an old man about what he sees, what he has seen, on the Black side? And I'm giving it to you straight-up.

We were not as confused and messed around early in the game. I think it would've been pretty hard to think of yourself as an 'upper class slave' or a 'lower class slave.'

I loved Malcolm X, I agreed with so much that the boy fought for, but I never felt comfortable with his 'house niggers' and 'field niggers' thing.

Surely there must've been 'house niggers' in the field and 'field niggers' in the house. Common sense would tell us that.

When I say that we were not as confused and messed around with, back then, I'm not trying to pat anybody on the back. I think I can attribute the lack of confusion to the times.

There wasn't a bunch of computers then, or sophisticated anti-African-American think tanks. Stuff was real primitive back then - shootings, burnings, lynchings. We knew who the enemy was.

Nowadays, if I were to say that one of the Black man's meanest enemies is the market driven economy, a lot of Black people would try to black my eye. Or just blink stupidly.

It's a whole new ballgame now and it's deadly.

I wouldn't want to try to pinpoint the exact moment-in-time that we went from the **Real Deal to Fantasy**, but I suspect it happened sometime during the '60's, when enough fertilizer had been spread to make people believe that racial justice was going to be achieved.

Of course it didn't happen, and it's not ever going to happen as long as African-Americans are considered a problem. That may sound like a mean assessment of the situation, but that's what reality can be like."

The old man paused to take a slow sip from his Chivas Regal glass.

"The African-American, then and now, recognizing what the Real Deal is, and always has, simply stockpiled some soul and held onto it for cold days.

I think that's what it comes down to, in terms of us dealing with hopeless conditions, serious despair, African-American Nihilism. Somehow, in some kind of way, spiritually, I believe, our ancestors laid out enough stuff for us to stockpile it, to feed on it when necessity demanded that we do so."

"You believe the spirits are responsible for our survival?"

"Daughter, I'll tell you the honest to God truth, I can't point my finger at any other energy source. I've spent many hours of my life trying to discover the secret of our will to overcome, many hours.

And, after all the fancy wrappings have been stripped away, we always wind up at a spiritual place called 'git up and git on!'"

Akosua and Kojo laughed at the old man's use of the vernacular.

"You know something? I've been disappointed in our intellectuals, our poets and writers, for years, because they've never made a serious effort in this direction.

Kojo, I've even taken your Daddy to task about this. I used to ask him, why is it we can go to the book store and pick books on 'Hindu Thought About the Other Side' 'Japanese Looks At the Cherry Blossom' 'Jewish Thinking on the Jewish Holocaust', but there's not one book on the 'Spiritual Conquest of the African Holocaust/Diaspora'.

He told me that he didn't have any books about that because no one had written one. Can you imagine such a thing?!

We ought to be swamped with books, pamphlets even, about the spiritual forces that we tapped to overcome the nihilism of chattel bondage.

I'll go a step farther and say that we need to have our asses kicked, pardon my French, Akosua, for not having a Holocaust/Diaspora Monument erected in all of the places we were shipped to.

CHAPTER 28

It's absurd that they would have monuments to Lassie, the Wonder Dog, and statues erected for the commemoration of every racist who ever showed his face, but not one serious monument to our people."

"Granddad, do you think a film could be a monument?"

"Let's take a look at it."

Kojo rewound the three tapes, drained the dregs of his orange juice and took a shower.

A balmy Los Angeles Basin night, the distant plinking of a stringed instrument. The Armenians must be doing a little '*do*' tonight.

He slipped into pajama bottoms, (Akosua always wore the tops), and stretched out on his bed, a full moon glaring through his bedroom window, locked his hands behind his head and mentally replayed the three video tapes and the one his grandfather had played on his mind.

That was some Heavy Drippin' Drama you dunked us in, ol' dude. Heavy.

Soul Reservoirs of Spiritual Energy — Billie Holiday. The tape was/ had been an hour of Billie Holiday's life, the focus on her drug addiction.

But even with the drugs she still had 'More of Something' than all of her peers, and most of the people who call themselves singers today.

And it wasn't just the voice, there was something else in the voice; a sound track of her experiences in life, the sound track for the experiences that many, many of our people have had. She was articulating something in a way that expressed what we felt/feel.

Granddad was right. A lot of our people don't seem to want to feel that deeply any more. And they had the nerve to have that little slender sister play Billie Holiday in "Lady Sings the Blues."

Seems that she would've been embarrassed to try to play Billie. O well....

And what made Richard Pryor, during his salad days, so funny? Kojo had sprawled in his chair, laughing aloud, alone at "Richard Pryor, Live!"

It wasn't funny hah hah. It was more like a subterranean feather tickling a Black nerve.

Yeah, the White people laughed too, but they were laughing at the brother...we were laughing with him.

Moms Mabley had that going for her too, a direct pipeline into the African-American funny bone.

"Redd Foxx in 'Vegas," the third tape, made him laugh at the way Foxx said things, the cool assumption he made while telling his jokes, that the 'In' people were definitely 'In.'

And he went out doing "Sanford and Son". Will the real Redd Foxx please rise from the sitcom?

The 'phone buzzing startled him. 12:45 p.m.. Akosua?

"Good evening."

"Yes, good evening Kojo this is Juna and I've just talked to Akosua and I'm very excited about the project it sounds like just the sort of thing I could drown myself in."

"Well, please, don't do that. But I'm really glad that you feel good about things. Incidentally, I wanted to talk with you about a musical group I saw in Copenhagen, Denmark, recently...."

"The One Earth Music group, Don Cherry II, NaNa Mayuto, Chatur Lal II, Otis Blackwell and Sister Kanda."

Kojo almost dropped the 'phone....

"You've heard of these people?"

"Kojo, we all know each other. The earth is a small village, remember? Well, that's enough of that, I have to go feed my cat. 'Bye."

He placed himself back in position on the bed, trying to recapture the mood. It was gone.

O well, what the hell, it was good while it lasted. Damn! I wanted to talk with that mad musician about the musical group, about using some of what they're about...guess I'll pass the buck to my baby.

Kojo and Akosua strolled through her house, checking out the renovations.

"It's amazing what these guys can do."

"I thought it was amazing too, until I really looked at the materials inside these houses.

This wall was nothing but heavy cardboard, what do you call it...? Plasterboard or something.

They slugged through that in an hour. The extra time they've spent comes from my absolute insistence that they do things '**Right**.'

Fortunately, I have a conscientious guy who seems to be paying attention."

"Looks like I'll be able to come home soon."

"Looks like you'll be coming home on Monday."

"That soon, huh?"

"It better be or else I'm gonna pick up a hammer and start nailing some heads! Come on, let's go out back, I've put a couple chairs out."

Kojo followed her out, taking in the huge space that had been hollowed out of the rear of the house.

"We can use this as a joint work space, or put a couple dividers up. And I've designed the back porch area as your private space, I used your office as the model.

And, of course, the bedroom has been left pretty much the way it was... except for the bathroom."

Kojo had smiled down into the sunken tub that was large enough for two people.

"I just don't feel I can kick back in a shower the way you can do it in a tub. Don't you agree?"

A hazy September afternoon in Echo Park. Akosua had chilled a bottle of Blanc de Blancs for them to sip as they worked on "My Grandfather's Eyes."

Kojo took note of the serious tone that dropped into Akosua's attitude, the minute they settled in.

After an hour of re-hashing the images, the transitions, suggestions for musical walls to surround the ideas...

"Juna called me last night, told me she had spoken to you."

"She's under control."

The details of what they felt was going to make the film a classical work.

Akosua took them into Part II.

"I listened to your Grandfather very, very carefully the other night."

An hour and a half later, the Blanc de Blancs sipped out, they leaned back in their chairs, drained.

"Akos', I think we got something here. It goes beyond 'screenplay.'"

"Remember, that's what you kept reminding me, let's make it more than a 'screenplay,' let's make it an '**<u>Experience</u>**.'"

"Do you think we've been hard enough on ourselves? Do you think....?"

"Kojo, I think we've put together a helluva piece and it'll be validated on Sunday."

"I'm not going to give them the full thing, I'm simply going to pitch the major idea of the thing at them and pray for the best. I've been working on a speech...."

"You've been what?!"

"Writing a speech..."

"Kojo, please take some advice from your better half. I can say that now. Don't write a speech, give a talk, pitch an idea, say some words, but don't give a speech.

What we have demands something fresh, original, straight from the heart. Remember, these are people who deal with canned laughter and over-rehearsed politicians all the time."

"Akos', come over here and let me molest you."

"You don't have to do it out here, do you? We could go inside... and take a hot bath...."

"You're wicked."

"I know."

❖

"Our Production Company"

"Questions? Do we have any strangers in the house? Anybody who doesn't know everybody else? Good. That'll save us the time it would take for introductions.

However, there is one person I would like to introduce you to, her name is Akosua Ferguson-Brown, my wife."

A few people looked stunned and then began to applaud.

"I thank you, we thank you for your applause of approval. Now, let's get to the business at hand...."

They had decided to get right down to business, to accustom the people who were going to be involved to punctuality.

"I hate these meetings where people take forty-five minutes to get into what it's about."

Kojo looked around the room. Wall-to-wall talent.

Thelma Nagata, D.J. Ross, Phillip Charles, Sid Burns, Ed Burns, Mac Weaver, Jackie F. Muhammad, Michael Sims, Juna, heavyweights.

"I don't think I have to give you guys a resume, we've all worked together at some point, so I know who you are and you know who I am."

Akosua made surreptitious study of the faces in the room. They were obviously Kojo fans.

"Now then, let me give you the briefest of explanations concerning the project."

Thelma Nagata, the future office manager pulled out a steno pad and ballpoint. Wowww, is the lady efficient or not?

Thirty minutes later he had presented the idea for his first film, given them a slice of the second and the hint of a third.

The floor was opened....

"Kojo, you're talking about a film production company that will produce excellent films."

"You got that right, D.J., and with good fortune smiling on me, you'll be the camera man for all of them."

"I like your idea of using sound effects, rather than a lot of dialogue. That's never been done with Black films."

"Sid, with all due respect, let me correct you. We're going to be making African-American films. That's a whole new ballgame, a real big distinction in mind.

That's one of the mean things that's been done with us for a long time, we've had the wrong labels slapped on our goodies."

"Sounds like the music is going to be the most important element of the film, the first one."

"Which is why we have asked the inimitable Juna to do the score."

"Were you wondering why I was here, Jackie?"

"Juna, I never wonder why you're anywhere that you are, wherever that might be."

Akosua slipped in suavely... "Now, now, now, sisters, we can't have Jackie F. Muhammad, the top P.R. person around and Juna, the top musician around, clawing each other to pieces, can we?"

There was a moment of silence while the people in the room looked at each of the antagonists with disapproving eyes.

"Now then, going right along...I'm going to assume, from this point on that everyone here is going to become a card carrying member of 'Our Production Company.'"

Akosua did a double take and smiled at Kojo's reaffirming wink. 'Our Production Company'. Perfect.

"If we have anyone here who wants to opt out...?"

Ed Burns, assistant director on thirty feature films, cleared his throat.

"I want in, definitely, but I think some serious questions need to be answered...."

"The first consideration is, of course, 'The Dream,' and you've done a hellified job of laying that on us.

"It's called pitchin', Ed, you know how it's done!" Philip Charles called out from the opposite side of the room.

The group shared 'Insider chuckles'....

"Right, now then, after the pitch, 'The Dream,' let's get to the most important question of all. Where's the money coming from to do "Grandfather's Eyes"?

The alert level of the group shot up 90%, every eye focused on Kojo. He took a subconsciously aggressive stance.

"Ed, as the politicians say...I'm glad you asked that question. The only answer I can give to you is an honest one... I don't know."

Akosua's jaw dropped with all the other dismayed reactions in the room. Kojo rushed on to say....

"No, I can't tell you at this moment exactly where it's coming from. But I'm asking you to trust me, at least on a month to month basis."

"Mac Weaver here, Kojo. . .let's say we all do trust you and everything and we wind up with a fabulous film, how do you get it distributed?"

"We'll have to cope with that just before we get to it. I have a sneaking suspicion that we may have to deal with the usual suspects."

Once again they shared 'Insider smiles'. They knew who the usual suspects were.

"Question? Put your hand down, Thelma, and stop pretending you're in fifth grade."

"Ahhh, it was a such a wonderful time in my life, O well...uhhh. . . do you have any fears that 'Our Production Company' will be called racist, by the usual suspects, because we have no Whites in the company?"

"I read you loud and clear. I've asked the people who are closest to me to participate in this venture. That's all. As we grow and find more like minded individuals who are willing to go through what we know we're going to have to go through…we'll consider them for inclusion.

You see, what I'm asking for is a very strong commitment from everyone here. And I wouldn't consider people who are not willing to take that extra step.

I know that what I'm asking for will be a sacrifice for all of you, financially and emotionally, but I know we can pull it off."

"Kojo, what about office space, 'phones, all that madness…?"

"Jackie, by the end of next month we will have offices in a fantastic Quonset hut sized loft on Slauson and Stanford, a half block east of Main street.…"

Juna gasped out… "That's in 'South Central Los Angeles!'…South Los Angeles."

Kojo, not certain if her gasp of surprise indicated approval or disapproval, moved on.

"By the end of next month. Once we've set up, we'll go into pre-production at the end of the following month, November. In other words, we'll be doing this on a month to month schedule.

In December we'll start getting into principal photography.

I'm going to be asking you brothers and sisters to be doing a lot of stuff for free that the 'Biggies' would pay you big bucks for, for free at first, but I guarantee you, we will all profit in the end."

There was a heavy moment of silence, broken by Juna's raspy voice.…

"We gittin' ready to kick some ass around here."

The room exploded with laughter. There was just something about the way she said it.

Kojo studied Akosua's sleeping profile and smiled. Looks like I picked a winner. Laced his hands behind his head and stared up through his bedroom window at a crescent moon and a sky bristling with stars.

I must be out of my mind. How can I possibly do a month-to-month schedule? Maybe I should've given us more breathing space. Maybe….

A small, clear voice whispered into his right ear…don't worry, everything will be cool. Everything will be cool…

He jerked his head toward Akosua to see if she were talking in her sleep. She was silent, sound asleep. The weight of the mystery in his life suddenly overwhelmed Kojo, he began to pray... silently.

"I beg my ancestors and I beg the Orisha, please don't let me go crazy...I beg my ancestors and I beg the Orisha, please don't let me panic...I beg my ancestors and I beg the Orisha...."

A calm settled on his head, made him release a dreamy smile....

I have Thelma Nagata as my secretary-office manager. D.J. Ross-camera man, Phillip Charles, the man who lit the inside of a barrel, using only the knot hole. Sid Burns for sound. Ed Burns, assistant director, Mac Weaver, assistant director. Juna doing the score, Jackie F. Muhammad, P.R. genius. Still photographer-Michael Sims. Yeah, we'll need a full book of photos for this one. And Akosua Ferguson-Brown, my co-writer, co-producer-wife. He unlaced his hands from behind his head. What the hell am I feeling antsy about? I've got a dynamite group ready and willing to get down with me and I'll pick up more along the way...what am I tripping for?

He folded his hands across his chest and settled into a dream ridden sleep. William Holden, Faye Dunaway, Ned Beatty, Peter Finch, the other guy with the aggressive Robert Duval jaw Chayevsky "Network". Beatrice Straight as the wounded wife in "Network"...

The opening scenes flickered in front of his closed eyelids, Peter Finch strolling around the file sections with a glass of whisky in hand as the credits rolled over the scene.

Big-time-stuff CBS-NBC-CNN, folks who decide which news is the news. Peter Finch trips out, hears God speaking to him, telling him that he should tell the truth.

It's all mixed up with Black militancy circa 1960 odd and cold blooded insights not the world of the dominated media, giant propaganda mills. The insight was hindsighted and foresighted. Kojo grumbled a bit in his sleep, reviewing the part of the Black militants bargaining for a piece of the media pie, while nourishing themselves on Colonel Sanders chicken buckets.

Even if it was true, I would've sacrificed that and focused on something else. But then, I'm not a White boy.

Selection, selection, that's the key to the whole business, making the juxtapositions mean something. He saw himself at a large, walnut painted desk, a pile of fantastic photographs on one side, a pile of cards with words that focused on concepts that were so profound that the cards quivered when he held them up.

The cards quivered and almost jumped from his hand whenever he touched the right picture, it felt as though they wanted to mate.

The right words - the right picture - selection. The dreams stood him up on street corners in New York, uptown and downtown, staring at the ridiculous rushing of the people.

"Network" took a hard look at manipulated behavior - "We're Number One!" - what does that mean? What does number two mean? Network.

Have to take another look at that. Faye Dunaway, the media bitch, William Holden, the ethical one. Schumacher.

How did he become so ethical squirming around in a pile of shit that deep? Yeah, that's a serious flaw there. Here's this guy, what's his name? Schumacher, the head of the news division, who has been on the scene since Day One, involved with the whole thing.

How does he get to be so ethical?

"Kojo?! Kojo?! Please dear...whoever you're talking with, could you save it 'til the morning?"

"Oh, sorry...guess I got a bit involved...."

He smiled at Akosua snuggling down into her pillow. Wonder how many of these conversations I had before you came?

The Chans were gracious about his moving.

"Well, c'mon now, Kojo, we wouldn't expect for a man to live away from his wife."

October 1st, Kojo was firmly installed, busy doing ten things at one time.

"Kojo, what about this loft that you proposed to use as an office?"

"It's a real deal. My friend, John Outterbridge, is getting ready to move back to North Carolina and he's leasing it to me for a year, with an option to buy."

"What will you use for money?"

"Well, he's giving me the first three months free and, after that, $800 per month."

"Man, that's what I call a friend."

"Yeah, John is a gem, always has been."

It was happening....

"Kojo, now you know if you talked to your Granddad it was bound to get back to the family. I think I may have something of interest for you, if you need money...."

"Dad, please don't play with my head like this. If I need some money....?!"

"Well, think you might be able to break away for a meeting with One Hundred African-American men?"

"One Hundred African-American Men? Your group...?"

"Yeah, one of the organizations I joined not too long after we moved out here. How does Saturday morning, about 10 a.m., suit you?"

"10 a.m. is fine."

"Good, I'll pick you up about 9:30. How's Akosua?"

"Busy, Dad, busy...."

"Sounds like you guys are onto something dynamite. Good. See you Saturday."

Kojo gently dropped the 'phone back into the cradle. One Hundred African-American Men. It was one of the few organizations that his father belonged to that he wasn't exactly enthusiastic about. They gave him the impression of being a collection of good time type, high rollers with low aims, somewhat "booshie".

But I shouldn't jump to too many bad conclusions, after all, Dad's been in the group for ages and I know he's about <u>Something.</u>

"Kojo, you want to take a lunch break with me?"

They sat under a beach umbrella, a thrift shop item that Kojo had gotten for ten dollars, "Compare Compari," and feasted on shrimp salad sandwiches and chilled white wine.

"Akos', I just got an interesting call from my Dad. He's inviting me to a meeting of One Hundred African-American Men on Saturday...."

"What's the deal?"

"I don't know yet. He's making little sounds about money but I don't have the slightest idea where it would be coming from."

"Well, I don't want to throw any curves at your head or anything, but the sooner we get our hands on a large sum of it, the better."

369

"Are we bankrupt already?"

"No, sweetheart, far from it. Everything is cool on the homefront, but I've been talking with Thelma about office equipment and stuff and she's running some interesting figures at my head. The lady is an organizational genius."

"Yeahh, she's something, ain't she?"

He noticed it as she wedged herself away from the table. Akosua is gaining weight.

"Akos', looks like we should be going on a little diet, huh?"

She came to pose in front of him, a slight bay window blocking his view.

CHAPTER 29

"You don't diet away babies, Kojo, you give birth to them."

He pulled her down on his lap and smothered her face and neck with kisses. It was happening.

One Hundred African-American Men held their Saturday meetings at the Crenshaw Club. They wandered in from early golf dates, tennis matches, aerobics workouts, jogging.

Well, I gotta say this much, they're fitness conscious anyway...

There were also a number of the One Hundred who gave some evidence of serious hangovers and Bloody Mary breakfasts, but in the main, he noted, they were a fairly representative collection of middle aged African-American men.

He recognized a few of the more public figures: Assemblyman Whatshisname, the middle echelon actors, six or seven doctors, lawyers, teachers, upper level civil servants, a stray airplane pilot or two, the owner of the best stocked and most Africentric bookstore in Los Angeles County.

"Dad, are there really one hundred men in this organization?"

"More like 65, but someone thought it would sound better to say one hundred."

"O, I see...."

"Said the blind man."

Enormous trays of scrambled eggs, sausage, bacon, toast and huge carafes of orange juice were laid out on a buffet table.

"Breakfast is served," someone announced, and the men made their way to the food, laughing and joking.

Kojo felt trapped. Thought we were supposed to meet at 10 a.m.

His father took note of him making a sly study of his watch and whispered, "Relax, Kojo, this the way the brothers do it, we haven't seen each other since the last meeting...."

Breakfast finished, (11:30 a.m., he noted), it was time for the business of One Hundred African-American Men.

The minutes of the last meeting were read, an update made on the fifteen college scholarships they were sponsoring, (Kojo sat up a bit straighter), the medical bills that had been paid for a couple of the Men with financial problems, the situation with the orphanage that they were sponsoring in Accra, Ghana; their financial state of being was put into perspective by an astute accountant who made certain that everyone understood that it was his expertise that multiplied their funds three fold, during the past year.

Kojo was fascinated by the casual manner the business was framed, yet how efficiently it was worked out. Brothers **be** a bit late, but they **be** taking care '**bidness**'. He looked up to discover, his father was speaking....

"So, rather than attempt to tell you what it's all about, I'd prefer you be given the story first hand. May I present my son, Kojo Bediako Brown."

He felt a little befuddled for a moment, as the applause drove him to the lectern. What the hell can I say to these guys?

It took him a few moments to unravel the tape, to know where to start from and where he wanted to wind up.

They weren't a difficult group to talk to, in some ways it was like speaking to 65 facets of his father.

"I don't have a prepared speech, because I didn't really expect to speak."

"Speak your mind," someone called out from the back.

He decided to go from his U.S.C. film school days; the frustration, the Eurocentric racism that was so deeply ingrained that the people who were guilty of it didn't even realize it.

The support that his mother and father gave him, his family. Coming out into a mean assed world that wasn't any less racist than U.S.C., and owned up to it.

The difficulties of trying to gain control of some percentage of the cinematic African-American image. What he wanted to do.

His recent trips to Ghana and to Denmark, the honor that was paid him in Copenhagen.

The story he wanted to tell in "My Grandfather's Eyes," the problems he was facing, trying to take it up.

After twenty minutes he dried up, he had gotten it off his chest, he had spoken his mind.

The applause startled him. What were they clapping for?

The Saturday meeting of One Hundred African-American Men was slowly melting, the business was just beginning. Father Brown came to steer him into a room where five of the One Hundred were waiting for him.

"Kojo, this is our screening committee: this is brother Franklin, brother Castle, brother Turner, brother Settles and brother Dirkson, our accountant."

He shook hands with the men and stood in place, feeling like a schoolboy in front of the class.

"Have a seat, Kojo, let's talk about what you need. And what we want."

He literally stumbled out of the room after an intense forty five minutes of information-exchange-interrogation.

They wanted him to do something quite simple, give them a hard based reason for granting him funds to get his show on the road.

The exchange indicated how little they understood about the above the line/below the line costs, but they understood money. And what they were concerned about was whether or not they would receive a decent return on their investment, within a reasonable period of time.

Brother Dirkson asked the toughest questions and took the most notes.

"Why do you want to make this film, Kojo, why do you want to make films period?"

"Because I have to.... Because our story needs to be told."

He had doubts about whether or not he had come off as well as he wanted to. His father stroked him out as they settled into the car.

"Kojo, it's o.k., it's o.k., I'm telling you, it's o.k. These brothers have been waiting to jump into some media action for a long time and you're the perfect scenario for them — young, educated, with the proper credentials, got a track record, traveled, been honored by a university in Europe, about to burn the world up, and you're my son to boot. What're you worried about?"

They embraced and clapped each other on the back.

"O.k., now then, enough of that. How 'bout tripping over to that seaside place you like for a couple tall ones?

You can give me a closer look at what you're planning, so I'll know who to lobby, when the time comes.

"Dad, you're too much, you know that?!"

"Yeah, I do know."

"Akos', did you get the message from your publisher? He seems to be excited about the outline, except, whatever it was you sent him..."

"Got it! They really seem to be in love with me these days. What's happening with One Hundred Men?"

"The accountant called this morning and wanted to clarify what I meant in paragraph six on page twelve. He's a serious little guy, that one."

"Dear Grace,

I've been so busy doing so many things that I haven't had the time to reply/write you.

I've gotten married since last we met, I may as well be up front about that. The basic reason why we got married is something I can be completely honest about. I needed to do it for ritualistic reasons.

No, please don't laugh, don't change the channel. I've known Akosua

Ferguson, now Brown, plus Ferguson, for more than two years, and it was time for us to do Something.

I'm telling you this honestly, so please be prepared. My relationship with Asiafo, the man in the forest, was my catalyst of getting married.

He was the one who said I had to do it. If wanted to get what I wanted.

I could lay out the rest of the stipulations, but it wouldn't serve any worthwhile function.

Please understand that I will always love you, in all the ways that we can love and that I wish you the kind of happiness, when your turn comes, that I'm experiencing.

I'm not married to the kind of woman who would become hysterical if I received an occasional note from Ghana, so don't hesitate, if you feel the urge.

Love,
Kojo

P.S. Looks like there's a little Kojo or Akosua on the way, about six months from now.

The loft was opened to them, John Outterbridge had gone to do more work down-home. Kojo and Akosua strolled through the space.

"We could build sets in here, you know that?"

"Looks like you could fly airplanes in here. This place is huge. You'd never have any idea that this was here, entering that ordinary sized front door."

'Bridge planned it that way. And check out the burglar proofing... all the grillwork on these windows that look like works of art."

"Now all we have to do is bring in some state of the art equipment and **git** busy."

They separated, peeking into odd corners, discovering things.

"Kojo! Kojo!"

"I hear you, but where are you?"

"Over here, behind the big panel."

"What is this?"

"It's a mini-kitchen, that what it is. It looks exactly like the kind of thing you'd want to use to prepare midnight snacks."

"Now I'm really beginning to understand what he meant when he said, I'm not going to give you a guided tour, I'll let you discover the place for yourself."

Six anxiety ridden days later Kojo received a call from his mother.

"Kojo, your father decided to give me a chance to have some of the fun...."

"What's up, Mom?"

"Looks like you are, my son, looks like you are."

"I don't understand...."

"I'm proud and happy to say that One Hundred African-American Men have just granted you 1.5 million dollars to do your thing."

Kojo suddenly saw stars flashing through his head. O God, don't let me punk-out here and faint.

"One point five mil? Is that what you said?"

"Exactly. The information came straight from the accountant to your father. Congratulations! Looks like you're in business!"

"You better believe it! Thanks, Mom, talk to you later!"

Kojo offered a silent prayer of thanks and tried to pull off a nonchalant stroll to the kitchen.

"Oh, Kojo, you want to have a snack out back, I'm making fried eggplant with a little Parmesan?"

"Yeah, that would be tasty 'round about now."

He had to face himself to handle the plates without rattling them. But at the same time he felt strangely calm, as though the news he had received was "natural."

"There's some white wine in the 'fridge."

"Why don't we have some Champagne?"

She stopped placing slices of eggplant in their plates to stare at him.

"Champagne?"

"Yes, what better way to celebrate this 1.5 million dollar grant I just got from <u>The Men</u>!?"

Akosua screamed and raced around the table to swing on his neck.

"Oh Kojo, that's wonderful! Fantastic!"

"Yeah, we can have Thelma begin to set up the office now, and open up a payroll, we're in business."

The loft made a unique business operation happen. There was privacy and open-ness. Thelma Nagata was in office heaven...

"My God in Heaven, there's enough space in here to run a train."

And within weeks a creative train was running. Pre-production was going on. Kojo assembled his staff....

"We are going to have to do this as well as it can be done the first time, because we won't have the resources to do it again. And again. And again."

Kojo and Akosua did locations, after hours.

"We're looking for all the physical elements in our scripts, we'll have to depend on the people to take care of the emotional and the spiritual."

The 'phones were ringing...

"Kojo, Line 4."

"Kojo Bediako..."

"Hi Kojo, Charley Bascom here. So, how's it going, pal?"

Charley Bascom? The hyenas have sniffed the scent.

"Charley Bascom, haven't talked to you for a while."

"Yeah, not since you turned down the golden chance to do the jazz series...."

He felt strong enough to wedge the blade in a bit. "It wasn't a 'golden chance' ...."

"Awwww c'mon, Kojo, that was just one thing on the road to many things. Uhhh, what's this 'Our Production Company' stuff? You didn't tell me you were going into business for yourself"

"You didn't ask, Charley, you didn't ask."

He could almost feel the neurotic anger come through the receiver. The man was not accustomed to having his psyche played with.

"So, I'm asking. What's the deal?"

Kojo, well aware of how accurate and informative the Hollywood Grapevine could be, decided to splash broad strokes in Charley Bascom's ear.

"That sounds great, Kojo, really great! There's just one thing missing. How's your distribution set up?"

"Charley, we'll have to talk about that at a later date. Right now I'm late for two meetings...."

"Sure, sure, I understand. Looks like you're onto something hot, guy. Why don't we get back at it at the beginning of the week?"

"Yeah, sure, beginning of the week, talk to you...."

Kojo hung up and smiled into Thelma Nagata's beaming face. You couldn't really call it revenge, but it sure felt good to give the moguls a taste of their own medicine.

It was happening. Our Production Company was a 24 hour a day operation. Members of the staff came and stayed. And stayed. To do the zillion things that were necessary to make a film happen.

Mr. Harvey and Mrs. Minerva Ferguson came.

"We just happened to be in the neighborhood."

Akosua winked to Kojo. Minerva Ferguson wouldn't be caught dead in this neighborhood. Just passing by....?

They gave them a tour of the facility. They were impressed. Harvey Ferguson wandered off by himself.

"Don't get lost, Harvey."

"I'll try not to...."

Mrs. Ferguson frowned at his reply. The man was becoming a bit sarcastic in his old age.

"Kojo. Akosua, can we go to some private spot?"

They looked at each other, private meant being fifty yards from the nearest 'phone.

"Sure, we can sit over here."

Akosua had put her thrift shopping expertise to work and scrounged a dozen comfortable Danish chairs and three sofas.

Kojo rushed to take a quick call and returned with pineapple juice.

"Sorry, had to get that. Did I miss anything?"

"No, I waited for you. Hmmm. . .this is delicious."

"Thank you."

They were in a flight pattern that Mrs. Ferguson knew nothing about, she made them feel antsy. They cloaked their impatience with frozen expressions.

'Phones were ringing, machines were clicking and clacking, Mrs. Ferguson was playing her scene.

"Akos', you look perfectly adorable pregnant, you know?"

"Uhh, Mrs. Ferguson, this is like in the middle of our work day, you wanted...."

"Yes, I wanted to know what kind of legal representation you have for your corporation?"

They exchanged dumb looks.

"Well, we know a guy...."

"Hmmm, just as I thought. I've spoken to my attorneys on your behalf, Green, Shafton and Clark."

"Wowww! They're pretty expensive....

"They would be if they weren't trying to earn brownie points for aiding and abetting a fledgling group of African-American film makers."

Kojo stunned her with a lip smacking kiss on the cheek. Akosua pulled her mother up from the sofa and hugged her.

Harvey Ferguson smiled at the warm tableau....

"Kojo, you need a ten car parking lot out back, I think my firm can do it for you."

It was Tuesday evening, one of those balmy-in-Los Angeles-November evenings that only seem to happen in Los Angeles, despite the earthquakes, the racial strife and the smog.

Akosua and Kojo had decided on a picnic in Griffith Park. They drove up past the golf course, around the "back side" of the park, to a section with only a few people.

"Kojo, you know something? Life is beginning to have an unreal, almost surreal quality about it with us."

"How so?"

"How so?! Well, look at what's happening. We have a fat bank account. All the people that you wanted to bring in for your film have come and more are on the way. You're being granted a serious amount of respect for your creative efforts, things are rolling with Our Production Company. I've just sold another book, we're in love, I'm pregnant!"

He shared the feeling. It was almost unreal. The snags that occurred were minor and easily resolved. Every obstacle seemed to remain in place for only a few minutes before it was overcome...Asiafo....

There was a large grained streak of doubt running parallel to an equally streaked grain of belief in the reasons why it was all happening.

Would the same things be happening if I hadn't met Asiafo? Is he really the catalyst for all this?

There were moments during the day, when he knew or felt that Akosua, the talented people around him were glancing at him with admiration, and he wanted to say - don't admire me, this is the way it's supposed to be, this is what Asiafo said would happen. Everything is cool.

"Akos', I know what you feel, believe me, I do. Looks like we have this section of the park to ourselves."

"Good. Who else comes to picnic on Tuesday, at 4:30 p.m.?"

They chose a spot under a large, low limbed tree, spread their blanket and settled in.

They were having catered goodies from the Nagasaki Cafe; bento boxes of vinegared rice, sushi, sashimi, nori leaves filled with tempura shrimp, wasabi.

"I love the way Japanese design their food to be eaten."

"Don't they do that in Africa, in Ghana?"

Kojo frowned involuntarily, the truth was difficult "**spit-to-swallow**."

"Oh, I'm sure some effort is made privately, you know, when people give dinners, but on the whole, my experience was not that great, aesthetically.

Fufu in a bowl, light soup they call it, with a piece of goat or fish slopped in it. The flavors could be interesting, depending on who cooked, but I never felt there was any effort made to do "pretty" with the food.

The other thing that puzzled me was the use of Palm Oil. Palm Oil in everything. It was kind of a drag because it got in the way of the other flavors.

You begin to ask yourself what does fish really taste like without this palm oiled based sauce?"

"Doesn't sound like you're such a great fan of Ghanaian cuisine."

"No, not really."

Sorry, Grace, I'll never forget your banku and groundnut stew with fish.

"Oh, Kojo, we forgot the beer."

"I'll get it."

He popped up from the blanket, nibbling a rice ball and moved for the car, parked a hundred yards away.

What could taste better than a cold Kirin right now?

Madness in the Park

He pulled the six-pack of Kirin from the cooler in the trunk of his car and began the long stroll back to their spot. The scene registered as a complete photo. A dirty, ragged man was standing at the edge of their blanket. He broke into a worried jog. What the hell is this? He came up behind the man, catching Akosua's eye. What does he want?

Kojo circled the man carefully and almost sighed with relief. It was just one of those wild and crazy guys who were running 'round the world these days. Kojo stared into the man's dead eyes. He's gone. What is he? Black man, about fifty, emaciated, gone. There were thousands of the same types all over Los Angeles, beneficiaries of the Reagan-Bush-close-up-the-mental-warehouse-years. He was disturbed by the man's stance at the edge of their blanket. He wasn't armed, but he was obviously gone. Kojo decided to try the sweet approach.

"What can we do for you, my brother?"

The man's unfocused eyes stayed on a distant target as he made the hand to mouth gesture for food.

Kojo felt a sudden rush of nervous perspiration pop out under his armpits.

He stared into the face of the man, trying to read something from the dead expression on his face. Nothing.

Kojo closed his bento box and handed it to the man.

"Wait, here's a beer."

The man took the bottle of beer and dropped it into the rear pocket of his filthy, grease-oil stained pants.

He opened the box and, with an incredible delicacy of finger play, dabbed a California roll into the wasabi and swallowed it without chewing.

He ate another bit of food and turned away from them and began to walk in a serpentine fashion, very quickly, as though he were late for an appointment.

Akosua moved closer to Kojo and squeezed him in a big hug.

"Kojo, I love you...do you know that?"

"I love you too," he whispered. He was perspiring heavily and his voice box felt constricted.

"That was one of the most unselfish things I've seen in a long, long time. You gave that man your dinner."

Kojo felt himself coming back, a little. The heart stroke was slowing down, the perspiration cooling.

He had fed the stranger. Was it the right stranger?

"Well, you know how it is, you have to go with the vibe sometimes. I always think, when I see dudes like that, it's him today, it could be me tomorrow."

"There, but for the Grace of God, go I."

"I heard that."

"Here, have some of my tempura."

Invitations started pouring in, attention from the moguls.

"Dan Dryson here. Sayyy, what's the deal with you? I've called your office twice awready...."

"Sorry, Dan, been meaning to get back to you. So, what can I do for you...?"

Bascom had the scent first, now they all have. Good. Let 'em pant for awhile. They know the quality of my work and what it'll bring in. Good. I'll get to 'em when I get to 'em.

The call to be social was a bit more difficult to deal with. One Hundred African-American Men sent a gold embossed invitation to their winter ball - "**THE MEN CELEBRATE**."

CHAPTER 30

"Well, of course, we have to make that."

Akosua's current book provoked public acclaim that she wasn't prepared for.

"Looks like the "Outlaws" have struck a little literary gold here." Their community wanted to take a look at the successfully functioning African-American couple with the supportive in-laws.

Jackie Muhammad was definitely on the stick.

"O.K., Kojo, Akosua, let me make a couple things clear. I'm the best, o.k.? So, go with me.

I'm going to promote you guys beyond the beyond. I see a somewhat royal touch here. Akos', as Queen of the literary scene and you, Kojo, as the African-American 'King of Cinema.'"

Kojo and Akosua, being somewhat shy by nature, slunk down in their chairs at the bold outline their P.R. person was playing out for them.

She pulled them back up with a well rehearsed pep talk.

"Look, Kojo, you want your film to make money so that you can make mo' bettah films.

Akos', you want your books to sell so that you will be able to call your own publishing shots.

I want to live up to my reputation, all Praises Due to Allah, and the only way we're going to be able to pull any of this off is by extending the current methodology of publicizing into another realm, an African-American realm.

'Dagbladet,' the Danish film magazine will be here tomorrow for a brief interview and lots of flicks. Are you guys ready?"

"Dagbladet....? Wow! how did you know about them?!"

"Kojo, Akosua, I have done a serious research job on you two. I'll be bringing in folks who've had your best interests at heart for years.

I've pulled the "Literary Gazette" in to do a piece on Akosua's father-in-law stocking her books in his store. There are angles, my sister, my brother, and I know them."

"Well, you know we start shooting at the end of the week and time will be tight. We'll only have three months to do what we have to do."

"Kojo, I know the schedule, and I know that you've engaged some of the heaviest talents in this industry. In addition to that, you have drummed your message in so hard that I have no doubt that we could do our jobs in the dark.

Now, what I'm saying to you is simple...let's put enough serious, honest publicity out there to guarantee your success.

Remember, in the Beginning was the Word (and publicity)."

❖

FADE IN (OUTLINE)
EXTERIOR - ANY LARGE AMERICAN CITY - NITE

A) A subliminal series of shots gives us a stroboscopic look at neon-city-life. We cover everything from idiots lighting cigarettes to cars whizzing along the speedways. Some things have a phosphorescent glow.

   The atmosphere is electric and stupid. The activities are ant-like, but unlike ants these activities are nebulous, that is to say, practically meaningless.

CUT TO:

B) EXTERIOR - SEASIDE AFRICAN VILLAGE - DAY

   Two babies (boy and girl) are playing at the shore line, suddenly turn to the CAMERA apprehensively...
   (APPROPRIATE MUSIC ACCOMPANIES)
   Note: it's all about contrasts, juxtapositions that say something psychologically interesting.

CUT TO:

C) Enslaved Africans chained together.

A self-righteous White preacher is preaching to them, reassuring them that the life they will be going into is better than the "pagan" life they are being taken from...Amen....

CUT TO:

D) (It's just cut to-cut to for the outline here. We will be using every creative transition and angle known to man in the actual script.)
INTERIOR - HIP HOP CLUB SCENE - NITE

It is Rap Time! It is Reggae Time! It is pop lock / what's left of break dancing. A montage.

CUT TO:

E) EXTERIOR – THE INNER CITY STREETS - NITE

A gang fight between two Black gangs is in progress. Uzi bullets, tracers, small arms fire, lots of blood. The scene could almost be a caricature of a Hollywood "urban action" movie, except that the blood isn't ketchup and the dead do not appear in other movies.

DISSOLVE TO:

F) EXTERIOR - COTTON FIELD - DAY

The sun is blistering and the enslaved Africans who are working in the fields are not singing bright songs.

MELT TO:

G) INSERT

A "baseball card collection" of Authentic African-American folk heroes (half male/half female) is flipped. The subliminal effect is to use just enough time to have the face and name register.

CUT TO:

H) EXTERIOR - LIQUOR STORE - DAY

We see a bedraggled, **drunked** out collection of men and women lounging around in the parking lot next to the liquor store.

They have reached the desperate stage of not being able to go too far from the source of their pain killer.

(The scenes go quickly. We jump on it and **git** on. Some of the satire / truth / honesty / irony / sarcasm, etc., will depend on the briskness of the pace to Say something).

SLICE TO:

I) INTERIOR - FASHION SALON - DAY

It is African/African-American Fashion at its best. The models are not bony-thin, nor are they jelly bellies, and the clothes are superb designs.

CUT TO:

J) EXTERIOR / INTERIOR -
AFRICAN REFUGEE CAMPS / AFRICAN-AMERICAN GHETTOS

The strife of war on both fronts is shown.

EASE TO:

K) The Pan-African scene / a montage-look at us all over, doing what we do. The Contrasts are automatic, stimulating.

SPIRAL TO:

L) African religious practices in various parts of the world - use one ritual and show how it is performed: America = The Religion/ Yoruba.

Brasil　　　=　　　Candomble

Haiti	=	Vodun
Cuba	=	Santeria / Lukumi
Puerto Rico	=	Santos / Santeria
Trinidad	=	Shango
Jamaica	=	Obeah / Poco

Aside from the widespread, indigenous belief systems of Africa, we'll look at the places in Europe and Asia that have been influenced by these religious systems.

The focus will be on Greece and their adoption of the Yoruba mythology, wholesale.

"Kojo, what time did you tell your Grandfather we were coming?"

"4 o'clock. I'm coming. Just want to finish these last two points."

M) Healthy African-American children / sick African-American children (what makes them healthy / sick?)

N) REAL VS. UNREAL

During the course of all the pre-production madness, Kojo felt compelled to get away for a few hours, to talk with his Grandfather-mentor about a few things... Akosua wanted to explore his feelings concerning the spiritual connections.

"Kojo, Akosua, ahhh, young lady, I must say...pregnancy becomes you."

"Thank you, Granddad, I think you're the first man I've ever received that compliment from...."

"Now hold on here a minute, Akos', I'm always telling you how beautiful you look...."

"But, Kojo, you know that's because you think I'm feeling a little dumpy and you want to pep me up a bit...."

"Akosua...."

"She's right, Kojo. . .we menfolks do stuff like that at times, 'specially if we're sensitive."

He ushered them in on a tidal wave of good vibes, exchanging hugs, kisses, an affectionate pat on Akosua's exploding stomach.

"C'mon in, c'mon in, you just missed your Aunt Rose, Aunt Deborah and Aunt Afiya by about ten minutes."

"Paying you a visit, huh?"

"Killing me with kindness would be more like it."

"Granddad!"

"Just joking, daughter, just joking! They came over to make sure I was eating properly and all that. They must've left a half ton of food in the kitchen, including half a turkey."

"I see what you mean about killing you with kindness."

"Don't mind them. Can I get you guys a drink of something? Water, pineapple juice, coke, Chivas Regal?"

Akosua took the lead.

"Granddad, why don't you pour yourself a drink? I'll get us something from the 'fridge."

"It's there, you know where it is...."

Kojo settled himself into his arm chair, affectionately gazing at his Grandfather, the neatly stacked stack of books next to his low slung "barber's chair," a reading chair he had designed for himself.

"Who wants to sit and read in a ram-rod position?"

"That's quite a lady you got there, Kojo, quite a lady."

"I'm beginning to appreciate that more and more each and every day."

Akosua returned with a tray loaded with ice cubes, two kinds of juices. Kojo smiled and made a snap decision.

"This is an afternoon off for us, I think I'll join Granddad and have some of his juice."

Granddad enjoyed the comment and poured two fingers of Chivas Regal into two glasses.

Akosua held her glass of pineapple juice up in a toast.

"Here's looking at you because I can't join you, but there's always next year. Cheers."

"Cheers!"

"Yeah, cheers!"

They sipped their drinks and were silent for a few moments. Grandfather Brown opened the floor.

"How's the movie thing going?"

The flood was channeled, they had someone who cared from the "outside," who could listen to their stories without being critical.

"It's always an uphill battle when you do an independent production. As you know, The Men granted us 1.5 million to do the thing, we could use twice as much."

"We're trying to stay away from the usual guys, in order to get more money, because they will immediately start putting their sticky fingers all over everything."

"We'll have to deal with them when it comes to distribution because they own all the theatres...."

"There are so many things to do when you set up an independent production company. All of the busy-busy stuff that would be taken care of by a bunch of gophers in a major league studio have to be done by us, all of us are gophers."

"So, things are going o.k., huh?"

Akosua and Kojo exchanged smiles. The old man had shuffled them to the bottom line.

"Uhh, yeah, Granddad, I guess you could say that. We start shooting next week."

"Good."

They sipped and relaxed. Akosua had noted earlier that being in Grandfather Brown's space was a soothing agent. He didn't make them feel as though they were compelled to start jabbering about all that they were about.

He offered them space and allowed them the chance to shade in the blank areas at their own speed.

"Grandfather Brown...."

"Call me Granddad, Akos', you're one of my daughters now."

"Granddad, we're going to be dealing with a recurring theme in our film, the presence of a certain kind of...of spirituality. We wanted to talk with you about that."

"Oh, I see...."

"Said the blind man...."

Kojo and his Grandfather laughed at their little "in" joke.

"Well, let's talk about what you want to know. If I know something about it, I'll tell all."

They settled back to think for a few seconds. What do we want to know. Akosua led off.

"Do you think that Africans, people of African descent, have a greater sense of spirituality than other people? And that this may have been a factor in our surviving chattel slavery."

The old man pursed his lips thoughtfully, took simultaneous sips with Kojo. When he answered her question, it seemed that his voice had taken on a darker texture.

"Akos', you know something? That's a question I started putting my mind on, about forty some years ago. I used to talk with Tanina, with my wife, about it. I'll tell, I'll share the conclusions we reached. Number one, I don't want to dig a grave for myself and say that we have a monopoly on spirituality. No, I wouldn't want to say that. But I will say this, if there was ever a race of people in the world who were forced to call on inner reserves of spirituality, of ancestral courage, it would have to be us. People sometimes forget that we had the Plagues, the Holocaust, genocide, slavery, Hiroshima, Nagasaki, and colonialism put on us at the same time, all through **'OurStory'**.

Somebody a whole lot wiser than me will have to explain the why-of-why we've had to go through all this, why we're still going through it, but one thing we all know is that steel is tempered by pressure. If we take spirituality as a form of steel, then we can certainly say we are a bunch of sharp swords."

They shared a smile at his wit.

"Everywhere I look around the world and I see people of African descent, I see a certain kind of "Ancestor Strength" that's being used to help meet their daily problems.

We seem to make slightly different approaches to our ancestors, to the Orisha, to God, but it comes down to the same thing in the end.

We've had to go deeper than most folks because of our historical circumstances. Was our spirituality a factor in surviving chattel slavery? I'd have to say yes. When you do a broad sweep, what do you call it, Kojo?"

"A Pan...."

"Hahh hah, that's the word. When you do a 'Pan' of the African spiritual scene, you can come away with some very interesting possibilities.... I'll just give you three or four random examples of what I mean.

Remember Fredrick Douglass — and that knock down-drag out fight he had with the so called slave breaker? Remember that a '**BOCOR**' had given ol' Fredrick a root that would protect him and allow him to overcome his enemies.

Think about Harriet Tubman and those so called 'spells' she used to have. Think about Nat Turner and Denmark Vesey and how touched they were by spirits.

Think about Boukman, the priest up in the hills in Haiti, who really kicked the revolution off. Toussaint L'Overture may have continued it but Boukman kicked it off. Think about Zumbi in Brasil, and the Quilumbo of Palmares. All of these things and so many more nobody could count 'em, tell me that we hooked into something quite deep, a long time ago."

Akosua was feeling enlightened, her research being validated by an authority.

"What about White people, Granddad, where do you put them on the spiritual scale?"

"Way down, 'way down. I sometime think that the White race got up on the wrong side of the bed. Now don't get me wrong, there are individuals, there have been individuals, I think John Brown was one, who could measure up to us spiritually, but on the whole, no go.

I see that as the reason so many young Whites skipping off to Eastern religions, to African religions, to obscure little islands in search of something their ancestors couldn't bequeath them. How would you feel praying to a great granddad who had been a slaver, a serial rapist, a robber, a killer and a mad man? I think you'd be on bad terms with your ancestors, if you had ancestors like that. Now, your question is, how did that happen? How do you wind up with a rogues gallery of people for ancestors?"

"Granddad, you stole the question right off the tip of my tongue."

"That is as much of a mystery as the reason why we've so often held the dirty end of the stick. As liberal as we all try to be, in our study of the White psyche, we inevitably reach the conclusion that you're dealing with a race of diseased minds, warped mentalities.

There is a folk tale that says that the '**It**' of the universe deposited growth matter on this planet. The Black growth grew naturally, the Yellow, Brown, but the White growth had something happen to it.

Remember now, this is just a myth, a folk tale...but it goes on to identify most of the terrible traits we find in Whites; their rapaciousness, greed, lack of sensitivity, self control, concern for nature, need to fight all the time, racist behavior...traits that came out of this growth and have been kept alive down through the centuries."

They were completely silent for a few moments, each focused on a different point.

"I was just thinking of the Danes I met, just a short while back, and how they fit the category - Whites - that you just talked about."

"Well, give them credit for trying, but unfortunately, they did their share of raping and pillaging too, back in their Viking days.

And they didn't get 'hold of those islands in the Caribbean by lottery. But give 'em credit for trying."

"I think about the White people I went to school with...there was always something I just couldn't understand about their mindsets. You know what I mean?"

Grandfather Brown took a sip of his drink and smiled at Akosua's comment.

"Yeahhh, I know what you mean, daughter, I know what you mean, if you've had a problem trying to figure out where they were coming from, just think about the job that our ancestors had, not even knowing his language, let alone where his head was.

I think that's one of the big reasons why we pray to those super human beings who had to come to grips with this weirdo every day of their lives."

The tone was jocular but the undercurrent was serious.

"Any objection to continuing this while we try to polish off a few loads of this ton of food these women have left me?"

"Akos', you awake?"

"Yeah, I'm awake but I don't feel like going with you this morning. I think I'm the victim of something called morning sickness."

"Can I do anything for you?"

"Yes, go to your exercises so that you'll be able to teach the newborn how to do Capoeira."

"I love you, Akos'."

"And I love you too."

Kojo slipped out of the house and shuffle-jogged to the small playground, ("Echo Park District Playground"), three blocks from them.

He felt a bit of nostalgia for the heavy smoker Harry *"Coff! Coff! Coff!"* and his three Schnauzers, the various nut cases and odd balls that bobbled around Barnsdall Park all day long.

The Echo Park District Playground was offering unexpected dividends — no dog dirt, a hard packed surface and very few people to bug him at 7:30 a.m.

A handstand against a tree trunk started him off

The film was called "The Island", it was Japanese and had the cruel, formalized beauty that the Japanese seem to love so much.

The story was lean and simple. A family lives on an island and must row five miles to a mainland to get water every day. Often twice a day, because they are farmers and the vegetables they raise are thirsty beings.

The film is almost silent, except for the constant slapping of oars, back and forth, back and forth.

Kojo slipped from one movement to another, almost allowing muscle memory to take over. Yeah, that's the best kind of workout, when you don't feel any strain or pain.

Forty five minutes later, the workout done, he loped up the hilly street feeling loose, ready for whatever the day had in store for him.

"Sheila Buttram just called, she wants to talk with you about your project."

They fell into each other's arms, laughing at the absurdity of it all. If you were bold enough to tell them kiss your ass, they would pursue you. If you kissed their asses, they would abuse you.

"So, now what do we have? Dryson has kicked in, now Buttram. They must smell blood."

"Or a damned good film about to be shot."

"Which reminds me, needless to say, that we're having a meeting this evening to talk about everybody's responsibilities. This thing has to go off on schedule and come back on schedule. How're you feeling?"

"Shaky, but o.k...."

"Think you might like to share a glass of orange juice with me?"

"Sounds like a winner to me."

After glasses or orange juice and a few returned calls...

"I'll get back to Buttram tomorrow."

They reviewed the structure of the shoot. Kojo had deliberately chosen two top flight assistant directors, Ed Burris and Mac Weaver, as his "wing men".

"I'll be handling the main thrust of the piece and they'll be doing the peripheral work, but nothing is going to be more important than the peripheral work. I've drummed that into their minds."

"I know, I've heard you."

"That was some heavy drama Granddad laid on us last night, huh?"

"You're used to it. He blows me away...."

"Really. Well, it's time for the producer-writer-director to charge off to the office. Thelma and the new girl have been gathering in extras since last week. I need to take a look at that, and also, we need to get **definites** on the equipment trucks and...."

"Kojo, you'll be late in a few minutes...."

"Aren't you going....?"

"Not today, let's say the pregnant woman took a day off."

"You are o.k.?"

"Yes, love, just pregnant, that's all."

"O.K., a quick shower and a shave and I'm off."

From the first day in December that they shot the first scene, Kojo felt that he was in a blurred version of Heaven.

Akosua came back strong after a week of "morning sickness," each element of the production team was functioning with maximum efficiency and it looked as though they were going to be able to start editing as they worked.

They "guerillaed" their way around, dropping off cameras and actors on a corner to do something exciting and creative before permits were requested. The actors and actresses, the extras, got into the groove. Once it was seriously explained to them, they got into it far enough to make suggestions, some of them constructive.

Trick bags were opened and goodies brought forth, an African village was found in South Carolina. Mac Weaver went and shot with rented equipment.

It was happening, Kojo's Our Production Company was shooting a film entitled "Grandfather's Eyes."

The moguls had re-connected.

"Now look, Kojo, let's not be difficult about this, I want to help you put your film out there."

"I know you do, Charley, I know you do."

They were constantly being pleasantly surprised.

"Ah yes, Akosua, this is your mother. Have you forgotten?"

"Oh, Mom, I'm sorry. You sounded like someone else..., and we've been so busy, I feel like I have a 'phone in each ear half the time."

"I understand."

"Well, what can I do for you? How's Dad?"

"Your father is well and reading the Sunday newspaper from front to back as usual but I think I can do something for you...."

A half-hour later Akosua floated from her workshop space, to Kojo, furiously juggling scenes and ideas, at the rear of the house.

"Kojo? Kojo? Can you stop for a moment?"

"Akos', what's wrong? Is it time?"

"Hahhh hahh, no silly man, I've got a lil' while to go yet."

"You had me shook up there for a second."

"My mother just shook me up."

"What's the problem this time?"

"No problem, not at all. The lady has put us in a position to get a few hundred thousand dollars."

"What?!"

"You heard me. It seems that a number of the sisters who are married to One Hundred African-American Men felt that they should get into a matching funds number, prompted by my mother, of course."

"Of course."

"So, there it is. She wants you to contact this lady, set up a meeting and pitch. Mom is telling me that the fix is in, it's just purely a matter of going through the forms."

"Well, I'll be damned."

"That's what I said."

They embraced, full of smiles.

"Akos', we're going to have to do something nice for your mother."

"We are doing something nice," she said, patting her rounded stomach.... "I'm off for a little afternoon siesta, want to join me?"

"In a little while, I have some things to straighten out... and the news you've just given me has charged my batteries."

She sprinkled a wave of her fingers and waddled to their bedroom. Kojo sat at his desk for a few minutes, found that his work energy was shot and decided to sit out back with a goblet of San Antonio Red.

Los Angeles sprawled beyond the borders of his view. It was the winter time, December, and the air was clear enough for him to see and breath. It's really weird that people only think about coming out here in the summer, when the place is suffocating from the smog.

He leaned back in his chair, shaded by the Campari umbrella, feeling full of himself. It's happening, it's all happening, my dreams are becoming realities.

He did a slow, emotional Pan of his scene. Yeahhh, it's looking good. When it gets to the point where Akosua's mother starts kicking in...

He glanced at the green and black coil, about 10 yards to his left, strayed his glance and came back to it. A snake. The coil wasn't moving, the head wasn't flicking about, it was coiled, motionless. Kojo sipped his wine, stared at the coils..., about three feet long, beautifully tapered, incredible coloring, black bottom and green top.

He made a quick mental review of all the zoos his parents had taken him through, the books on herpetology, trying to place the snake's coloring in a category. Is it poisonous? Black and green, what's that? He felt a kind of chilled fascination at the sight of the snake, smothered in centuries of myth and fear. He glanced away for a moment, sipped his wine and, when he turned back to the snake it seemed to be much closer to him. Was it moving? Is it closer?

Kojo made two quick decisions. If it comes closer I'll throw my glass at it. If it stays where it is I won't bother it. Snakes have a right to life too.

The raspy sound of a voice that seemed to come from nowhere froze his blood. The only time he could remember having that feeling was seeing the Hitchcock monster thriller - "Psycho" - when Tony Perkins, charges Janet Leigh in the shower with a butcher knife.

"Feed me," the voice rasped.

Kojo gripped the arms of his chair. No, this couldn't be the stranger that Asiafo spoke of, this was a snake.

"Feed you what?" he asked, his voice trembling.

"A large rat."

Kojo placed his glass on the table, edged up from his seat, being careful to stay on the far side of the snake.

"'When?"

"Tonight," the snake whispered in a raspy baritone and slithered away.

Kojo couldn't control his trembling, the sudden film of sweat that coated his face. He looked around in all directions.

CHAPTER 31

People would think I'm out of my mind, out here talking to a snake. No, I couldn't've been talking to a snake, snakes can't talk. A rat. He wants a rat. That's what snakes eat, rats.

The trembling gradually stopped as Kojo began to reason with himself. It wasn't a mirage, it wasn't somebody doing ventriloquism, it was real.

A stranger. I'm supposed to feed a stranger. No one said anything about the form of the stranger, or the shape. He thought back to the ragged, crazy looking man in the park.

I'm supposed to feed a stranger four times a year, that's the deal.

Pet Store?

A rat. Where can I find a rat? The Echo Park Pet Shop. It's a perfect time... Akos' is napping. Kojo tiptoed through the house to peek at his wife. Good. She's sleeping like a baby...pun.

The Echo Park Pet Shop, six blocks east of them. He decided to jog it, rather than run the risk of starting the car and waking Akosua.

Hope this place is open. Yes, of course it's open, Sunday is their big day.

He jogged easily, his mind tingling with ambivalent thoughts. This can't be real...I can't be running down the street to buy a snake's dinner. The thought stunned him to a shuffling walk....

A snake spoke to me in my back yard. No, that couldn't be, snakes don't talk. Asiafo has sent me a snake to feed. He revved himself back up to a jog. Asiafo sent me a snake to feed, a stranger. He felt like screaming. Or turning around and running back home.

What will happen if I don't feed the stranger, the snake?

"Yessir, may I help you?"

"I want to buy a rat."

Kojo felt a sour taste well up in his throat, thinking about his errand.

"This way, please."

The salesman led him into an off room.

"We keep them here so that the children won't come in and harm them. Now then, what did you have in mind?"

White rats with pinkish eyes, fattened for sale, cages of them.

"I'll take that large one there."

"Good choice, I call him ol' Dan. Rats are very intelligent, you know?"

"Yes, I know."

The thought jarred him. — Should I kill it or....?

"I see that you don't have a cage for your pet, would you care to...?"

"Yes, I'll take that one over there." The rat was going to be alive. He paid, placed the caged rat in a large paper bag and started back home.

God, I hope Akosua isn't awake, I'd have a helluva time trying to explain this rat. Wonder if she's afraid of rats?

He tiptoed back into the house. Good, still sleeping.

He went to the kitchen, cut a length of string from a ball of twine and tied it around one of the rats rear legs. The large white rat, genetically domesticated, only sniffed at the string tied to its leg.

Kojo found a short stick in the yard, staked it in the place where he had first seen the snake and tied the rat to the stake. The rat scurried around the stake, obviously looking for food.

So, you're hungry, huh? He hurried back inside to get a slice of bread and a dish of water. What the hell, the condemned rat ate a hearty meal.

He paused to gulp a glass of wine before slicing the bread. He felt shaky, disoriented. What the hell am I doing?

He carried a small dish of water and a slice of bread to the yard, trying to place the whole business in perspective.

If I don't do this I'll cut off my flow. If I don't do this I'll cut of my flow....

He came to a stunned stop at the stake. The rat was gone. He dropped the water and bread, squatted and studied the turf.

The stake was there and the string had been untied. The ground showed evidence that the rat had scratched and struggled. The snake got him, but who untied the string? Snakes don't untie strings....

"Kojo! telephone!"

In the weeks following, the law firm of Green, Shafton and Clark were kept busy tying up neat little bundles of deals, contracts, agreements.

Mrs. Minerva Ferguson's Women's Auxiliary kicked in with $300,000.... "We want some of the action". The normal snags of movie making occurred, but nothing proved insurmountable.

Kojo felt like a man on the crest of a wave, literally. The film was being made. Frank Goldstone and Dan Dryson were trying to out-bid each other for the chance to distribute the work, it was happening at a pace that he could never have predicted.

Kojo and Akosua Ferguson-Brown were **HOT!** Ms. Muhammad, the P.R. expert, kept their faces and doings in the trades, the local papers, and chipped away at the major league magazines.

"Kojo, don't worry about a thing...by the time your film comes out, people will be panting to see it."

Juna, the musician, jumped into her creative trench and was obviously scoring a masterpiece of a score.

"I've invited the One Earth Musical Quartet, with Kanda, to participate in this musical feast I'm preparing. I find this very interesting work to do, you know what I mean? 'scuse me, I must go, my cat wants to get out."

The still photographer for the film put it well when he told Kojo, "I've never been a part of a set that had vibes this good. Never."

But late at night, after the last scene had been shot, the lights clicked off, Kojo sat in the dark, imagining that he could see the black and green snake, that he could hear him say, "feed me."

The thought of him going to buy a rat for a snake that said, "feed me," made him feel as though he had done something vaguely dirty.

Why should I feel like this? It's just part of the program. If it wasn't this, it would be something else. If I don't do what I was supposed to do, the thing wouldn't work. Or would it?

He felt tempted to disregard the agreement he had made with Asiafo. What sense does it make? I'm just being superstitious, that's all. But he couldn't shake off the obligation he felt.

I agreed to get married within three months. I did it. I agreed to feed a stranger four times a year. I've fed two strangers this year, that nut case in the park and the snake. Was the nut case really a stranger, or just a crazy man begging for sushi in the park?

The snake was definitely a stranger, I don't even have to think twice about that. But was the nut case a stranger? Have I only fed one stranger...? The snake, definitely. But was the other man a part of the situation? What if he wasn't a part of the situation? Am I still obligated to feed three more strangers before the end of the year, rather than two?

Secretly, he prayed against the idea of snakes as strangers. Please, don't send me more snakes.

In addition he was beginning to feel a secret guilt. What if I told Akosua that I married her because it was part of a deal that I made with a man in the forest?

How could I tell these intelligent people I'm working with that it's all happening because of a deal I made with a man in the forest? Is it really happening because of the deal I agreed to?

He carefully thought out a way to rebel against the deal, and quickly shelved it. How can I rebel against something that's paying off like this? But what is paying off? Would it happen anyway? That was the thought that nagged him. If I had come back from Africa and jumped on the stick the way I did, maybe it would be happening just the way it's happening. Maybe....

The last month of the year found them blazing away, creatively.

"It's like a pure distillation, I'm telling you, Kojo, like a pure distillation."

"Funny that you would see it that way, I think of it like having a baby."

"Without any morning sickness I hope."

"Definitely."

Once again the snake came unexpectedly. It came to him during his morning workout in the Echo Park District Playground. He was doing his usual handstand against the trunk of a tree when he spied the familiar coil of black and green. He came down from his handstand and tried to ignore the snake.

He did a slow Pan of the playground — a grandmother type pushing a baby buggy through.

"Feed me."

Asiafo, "Feed me..."

The by now familiar raspy voice grated Kojo's nerves, made the hair on the back of his head stiffen.

"I already fed you!" he replied, angry with himself and the gruesome situation.

"Feed me!" the snake rasped again.

"Feed you what?! Where?!"

"A rabbit, in the yard," the snake answered and slithered away. Kojo stared at the disappearing reptile with angry tears in his eyes.

"So, I'm supposed to feed a stranger four times a year, right? For how many years?! And you're no stranger, you're a damned snake and I've seen you before! You're not a stranger!"

Kojo turned to stare into the curious faces of two mothers bringing their toddlers to the playground.

Bet they think I'm just another crazy on the loose. Who knows? Maybe I am. A fuckin' rabbit!

The movie was fixed in his mind, he could see the beginning, the middle and the end of it. It was the story of a man who had made a promise to a supernatural force, a promise he didn't want to keep.

How do you make a story like that interesting? I've supplied the damned snake with a rat and a rabbit. A strange man comes to the back door with a sign in his hand, "I will work for food."

A stranger - "I will work for food". Why food? Why not money? And, of course, we had to let him work...for food.

Feed the stranger four times a year. Which stranger? How many years? The strain of his thoughts was beginning to make him noticeably irritable.

Akosua wrote it off to being pressures from the film making. They were well into it now, all of the elements were **cohesing**. Kojo had the center and his two assistants were on the wings.

Kojo saw it as a neat job of sewing elements together.

"We want to have a seamless work, a work with all of the signposts pointing very artistically to a clear and definite logic."

He worked out a distribution deal with Charley Bascom.

"It was either him or one of the others. They're all the same. The thing about Charley is that he's a bigger asshole than most. And that's what we need."

Busy, busy, busy...the office in the loft suddenly seemed smaller with the influx of workers. The home 'phone rang constantly.

"Kojo, you think we should ask the sister to back away from the P.R. pistol for a minute?"

"It's too late now, she has us booked until you go to the hospital."

Kojo Bediako Brown was the head of the operation, but he knew how to relegate authority. "My Dad gave me an excellent piece of advice, years ago. Don't work with people you can't trust."

And during the course of one casual interview with a local columnist, he almost put his foot in his mouth. The question that provoked the problem was, "And to what do you attribute your success?"

Asiafo's manic laughter, the green and black snake, the demands on him almost caused him to blurt out the story of the deal.

Akosua took note, "What was that all about? Sounded like you were about to say something other than...'I attribute my success, such as it is, to my family and my wife.'"

"Awww, you know how it is, I just had my mind on a half dozen things at one time."

A rabbit in the yard. Back to the pet store.

"Welcome, looks like you're building up quite a collection, uhh—Mr...."

"Jones."

"Uhh, Mr. Jones. Well, we have the white bunnies here, and the great Belgian hares over...."

"I'll take a bunny."

"Very good, sir. Will that be all for you?"

"Yes."

That's all, too much. Where can I hide a rabbit?

He sat in his car, trying to find an angle. If I take it to someone's house, they'll be sure and ask Akosua, one day, what happened to the rabbit?

He drove aimlessly to the ocean. It was 8:00 p.m. He left the rabbit in the back seat of his car with a half dozen carrots, a bowl of water and strolled along the beach.

It was a rare short day, but they had worked all night, the night before. Damn, what a helluva crew I have. They're willing to do it until it's done right, that's the only way.

The clear December ocean air was bracing, caused him to dig his hands deep into his pockets. How do I do this? Keep the rabbit in the car until Akos' goes to sleep? What?

The absurdity of the dilemma caused him to laugh aloud. What kind of madness is this?

He turned away from the ocean to walk back to his car, the problem still unresolved.

He opened the car and looked at the rabbit on the floor, contentedly crunching on a carrot, little black pellets scattered about.

Dammit! Rabbit crap. Now I have to get the car cleaned. He drove off, thinking about his problem and the future scenes to be shot. It should be a wrap by the end of next month.

"Yes, of course, some people will look at the film as though it were some sort of odd thing, a documentary perhaps. But that's the risk one has to run whenever you do anything new and different."

"Can you give us some idea of the basic story of your film?"

"Well, actually there are three interwoven stories, and they are viewed by the eyes of a wise old man."

"You're listening to "Family Ties" on KPFK, 90.7 on your radio dial and our guest this morning is brother Kojo Bediako Brown, the writer-director-producer of a film that will be released sometime within the next three months...."

"That'll be closer to six months...."

After all that worrying, it was all for nothing. Akos' had gone over to her mother's, had a late dinner and spent the night in her old room, making her mother ecstatic.

And the greedy snake got his rabbit the minute I turned my back. Or else he escaped.

"Hah hah. . . about six months. O.K. This is Rick Sands of "Family Ties" and we invite your questions for our guest, Kojo Bediako Brown. Ah hah! I see a red light on one console. Go ahead, caller, you have a question for brother Brown?"

"Yes, my name is Kwame Sekou Toure 'The Second', and I want to ask the brother if the film he has almost completed is going to be a Negrocentric thang or a Black thang?"

"Brother Brown, how would you respond to that?"

"I'd simply like to say that we don't see the film as a Negrocentric or Black thang, but rather as an African-American statement."

Amazing how...how parochial some of the brothers can be.

"Thank you, brother. Next caller, go ahead please...."

"Uhh yes, my name is Latisha Khalidifa and I'm calling to congratulate the brother and sister Akosua for pulling together in the way that they've done. Far too often we have the sad story of the brother who has made it, turning to the White girl as though she represented the pinnacle of some kind of achievement. I've just finished reading a wonderful story on brother Brown and sister Akosua in 'African-American Life', talking about the sister's literary accomplishments and the success that the brother has been having. I think what 'we as a people,' must address ourselves to is the idea of entrepreneurship, no matter whether it be in wholesale goods or the visual media, such as film making...."

"Uhhh, sister Latisha, we appreciate your observations and comments, but I'm afraid we've come to the end of our time.

Once again, this is Rick Sands and you've been listening to "Family Ties," 90.7 KPFK, on your radio dial. I'd like to thank our guest, writer-producer-director Kojo Bediako Brown, for sharing his gems of wisdom this morning. 'Til next time, remember...keep the family ties together."

From the radio station to the office to answer a dozen calls, a meeting with the assistant directors.

They all felt they were involved with something new and extraordinary. The assistants were being given the opportunity to stretch their imaginations to the max, within the framework of Kojo's design.

Have to sit with Juna for an hour. The thing looks like it's almost ready to go into the editing room.

Suddenly the late nights that frequently saw then yawning at dawn were coming to an end. The middle section had seemed glacial, but now the ending was a pebble starting to avalanche. Akosua had retreated to the office setting.

"You don't need a pregnant woman on the set."

It was a whirlwind feeling. And it was compounded by the drummed up drama of the holiday feeding frenzy. There was something seriously ludicrous, he felt, about people racing around Beverly Hills, to one shopping mall after another, to take themselves further into debt.

No wonder the Japanese are able to kick us in the ass so hard. While we run around pretending that a little red faced man, with a white beard, wearing a red snowsuit, is going to make us happy, the Japanese are lined up at the savings window. And what was it really about? Something that had to do with Jesus Christ's birthday. That seemed to be the last thing anyone carried a feeling for.

Akosua felt like a traitor because she was forced to join the frenzy for a minute.

"If I don't get them something they'll think that I've become anti-Claus or something."

Kojo didn't have that problem. Stray members on the fringes of his family celebrated Christmas, but for him, for his family, it had always been Kwanzaa and New Years/Yemanja at the beach.

"Kojo, don't even think about all those sick Euroholidays...that our people have been conditioned to celebrate. "Thanksgiving" is the most terrible example...."

No, it wasn't the Christmas buying frenzy that he was concerned about, he was concerned about bringing the film in, a few dollars under the budget.

So far so good. They had pulled the belt as tight as it would go, no one had goofed off and the results were about to be taken to the editing room.

Kojo left the office-loft feeling almost euphoric. It's all happening, it's all happening, my vision is becoming a reality.

My wife is going to have a baby, we're going to have a baby and get rich too. He made an impulsive stop at Trader Joe's in Echo Park.

Be a nice thing to take a good bottle of white wine home. Wonder what Akos' is doing for dinner?

❖

"Akos', put all of it on hold for an hour, the 'phones, all of it. We're going to have dinner, sip some wine and lap up the sunset."

"I'm with you all the way...."

It was the first time in weeks that they were able to share their lives without interruptions. They knew it would only be for a moment or two, but that made it even more precious.

Kojo studied his wife's movement as she walked out into the yard. Her shape has changed but she's still graceful. How many months? Seven months. It won't be long now.

"Linguine and clams? How did you know I wanted pasta?"

"I know my man," she answered and gave him a lascivious wink. They ate and drank, keeping the unwritten/unspoken rule of No Business this evening.

Linguine and clams, garlic bread, antipasto, a good French wine. The lush colors of Fellii's "Roma," the art of Marcello Mastroanni, Giancarlo Giannini, Sophia Loren and Vitorio de Sica, Victor Storaro...flooded his senses as the flavors of the food mingled in his mouth.

"Akos', if you weren't an African-American woman, you'd be the best Italian cook in California."

"I don't see a contradiction there...."

They shared the laugh and sipped their wine.

"Bread, Love and Chocolate." "Dark eyes." "La Dolce Vita." "Rimini." "Bitter Rice." "Mambo." Wonder what happened to Silvana Mangano? Last thing I saw her in was "Dark Eyes," the Italian-Russian thing with Marcello Mastroanni.

That's what I'd like to do, an African-American-Senegalese thing. Or an African-American-Ghanaian film. Or maybe an African-American-African-Brasilian thing.

"What's the secret little smile about sweetheart?"

"Oh, I was just thinking about all the good things happening to us."

Akosua circled the table to drape her arms around his neck...

"Kojo, I love you so much...."

He led her around the chair to sit on his lap.

"I'm too heavy."

"No, you're not too heavy."

They held each other. Kojo placed his hand on her stomach. Such a hard, tight ball. Akosua nuzzled her nose into his neck. Kojo, looking past her shoulder into the border of flowers, shivered when he spotted the black and green blur of the snake.

For a moment he felt a deep sense of revulsion about himself, the dirty deal had made, in order to claim fame and fortune.

And I can't lie to myself about it, not after feeding the damn thing rats and rabbits. I'm in it as deeply as I can be.

"Kojo, I'm going to take a shower and a little nap. You want to join me?"

"Just as soon as I polish off another glass of this Vouray."

She planted a solidly erotic kiss on his lips and strolled into the house, winking at him over her left shoulder.

Just look at this woman..., seven months pregnant and she's become sexier every day.

CHAPTER 32

The Snake. The Snake.

He stared at the bordered underbrush. I did see it. What the hell is it hanging around out here for? He sipped his wine, frowning at the sunset.

A month later, into the New Year, while doing his early morning Capoeira workout, the snake appeared, casually flicking his forked tongue.

Kojo froze in place. Now what?

"A goat."

Was he actually speaking or were the sounds coming from some sort of vibration?

"A goat."

"No! no! I am not going to feed you again!"

The snake slithered away. Kojo stood in place, trembling, sweating, the workout forgotten. Why me? Damn!

He draped a towel around his neck and started the uphill walk home. I've already fed the damn thing four times. But that was last year a small voice whispered at the back of his head. Last year, this is a New Year.

The New Year meant a few crucial scenes for "Grandfather's Eyes" had to be re-shot, the editing completed, arguments happening with Charley Bascom about the final cut.

"Kojo, you've got to admit, it's a pretty rare situation we have here, where the guy who's responsible for making the distribution deal of the decade, doesn't really know what the fuckin' movie is about and has no say so about the final cut."

"You begged into the picture, Charley, remember?"

The music was going straight ahead, with magical Juna and the One Earth musical group.

Yes, it's all coming together...why should I cater to a damned snake? I must be out of my mind.

Shower, shave, off to the loft....

"Kojo, Jackie has me scheduled to speak to a women's group this afternoon, and then I have the literary number to do this evening."

"Good, I'm glad she decided to focus on your side of the screen for awhile, she was wearing me out."

"She'll get back to you next week, have no fear."

"Does the woman ever sleep?"

Agreements made, contracts to read, an appointment with the lawyers, Green, Shafton and Clark, a visit to the hospital to cheer up Thelma Nagata, the super office manager who was recovering from a slight case of fatigue. Editing, things to do.

He backed out of the driveway and almost rolled over the three year old . The mother's scream froze his foot on the brakes. He watched the woman snatch her baby up and scurry across the driveway. They exchanged mean looks.

You almost ran over my baby....

You shouldn't allow your child to walk across driveways by itself...idiot!

He felt un-nerved by the experience. God, how would you feel, killing a baby?

The thought caused him to become more cautious at stop signs, drive a little slower than usual through the city streets.

Well, the "Hollow Day" madness is behind us for a while, let's see what the New Year has in store.

He came off the freeway at Slauson and immediately pulled over to let the screaming fire truck pass. Always something happening in South Central L.A. He was surprised to see the truck make a blistering right turn a few streets ahead of him, his street.

He accelerated. What the hell is this? He turned the corner to find it blocked off, fire trucks and police cars in the way. He backed up, whipped around to the next street and ran back to the loft.

"Let me through here, I'm the owner!"

"Sorry, pal, no one comes through 'til the fire department finishes their work."

"But, I'm the owner!"

"It doesn't matter who you are, you can't get through here."

For a split second Kojo thought seriously of punching the policeman in the face. It was a moment that he didn't surrender to.

"Let him through, officer," one of the fireman called to the policeman.

"You say you're the owner?"

"Yes, what happened?"

The fireman strolled to the side of the building with him, the neighborhood folks, excitement past, drifted away.

"Well, number one, the damage isn't all that great, luckily. It's more a case of more smoke than fire."

"Can we go inside, any damage there?"

"Most of the fire was contained in the rear here, looks like an electrical short circuit fire, offhand, but we haven't completely checked the premises...."

Kojo took a deep breath and released a sigh of relief to find the office and office equipment intact, except for a few large puddles of water.

"You were lucky, somebody spotted the smoke right away and called in."

"Yeah, I really appreciate that."

Efficiently, the firemen cleared the space, rolled up their hoses and left Kojo to look closely at the scene.

We were really lucky. I'll have to give Thelma a bonus, when she gets out of the hospital, for spacing these metal file cabinets and insisting on the proper covers for everything.

A fire, electrical short circuit...hmm. And where is everybody? 11:00 a.m., Sunday morning...wowww! I must be slipping. Even the members of Our Production Company have to take some time off.

He strolled through the space, consciously trying to block certain thoughts out of his head.

Almost ran over a baby this morning...a fire in the office. No, no connection, all of it just pure coincidence. He sprawled on one of the office sofas, wishing that he had someone to talk with.

What's wrong with me? I got hundreds of people to talk with. He called his parents.

"What're we doing? Just sittin' around, waiting for you and Akosua to pay us a visit."

"See you in fifteen minutes."

He secured all of the exits and tripped off to try to get a few answers to a few questions.

❖

"Dad, you were into herpetology at one point, weren't you?"

"Yeah, you know how it is when you run a bookstore, you'll have things grab you for periods of time. You pick up a book about something you didn't know anything about and one book leads to another book, the next thing you know you're some kind of authority.

Your mother was one of the country's hippest hypnotists at one point. Nzingha, remember your hypnotic period?"

"Make fun if you want to. If I had had more time I probably could've hypnotized you, even."

"That would be the day!"

Kojo laughed with his parents, the pressure forgotten for the moment.

"Kojo, you staying for a late lunch?"

"By all means."

"Well, let me go whip something together."

"Make it hypnotic!"

She playfully spanked her husband on the shoulder leaving the room. Mom and Dad. I hope Akosua and me are like you two when we mellow out.

"Now, what's this thing about the snakes?"

"Uhhh, well, we're dealing with a couple scenes that deal with the snake...."

"Uh huh, well, where do you want to start?"

Kojo toyed with the idea of beating around the bush, abandoned the idea and decided to head straight in.

"How often do snakes eat?"

His father gave a curious look for a moment.

"A lot depends on the size of the snake, the type of snake and the size of the meal. A fair sized anaconda can swallow a small deer and not need to eat for three or four months."

"So, theoretically, a certain kind of snake, of a certain size would only have to eat...maybe three-four times a year?"

Father Brown pursed his lips, frowned a bit, considering the question.

"Yes, theoretically, there's no evidence of greed in snakes, unlike some other species of beings...."

Kojo gave his father a full look of attention, his signal that he wanted to know more...more....

"The snake is a very interesting figure in everybody's mythology. We have the Christian thing with the snake in the Garden of Eden, of course, and a whole bunch of other cultures with similar myths.... They've always been considered to link to something evil. I guess it's based on the way they look and move. They're feared and worshipped, hated and worshipped. Did you ever see the documentary of a group of people in Burma, they called it back then, who made a pilgrimage once a year to a cave where some kind of giant species of snake lived? I don't remember if it was a cobra or not, but it was huge."

"What color was it?"

"White, I remember that, white and huge. Anyway, a woman was designated to lure the snake out of the cave and kiss it on the head three times. I think the reason for doing it was to ensure that they would have a successful harvest. Or something like that. Tiny Asian woman, making moves like a snake herself, feints back and forth at the mouth of the cave, after a few minutes the snake lunges out at her. Huge thing, it must've been nine feet long and thick barreled. The snake strikes at the woman and she dodges, the snake strikes, she side steps. It was like watching a Balinese temple dance. After a few attempts to strike her, they settle into a calm state. The snake, who was holding himself higher than her, lowers his head and she makes the first kiss."

"I never saw this, I'm sure I would've remembered if I had."

"I'm sure you would have. The second she kisses the snake's head he is aroused again, rears up and strikes at her. He misses, and they get into a little dance again. Three times she did it, three times. I thought about all kinds of crazy things, trick photography, stuff like that. But no, this was real. After she had performed the last kiss she backed off and the snake slid back into the cave. It looked like it had been choreographed. When they did the close up of the woman you could see venom all over the front of her clothes. Maybe it was a giant species of spitting cobra. I don't know. But I will never forget the sight of this sticky stuff on the front of her dress and the totally drained expression on her face. She looked as though she had been in a fist fight with a giant snake and won."

Silence closed in on them for a moment, each thinking about the scene.

"Yeahhh, that was a helluva piece of film. If my memory serves correctly, I think I saw it at one of those herpetology sessions I used to go to, years ago. Incredible thing about the snake, it has always been considered an evil messenger, a force for evil. There is no record anywhere, that I know of that offers us a picture of the 'good snake.'"

Kojo felt a slight chill grip the back of his neck.

"But snakes do a lot of good, they eat rats and...."

"That's right, they help stabilize the balance that makes nature work the way it does. But once we take the creature out of the desert and the fields, he becomes an evil demon, in league with wicked spirits."

"How do you feel about that? That the snake is a messenger of evil and all that...."

Kojo smiled at his father's meditative pause, he acts just like <u>his</u> father....

"Kojo," his voice took on a more serious note, "I'll be perfectly honest with you. When I was younger and less romantic, I was tempted to look for logic in everything.

Now that I'm older, and I've experienced so many unbelievable things, I find myself believing in things that I would've laughed at years ago. If someone had told me about a little woman in Southeast Asia kissing a giant snake on the head, I would've looked for some "logical" reason for it. Now, I see it for what it is. To get back to your question. No, I don't think that snakes are inherently evil...but...."

"Yes, but?"

"But I have to feel that there must be a bit of fire in that smoke, somewhere. I mean, if people all over the earth have come out with negative stuff about the serpent they must know something. Or they've found out something. I put a special trust in the so called "primitive" people, these are the ones who've lived in the same environment with the snake, they know him. And if they have a mythology that stresses his evil side...well...."

"If you gentlemen can put your snake talk aside we can have lunch. Kojo, would you like a glass of white wine?"

"Oh my God! Akos'?! What happened?"

"Just a clumsy move, that's all. I was coming in from the back yard and tripped up the steps. The problem is this balloon in front of me, I couldn't see the steps."

No big thing, a little gash on the head, a warning to be a little more careful.

Kojo folded her into his arms.

"Be careful, baby, please, I don't want anything to happen to you."

I almost ran over a baby. We had a fire in the office. Two or three other potentially disastrous things have happened. My wife stumbles up the steps and gashes her head. O.K. Asiafo, you win.

He went for his workout a half hour earlier, feeling antsy. The workout was half hearted. He had his mind on half a dozen other things. How in the hell do I communicate with this damned thing, to tell it that I surrender?

You want a fuckin' goat, you got it.

He finished his workout, draped a towel around his neck and sat at the base of a tree, waiting.

What if the damned thing is angry with me? What if it doesn't come back? How can I square myself?

After a half hour of anxious waiting he reluctantly decided to pack it in for the day. He looked over his shoulder at the last place he had seen the snake. Now what?

The rest of the day was spent dealing with one small catastrophe after another.

"Kojo, would you believe it?! These idiots have sliced through our telephone lines! I knew something like this was going to happen when I saw them digging up our street. Idiots!"

"Thelma, be cool. How long will it take them to put us back in business?"

"Tomorrow, at the earliest. The day after, at the latest."

"Be cool, we shall overcome."

Kojo replaced the 'phone in its cradle, tilted his chair back, tented his fingers under his chin and frowned.

I goofed. I should have done what I was asked to. What does he want? A goat?

Later that day, after a full day in the editing room, and a light dinner of curried fish, Kojo sprawled in his back yard chair.

"Kojo, I'm going in, I feel like reading a bit. You want anything?"

"Nawww, I got a big glass of San Antonio Red, that's about all I need for the moment. Hey, looks like that cut on your head is almost gone."

"Yeah, I'm using aloe vera, miracle stuff"

"Good, be with you in a bit."

He watched her go into the house, feeling melancholy, blue. He and Ed Burris had carefully studied crucial footage and discovered a gruesome number of mistakes.

"Wow! How did that get in there?!"

He sat up slightly as the snake slithered across his line of vision. The snake gathered itself into a tight coil, ten yards in front of him and seemed to be waiting.

Kojo slugged half his wine down, tried to avoid looking at the snake for a minute and then suddenly asked in an irritated tone, "Where? What time?"

"Griffith Park, near the tennis courts, dawn tomorrow."

And slithered away. Kojo remained in place, gritting his teeth. Damn! Where in the hell am I supposed to find a goat at dawn?

He ground his teeth together, annoyed with the idea of being forced to do something he didn't want to do. No sense acting stupid about this, I have to do what I have to do. Let's hope the pet store has a damned goat.

The clerk who had sold him the rat and the rabbit was quite willing to open shop for him before dawn, for an extra hundred dollars.

"Uhh, are you making an ebọ, Mr. Jones?"

"A what?"

"A sacrifice."

"I suppose you could call it that."

He had left Akosua reeling from a heavy dream sequence....

"You going up to the park to jog at this time of morning?"

"I need it. I haven't been paying too much attention to my exercise program lately, with the editing and all. And dawn is a good time to go clear your head."

"Yawwwn, run a lap for me."

He drove carefully through the heavy fog, a cold anger welling up in him. Damn....

Shadowy figures jogged along the bridle path paralleling the road. Serious joggers up here.

He parked the car and pulled the small goat out of the rear. First it was rabbit crap, now I got goat shit to clean up.

He dropped a short length of rope around the goat's miniature horns and pulled him along.

Beautiful, small, fawn colored animal, with that typical crazy looking goat gleam in his eyes.

He sat at a picnic table near the tennis courts, allowing the goat to graze, as he looked around in the hazy fog, gradually brightening to a dull blue in the east. It'll be dawn in a half hour. What should I do? Well, I've staked the rest of them out, guess I'll do the same with this one. He tied a firm knot around the leg of the picnic table, took a last look at the grazing animal and started walking away. I've got my stuff on, I may as well do a lap. A lap around the Griffith Park bridle path, not a marathon, but an interesting run, full of mushy spots that tortured the calves and made the jogging a challenge.

Kojo did a brief warm up and made a snap decision to run the path counter-clockwise. A hundred yards into his run felt the shadow of three huge men running, grunting as they ran, slugging imaginary opponents in front of them.

Whoaa, this is the boxers roadwork hour, and the anorexic ladies, the exercise freaks, the mad joggers, all the people who think they have a vested interest in being here.

He smiled at his reasoning. What the hell am I doing here?

The sun popped over the edge of the horizon as though it were being squeezed out of a tube.

The last wisps of hazy fog dissipated. Kojo settled into a comfortable stride and took in the scenery as he jogged. The early golfer. God, what a strange game. There must be something to it, if so many people love it the way they do.

The coyote, making cat-like movements, thirty yards to his left front, intrigued him.

He knows that I don't have a weapon, that I'm simply an innocent jogger who wishes him well. Animals have more sense than people.

By the time he returned to his starting point, so many things had whirled through his mind that he almost jumped in his car and drove off.

The goat. It was a half hour past dawn, the fog was gone and the sun's rays promised a hot day. Kojo ran to the picnic table where he had tethered the goat. He picked up the end of the rope that had been wound around the goat's horns. The rope had been untied, the way the rat and the rabbit had been untied. Kojo dropped the rope and strolled to his car, humming a tuneless little tune. He felt greatly relieved.

February, the second month of the New Year, and Our Production Company was on the verge of releasing its first feature film, "My Grandfather's Eyes."

"There's still some editing to be done, but basically we have what I was shooting for."

It was post-production time, time to make sure all the eyes have been dotted and all the tees crossed.

Kojo and Akosua frequently fell into each others arms at the end of the day, delightfully fatigued.

"Akos', have I told you about my five-year plan?"

"No, tell me about it."

"I want to make four films over the next five years. When this is finished, I want to take a three month break and jump right back into the saddle."

"Sounds somewhat ambitious to me."

"Yeahhh, it does, doesn't it?"

They felt something magical about the fact that they had worked like fiends to come up with a film.

"Let's hope it's world class."

"How can you doubt it, with the people you've had work on it."

"You're looking at my five year plan repertory group."

"Do they know that?"

"Well, not yet, but I suspect most of them have heavy suspicions. You know, I've always admired the way Bergman, Wertmuller and a couple other European film makers have kept the same crews together for years.

"Yeah, that's true, isn't it? Seems that the only time we've done that is on T.V., never in movies.

You ever see any of the old Milton Berle, Sid Caesar, Imogene Coca, Jackie Gleason things?"

"Once or twice my parents took me to see a revival of Sid Caesar's "Show of Shows", ten of his best. They laid me out."

The show was back on the road, the film, "My Grandfather's Eyes," was scheduled for Spring release.

Jackie Muhammad had gone toe to toe with Charley Bascom and won.

"Where in the world do these Neanderthal thinking White men come from? You know what he had in mind for the publicity poster, the thing that's going to lure people into the darkened theatre?

He wanted an Uncle Remus figure with a little boy perched on his knee, kind of a take off on "Song of the South". Can you believe that?

We had to circumnavigate his madness to put things on the proper track. All praises due to Allah."

The law firm of Green, Shafton and Clark ran interference in negotiations concerning the split between the film maker and the exhibitor.

"Mr. Brown, I'll think you'll be pleased to know that Mr. Bascom has finally accepted your terms. We'll have contracts for you to sign in the coming week."

Contracts, loose ends, endless details. The film, "My Grandfather's Eyes" due for general release in May.

"Akos', why don't you pack your notebook and let's take off for a few days. I don't know about you but I need a break."

"I'm with you, where to?"

"Huatabampo."

"Let's go."

❖

Friday morning, 5:30 a.m., they joined the early commuters, feeling bright and eager to leave the problems, the frustrations, the city, behind them. Kojo drove the first lap, one hand on the wheel, one hand gently rubbing Akosua's swollen belly.

"Is it my imagination, or do I really feel somebody kicking my hand?"

"Nothing imaginary, the action inside here is alive."

San Bernardino, straight through the Imperial Valley, kicking off into Yuma, Arizona for the first leg. They were going to cross over from Nogales, Arizona into Nogales, Mexico.

They traveled well with each other trading a sentence from time to time, feeling at ease, free.

"Are we stopping at Gila Bend?"

CHAPTER 33

"If you want to?"

"Yeah, I think it would be kinda fun to re-trace our steps, sniff at the tracks again."

"Hahhahhah...well, I guess that's one way to think about it."

The Gila Bend Hotel proprietor was there and welcomed them.

"Welcome back to Gila Bend, didn't think I'd see you folks again so soon."

A shower, change of clothes and a stroll into the desert. They stood, arms linked, staring up at the sky.

"Kojo, do you know how I feel right now?"

"No, tell me."

"Like the heavens, like the sky, like the stars. I feel majestic. At this moment I feel like the Mother of creation. I'm sure it has something to do with this life I'm carrying inside of me. I'm sure that has something to do with it.

I've never felt this grand before, you know what I mean?"

"I think so."

"I can look up at the sky and imagine a cosmic woman giving birth to all of this. I've never bothered to give the matter a whole lot of thought, but tonight, right here, I have to believe that God is a woman."

Kojo stared at her profile, not knowing what to say. A coyote howled in the distance.

"Let's go back."

The road to Tucson made them think about cowboys and Native Americans.

"The criminal shame of it is that our brothers, the Indians, were dogged out by the brothers, by the Buffalo Soldiers they called them.

Yeahhh, they sicked the Black man on the Red man and just stood back and chuckled.

Dad has a bunch of books on that period. Incredible time frame. They couldn't figure out what to do with the best cavalrymen in the Union Army, so they shipped them out here to the desert, with poor equipment, poor horses, lousy officers...."

"Isn't this where that Black lieutenant, what's his name? Flare or Fillips?"

"I'm not sure, but I think it was Flipper."

"Right Lieutenant Flipper, the first Black graduate from West Point. They sent him out here and then ganged up on him for going horse riding with a White girl."

"I remember that, vaguely. They busted him, the whole bit. But if I'm not mistaken, they restored his stuff many years later."

"Justice, huh?"

An ice cold draught beer for Kojo, a warm orange juice for Akosua, southward to Nogales. The border, a few dollars spent to speed up the process.

"Down here they call it 'La Morbida,'...'the bite.'"

"In Ghana they call it 'dash.'"

"Same thing all over the world, gimme some money."

The Sonorran desert spread open in front of them once again, hot and merciless. They drove, sipping water and panting from the heat.

"A bit warmish, eh?"

"I should say, rather_rrr_."

"It won't be long for this, right after Hermosillo, we'll start edging over to Guaymas on the ocean side."

"I remember."

Hermosillo, the supermarket, for canned peaches, white wine, apples.

"It could be an American, supermarket, Huh?"

"It is an American supermarket."

Guaymas. They pulled the salty tang of the sea into their noses like a rare drug.

"Looks like we can breath again."

"Yeah, the desert doesn't give up a lot of cool air does it?"

The Hotel La Mar for their first soft evening at the ocean and a dinner of Huachinango ala Vera Cruzano.

"Mmmmm. . .I love the way they do this fish."

Everything had been placed on hold for their trip, it was a trait that they were beginning to admire in each other, the ability to let go.

Huatabampo seemed to drift into view from behind a sand dune.

"This is truly what I call a picturesque place."

"I've been searching for that word for miles. Yeahhh, that's what it is."

They did a round about of the city's plaza and headed for the Huatabampito Hotel, "Suite #6."

Mr. and Mrs. Chavez, plus their stair-step-collection-of-six, were there to greet them.

Mrs. Chavez grabbed Akosua in a python embrace, rejoicing vicariously in her pregnancy.

Mr. Chavez looked the situation over and offered Kojo a macho hug and a bit of whispered wisdom.... "Only we men can do these things.... Comprende?"

The welcome section over, they were left to themselves.

"La cena estaba seis, por favor."

"I got the por favor, what's the other?"

"She says dinner will be at six."

"O Lord, here we go."

They had four days to chill out and they were going to take advantage of it.

"Akos', you know something? When we left here the last time I felt like I had been recharged."

"I know the feeling, my man, I know the feeling."

Days and nights on the Huatabampito blended, became a tapestry. From the first evening meal, ("Sopa de Huatabampito"), to the following breakfast of shrimps and eggs, they drifted from one warm vibe to the next.

They sprawled on the shore of the sun warmed water, Akosua smiling at the sight of her bulging belly in a bikini. Kojo gazed at the creamy clouds and the baby blue sky and wished he were a bird.

What is so important about being down here anyway? Slugging our way through all of this gravity, sucking up everybody's garbage.

And when the poetic feelings threatened to overwhelm them with emotions they didn't feel capable of dealing with, one of the Chavez children would quietly inform them that it was time to eat.

Thoughts, food, sleeping, careful love making, dreams.

Kojo seriously considered another week of indulgence.

"We can't do it, Kojo, we can't do it, as much as we'd like to. I have stuff to do and you know you have things to do. The first preview is next month, isn't it?"

"You got that right."

Charley Bascom had insisted on at least one preview....

"C'mon, Kojo! Gimme a break for God's sake! I'm the distribution guy of the century, you're getting the lion's share of the percentage...you have to give me a preview, an idea of what's in this "Granddady's Eyes".

"**My Grandfather's Eyes**", Charley, that's the title, don't forget it, o.k.?"

"Sorry, Big Guy, no need to get testy about it."

The traditional preview in Pasadena, with opinion cards. O.K., let's see what a cross- section of people think about the film. It's a done deal in any case.

The drive back was truly anti-climatic.

"This is what is known as the downside, huh?"

"You're right, but we're going to be looking at the bright side of the downside, we have 'a film in the can.'"

The preview audience was composed of industry people, invited guests and people who had simply decided to sneak a peep at something called, <u>My Grandfather's Eyes</u>".

Charley Bascom's entourage was strategically scattered throughout the audience. Bascom wanted to make certain, beyond the opinions offered on the cards, that he was made aware of unusual laugh spots, where sad angles intruded, what effect the work had on different people in the audience... mainly White.

The cast and crew of Our Production Company formed a tight core in the center of the theatre audience. They seemed to be saying, with their circle-the-wagons-attitude, we did it, now come and get us.

After the first ten minutes, the prologue, Kojo felt like a man holding his breath under an iceberg.

Akosua started his flow again by grasping his hand. Yes, it was happening, they had put the far reaching vision of the old man's eyes on film.

The ways he looked at the world became more than a peek through one pair of glasses, there were facets, sections that were almost <u>Cubistic/</u> Picassoian.

They had created a work of art, and if there was any doubt, it was dispersed by the musical score that Juna and the Earth One group had put together.

Two hours and ten minutes later the film came to an end, technically; but it was apparent to all those present that the ending was just the beginning.

The audience, led by Our Production's people, applauded long and hard. Charley Bascom rushed over to offer his version of congratulations.

"Why didn't you tell me you were putting this kind of thing together?"

The word was out. A day later the trades were heralding a "latter day Spike Lee."

"They really get to me with that stuff. Why can't they accept Kojo Bediako Brown for who he is, and Spike Lee for what he was. They must always pigeonhole us. Why?"

"You know why. But be cool, you don't want to angry up your ambiotic fluid, we've only got a few more weeks to go, right?"

"About five, to be exact."

"So, be cool, let them say what they feel comfortable with. We know what the real deal is."

Sunday afternoon in the Brown house. A half dozen calls to deal with, more details to be worked Out.

"Kojo, Jackie wants to set up a press conference in Chicago for the opening there. Are you game?"

"That's next month, right?"

"April, right."

427

"Sorry, that's too close to your time. This is a first for both of us and I'm determined to be on the scene when 'your opening' takes place."

More details.

"Juna called, she's having second thoughts about the last 45 seconds of music in the film...."

"What kind of second thoughts?"

"Not really second thoughts, she's just on an anxiety trip."

"Cool her out, I beg you."

"No problem."

"Did you read the review in the Times?"

"I glanced at it."

"Well, I won't burden you with the whole thing, about comparing you to Buneul and Cocteau. What he does get to, that's quite interesting, is this: 'Rarely, if ever, do we find ourselves faced with a true trace of Africentricity, which means that a creative person of African descent has traced his root lines to a primeval source,' etc., etc. Crazy, huh?"

"Yeah. You know I think it drives some White people crazy when they realize, after all the cultural imperialism, and other kinds of whippings they've laid on us, that we ain't them and we ain't about to become them."

"You do sense a little hysteria there, don't you?"

"Really. What they don't realize is that my Grandfather is pleased and that's enough for me."

"I'll second that vote. Oh, are you going with me this afternoon?"

"Where?"

"Well, my mother and your mother put their heads together for a baby shower. Looks like they've discovered each other."

"Well, you know they say opposites attract. Go do it. I'm going to hang out here today, maybe look at a couple movies, sip a little vino."

"Have fun."

An hour later, after talking to four members of Our Production Company: Jackie Muhammad, Juna, "Juna, don't worry, everything is fine, Akosua will be talking with you in the coming week."

"What day?"

"Uhhh, Monday, it'll be Monday for sure."

"Are you sure...?"

"Yes."

Kojo selected a movie from his collection - "Mississippi Masala," and settled into ninety minutes of one Indian director's idea of what Indian-African-American relations might've been, 'way back when.

Hmmm, not bad. Not bad at all. I don't believe it but it was nice. Denzel was at his usual good self and the Indian girl with the luscious growth of hair made a suitable sexpot. The thing of the Indian presence in Uganda was over-simplified, but what the hell could you expect from an Indian film maker? Thank God Idi Amin died, too bad he couldn't have been killed.

He was tempted to put one of the Cary Grant movies on, decided not to, poured himself another goblet of the San Antonio Red, drifted out to the back yard, slightly buzzed, feeling egotistical.

We've got a helluva movie on our hands, a helluva movie.

He flexed back on the steps of the back porch, sipping his wine and trying to see into the future.

The curling, spiraling piece of thick black and green rope seemed like a mirage for a moment, 'til it coiled five yards in front of him. They stared at each other. Kojo felt a sudden chill. Now what?

CHAPTER 34

The snake slithered away. Kojo stared at the slight depression that the snake had made in the grass. Now what?

He stared at the space the snake had vacated. What do I do about this? I need to talk to somebody. He worked his way carefully through a Rolodex file of people. Mom and Dad? Yes, of course, they would understand, but how could I tell them this crazy shit?

Granddad, yeah, he would understand it too, but how would I go about explaining that I had made a deal like this, in order to do my film?

Akosua? No, never, she would feel used. I think I would feel used if someone told me that they married me because they had made a deal.

He mentally wrote, and scribbled off a half dozen other names, friends. No, this one is on me.

Monday morning. Capoeira time....

"Akos', how do you feel?"

"Oh, just a little green about the gills, but not bad."

"Anything I can get you before I make my run?"

"It would be great if you could do a fast forward of this pregnancy."

They shared a big smile.

"I wish I could, sweetheart, believe me, I wish I could."

He leaned over and kissed her gently.

"I won't be long. I just felt an urge to go up to the bridle path today."

"I'll be going with you, again, one of these days."

A final peck on the lips and off to Griffith Park. 7:30 a.m., the beginning of commuter traffic.

Kojo joined the flow, heading north on Riverside Drive, pleased that he wasn't a member of the herd, that he didn't have to pay dues to the clock.

"Kojo, whatever you do, try to stay out of the herd. Once you become a labor unit you're dead, you'll be working your life away instead of doing your life's work."

Thanks, Dad, that was the best piece of advice you've ever given me. He glanced at the man biting his nails in the next lane, the woman splashing make up on her face in the car ahead of him, the air of tension evident beyond the steel frames of the vehicles.

Impatient drivers blew their horns, they cursed other drivers, the streets were electric with hostile vibes.

Kojo released a pent up breath as he drove into the park. Thank God, I'm out of that madness for a minute. He drove slowly, enjoying the greenness of the park, smiled at the chubby couple laboring up the slight incline into the heart of the park. Poor babies. Tennis players, power walkers, joggers, people trying to be healthy. He parked, did a brief warm up and started his run on the bridle path.

He felt strong, full of energy. Damn it feels good to be in good shape. He fell into a comfortable groove and ran easily, using his run as a sightseeing tour. The early morning golphers, people romping with their dogs, horsy types bouncing along on their thoroughbreds.

After the run, breathing easily, he decided to drive to the "backside" of the park, the place where he and Akosua did their picnics.

A man with a guitar sat on a picnic table two hundred yards away. Good. He has his thing to do and I have my thing to do.

Capoeira alone — shadow movements; the ginga, that basic dance step that has so many variations. Besoa, the front "blessing" kick, the Meia Lua de Frente, the half-moon slicing kick to the front, Meia Lua de Compasso, the spinning half moon compass kick, Au-Au-Au-Au-the cartwheel-somersault.

Forty minutes later, after going through as many movements as he could remember, with variations, he wandered over to a picnic bench and sat down, feeling a little winded, but exhilarated.

He took casual notice of the tree limbs scattered around. They're trimming dead wood....

Beautiful day, Spring in Southern California. He did a slow Pan of the green hillsides surrounding him, the woodsy atmosphere. Hard to believe that we're in the middle of a big nasty city.

It seemed to be a piece of one of the dead limbs until it moved in his direction, red and black slithering toward him. Kojo froze, feeling scared of this thing that Asiafo had put into his life.

The snake coiled, flicking its forked tongue out from side to side, listening to movements.

"Feed me."

The horrible rasping sounds grated in his ears.

"I've already fed you."

"Feed me."

The same rasping sound, like hard scales being scraped against metal. Kojo felt the perspiration trickle under his armpits. He made a quick decision.

I have to do what he wants if I want to keep the flow going. Remember what happened the last time. I'm too deeply in the game to back down now.

Kojo felt the words struggle out of his throat, he felt himself choking.

"Feed you what and where?"

The snake seemed to make a dancing movement with its head.

"Your first born, here, next month."

Kojo leaped from the table, grabbed a piece of dead tree limb and began to beat the snake to death quick, sure blows up and down the length of the snake.

He felt mad and sick. The primeval fear that has made the snake a despised creature filled him with dread, forced him to pound the snake until it was a long bloody pulp.

The guitar player ran to his side...

"O my God! What happened?! Did it attack you?"

Kojo stared at the limp, bloody thing on the ground and nodded...

"Yes, yes, it attacked me."

He threw the stick away and walked slowly to his car, feeling nauseaous.

It took a great effort to keep him from cracking up during the following days.

He was obviously nervous and disturbed. Akosua noticed it, talked about it with her mother and her mother-in-law.

"You should see this man, he's a bundle of nerves, you'd think he was having the baby."

Kojo felt compelled to do all the things he had to do, attend the meetings, discuss the publicity campaign for the film, deal with people, but he did it mechanically, like a man on a treadmill, with no possibility of getting off. He nursed the secret feeling that something dreadful was going to happen to him. Or Akosua. Or the baby.

He spent days at the beach, staring at the water, waiting for something to happen, for some sign.

Akosua tried to pull him out of himself.

"C'mon, Mr. Creepy, let's go for a picnic up in the park, we haven't been up there in a while."

The idea of the park made him feel cold waves up and down his spine.

"Why not the beach? We haven't done a picnic at the beach in a while."

"Suits me."

Three days after a false baby arrival alarm....

"Akos'?! What's wrong?! You o.k.?!"

"I don't know, feels like something is about to happen...."

The letter came. It was from Grace and Kojo was fortunately, the one to pull it out of the mailbox. He made a mental note to talk with Akosua about the ex-ladyfriend in the Motherland.

She's a sweet sister but I don't think she'd like for the correspondence to continue, I don't think I'd dig it if she was receiving letters and writing an old flame.

He closed himself in his study to read the letter.

"Dear Kojo,

Long time, eh? I hope all is going well with you and your work. Things are going on pretty much as usual. I'm doing well and trying to do better but, as you know, in Ghana here, one must be careful not to cause too much envy.

You know what degree they will give me? It's called a Ph.D., "pull her down".

From this point I will limit my correspondence to Christmas cards.

Why? Well, I started thinking of how I would feel if you were my husband and you were receiving letters from some woman in Africa.

I hope you can appreciate my feelings about this matter."

Kojo paused and stared up at the ceiling, God, I wish I could've married both of them.

"Now then, the news, as they say on the Ghana Broadcasting Corporation, (G.B.C.),... I went to visit Auntie Eugenia in Tsito last week and she was full of news. She told me to tell you that the headmistress was engaged to be married.

What does that mean?

"The most devastating bit of news concerns that "Wild Man of the Forest," Asiafo, the one you made your "deal" with. He was found dead, his skull crushed, on the outskirts of the village.

There is a great suspicion that one of the members of the family that lost a family member to him may have done it.

The consensus seems to be "good riddance".

I have to tell you honestly, I was a bit surprised when you told me of your "deal" with this man. I couldn't come out openly and say to you, Kojo, I think it's a bit of rubbish because you seemed so totally taken in by the possibilities that were being offered you.

Well, in any case, whatever the obligations were I think you should think that they have effectively ceased at this point.

The man is dead. The proverb says, "You can't put food in a dead body's mouth."

Kojo felt the tears sliding down his cheeks before he realized he was crying. All the weeks and months of tension, of feeling sick of the "deal" and the terms he had to meet, began to flow out of him...

"I will be traveling to Cuba and possibly the U.S. sometime next year. I hope that we can get together and "do lunch," as you say in Hollywood.

'Til then, all my best,
Grace"

Kojo folded the note carefully and put it in his shirt pocket. I'm free, I won't have to feed the damned snake any more.

He shook his head, trying to reason with himself. Was I hallucinating? Did I actually make sacrifices to a snake? Have I been successful because of the deal? What now?

Was it pure coincidence that Asiafo had his head crushed when I killed the snake? I'll have to find out what day he was killed.

Speculations were cancelled by an urgent knocking on his door.

"Yes?"

"Kojo, I hate to disturb you but I think it's time for us to go the hospital."

The film, "My Grandfather's Eyes" was finished, edited, scored, distributed, (it received an especially warm reception in Copenhagen, Denmark), and applauded.

Akosua Ferguson-Brown gave birth to an 8 pound 4 ounce boy who was named Kwabena Bediako Brown.

Kojo's following films, "Secret Music" and "Drylongso" removed him from the stereotyped shadow of the White media's definition of a Black writer-director-producer.

"Akos', listen to this; "Kojo Brown's "Drylongso", an almost indefinable word of African origin, appears to substantiate his appeal to people in general, rather than Black people only.

The high level of his art should make all of us appreciative of that fact. He shows all of the qualities that made Ingmar Berman and Federico Fellini powers in their day."

"They can't stop comparing you to White boys, no matter what, huh?"

"Seems that way, even when they're supposed to be passing out compliments."

The Browns were on a roll. Akosua's books, finely written examinations of the finite play between the sexes were critically acclaimed and Kojo was following his five-year plan in his third movie.

Their son was five years old and precocious. His grandparents were the first to take note of the boy's interest in snakes.

"Kojo, looks like your son has a keen interest in snakes. Notice what happens when I open that big book on reptiles? He stares and points at them as though he knew every one of them."

'Close the book, Dad, I don't want him to become interested in snakes."

"But why, what...?"

"Please, Dad, just close the book, I'll explain it to you one day."

❖

END

POST SCRIPT...

Dear Kojo,

Charles has returned. He is older, has suffered serious psychological wounds from the war in Rwanda, but aside from that he is feeling full of "piss 'n vinegar", as you say in America.

He came back to me unexpectedly, which is the way things like that happen and, once again, I must admit that your presence helped prepare his coming.

I am happy that matters have turned out in the way that they've turned out for us. I must admit that I couldn't have imagined a scenario to fit our circumstances.

God does, indeed, work in mysterious ways. Ghana is going on, sometimes ahead, sometimes behind, but always, on. We discover new things, people, ways and means every day.

Please be aware, we have found, according to the villagers of Tsito, that Asiafo left a son behind. Natshiwee.

I don't know what else to say...

Love, Grace -

Printed in the United States
By Bookmasters